THE ORIGINS OF
CHINESE COMMUNISM

DATE DUE

The Origins of
Chinese Communism

Arif Dirlik

New York   Oxford
OXFORD UNIVERSITY PRESS
1989

Oxford University Press

Oxford New York Toronto
Delhi Bombay Calcutta Madras Karachi
Petaling Jaya Singapore Hong Kong Tokyo
Nairobi Dar es Salaam Cape Town
Melbourne Auckland

and associated companies in
Berlin Ibadan

Copyright © 1989 by Oxford University Press, Inc.

Published by Oxford University Press, Inc.,
200 Madison Avenue, New York, New York 10016

Oxford is a registered trademark of Oxford University Press

Library of Congress Cataloging-in-Publication Data
Dirlik, Arif.
The origins of Chinese Communism / Arif Dirlik.
p. cm. Bibliography: p. Includes index.
ISBN 0-19-505453-9 ISBN 0-19-505454-7 (pbk.)
1. Communism—China—History. 2. Chung-kuo kung ch'an tang—
History. I. Title.
HX416.5.D57 1989
335.43′0951—dc 19 88-17460 CIP

2 4 6 8 10 9 7 5 3 1

Printed in the United States of America
on acid-free paper

To Nedim and Murat,
With my joyful appreciation of
their precocious social consciousness
—and loving dispositions.

PREFACE

The origins of the Communist party of China have received little attention from students of Chinese Communism. Most historians have not deemed the subject significant enough to warrant detailed study. The exceptions are easily identifiable: Sima Lu's *Zhonggongdi chengli yu chuqi huodong* (The Founding and Initial Activities of the Communist Party of China) (Hong Kong, 1974), Ding Shouhe's *Cong wusi qimeng yundong dao Makesi zhuyi di chuanpo* (From the May Fourth Enlightenment Movement to the Propagation of Marxism (Beijing, 1978), and Li Xin's *Weida di kairui* (The Great Beginning) (Beijing, 1983). The first work, which is, to my knowledge, the first to address certain fundamental questions about the origins of the Communist party, has never received the attention it deserves. The other two are too recent to have made an impact on scholarship, at least partially because they themselves are products of the same political and intellectual trends that are responsible for the present study. Our understanding of the origins of Chinese Communism still rests, consequently, on studies that have incorporated the topic into broader inquiry about the history of Chinese communists. The present study represents an effort to remedy this situation.

Our understanding of the origins of Communism in China has been based in the past on studies that may be classified into one of two categories. The first category consists of works concerned with the unfolding of Communism in the 1920s, and emphasizing Soviet involvement in China. This category includes early studies of Chinese Communism, such as C. Brandt's *Stalin's Failure in China* (New York, 1958) and A. Whiting's *Soviet Policies in China, 1917–1924* (Stanford, 1953). Both the subject matter (the revolutionary movement of the 1920s) and the environment in which these books were written (the Cold War years) predisposed these studies to emphasize the Soviet role in the Chinese revolution, portraying the origins of Communism in China as an extension of a Communist movement emanating from Moscow. The complexities of the context of radicalism in which Communism took root in China were largely pushed into the background.

A counterpoint is to be found in the second category of studies, which stressed the indigenous roots of Chinese Communism. The classics in this category are B. Schwartz's *Chinese Communism and the Rise of Mao* (Cambridge, 1951) and M. Meisner's *Li Ta-chao and the Origins of Chinese Marxism* (Cambridge, 1967). These studies, in reaction to the Cold War portrait of Chinese Communism as a mere offshoot of an international Communist conspiracy based in Moscow, were concerned above all to explain the emergence of an indigenous Communist movement in China under Mao Zedong's leadership after 1927—Schwartz's work directly, Meisner's indirectly. As Meisner's work, especially, makes clear, an anti-imperialistic nationalism, which characterized Chinese Communism under Mao, provided in these studies the framework within which to explain the origins of Chinese Communism as well; nationalism, more than anything else, accounted in this presentation for the Chinese attraction to Communism from its very origins. This presentation proved particularly attractive to students of Chinese Communism because it viewed that movement as stemming from within Chinese history— and accorded with prevailing Maoist historiography (at least in the People's Republic). It is fair to say, I think, that this version has been the dominant one among students of Chinese history for the past two decades.

These accounts share a common point of departure in the 1917 October Revolution in Russia which, they agree, provided Chinese radicals with a new strategy of revolution, if not a new way to perceive the world. Their major difference lies in the explanations they offer for the Chinese attraction to Marxism (or Communism—the two are not carefully distinguished in either case). In the one version, Soviet intervention in China, along with the material advantages offered by the Soviet Union, attracted Chinese intellectuals to Communism. In the other version, the Chinese attraction to Communism is a consequence of the power of Marxism-Leninism to answer revolutionary yearnings born of China's world situation. Both interpretations view the origins of Chinese Communism from the perspective of later developments, and pay only meager attention to a contemporary Chinese perspective on Communism, and to the mechanisms that went into the making of the Communist Party of China when it was established in 1921.

These questions provide the point of departure for the present study, which covers a four-year period between the October Revolution of 1917 and the founding of the Communist Party of China in mid-1921. It examines in detail the ideological and organizational developments in these years that brought radical intellectuals from no appreciable understanding of Marxism, and even a negative appraisal, to a conclusion that only in a Marxist-inspired Communism lay the solution to China's problems. I was convinced of the necessity of reexamining the emergence of Chinese Communism not only by recently accessible materials that suggest a more complex picture of the origins of the Party than has been previously possible, but also by certain fundamental anomalies in our current understanding of the problem. The problematic relationship between the October Revolution, Marxist ideology, and Communist organization has more or less been bundled into an "entangled web" in existing historical explanations. This study undertakes to disentangle this web.

This study was also conceived as a study of the May Fourth Movement in China, an intellectual and political watershed in modern Chinese history. The years during which the Party came into existence were momentous years in Chinese radicalism. As this study tells the story (and as we have long known, albeit in a fuzzy way), the origins of Communism in China were inextricably intertwined with the developments of the May Fourth period. The elucidation of the relationship of Communism to the May Fourth period also sheds some new light, I hope, on the May Fourth period itself, especially on the ideology and organization of student activism in these years. This elucidation underlines, above all, the importance of socialism, which was not peripheral to May Fourth thinking, as past studies imply, but a central concern of contemporary radical thinking.

In the broadest sense, this study seeks to get at questions of radical organization, the relationships between ideology and organization, Marxism and Communism, in which I have had longstanding interest as a historian and individual. The process of the Party's founding in China has much to tell us, I believe, about the nature and processes of radical politics in general. The transformation of a diffuse political and cultural radicalism into organized political activity among May Fourth radicals has been parallelled in my own personal experience in the political movements born out of the radical culture of the 1960s, not just in the United States but around the world, including my country of origin, Turkey. Despite widely different social and political contexts, the experiences of May Fourth radicals often read like experiences of radicals in these other instances of intense radical activity: a sense of crisis born out of internal and external developments; the search for alternative forms of cultural expression and social organization to overcome an alienating social environment; a profound confusion of social with individual goals; and, above all, diffuse radical activity, frustrated by social, cultural, and political oppression in its pursuit of self-realization through experimentation with new social forms such as study societies and communes, finding ultimate expression in self-negating restrictive political organization or descent into social hedonism. If these radical movements differ in their consequences, the differences lie not in the dynamics of radical activity, but in the social and political contexts that offer different possibilities for and limitations to radical expression.

In a study that is self-consciously historicist, the case for the general implications of the establishment of Communism in China may be presented only implicitly. To historicize, however, is not necessarily to trivialize. Indeed, I believe that it is only with a minute investigation of the processes of radical politics in this historical case that its universal implications are best revealed. So far as I am aware, the approach utilized in this study of Chinese Communism is parallelled in only one other study of the origins of a Communist Party, Allan K. Wildman's study of the origins of the Russian Social Democratic Party (the context for Bolshevism) in his *The Making of a Worker's Revolution* (Chicago, 1967). While that study does not delineate the conceptualization of the problem with the explicitness of the present study, its findings concerning the relationship between ideology and organization in the emergence of a socialist movement in Russia in the 1890s closely parallel what I offer below with regard to the Communist Party of China. It also shows, much more clearly than the present study does, that the vitality of the socialist movement rested ultimately in its relationship to a social context of which a burgeoning working class in ferment was a conspicuous element.

A few words are in order here to anticipate the conclusions of this study so as to place it within the context of existing explanations of the origins of Communism in China. I think the available evidence indicates the correctness of Cold War assumptions that the Communist party of China was a product of direct Communist International intervention. This view in recent years has been gaining currency among historians in the People's Republic of China as well. This study goes beyond them to provide an explanation for the success of the transplantation. Unlike Schwartz and Meisner, who also stressed internal developments over external intervention, I trace Chinese receptivity to the Bolshevik message not to ideological predispositions but to problems which radical activism in the May Fourth period presented to Chinese intellectuals; not the least being their relationship to society, in particular the burgeoning labor movement. Ultimately, I believe, the emergence of Communism in China coincided with the coming of age of urban capitalism, with all its attendant social problems. The distinction between external and internal increasingly lost its significance, I suggest, in a society that appeared more and more to be part of a world market of commodities and ideas.

In a basic sense, then, this study incorporates existing historical explanations in order to transcend them by resolving the anomalies with which they present us. The historicist tack also makes possible, I think, the explanation of certain phenomena in the history of the Communist party that have remained blurred in more general explanations, with the result that questions pertinent to understanding later developments in Chinese Communism have also been blurred. These questions range from the relationship of the Party to the Guomindang in the 1920s to the relationship between theory and practice (or Marxism and Communism), and possibly even to certain developments in post-1949 China, as some Chinese historians have suggested.

There is another reason for employing the historicist strategy to examine the experience of radicalism, and the context of radical culture, that made it possible for some radical intellectuals to become Communists. It is possible that, given the conjuncture of world developments and internal developments in Chinese society, the appearance of socialism and Communism were inevitable in China at this time. It is also important to remember, however, that very few people in China became Communists. Communism was an important ideological commodity in the world following the October Revolution, and it easily impressed radical Chinese intellectuals looking for ways to cope with China's plight as a society. The road to Communism, however, was not for that reason easy; it was long and arduous. To listen to what Communist ideologues and many students of Communism say of it, conversion to Communism seems like the easiest thing in the world for people caught up in the grand motions of history, be they invisible social forces or ideological dispositions. However, to become a Communist is not easy. It is both dangerous and alienating; for the idealistic Communist, it is even dangerous to be a Communist under so-called Communist regimes. It means exposure to persecution and bodily harm; this would be the fate of many who participated in the founding of the Communist Party of China. It means resignation to a sub-rosa existence, alienated from colleagues, friends, and even kith and kin. It even means alienation from one's own values—the very values that justify Communist commitment but must be suspended temporarily in the name of long-term goals. There is, in other words, a tragic element to Communism. Our appreciation of why and how people become Communists, in China or elsewhere, must remain limited to the extent that we ignore this human element.

While existing materials do not permit detailed inquiry into the psyches of early Chinese Communists, we may at least begin to make a preliminary inquiry by taking account of the processes whereby Chinese radicals turned to Communism. This is a major reason that the discussion of radical culture and the organization of radical activity in the May Fourth period plays a prominent part in my account. My intentions are not merely sociological; I seek also to address the experience of radicalism that lay at the roots of Communism in China.

The thesis presented here might have been possible but not very likely only a few years ago. I owe a debt of gratitude to works whose approach to the problem I challenge, especially those of Schwartz and Meisner, whose own theses on the origins of Chinese Communism raised questions that have influenced the making of this study. In a more immediate sense, this study has drawn inspiration in more ways than one from the recent deconstruction of Maoist historiography in China. Chinese historians have engaged in a furious effort in recent years to re-evaluate the origins of Communism in their country. Although my thesis differs from those in current party histories, it was made possible largely by the same historical writing and investigation that has brought forth new ideas and materials. The work on the origins of Chinese Communism by Sima Lu, cited earlier, is the only one I know that addresses a pivotal question in this study: the role that May Fourth study societies played in the founding of the Party.

To a few individuals I owe a special debt of gratitude. The approach used in this study began to germinate imperceptibly in many delightful and contentious conversations over radical politics with my former colleague at Duke, Bernard Silberman, now of the University of Chicago. Maurice Meisner, a historian for whose work I have the greatest respect, has given me invaluable encouragement by graciously recognizing the validity of my arguments, many of which are directed at his own work. My Duke colleague Laurence Goodwyn has unfailingly stimulated my thinking on problems of radical activity. Professors Cai Shaoqing and Lu Zhe, of the Department of History at Nanjing University, gave me invaluable help with the collection of materials while I spent a year there in 1983–1984. To Professor Lu I owe a great debt not only for confirming trends in my thinking, but also for bringing to my attention materials of which I was previously unaware. Finally, I owe gratitude to the sad memories of two committed radicals, one an acquaintance for an unfortunately brief period, the other a former student and friend: Malcolm Caldwell and Cesar Cause. They were both brutally murdered within a year of each other in distant parts of the globe, when the ideas that have gone into the making of this study were first beginning to take shape in my mind. Their experiences and their fate have left an indelible imprint on my appreciation of radical politics.

Thelma Kithcart and Dorothy Sapp of the Department of History, Duke University, were of invaluable help in the preparation of the manuscript in its final stages—which was but the most recent instance of the assistance they have provided over the years. I acknowledge it with gratitude and affection. Thanks are also due to my editors at Oxford University Press, in particular Paul Schlotthauer and Martha Ramsey, for their meticulous editing of a lengthy manuscript.

A number of organizations have provided me with support over the years for research and writing on Chinese socialism which contributed directly or indirectly to this study. A fellowship from the National Endowment for the Humanities in 1978–1979 helped me embark on the study of socialism in China. A Duke University Research Grant that enabled me to go to China in the spring of 1984 helped me enormously with the collection of materials. A summer grant from the Hoover Institute on War, Peace and Revolution for a projected study of anarchism in China helped me with the discovery of sources that have also contributed to this study. I would also like to thank the gracious staff of the Hoover Institute East Asia library, especially Julia Tong, who have been unfailingly helpful on every occasion I have spent utilizing the resources of that excellent library. Finally, the writing of this study was made possible by a grant in 1985–1986 from the Joint Committee on Chinese Studies of the American Council of Learned Societies and the Social Science Research Council, financed in part by the Ford Foundation, the Andrew W. Mellon Foundation, and the National Endowment for the Humanities.

During the years of research and writing that have gone into the making of this study, my personal life has undergone important changes. I am grateful to my children Nedim and Murat for the fortitude with which they have dealt with those changes; to them, with love and appreciation, I dedicate this study. During the period of the writing, my dear wife Roxann was there whenever I needed her—which was all the time. To her I owe more than I can express in words for the intellectual and emotional challenges she has brought into my life.

A final note here on a technical question. In my translations from the Chinese original, I have opted for literateness over literalness. Literal translations often make the original authors sound like half-wits. I have tried to read the texts in accordance with my understanding of the context, and bring to them a fluency that is sometimes lacking in the original.

Durham, N.C.   A. D.
January 1988

CONTENTS

THE ORIGINS OF
CHINESE COMMUNISM

1

Perspectives and Perceptions: May Fourth Socialism and the Origins of Communism in China

The early history of Communism in China often reads as the triumphal march of Marx-Leninism into Chinese radical thinking, in which Non-Bolshevik socialisms appear in a lurking, shadowy way. Historians have recognized their presence during these years but usually assigned them to the historical pale, as marginal encumbrances with no significant bearing on the central ideological developments of the time. The ultimate victory in China of a Marxist-inspired Communist revolution has blurred in historical memory the important role of these other socialisms both in the origins of Chinese Communism and later in the Chinese revolution.

This blurring of historical memory is readily evident in the treatment historians have accorded anarchism. During the years around 1919, the May Fourth period, anarchism pervaded radical thinking on social and cultural change, and "communism" was identified with "anarcho-communism." Anarchism, moreover, served as "midwife" to Marxism; the majority of those who turned to Bolshevism after 1920 went through an anarchist phase in the course of their radicalization, as they acknowledged freely in later years. Yet students of early Chinese Communism have rarely tried to account for this "anomaly" in the Chinese attraction to Communism. Chinese historians portray anarchism as a residue of pre-Marxist petit-bourgeois intellectual inclinations that was rapidly marginalized when Marxism appeared on the scene. While in recent years there has been a tendency to attribute greater staying power to anarchism, they have continued to treat it as an undesirable intruder, a baneful influence that some could not purge from their minds. With a few exceptions, Western scholars have been even more adamant in treating anarchism in the May Fourth period as an inconsequential historical remnant. The two seminal studies of early Chinese Marxism that have done much to fashion our views of this period, Benjamin Schwartz's *Chinese Communism and the Rise of Mao* and Maurice Meisner's *Li Ta-chao and the Origins of Chinese Marxism*, scarcely mention anarchism. When they do, they merely relegate it to the past as (to paraphase Meisner) an anachronistic impulse that played no dynamic role in May Fourth thinking.[1] Even compelling evi-

3

dence of anarchism has been explained away, as when Meisner states that "Li Ta-chao . . . looked with great favor upon Kropotkin's theory of 'mutual aid': but the influence of Kropotkin was most strongly evident only after Li had already declared himself a Marxist in 1919, and he then used the idea of 'mutual aid' for the explicit purpose of reinterpreting the Marxist theory of class struggle."[2] It is puzzling why Li's anarchist-inspired reinterpretation of a central Marxist idea should imply anarchist anachronism rather than point to a serious need to qualify his self-proclaimed Marxism; suffice it to say here that such facile dismissal of anarchism in the historical literature on Marxism is common.

These views have not gone unchallenged. Some historians, pointing to the earlier popularity of anarchism, have argued not only that it remained influential through the May Fourth period, but even that anarchists paved the way for acceptance of Marxism by introducing the vocabulary of socialism into the language of Chinese politics.[3] These historians have done their case a disservice, however, by basing their arguments mostly on evidence from before 1911 rather than from the May Fourth period. The challenge, therefore, remains speculative and the case tentative, if not tendentious. A recent study by Robert Scalapino of Mao Zedong's early years has put forward a convincing argument for anarchist influence on Mao at this time, but this only underlines Mao's idiosyncracies as a Marxist, and leaves the broader issue open.[4]

Our failure to come to terms with the significant role of anarchism has distorted our understanding of this period and thus seriously flawed our understanding of the origins of Chinese Communism.[5] Not only did anarchism pervade radical thinking during the period when Marxism was introduced (or re-introduced) into Chinese thought, but anarchists played an important part in the early organizational activities that culminated in the founding of the Communist Party of China in 1920–1921. Yet these well-known facts have not received a serious hearing among historians who, with their attention firmly focused on the evolution of Marxism, have not deemed it problematic to relegate to marginality the questions raised by anarchism—presumably because it was a socialism without a future. A similar fate has befallen other non-Bolshevik socialisms that were popular in the immediate May Fourth period.

In this study I will examine systematically the relationship between Marxism and non-Bolshevik socialisms in May Fourth thinking, and consider its implications for our understanding of the origins of Chinese Communism. I believe that prevailing views of this subject are based on evidence drawn more from ideological memories, reorganized when the Party was organized, than from contemporary testimony. Indeed, they draw their plausibility from a teleological hindsight which is premised upon the rapid diffusion of Marxism in Chinese radical thinking with the founding of the Party and perceives in every sign of interest in Marxism in preceding years confirmation of an inevitable progress toward a Communist identity. This teleological hindsight has resulted in a reading which glosses over, even suppresses, historical evidence that suggests a more ambiguous picture. The recognition that non-Bolshevik

socialisms, in particular anarchism, pervasively influenced May Fourth thinking introduces many ambiguities into the ideologcal identity of radical intellectuals during this period and calls forth a radical rewriting of our understanding of the origins of Communism in China, especially where it concerns
the relationship between Marxist ideology and Communist organization.

As the point of departure for this discussion, I would like to summarize
briefly what I consider to be the conventional wisdom on the origins of the
Communist movement in China. This "wisdom," traceable to the works by
Schwartz and Meisner cited earlier, has shaped textbook accounts and may be
found readily in more specialized studies as well.

> The Communist movement in China was a product of the influence on
> Chinese revolutionary intellectuals of the Russian Revolution of 1917.
> Chinese intellectuals had been vaguely familiar with Marx and Marxism
> for nearly two decades before 1921, but had found little in the Marxist
> ideas they had encountered to excite their revolutionary imagination. It
> was the Russian Revolution that dramatized for them the significance of
> Marxism as a global ideology of revolution. The shock waves from the
> Russian Revolution carried to China the revolutionary message of Marx-
> ism as it had been formulated by Lenin. Under the influence of the Rus-
> sian Revolution, radical intellectuals turned to the study of Marxism.
> Marxism, of Western origin and yet critical of the contemporary West,
> found a receptive audience among intellectuals who were intellectually
> drawn to the West but felt frustrated with the West because of the ag-
> gressive activities in China of the Western powers. This frustration ex-
> ploded with the May Fourth Movement of 1919, following which the
> appeal of Marxism expanded visibly. In the Leninist constitution of the
> Russian Revolution, May Fourth intellectuals discovered a solution to
> their problems, and the most important "text" on the Marxist idea of
> revolution. The revolutionary government of the new Russia, through
> the Communist International (hereafter Comintern) it had recently
> created, intervened in the Chinese revolution directly to ensure that the
> lessons of the Russian Revolution were not lost on Chinese revolution-
> aries. With the help of Comintern advisors, Marxist intellectuals founded
> the Communist Party of China in July 1921.

This account represents a ground plan that has structured our understanding. The two events that frame the account, the Russian Revolution and
the founding of the Communist Party, dominate this plan. The narratives
with which historians have filled out the historical space between these two
events vary in tone and texture but share a common plot. The central theme
in this plot is the diffusion of Marxism in Chinese thought in the years 1917–
1921: Marxism entered Chinese thought under the influence of the Russian
Revolution and, having achieved sufficient density (in terms of adherents and
their ideological commitments), precipitated into the Communist party. The
May Fourth Movement served to promote the diffusion of Marxism in Chinese radical thinking. Comintern aid served as the catalyst in the precipitation

of ideology into organization. (It is important to note that Marxism in this account refers, explicitly of implicitly, to the Marxism of Lenin, or "Marx-Leninism.")

The problem with this account lies not in what it says, but what it does not say. The account is satisfactory as a surface reading of the historical developments that attended the emergence of the Communist movement. The problems concern the historical explanation embedded in this narrative structure. This reading ignores the subsurface ideological and social structures within which the Communist movement acquired its identity and is satisfied to restrict its vision to a perspective defined by Communism's *emergence*.

This narrative act of suppression in historical consciousness of non-Bolshevik socialisms parallels the suppression of rivals to Communism in history. This account assumes as its primary task the delineation of the *ideological* evolution whereby the "influence" of the Russian Revolution was distilled into the reality of the founding of the Party. In the process, the account renders silent all that did not contribute "positively" to the progress of Communism, just as it underlines all that seemingly contributed to that progress. Thus it marginalizes questions that have significant import for understanding not only the historical process but also the two events that frame it. These questions are audible in this account only in its silences, as part of the background noise of history.

These silences pertain most importantly to the relationship between Marxism and competing ideologies of social revolution, in particular anarchism, which in the immediate May Fourth period provided the ideological counterpoint to Marxism. The point here is not merely that radical thinking at the time was more complex than the account makes it out to be. These silences, rendered audible, not only cast the account in a different phraseology, but recast the problematic of early Communism: the question is no longer simply why and how it emerged in China, but how it emerged victorious over its more popular ideological rival when the latter showed no signs of dying a natural death but, on the contrary, was reaching the zenith of its popularity in radical thought. Phrased somewhat differently, the validity of the account's historical explanation can be sustained only by its denial of historical significance to alternative ideas of social revolution, just as the Communist movement in China was to prove its viability historically by suppressing its competitors. This was not merely a Marxist suppression of non-Marxist socialisms. Perhaps most significantly, in its presentation of the Party as the "natural" outgrowth of the diffusion of Marxism in Chinese thought, the account covers up the suppression to which Marxism itself was subjected by its subordination to the prerogatives of Bolshevik organization.

What is lost in the process is a sense of history. Seemingly a narrative in time (and space), this account in actuality abridges both time and space through the medium of ideology. Rather than present the two events (the Russian Revolution and the founding of the Party) in terms of a historical process, grounded in the perceptions and activities of the subjects of history, the account presents the historical process as mere intermediation. Historians' efforts to uncover ideological factors that may have predisposed Chinese intellectuals to receiving the message of the Russian Revolution, rather than restoring historicity to the process, has only added an element of teleological inevitability. The four-year interlude between the two events appears as an undifferentiated temporality, marked only by forward leaps in the inevitable progress of ideology. And the human agency that *translated* the one event into the other appears simply as the medium through which the one event was *transmitted* to the other. Studies of early Chinese Marxism typically display less concern for the conscious activity that implanted Marxism in Chinese thought than for the modulations Marxism went through as it was transmitted to China through the medium of unconscious ideological predispositions. This may have much to tell us about the history in ideology. It says much less about the ideology in history.

Three prominent features of this account are crucial. In the first place, the account puts external influence above internal developments in Chinese thought and society; internal background is often presented as no more than a "predisposition" of one kind or another that makes the external influence inevitable. The Russian Revolution is thus endowed with the status of a transformative event in Chinese history.

Secondly, the terms of the account are abstractly ideological, and evolutionary rather than dialectical. The diffusion of Marxism in Chinese thought appears as a consequence of the Russian Revolution, and a premise of the founding of the Party: Notwithstanding certain qualifications by its authors, the account presents the diffusion of Marxism between these two events as an ideological evolution which followed an unbroken path, gathering adherents and strength as it went along.

By the same logic, finally, the account isolates ideology from organizational activity, and assigns priority to the former. The interest in and/or accumulation of knowledge of Marxism leads with the force of inevitability to organizational activities that culminate in the founding of the Communist party. A certain conception of the relationship between ideology and organization—that ideology determines organization—is re-presented here as the logic of history—that ideology precedes organization temporally. This same conception imposes a one-dimensional meaning on ideology: that Marxism, even without the benefit of organization, carried the same meaning for everyone; in other words, that a Marxist ideological entity emerged prior to Communist organization and served as its basis.

I will address the questions raised by these features of the account at length in the final section of this chapter, for they provide the *problematic* around which this study is structured. Before proceeding it is only necessary to note that this inquiry brings into sharp relief a further problem: the evidential basis for our understanding of the origins of Communism in China. This understanding rests entirely upon our appreciation of the appeal of Marxism to those who emerged early on as leaders of the Communist movement, Li Dazhao and Chen Duxiu. Chen Duxiu, as is well known, opted for a version of guild socialism under the influence of John Dewey and Bertrand

Russell, and did not convert to Marxism until sometime in early 1920. This leaves only Li, who responded with enthusiasm to the Russian Revolution in 1918, and "declared" himself a Marxist in 1919. Li's experience, in other words, provides the sole basis for our notions of Marxist thought in China before 1920; indeed, it is not an exaggeration to suggest that the conventional account is little more than a re-presentation, as historical process, of the biography of Li Dazhao. While no one, with the possible exception of Schwartz,[6] has suggested that we may generalize from Li and Chen to other early Marxists, their cases have tacitly served as paradigms of conversion.

It is problematic to read from the cases of Chen and Li into the conversion of their younger followers (most of whom also happened to be their students), and not only because there is even less evidence in their case of any serious interest in Marxism before 1920. There is compelling evidence that Li and Chen, once they had become Marxists, used their considerable intellectual prestige, and their personal relationships, to convert those who became China's first generation of Communists. Thus their experiences differed fundamentally from those of Li and Chen.

Furthermore, the case of Li Dazhao is not as nonproblematic as has been made out. Meisner's biography, brilliant as it is, succeeds in confirming Li's self-proclaimed Marxism only by overruling or rationalizing contradicting evidence, especially evidence that raises serious questions about Li's understanding of the Russian Revolution and Marxism. On occasion, as in the example cited earlier, highly suggestive textual evidence—that Li's Marxism was not all he claimed—has been dismissed. Whatever our final verdict may be on this body of evidence, there is no question that its problematic nature calls for further consideration.

The thesis that guides this study may be summarized briefly as follows. Viewed from a contemporary perspective, the immediate question pertinent to understanding ideological developments in the May Fourth period concerns not Marxism alone, but the immense (and sudden) interest in socialism in general. This perspective de-emphasizes the "influence" of the Russian Revolution on Chinese radical thinking—since May Fourth socialism, as far as it knew of the peculiarities of Bolshevism, was wary of the revolutionary strategy that had brought the Bolsheviks to power. External events, especially the appearance of a worldwide "tide" of social revolutions, were of crucial importance in drawing Chinese attention to socialism. The Russian Revolution was recognized as the most important of these events, a revolution unprecedented in its compass, and a paradigm for a new age of revolutions; however, the advocacy of socialism became plausible because of developments within Chinese society, the effects of which became recognizable with an unprecedented sharpness in 1919: the emergence of labor and capital, with all the attendant social problems.

The consequence of this recognition was that distinctions were blurred between the problems of China and those of other societies around the globe, a blurring which came easily to a generation nourished on the ideological cosmopolitanism of the New Culture Movement. Global problems were China's national problems, and China's national problems were global problems, all of them rooted in the capitalist world system. Awareness of worldwide social conflict resulted in a new reading of China's problems, in other words, while the evidence of social conflict within China endowed worldwide developments, including the Russian Revolution, with an immediacy of meaning. Social revolutionary ideology, which *as* ideology had a history of nearly two decades in Chinese radical thinking, had found its substance. In this context, socialism, with its promise to end the conflicts created by capitalism, found a ready audience.

This new awareness did not point automatically to Marxism or the revolutionary strategy of the Bolsheviks. The most fervent advocates of socialism in the immediate May Fourth period valued it because it promised not revolutionary violence but the possibility of avoiding the violence that capitalist society generated by dividing society into conflicting classes. Interest in socialism stimulated interest in Marx, as "the founding father" of socialism, and in Marxism; but the insistence of May Fourth socialists that socialism promised the resolution of conflict, not further conflict, also "obstructed" the progress of "Marxism," as some Chinese historians have argued. Similarly, while May Fourth socialism pointed to a Bolshevik-style Communist party as a possible option, the Communist Party of China did not emerge spontaneously out of the diffusion of socialist ideology. Rather, diffuse socialist ideas inspired radical activity, which in turn led to frustrating experiences—convincing some Chinese socialists of the hopelessness of peaceful strategies of change. It was not an abstract attraction to the Russian model of revolution, moreover, but direct Comintern intervention in the Chinese revolution, that in the end decided them in favor of a Bolshevik-style political movement. Only at that point, in 1920, when activities began toward the formation of the Party, did May Fourth socialists have to face the question of a Marxist ideological identity. The Communist party, in other words, was the condition for the emergence of Marxism as an identifiable alternative in Chinese socialism.

I will discuss this process in historical detail in the third part of this study. A few comments will be useful here on the conceptual considerations that underlie that discussion. I question not the significance of ideology in the formation of the Party, but rather historical explanations that assign priority to ideology and isolate it from organizational activity. As I noted earlier, a certain conception of the relationship between ideology and organization—that ideology determines organization—is re-presented in these explanations as the logic of history—that ideology precedes organization temporally. This conception is not the only one possible; indeed, it is as mechanical as its opposite—that organization determines, or even renders superfluous, ideology. The one view is idealistic in the extreme, even if its proponents include Marxist ideologues who will not extend to themselves the critical materialism they readily apply to others. The other view, a kind of inverted materialism, confounds social existence with the organizations that give it coherence, and ig-

nores not only that consciously motivated human activity is originally responsible for the choice of organizational forms, but that these forms themselves,
far from being autonomous determinants of consciousness, are ideologically
fashioned to express certain conceptions of social order.

What I propose instead is a dialectical conception of this relationship that
restores temporality to both ideology and organization, that re-presents the
relationship as a dialectical process and, therefore, shifts attention to the human activity that constituted the historical process by intermediating ideology
and organization. The focus here is on ideology as ongoing activity rather
than finished intellectual system, and on organization as construction rather
than finished structure. The revolutionary activity that constituted this process
involved rupture and suppression as much as synthesis and development. The
development of ideology required the suppression of its own ingredients, just
as its tangible expression—organization—restricted, as it formed, the very activities that went into its formation. The process, therefore, should be understood not merely as evolution, but more fundamentally as the working-
out of contradictions. The dialectic between ideology and organization has
important implications for our understanding of the origins of the Communist
movement in China and the direction it took in its early years. It also tells us
a good deal concerning the role of ideology and organization in the emergence
of radical movements in general.

The origins of the Communist movement in China lie obscured in complex
relationships among Chinese intellectuals in the May Fourth period which
Meisner has described as "a tangled web of obscurity."[7] Meisner did not undertake to disentangle these relationships. Neither have other students of early
Chinese Communism; their views of this period have, for the most part, been
derivative of his study and Schwartz's *Chinese Communist and the Rise of
Mao,* a work which also steers clear of questions raised by these relationships, indeed obscures them. Historians have been satisfied to recognize these
relationships, and proceeded with the "real" business of tracing the emergence of Communism, as if these relationships had no direct bearing on their
analyses and were simply marginal elements of the historical environment.

As Chinese historians have begun to recognize in recent years, in these
tangled relationships we find not only the conditions for the emergence of
Communism, but the very "moments," ideological and organizational, out of
which the Communist movement was forged. Of these relationships, two are
of crucial significance. First is the relationship of Marxists to other socialists,
in particular the anarchists, who participated directly in the initial efforts toward the founding of the Party. One participant in these events has recalled
recently that "Marxism-Leninism was only one among the hundred schools"
of this period.[8] Marxism was not merely one among the competing socialisms of the immediate May Fourth period, we might add, but the weakest one,
in both the number committed to it and, even more so, Chinese intellectuals'
familiarity with it; and Leninism was virtually nonexistent as ideology. Placing
Marxism against its socialist competitors brings into relief the distinctive elements of Communist ideological and organizational activity, which elevated

this weak Marxism to supremacy in Chinese socialism within a matter of years. In doing this, moreover, it is necessary to recognize first that this inter-socialist competition was very real. Marxists, in their efforts to discredit rival socialisms, tried at the time to portray them as backward expressions of a defunct Chinese culture or of outmoded class interests.[9] Some historians, Schwartz among them, have accepted such portrayals at face value.[10] This view ignores completely that as the Party was organized in 1920–1921, its founders devoted more energy to suppressing anarchism and, to a lesser extent, guild socialism, than to refuting their non-socialist critics.[11]

Of related, and equal, significance is the relationship of Communism to the concatenation of events we have come to term the New Culture and May Fourth movements. Lucien Bianco has remarked that "the founding of the CCP [Chinese Communist Party] can be seen as an extension of the May Fourth Movement."[12] This observation has a profound truth to it, though it remains to be spelled out. Developments set in motion by the May Fourth Movement did indeed provide the groundwork for the Party. In this case too, however, the process was not evolutionary but dialectical, for the building of the Party would in the end require a rupture with its May Fourth legacy.

If ideologically the Communist party benefited from the intellectual conditions prepared by anarchism, it benefited organizationally from the existence of study societies, which had emerged with the activism generated by the New Culture and May Fourth movements, in which anarchist ideas played an important role. These societies, loose associations of intellectuals devoted to ideological inquiry and debate, articulated in their constitution the "tangled" relationships of the period. They provided a direct link between the May Fourth Movement and the founding of the Party. And they provided the immediate social context within which ideological issues were clarified, and the tangled web of May Fourth socialism sorted out into various strands— some of them tattered beyond repair in the process.

In their origins, these informal study societies were not Communist in leadership or intention; their primary goal was to pursue the intellectual and social issues the New Culture and the May Fourth movements had brought to the forefront of Chinese intellectuals' consciousness. Membership was based on the personal networks that had been established within the new educational institutions and journalism which provided the context for the May Fourth movement in general. Ideological labels are not appropriate for these ideologically and organizationally diffuse coteries; but to the extent that they displayed a social revolutionary orientation, their ideas were infused with the vocabulary of anarchism.

The Communist movement in China emerged out of the reconstitution of such associations across China's major urban centers into a coherent organization in accordance with Bolshevik principles. It is doubtful that the Communist movement or ideology could have assumed the coherence it did as rapidly as it did without these societies having prepared the ground organizationally. When the Comintern initiated the founding of a Communist party, the few who had shown Marxist inclinations in 1919 were quickly able, by

the weight of their prestige, to transform into political cells the study societies they had either founded themselves or had contact with through personal
connections of one kind of another.

The dialectic of Communism's emergence is most readily apparent in the
process whereby these societies were converted in 1920 from ideologically
and organizationally loose associations of intellectuals into the coherently
organized political cells of ideologically committed activists out of which the
Communist movement was to take shape. In 1920–1921, "the organizational
and ideological foundations for the Communist Party were laid"—not because these foundations were created at this time, as Meisner's statement suggests, but because at this time the organizational rupture was initiated that
led directly to the Party's founding within the year. The laying of the foundations of 1920 meant for the Communists the reorganization of the May
Fourth legacy. This meant the parting of the ways for Chinese socialists who
were unable, once confronted with Communist demands for organizational
coherence, to sustain either the personal relationships that had once held
them together, or the universalistic humanitarianism of May Fourth ideology
that had hitherto countered the tensions in their eclectic socialism.

These organizational developments were crucial to the unfolding of Marxist ideology. The emergence of Marxism as a distinctive ideology of action in
China coincided with the organizational rupture initiated in 1920. Ideology
was not a passive element in this rupture; it not only legitimized the transformation of study societies, constituted out of personal networks, into political
cells organized in accordance with impersonal rules, but even more importantly, it endowed that transformation with meaning and direction. Nevertheless, I will argue that until this transformation got under way, it is meaningless to speak of Marxism as a distinctive current in Chinese socialist
thinking, because only a rare Chinese intellectual before 1920 was conscious of
him/herself as a Marxist. And even in those cases the assertion of Marxist
commitment was not matched by clarity of ideological expression. As one
Soviet author has put it, "It was in the course of enthusiastic struggles against
bourgeois reformists and anarchists that *believers* in socialism reached an
important conclusion: that Marxism was not merely a European theory but
an international one, completely appropriate to Chinese conditions" (emphasis mine).[13] We might point out that these "struggles," with guild socialists
and anarchists, got under way in 1920, and were part and parcel of the organizational struggles for supremacy during which the first coteries of Marxists
came into being in China. In other words, the diffusion of Marxism as ideology (or, the "belief" in Marxism) coincided with, and was indistinguishable
as a process from, the organizational emergence of the Communist party.

I do not mean to suggest here that we should abandon explanations based
on ideology in favor of explanations based on the inner workings of these
organizations. As I will argue later, the growth of interest in Marxism and
the search for coherent organization coincided historically in the years 1920–
1921. The relationship between ideology and organization was a dialectical
one. Ideology played an important part in bringing organizational coherence

to informal associations. In the process, ideological commitment replaced intellectual interest or personal relationship as the criterion for membership. Marxist ideology proved relevant to Chinese intellectuals at that point when the study societies, having fulfilled their role as social spaces in which intellectual issues could be aired and clarified, pointed to the need for the kind of organization that could serve as a means for political action. Marxism's immediate impact was to provide guidelines for the constitution of a formal organization, with disciplinary powers over its membership. This reconstruction did not end disagreement or conflict, but brought it within well-defined boundaries, with the coherence of the organization as its reference point. Those who, for intellectual or political reasons, held ideas that differed from the organizationally defined ideology had one of two options open to them: to leave the organization, or to subordinate their divergence to organizational discipline. Marxist ideology, in other words, served as the architectonic principle of the emergent Communist organization. Ideology, moreover, did not serve merely as an organizing principle but defined the nature and the direction of the political activity to which the organization was to be committed.

The organization, on the other hand, by placing limits on interpretation, disciplined ideological activity and endowed it with coherence. The study societies, however diffuse their origins, served as vehicles for ideological propagation. At the very least, they made it possible for the first few Marxists to spread their ideas over the face of China. Once study societies had been converted into a political organization, this organization could also serve as a coordinator of political and ideological activity on a national scale, and was able to exert an influence in China out of all proportion to the actual number of members. Thanks to this organization, in the 1920s Communists appeared as a beacon of coherence in a sea of political and ideological chaos.

The place of organization in the origins of the Communist movement is important in two other respects. In the first place, Bolshevik organization held considerable appeal for May Fourth radicals, not just among anti-Communists such as Dai Jitao, but even for Chen Duxiu and Li Dazhao, the founders of the Party.[14] Many a Chinese intellectual expressed concern in these years over Chinese inability to participate in organized action. This was possibly a basic reason for the immense popularity in the immediate May Fourth period of Kropotkin's idea of "mutual aid," which appeared as a functional principle—more than a utopian promise—for realizing group life, a fundamental concern of May Fourth radicals. And China's intellectual and educational leaders, beginning with Cai Yuanpei in Beijing University, made efforts to establish associations among youth that could bring to them habits of cooperation and organization. In the literature of the period, discussion of ideology, *zhuyi* (literally "ism"), was frequently linked to the problem of concerted action; in other words, it was perceived in its relationship to organization. In Marxism, seen through Bolshevik lenses, Chinese intellectuals discovered not just a social theory, but an ideology of action—an organizational ideology that provided not just common goals or a utopian vision (for which there were alternatives) but, more importantly, a unifying principle for concerted action. It was here that the role of the Russian Revolution was most catalytic. The Revolution's impact was not so much in abstract ideological "influence," but in the Comintern's direct intervention in organizing ideologically uncertain radicals into a unified group. The victory of Marxism over its socialist rivals was not ideological, the ascendancy of truth over false consciousness, as Chinese historians would have it, but organizational: by guaranteeing ideological discipline, the Communist organization allowed effective social and political activity. It offered possibilities of action that were foreclosed to its competitors, in particular the anarchists, who were not willing or able to organize to the same level of coherence. The experience, however, was to have considerable influence over the Guomindang.

The question of organization is important, secondly, from a long-term, broader, historical perspective. Just because the Bolshevik possibilities for action held an attraction for Chinese radicals does not mean that in the May Fourth period they were attracted to Bolshevism pure and simple. Indeed, despite the rather vague understanding of Marxism in the early May Fourth period, Chinese attraction to Marxism was initially characterized by considerable openness, with regard to both its revolutionary premises and its implications for China. This openness was lost as the interpretive possibilities inherent in Marxist theory were restricted to accord with organizational prerogatives.

There was, in other words, a price to be paid. The conversion of study groups into political cells divided radical ranks in China, because clear ideological lines were drawn between the various socialisms. The Communists themselves repudiated the critical perspectives on Marxism offered by other socialisms, which were themselves rooted in alternative readings of Marxism. In terms of revolutionary practice, this repudiation of alternative socialist visions compromised the democratic goals of political activity; ideologically, it meant the restriction of the capacity for critical self-consciousness. Furthermore, the ideological discipline that the organization guaranteed also made for an ideological narrowness that diminished revolutionary flexibility and, to some extent, blinded Communists to the realities of Chinese society. Ideological cliches replaced a burgeoning Marxist inquiry into Chinese society that would not be revived seriously until it became evident in the later 1920s that the revolutionary strategy based on those cliches had failed. This ideological discipline also facilitated control of the Party by the Comintern, which from the beginning defined its ideological content and, therefore, its political goals.

The question of organization, in other words, has important implications for our understanding of the course Marxist ideology would take in China and, by extension, our understanding of Marxism as a global philosophy of social revolution. Failure to appreciate this point has often led analysts of Marxism in China and elsewhere to look in ideology for problems that reside more properly in the relationship between ideology and its organizational context, which is at least partly a consequence of circumstances over which the ideology has no power. It is not surprising that the more flexible and creative interpretations of Marxism in the early 1920s (and later) in China were undertaken by Marxists who remained outside the Party or abandoned it after a brief flirtation. That the Party has repudiated the Marxism of those who would not abide by its organizational restrictions does not make them any the less Marxist; it only points to the Party's efforts to control ideological interpretation. The Communists themselves were not to reevaluate their assumptions concerning Chinese society until after 1927, when the Party's policies, first having given it enormous power and prestige, had brought it within a few years to the verge of extinction.

This study seeks to demonstrate the thesis just outlined through a reconsideration of three questions crucial to our understanding of the origins of Communism in China: the question of the influence in China of the Russian Revolution; the question of Marxism in the immediate May Fourth period, by which I mean basically the year 1919; and the question of the organizational activities in 1920–1921 that culminated in the founding of the Communist party of China in July 1921. The discussion draws heavily on historical materials that have become available in the People's Republic of China in recent years, especially materials pertinent to anarchism in the May Fourth period and anarchists' participation in the activities that were to lead, ironically for them, to the victory of Bolshevism. These materials do not simply add to the evidence already available; they enable us to reread formerly available materials from a new perspective.

PART I
Chinese Radicals and the
October Revolution in Russia

Prologue

The October Revolution in Russia in 1917 was a turning point in the history of socialism. The Revolution restored "revolution" to Marxism, which by the early part of the century had come to be identified with nonrevolutionary social democracy. As a consequence, revolutionary Marxism during most of the twentieth century has been identified, in popular images of Marxism, with Bolshevism, which has served as a measure of the revolutionariness of socialists. The Revolution also had an immediate impact on Third World revolutionary movements; in its aftermath, Marxism in its Leninist interpretation entered the ideology of struggles against imperialism from China, Korea, and Vietnam to Latin America, giving rise to the ideology of national liberation. In China, Marxism provided not only an ideology of revolution but also a model, first of revolutionary struggle and then of socialist nation-building which, in spite of problematic consequences, has left an indelible imprint on the course of Chinese history.

The October Revolution impressed its contemporaries as the first new paradigm of revolution to come along since the French Revolution, the fulfillment of European socialists' nearly century-old dream of social revolution. The French Revolution had heralded the age of political revolutions, contemporaries believed; now the Russian Revolution opened up the age of social revolutions, which would finally complete the revolutionary transformation of society. Around the turn of the century social revolution had been identified, in its evolutionary reformist guise, with Marxist social democracy of one kind or another and, in its immanent revolutionary guise, with anarchism. With the October Revolution, revolutionary social transformation came to be identified with Marxism, which in the years following, took over anarchism's status as the preeminent ideology of social revolution worldwide. In China as well, in the early 1920s, Marxism quickly superseded anarchism in radical thinking.

All this is clear, however, only in hindsight. Radical revolutionaries around the world responded to the October Revolution with an enthusiasm invoked more by the apocalyptic visions of social transformation the Revolution inspired than a clear perception of its ideological intentions. Concerning these, there was considerable confusion. Part of this confusion was implicit in the condition of revolution itself. The Revolution opened up the floodgates of social radicalism which, in the vastness of Russia, did not always follow a uniform course; even the few on-site observers such as John Reed could not keep track of the different courses the Revolution took in different parts of Russia.

This problem was exacerbated by the confusion introduced into images of the Revolution by its foes and friends alike. Anti-Bolshevik governments, from the United States to Japan, not only blockaded news of the Revolution (as part of a literal blockade and, from August 1918, invasion) but did their best to distort its nature. Especially noteworthy is the loose use of the label "anarchist" to describe the new Bolshevik government. This practice branded them as creators of chaos, but also led to more serious ideological confusion in popular images. Radicals who, in their anti-capitalist enthusiasm, read into the Revolution their own variegated, and conflicting, aspirations, compounded the confusion. Even anarchists, from Peter Kropotkin to Emma Goldman, initially supported the Revolution as a social revolution (though suspicious of its possible consequences), thus adding to the confusion between Bolshevism and anarchism. If anything unified radical responses to the Revolution, it was not a clear appreciation of its nature, but a feeling that "the enemy of my enemy is my friend." The October Revolution promised to bring down the enemy of all socialisms, capitalism, and must, therefore, be supported by all socialists against the efforts of capitalist governments to bring it down. A worthy goal, this did a good deal to blur the socialism of the Bolsheviks.

Socialism in China had a history of nearly two decades when the October Revolution erupted. Social revolutionary thinking in China paralleled, in its basic goals, the European and American thinking that had inspired it, mainly through the intermediacy of Japanese socialism. The two major trends were a "social policy" socialism, and anarchism. The former was characteristic of the thinking of Sun Yatsen and his close followers in the Guomindang, and of Jiang Kanghu, founder in 1911 of the first socialist organization in China, the Chinese Socialist Party. They advocated a socialism—inspired for the most part by European and American non-socialist social reformers—that sought to control capitalism in order to achieve a peaceful and egalitarian social development under government supervision; what might more properly be called "non-capitalist development" rather than socialism. Anarchism was associated primarily with a group of intellectuals who had converted to it while students in France before 1911, and a group of Cantonese intellectuals who after 1911 organized anarchist societies in Guangzhou (Canton) Shanghai, and elsewhere. Anarchists advocated a social revolution that was more authentic because they believed in both imminent social transformation and a popular mobilization to that end. Anarchist activity took the form primarily of cultural and propaganda activity, but they were also the first among Chinese radicals to engage in labor organization.

Anarchism was the most popular socialism in China on the eve of the October Revolution. After 1911, Sun Yatsen and Jiang Kanghu had been forced to leave China for political reasons. Anarchists had also been subjected to government persecution but had survived, mainly because they were less dependent on organized activity than other socialists. Their popularity increased with the New Culture Movement, conventionally dated from 1915, which was initiated by prominent intellectuals to transform China culturally. The leaders of the Movement, disappointed by the failure of China's Republican experiment after 1911, had come to believe that cultural change must take priority over all other change, and sought to nurture the growth of a new generation of Chinese attuned to the culture of the modern world. The antipolitical thrust of the Movement, and its emphasis on individual cultural and social liberation, created fertile grounds for the spread of anarchist ideas among Chinese youth. Though the leaders of the Movement were not themselves anarchists, anarchists participated widely in the Movement and had considerable impact on its thinking.

When the October Revolution erupted, Chinese radicals were ill prepared to understand or appreciate it as a Marxist revolution. Chinese confusion was even worse than that worldwide because they received their information secondhand from foreign sources. And the warlord government (which even sent a warship to Vladivostok to join the allied invasion of Russia) did its best to distort the picture, referring to the Bolsheviks as "extremists" (*guojipai*), an appellation associated in China primarily with the anarchists. But the confusion cannot be ascribed only to these causes, as Chinese historians suggest. Anarchists in China initially claimed the Revolution for their own, shaping initial radical reactions to it. Its nature was uncertain even to Li Dazhao, who supported it enthusiastically (and therefore later gained the reputation of being China's first Marxist). His uncertainty, due partly to the influence upon him of anarchist readings of the Revolution, also reflected a worldwide radical uncertainty. He was an avid reader at this time of the radical press that supported the Revolution, such as the *New Republic,* and American socialists such as Morris Hillquit (lawyer, author, and a socialist candidate for mayor of New York), who had responded to the Revolution with enthusiasm. Li's appreciation of the Revolution, more apocalyptic than substantial (as Meisner has pointed out), equalled in its enthusiasm Hillquit's greetings in November 1919: "Hail, Soviet Russia! The bright proletarian hope, the symbol of the new world spirit and new world order."[1] The vocabulary in which Li described the Revolution owed more to anarchism than Marxism.

This part will discuss the Chinese reception of the October Revolution in 1918–1919 and the Revolution's immediate impact on Chinese radicals. Three features of the Chinese response emerge. In the first place, the most conspicuous feature of the liberal and radical press reports was sympathy for the plight of the new Soviet Union under Allied aggression. Even those who were noncommittal on the revolutionary undertaking itself often expressed the belief that the new government should have a chance to pursue its goals. This sympathy turned to admiration in 1919 as the Bolshevik government proved able not only to ward off internal and external enemies but at the same time to institute a new structure of socialist government.

Secondly, Chinese radicals, beginning with the anarchists in the spring of

1918, hailed the Revolution as the harbinger of a new age. By early 1919, anarchists had grown wary but admiration had grown in other circles, including New Culture radicals such as Li Dazhao and Chen Duxiu, and some of Sun Yatsen's followers in the Guomindang. Admiration, however, did not imply a simultaneous approval of the Bolshevik model of revolution for China. In 1919 Li Dazhao came closest to suggesting that this model might be the only way out for China. Most of the other writers on the Revolution, though sympathetic to the Bolshevik undertaking, pointed to it as "negative example" of what might befall China if those in power did not heed the calls for fundamental reform. In these cases there was also a genuine interest in the new Bolshevik institutions as possible models for China.

Finally, the Chinese who wrote on the Revolution in 1918–1919 knew very little about its ideological foundations or its leaders' ideas. The Revolution was perceived within the context of the "tide" of revolutions that had erupted in the aftermath of World War I, and therefore seemed proof less of Bolshevism's virtues than of the necessity, worldwide, for social revolution to alleviate the problems created by capitalism. The revolution in Germany and labor movements in the United States and Great Britain also drew considerable attention. The Revolution provoked interest in Marxism, but Chinese writers refrained from identifying Marxism with Bolshevism, about which they knew very little. While Lenin and Trotsky were of immediate interest as revolutionary leaders in 1918, the Chinese knew very little about them, and there was little indication of any awareness of the momentousness of Lenin's interpretation, or reinterpretation, of Marxism. Lenin received attention from the anarchists in 1918, and by 1919 there was no question of his importance in the October Revolution. Yet he did not receive conspicuously more attention than other contemporary socialist leaders. For example, in the various articles on socialism and the Revolution published in the influential *Eastern Miscellany* (*Dongfang zazhi*) in 1918, Lenin appeared as an incidental figure in the revolutionary movement in Russia, even more so in the history of socialism; on the other hand, one article hailed Karl Liebknecht, another contemporary socialist leader, as "the Martin Luther of our Day."[2] When Liebknecht and Rosa Luxemburg were killed in the Spartacist Uprising in January 1919, a parade held in Guangzhou to commemorate them drew thousands; even if some spectators thought, according to one participant, that the pictures on the placards were of a recently deceased missionary couple![3]

If Chinese radicals were not fully cognizant of Lenin's importance to socialism, they knew even less about his ideas on revolution, including his ideas on revolution in the age of imperialism, the nationalistic appeals of which have been adduced in the past as an explanation for the Chinese attraction to Communism. Familiarity with Lenin would come after, not before, 1920.

2

A Revolution Perceived: The October Revolution through Chinese Eyes

Influence is an astrological concept, not a historical one. To render the concept historical, it is necessary to take as the point of departure for analysis not the influence, but the influenced, who appropriate for themselves an event or an idea outside their own history that is not of their making. This process of appropriation raises immediate questions concerning the meaning of influence.

Such was the case with the October Revolution in Chinese eyes. Except for an occasional Chinese, the Revolution did not appear in 1917–1918 the earthshaking event it was made out to be in later years. Those who did appreciate its revolutionary nature were not, therefore, transmuted into Bolsheviks; rather, they read into it their own concerns, and expressed their appreciation in a vocabulary they were familiar with because of the course Chinese radicalism had taken in the years before 1917: the vocabulary of anarchism. Chinese radicals who first received the message of the October Revolution found in it something it was not. They would not concretely grasp it until after they ceased to describe it in a vocabulary derived from a radical tradition that was contrary in some of its basic premises to what Bolshevism represented. This initial confusion was to leave its mark not only on their immediate appreciation of the Revolution but on their understanding of Marxism as well.

News of the Revolution reached China immediately after it had broken out, but throughout 1918, reporting on Russia remained sporadic and emphasized the Revolution's political and military events rather than ideology. There is little indication that in this reporting the Revolution carried a qualitative significance beyond that of other major world events following World War I. As stated in the Prologue, and as one historian of the period has put it, these reports displayed little comprehension of the Revolution's basis. When a special significance was attached to it, this significance was couched in terms that distorted its Bolshevik ideology. In the words of this historian:

> Because of a variety of restrictive conditions, reports on the Russian October Revolution in Chinese publications of the time (which were for the most part organs of bourgeois and petit-bourgeois parties and groups)

left something to be desired. Most of them were for a long time unable to comprehend the nature or the historical significance of the Revolution. They could not even distinguish clearly the basic differences between Bolsheviks, Mensheviks, and other parties such as the Social Revolutionary Party.[1]

Chinese historians have blamed this situation on distortions by the Chinese and foreign bourgeois press. Government repression of "extremism" in China cut Chinese radicals off from direct sources on the Revolution and led to their reliance on the bourgeois press of Europe and Japan. Within China, most of the reporting was done by the bourgeois and petit-bourgeois press, which similarly misrepresented the Revolution in accordance with their own ideological proclivities.

The seriousness of press censorship in China, about which there is no question, hardly changes the fact that up to the eve of the May Fourth Movement in 1919, the Chinese did not have a very clear idea of the Revolution's nature, and that the bourgeois rather than the radical press, with one very significant exception, displayed the greatest interest in the Revolution. Distortion in the press was probably a product less of ideological intention than uncertainty. Indications of this uncertainty may be gleaned from the reporting in the influential *Eastern Miscellany*.

Over the year following the Revolution, this periodical published five pieces that dealt directly with the Revolution and a sixth piece on socialism that referred to Russia in passing. Of these six pieces, only one—a translation from Japanese comparing the Russian and the French revolutions—was visibly anti-Bolshevik. The author was evidently against revolutions and perceived in the Russian Revolution a threat to order worldwide. (At the time this piece was published Japan had already dispatched an invasion force to Russia.) He compared the Russian Revolution unfavorably to the French: its lack of an ideological, social or political center, he believed, enhanced its potential for creating disorder. Bolshevik victory in November 1917 represented the transfer of power in Russia from the middle class to "uneducated extremists."[2]

The worst that may be said of the other five discussions is that they were explicitly noncommittal on the Revolution and give little prominence to Lenin and the Bolsheviks. A translator's note challenged the Japanese author's term "uneducated extremists," pointing out that Lenin was a "famous economist" and Trotsky a university graduate well known for his oratory. An editor's preface to a translation of the brief autobiography of Catherine Breshkovskaya lauded the Revolution as the victory of republic over autocracy.[3] A similar preface, this time to a long history of land reform in Russia, pointed out that the Revolution consisted of two revolutions, a political and an economic one, the first aiming to create democracy, the second to replace capitalist society with a new kind of egalitarian society.[4]

These discussions were wanting in that they failed to recognize the significance of Bolshevism in the Revolution or the history of socialism. Two articles, on the history of Russian "socialism" and on contemporary Russian political parties, barely mentioned Lenin and the Bolsheviks, though the former did discuss the split between Bolsheviks and Mensheviks in 1903, distinguishing them merely as "extremists" and "moderates."[5] The article on land reform mentioned Lenin and the Bolsheviks only in passing, describing them as advocates of collectivization who, like all social democratic disciples of Marx, were not as popular with the property-minded peasants as their opponents, the social revolutionaries. Liu Dajun's article on socialism, the only one to express open admiration for socialism (elliptically, in its suggestion that the Chinese choose the best features of all available socialisms), described utopian, state, Christian, Fabian, and anarchist socialisms in addition to Marxist (scientific) socialism, but did not have anything to say on Lenin or Bolshevism.[6]

It is not surprising, given the conditions of press censorship, that these discussions were noncommittal. In 1918 the Russian Revolution was still an attempted revolution, not a successful one. Its future was uncertain, its concerns unclear. Chinese reports on the Revolution in 1918, like those worldwide, showed some recognition of its leadership and ideological ancestry, but this was too vague to allow an ideological stand. Most prominent in the reports was a concern with "extremism," which was by no means universally feared or condemned. Even those who condemned "extremism," moreover, such as the Japanese author just quoted, were compelled to recognize that social inequality, and the disorder created by World War I, had produced the Revolution, not the "extremists."

Under the circumstances, Li Dazhao's enthusiastic response to the Revolution seems all the more remarkable as the solitary recognition of its significance. As is well known, in a series of articles he wrote starting in July 1918, he hailed the event as a new kind of revolution, a social revolution that marked the beginning of a new era of revolutions, and a new stage in world history representing the victory of the common people.[7] These articles provide an important ideological link between the October Revolution and the origins of Marxism in China.

The significance we have attached to these articles as a step in the growth of Marxism in China is at odds with their vagueness, which was as pronounced as anything to be found in the *Eastern Miscellany*. Meisner has pointed out that there was nothing particularly Marxist in the way Li comprehended the Revolution at this time.[8]

I would like to take this a step further and suggest that not only was Li's comprehension not Marxist, but his discussions of the Revolution at this time were infused with the vocabulary of anarchism. When he described the Revolution as the victory of the "common people" or of "laborism," and wrote that it sought to resolve the question of "bread," he expressed views that within the Chinese context were clearly of anarchist inspiration.

Meisner has argued that Li's enthusiastic response to the Revolution was a consequence of his chiliastic proclivities, which led him to see in it an imminent "gigantic historical transformation." Similarly, he attributes Li's par-

ticular perception to an innate populism that had long characterized his thinking, as evidenced by an anti-urban bias in his earliest writings on the problem
of changing China.

This interpretation, which has at least one eye firmly focused on the future of Chinese Marxism under Mao, leads Meisner to dismiss suggestions in
the evidence of Li's life that his response may have been shaped by dormant
intellectual resources the Revolution awakened. The fact that Li's intellectual
development before 1918 remains fuzzy calls for circumspection in interpret-
ing the available evidence. When he was a student in Japan during 1913–
1916, according to Gao Yihan, he was deeply interested in the works of the
Japanese Marxist Kawakami Hajime, "his hand not releasing the volume days
at a time."[9] This does not prove that Li became a Marxist at this time; Kawakami himself did not become a Marxist until sometime in 1918–1919. Nevertheless, familiarity with Kawakami's works may not only have helped Li propagate Marxism in the aftermath of the Revolution, but shaped his response to
the latter. Kawakami wrote extensively on the question of social change, which
he viewed in strongly ethical terms.[10] Li's first article on Marxism in 1919,
in which he "declared" his Marxist commitments, drew almost exclusively on
Kawakami as a source on Marxism. Li's approach to Marxism was characterized by ethical concerns similar to those of Kawakami.

Even more intriguing is the possibility of anarchist memories in Li's thinking. Before he left for Japan in 1913, he had some sympathy for the Chinese
Socialist Party of Jiang Kanghu, whose socialism was deeply imbued with
anarchist thinking. At this time, he was also influenced by Tolstoy, which may
explain the anti-urban, antipolitical and pro-peasant feelings of his earliest
writings.[11] The ideas Li articulated when he first expressed those feelings, in
his 1913 essay "The Great Grief," had a precedent in the writings of Liu
Shipei, who had also been influenced deeply by Tolstoy's anarchism.[12] There
is no direct evidence that Li had read Liu's writings, but neither is it sufficient to conclude, as Meisner does, on the basis of Li's opposition to the anarchist advocacy of assassination, that he was opposed to anarchism. Many
Chinese anarchists were opposed to assassination; conversely, Li's opposition
to assassination did not preclude admiration for Kropotkin in 1918–1919.
The possibility of anarchist influence on Li's thinking, moreover, does not
negate his populism. Within the Russian context of the 1860s, anarchism and
populism emerged from the same intellectual sources.[13]

The evidence that a prior exposure to anarchism may have contributed
to Li's response to the Russian Revolution in 1918 must remain circumstantial. The evidence for the role of anarchism in 1918 is more direct. Li was
not in fact the first Chinese in 1918 to hail the Revolution as the harbinger
of a new era of history. That honor actually belonged, ironically, to the anarchist journal *Labor* magazine (*Laodong*) (the first journal in China to use
"labor" in its title), which was published in Shanghai during the first half of
1918, and was the most important Chinese source on the Revolution at the
time. Unlike other journals, its coverage extended beyond news reports to
the evaluation of the Revolution's nature and historical meaning.

The two discussions of the Revolution in the second issue of *Labor* (April 1918) are among the most detailed reports on the meaning and the ideology of the Revolution published in China in 1918. (This issue was also the first of any Chinese journal to celebrate May Day.) Significant was an article by an Yi Cun entitled "The Political Strategy of the Extremists in Russia" ("Eguo guojipai shixingzhi zhenglue"), which described the internal and external policies of the Revolution. Quoting Trotsky, the author described the Revolution as "a revolution in the broad sense" (*guangyidi geming*), which meant first, that it was not restricted to politics but extended to the economic realm, and second, its aspirations were not merely national but global. "The revolution accomplished by the Russians is a world revolution, it is a social transformation (*gaige*)."[14] It was a revolution, he observed, that bureaucrats and the wealthy feared but laborers and the poor welcomed. There is little question about the sympathies of this author, who referred to the revolutionaries as "brothers" (*xiongdi*) and "compatriots" (*tongbao*).

A similar tone pervaded an article by Chi Ping, "A Brief Account of Lenin, the Leader of the Russian Social Revolution" (*"Eguo shehui gemingzhi xianfeng Lining shilue"*), which described Lenin as "the most enthusiastic proponent of universalism" (*datong zhuyi*) in the world. As had Yi Cun, this author stressed as the Revolution's goals the immediate termination of the world war and the redistribution of property to relieve the poor. He called the revolution in "our neighbor Russia" a "social revolution to make equal the rich and the poor." More significantly, he stated that "while people fear these two words, social revolution, it is nothing but a natural tendency of the world."[15] An essay in the third issue of *Labor,* "An Analysis of Lenin, the Reality of the Russian Revolution" ("Liningzhi jiepei, Eguo gemingzhi zhenxiang") made a similar statement, anticipating Li Dazhao by two months. "The French Revolution gave birth to the civilization of the nineteenth century, the Russian Revolution represents the tendencies of the twentieth century."[16]

In ensuing issues (the last one was the fifth, in July 1918) *Labor* published other discussions of the Revolution, including one on the various socialist groups in Russia, an article on the consequences of peasant liberation, and brief biographies of Trotsky and Breshkovskaya. These discussions were interspersed with many articles on labor and anarchism. Prominent among *Labor's* causes was Tolstoy's "laborism" (*laodong zhuyi*), which Li Dazhao hailed a few months later as a basic feature of the Revolution.

On the basis of earlier articles, it is possible to state that *Labor* discussions portrayed the Revolution as being in perfect harmony with anarchist aspirations. An article in the first issue, which was devoted to labor's struggles against the war in Europe, termed the ideology of the Revolution "anarcho-communism" (*wuzhengfu gongchan*) first, and freedom, equality, and universal love second. The same piece stated that the goals of the Revolution were the establishment of anarchy, the abolition of private property and religion, and the termination of the war.[17] The articles in the next issue echoed these views, depicting Bolshevik policies as efforts to get rid of laws, and Lenin as a thoroughgoing internationalist "who had no conception of national boundaries." The article on Lenin in the third issue did point out that the Bolsheviks traced their lineage to Marx, who had been at odds with anarchists, but the overall impression of harmony with anarchist notions remains.

The mere fact that Li Dazhao's initial opinions on the Revolution were first enunciated by others in *Labor* is no reason to assume that this journal was the source of his views. It is difficult to think, however, that he would have been unfamiliar with this journal and its contents. *Labor* was not an obscure, marginal journal. It was edited by Wu Zhihui, prominent anarchist and intellectual. Its contributors included Chu Minyi (a prominent writer for the anarchist *New Era* published in Paris a decade earlier), Huang Lingshuang, Hua Lin, and Yuan Zhenying, who were not only prominent anarchists of the May Fourth period, but Li's colleagues as teachers and students at Beijing University (Beida), active in the university's political life. The journal publicized the goal of "labor-learning" (*gongdu*), in which Li was quite interested. As China's first publication on labor, it was unlikely to have escaped the attention of anyone interested in social questions. Chinese historians, who criticize it for its "petit-bourgeois" distortions of the Russian Revolution, recognize it nevertheless as a publication that paved the way for the May Fourth Movement.[18] If this evidence is circumstantial, Li himself provided direct evidence of his familiarity with the journal when, in an article in 1920 on the history of May Day, he not only cited this journal of "two-three years ago," but quoted from its May 1918 issue celebrating May Day.[19]

The point here is not merely that Li was influenced by *Labor*'s presentation of the Russian Revolution as an anarchist one. The Revolution struck Chinese intellectuals from the beginning as a *social* revolution, the first of its kind in history, and it was perceived in the May Fourth period in anarchist terms because only anarchists advocated social revolution insistently, and consistently. To the extent that the Chinese recognized the Revolution as a social one, therefore, it probably initially aroused interest in anarchism, not Marxism. There is some evidence to support such a conclusion. As one Chinese historian has said of radicals in Guangdong,

> At the time (before the May Fourth Movement), quite a few people thought that the victory of the October Revolution in Russia was the victory of anarcho-communism. Radicals who were dissatisfied with the situation in China and wanted a revolution began, therefore, to believe in anarchism.[20]

Lest this be viewed as an idiosyncrasy of Guangdong where anarchism had strong roots, we may note that Shao Lizi, prominent Guomindang member and Communist, recalled the same tendency in Shanghai.[21]

This reading of the impact of the Russian Revolution may help explain an apparent anomaly in Li Dazhao's thinking. Meisner has observed that Kropotkin's concept of "mutual aid" began to appear with increasing frequency in Li's writing following the Revolution.[22] If Li, like many others around him, perceived the Revolution as an anarchist social revolution (and at the time there was in China no other concept of a *revolutionary* social revolution), the "anomaly" ceases to be anomalous.

The social revolutionary orientation in the May Fourth period, as much mood as idea, included everything from individual liberation from the family, to the abolition of the state and of distinctions between rich and poor, to the creation of a world of mutual aid and fraternity. Anarchists did much to provide the language of this orientation, which George Lukacs once described (in reference to his own Hungarian context, contemporary with the May Fourth period) as a "Messianic utopianism." The Russian Revolution powerfully invoked this mood. Li Dazhao's initial discussions of it were couched in a language of Messianic utopianism, as were the responses of others among his contemporaries. Indeed, it is less surprising that Li confounded the Revolution with anarchist visions than that anarchists should have done so, since they knew more than most of their contemporaries about the divisions between Marxists and anarchists.[23] We must remember that what the Chinese saw in 1918 was a revolution in its liberating moment, when it seemed possible to legislate away all the evils of the past, not a revolution breaking up on the shoals of reality. Many a European anarchist greeted the Revolution with similar hope. Kropotkin, Russian and anarchist, hailed the Revolution from exile in Europe and, soon after, returned home to participate in it. (What befell him there would contribute significantly to dampening initial anarchist hopes.)

The Revolution's immediate impact on Chinese consciousness, therefore, was to promote the idea of social revolution, which, in the Chinese context, meant the diffusion not of Marxist but anarchist ideas and vocabulary of revolution. This situation was to change following the May Fourth Movement, but not as dramatically as has sometimes been claimed. Nor do these changes indicate that Chinese radicals acquired a firmer grasp of the ideological basis of the Revolution or, least of all, as I shall argue, that they converted to a Bolshevik or Marxist strategy of revolution.

By the early May Fourth period, attitudes toward the October Revolution displayed greater complexity. Anarchists continued to invest it with hope as a step toward human liberation, which prolonged confusion over the nature of the Revolution. At the same time, there was growing wariness of the Bolsheviks as they turned to the tasks of state-building, especially as evidence of their suppression of anarchists proliferated.

Increasingly visible, however, was another attitude. Others, mostly socialists, admired the Bolsheviks' ability to set up a new, and effective, government structure. In this view, the Revolution was a necessary consequence of the circumstances of Russian society; the revolutionariness of the Bolsheviks had already given way to more moderate policies as they turned to political and social reconstructions, and they were lauded for their attention to social justice and welfare.

Under the circumstances, the confusion between anarchism and Bolshevik revolutionism persisted. As of 1919, anarchists had not given up hope in the future of the Revolution, but had come to hold a more somber view of it. It had become clear not only that the Bolshevik government had no intention of establishing an anarchist society, but that it was willing to compromise its principles in order to deal with the exigencies of revolution. Anarchists suspected the Revolution for what caused others now to favor it: its establishment of a new state structure. Its suppression of anarchists was no doubt an important factor in changing anarchist minds. In its February 1919 issue, the short-lived but important anarchist journal *Evolution* (*Jinhua*) published a piece entitled "The Russian Extremists" ("Lun Eguo guojidang") by a Ji Zhen. According to the editorial note, the piece was a translation by Ji Zhen from a longer article by a "Russian comrade," Yules Fordmaun(?), entitled "Who are the Bolsheviks?" The article bemoaned the continued confounding (in Europe) of Bolshevism with anarchism, and described Bolshevism as "piratism" (*qiangdao zhuyi*). Bolsheviks were not anarchists; they were not even Marxist socialists, because to describe them as socialists was to concede that socialism allowed human beings to "eat one another" (*ren shi ren*). Many Marxists, the author added, denied unequivocally the Marxism of the Bolsheviks.[24]

Anarchists also began to stress their differences from the Bolsheviks. Another article by Huang Lingshuang in the same issue of the journal criticized the liberal *Renaissance* (*Xinchao*) magazine for describing the Revolution as a "new world tide."[25] Huang argued that not Russian-style "collectivism" (*jichan*) but anarchist "communism" (*gongchan*) represented the tide of the contemporary world. While all socialists advocated the socialization of production, he observed, they differed over distribution. State socialism, scientific socialism, social democracy all made the state the agent of distribution; only communism advocated the principle "from each according to his ability, to each according to his need." Anarchism represented the contemporary trend in socialism because anarchism was the "friend of individualism" (without, he added, being individualistic in the capitalist sense). Huang cited a Japanese author, Fuse Katsuji, to argue that Marxism, the theoretical basis of the Russian Revolution as of all state socialism, no longer had much of a following in Europe.

Huang's arguments, which had first appeared in Chinese socialism in 1913 in the debate between the anarchist Shifu and the socialist Jiang Kanghu over the relative virtues of Marxism and anarchism,[26] would become standard arguments in the anarchist attacks on Marxism with the intensification of hostility between the two groups following the founding of the Party. During the immediate May Fourth period, they shaped the views toward the Soviet Union of many who were influenced by anarchism. The criticism of the Soviet Union initiated by *Evolution* would continue unabated in anarchist journals, and in the many contributions anarchists made to other important publications.

Anarchist attitudes toward the Soviet Union, however, retained considerable ambivalence. Anarchist opposition to the Soviet Union would not congeal until after Kropotkin's death in Russia in 1921, and the founding of the Communist party of China later in the same year; even then, anarchists' suspicion did not prevent them from flirting with Marxists in China or with the Soviet government. Conflicting reports concerning Kropotkin's well-being, rife in 1919, agitated the anarchists (as well as others such as Li Dazhao) and made them suspicious. Chinese historians have argued that anarchists' criticism of the Revolution, and the rumors they spread with regard to Kropotkin, were responsible for distorting the nature of the Revolution in the May Fourth period. On the other hand, it is important to note that anarchists such as Yuan Zhenying, Liang Bingxian, and Xie Yingbo, through the many translations they contributed to the anarchist and non-anarchist press, played an important part in spreading news of the Revolution at this time.

Anarchists, moreover, did not hold a uniform view of the Soviet Union. In the second issue of *Struggle* (*Fendou*), an anarchist who identified himself as A.D. attacked the Bolsheviks, in the name of "peace" and "humanity," for having substituted "state capitalism" for the "capitalism of the individual," for ruling by "might" (*giangquan*), and for their continued advocacy of war in the form of "class warfare." He was criticized in turn by an anarchist who identified himself as A.A. (Zhu Qianzhi, who, ironically, held a Stirnerian view of anarchism). While Zhu himself did not approve of the methods of the Bolsheviks because they fell short of a true social revolution, he argued nevertheless (as Emma Goldman had in the United States) that the Revolution must be supported by anarchists because it represented an important step forward in worldwide social revolution. The opposition to class warfare was especially vacuous, he argued, since social revolution had no option other than class struggle.[27] Zhu probably expressed the views of many anarchists at this time when he wrote in the May Day issue of the *Beijing University Student Weekly* in 1920 that

> since Lenin and Trotsky beckoned, class struggle, which everyone had thought to be utopian until then, has become a reality; the working class has awakened from its dreams to realize that social revolution is inevitable, that class struggle is the only real path to the liberation of the proletariat. From the perspective of anarchism, the revolutionary strategy of the Bolsheviks [*guangyi pai*] is not thorough enough, but from this other perspective, it is the beginning of the liberation of the proletariat. It has opened up the floodgates of social revolution, it has substituted the red banner for the white flag. Is this not the victory of laborers? Is this not the transition to social revolution?[28]

Some anarchists went even farther in equating anarchism with Bolshevism. Particularly prominent in this regard was *Fujian Star* (*Minxing*), published in "the Russia of southern Fujian," as the area around Changzhou was called under the command of General Chen Jiongming, who gave support to the Cantonese anarchists who had followed him there. In December 1919, Liang Bingxian, editor of *Fujian Star* and a prominent anarchist who had earlier in the year translated the new Soviet constitution into Chinese, described the ideology of the Bolshevik Revolution as "only-laborism" (*weigong zhuyi*). Liang argued on the basis of the Soviet constitution that the Bolsheviks' social revolution was to make labor and laboring into the criterion of citizenship in the new society. While he recognized that socialists had been divided over "collectivism" and "communism," they had all been one in advocating "laborism"; there was little difference in this regard, he pointed out, between Marx, Proudhon, Bakunin, Tolstoy, or Kropotkin. He recommended Bolshevism and the International Workers of the World as the "two great organizational means" to achieve social revolution in the contemporary world.[29]

The proliferation of radical journalism around the time of the May Fourth Movement guaranteed not only more extensive reporting on the Soviet Union, but also that the Chinese public was introduced to variegated perspectives on the nature of the Revolution. Still, reporting remained sparse and unsystematic. According to one recent count, between 1919 and May 1920, newspapers and periodicals in Shanghai published eighteen pieces on the Revolution (most of which had little to do with the Revolution per se).[30] The *Morning News Supplement* (*Chenbao fukan*) in Beijing, a major source of discussions of Marxism and the Russian Revolution under Li Dazhao's guidance, published during this same period one original piece and six translations (including the declaration of the first congress of the Comintern).[31] These findings could probably be raised a little, though not much, higher, by including discussions of the Revolution that did not carry it in their titles, but they are indicative of the general level of reporting. Furthermore, while these reports represent an improvement over 1918 both in numbers and in sophistication, they are not very impressive when viewed in context. It is necessary to remember that they were part of a broader interest at this time in revolutions around the world; indeed, it might be possible to conclude, on the basis of numbers alone, that the Chinese press was less interested in the Russian Revolution than in other dissident and revolutionary movements. The reports were both meager and haphazard when contrasted with the explosion of publications on the Revolution starting in the spring of 1920; between September 1920 and April 1921, *New Youth* (*Xin gingnian*) alone would publish thirty-seven such pieces.[32] Reporting on the Revolution in the immediate May Fourth period remained dependent on foreign sources (mainly Japanese, American, and English), and the picture they provided was not such as to create an overwhelming desire among Chinese radicals to follow in Russia's footsteps.

Government suppression of the radical press possibly continued to curtail reports on the Revolution. The otherwise incompetent military regimes in China proved quite effective in suppressing radicals. Government reports from early 1919 reveal its vigilance against "extremist" propaganda. As early as February 1919, one government report stated that Lenin's Bolshevik government had dispatched to China Russian and German communist agents, as well as Chinese workers who had converted to Communism in Russia, arming them with funds and propaganda materials, to establish contact with Chinese socialists and to propagate "extremist" ideology.[33] In early 1920, the government reported that it had confiscated eighty-three "extremist" publications.[34]

The list of these indicates that they were mostly anarchist, though included was a "State and Revolution." If this was Lenin's *State and Revolution,* it possibly did not make its way past the government; *State and Revolution* was not published in China until late 1920 and, as far as I am aware, there was no reference to it in publications of the May Fourth period.

The Chinese government continued to suppress publications that promoted "social change, family revolution, and the 'sanctity of labor'," and threatened filial piety, order, and social customs.[35] In the May Fourth period almost every publication in China advocated family revolution, and threatened order, customs, and fiilial piety. The government seemed especially on the lookout for journals that promoted the cause of labor and social revolution. A news item in *Evolution* in February 1919 reported the recent proscription of a "Three-two Society" (*Saner xueshe*) (the "three" referred to the three oppositions to government, family, and religion—*wuzhengfu, wujiating, wuzongjiao;* the "two" to "from each according to his ability, to each according to his need").[36] The proscription order stated that while "real" state socialists could be allowed to exist, "anarchists" such as those of the "Three-two Society" must be proscribed because of their potential harmfulness to state and society. According to the anarchists themselves, the "Three-two Society" was the brainchild of the socialist Jiang Kanghu and had ceased to exist some time ago. The proscription nevertheless provides evidence of the government's readiness to proscribe journals of the anarchists, the only prominent group at this time to advocate social revolution. Anarchist journals were routinely shut down almost as soon as they started publication, a major reason for the relatively short life of most of them. Anarchists were not the only targets of censorship; in the course of the year Mao's *Xiang River Review* (*Xiangjiang pinglun*) and even a relatively liberal journal such as the *Weekly Critic* (*Meizhou pinglun*) were suppressed.

Vigilant as they were, authorities seemed oblivious to the very significant political differences among publications that advocated "social change." The reading public was similarly confused. In early 1920, Chinese authorities were joined by foreigners in the search for radicals, when the American government instructed its consuls in China to root out "Bolshevist" activity. Most of the "Bolshevists" they discovered turned out to be anarchists, though the consuls themselves displayed no recognition of the differences between the two.[37] These activities perpetuated confusion over Marxism and anarchism long after Chinese anarchists had begun to turn against Bolshevism.

Where the Russian Revolution was concerned, another, perhaps even more insidious, kind of censorship may have been at work: a journalistic self-censorship caused by emerging divisions within the intellectual leadership of the New Culture movement in response to the challenge of social revolutionary ideas. In one of Li Dazhao's essays in his July 1919 debate with the liberal Hu Shi over "Problems and Isms," he recalled that when he had published his "Victory of Bolshevism" in *New Youth* in November 1918, the sociologist Tao Menghe had complained that it had "created problems" for the journal.[38] New Culture liberals such as Hu Shi and Tao Menghe had little patience for anarchism or Bolshevism, which may explain why, in spite of the enthusiasm of Li Dazhao and the tolerance of the editor Chen Duxiu, the most important New Culture journals such as *New Youth* and *Weekly Critic* were not prominent in publications on the Russian Revolution during the immediate May Fourth period. Li Dazhao, ironically, would find greater freedom to promote study of the Russian Revolution in a publication such as *Morning News Supplement,* which was associated with supposedly "conservative" Progressive Party (*Jinbudang*) members—who were themselves intensely interested at this time in questions of social change and socialism!

Under the circumstances, those who were sympathetic to the Russian Revolution, or believed the Chinese had something to learn from it, devoted their efforts to creating conditions for free discussion of it to educate the public. This was the case with Li Dazhao. If Li's writings in 1918 had been inspired by anarchist writings on the subject, he did not follow the anarchist lead now in renouncing the Revolution. In 1919, Li did not write much about Russia and Bolshevism, certainly nothing to match his encomia of 1918. The evidence of his publications suggests that his attention was now focused on Marxism. As early as November 1918, in "The Victory of Bolshevism," citing an English journalist, he had described the Bolsheviks as "revolutionary socialists" who upheld the ideas of "the German socialist economist Marx." A few months later he would begin to publish his first important pieces on Marxism. His most important writings over the year following the May Fourth Movement were on Marxism, not Bolshevism.

Li's writings on Bolshevism around the time of the May Fourth Movement took the form of encouraging its study. In "Another Discussion of Problems and Isms" (cited earlier) he explained that his discussions of Bolshevism in late 1918 had been intended primarily to educate the public by overcoming its fears of Bolshevism and to clear away rumors created by anarchists concerning the welfare of Kropotkin and the "nationalization of women" in the Soviet Union. A brief piece he wrote in March 1919 refuted a suggestion that "extremism" had no future outside of Russia and eastern Europe, arguing that without "extremism" there was no way to overthrow the injustices of present-day society. He recommended that the best way to overcome fears of "extremism" was to find out what it was all about.[39] This theme pervaded his writings of 1919, usually within the context of his discussion of other subjects.

Rather than write about the Soviet Union himself, Li would seem to have devoted himself to promoting such reports in publications where he had influence, such as the *Morning News.* On March 1, 1919, *Morning News* published an article by Ruo Yu (pseudonym Wang Guangqi) entitled "Research on Russia" (*"Elosi yanjiu"*), which refuted the rumor that the Bolsheviks were "nationalizing" women. It is possible that Li had put Wang up to writing the article; he recalled later that he had found out from an article in the *New Republic* that the Bolsheviks had created the rumor concerning the "nationalization of women" to discredit anarchists.[40] The article by Wang, even though written from an anarchist angle, referred to the Revolution as a "great event of the twentieth century" that the Chinese should study carefully. It recommended that "if the ideology of the extremists has any truths to it, we should adopt some of them; if their ideology has no truth to it, we should refute it." It also observed that newspeople had a great responsibility to inform the public and suggested they study Russian papers for information. Li may have been responsible himself for penning a short piece published in *Morning News* in April that criticized the use of the term "extremists" to describe the Soviet leadership. He explained that the proper term was "Bolsivike," which meant "majority" (*duoshu*) or "broader" (*guangyi*) group, and should best be transliterated into Chinese as *buersiweike*.[41] And he raised similar themes in various articles that did not directly address questions of the Russian Revolution, such as "The Crucial Battle between Old and New Thought Tides" ("Xinjiu sichaozhi jizhan"), and "Dangerous Thoughts and Freedom and Speech" ("Weixian sixiang yu yanlun ziyu"). The former article ended with the ominous warning that suppression of freedom by the Romanovs in Russia had only served to nourish the revolution.[42]

In 1919, Li was not the only Chinese concerned with the confusion, or with the commonplace references to Bolshevism as "extremism" or, in the authorities' favorite expression, "flood waters and wild beasts." An article in *Morning News* in April, after discussing the Revolution at some length, complained of the prevalent confounding of Bolshevism with anarchism, with the French Confederation Générale de Travail and the American International Workers of the World, and pointed out that Bolshevism was the "socialism of Marx."[43] Another major promoter of the study of Bolshevism at this time, the Guomindang theoretician Dai Jitao, wrote in his *Weekend Review* (*Xingqi pinglun*) in June that the term Bolshevism, made into "extremism," aroused great fear not only in the government but even among educators, none of whom made an effort to understand it. He went on to explain its meaning, (contrasting it to Menshevism) and described the Bolsheviks as believers in Marxism.[44] It is interesting, however, that such correctives seemed to have little effect even on the journals that published them; the occasional piece on the Revolution in *Morning News* still used the term "extremist party" to describe the Bolsheviks. As late as November 1919, Dai Jitao complained about those who not only spread ignorant fear about the Soviet Union, but also labeled as "dangerous people" the few who made an effort to understand that country.[45] In spite of anarchist opposition to Bolshevism, and the efforts of Li, Dai, and others to dissociate anarchism from Bolshevism, moreover, the idea that Bolsheviks were anarchists (possibly in a common loose sense, as chaos-makers) seems to have persisted as a general impression. In notes appended to his translation of William Bullitt's report on the Soviet Union, in the February 20, 1920 issue of the *Weekend Review,* Dai complained about "dumb" Chinese who still thought that Bolsheviks were anarchists even though the anarchists in Russia were opposed to the Bolsheviks, who were "pure Marxists."[46]

This confusion was a consequence in part of the ideological eclecticism that characterized the publications in which these reports appeared, including those of Dai and Li. The publications that reported most extensively on the Soviet Union in the May Fourth period were those whose publishers would turn anti-Communist with the founding of the Party. Anarchists continued to publish on Russia, but their writings were published for the most part in non-anarchist publications. *Morning News Supplement* in Beijing was an important source under Li Dazhao's guidance, and the *Weekly Critic* published an occasional piece, but the majority are to be found in publications, mostly in Shanghai, that were connected with various political parties and groups which had little to do with Communism. Prominent among them were *Awakening* (*Juewu*, a supplement to the *Nation Daily*), *Construction Weekly* (*Jianshe zhoukan*), *Weekend Review*, *Reconstruction* (*Jiefang yu gaizao*), *The Citizen* (*Guomin*) and, from early 1920 on, *The World of Youth* (*Shaonian shijie*).[47] *Morning News* and *Reconstruction* were associated with guild socialists and social democrats who had earlier been connected with the Progressive Party and were leaders now in the Research Clique: Zhang Dongsun was the most prominent figure in the publications of the Research Clique. *Awakening, Construction Weekly,* and *Weekend Review* were Guomindang organs which in their politics espoused the Three People's Principles of Sun Yatsen. *The Citizen* was the organ of the Student National Salvation Association and *The World of Youth* was a publication of the Young China Association (*Shaonian Zhongguo xuehui*), led by Wang Guangqi. There was no Communist organ in China in 1919, and later Communists published mostly in these publications, without any clear identity of their own.

The most prominent feature of these publications, as of May Fourth journalism in general, was their ideological eclecticism. Their association with various political groups on the Chinese scene did not mean that they closed their doors to different views. Anarchists and future Communists blended easily in their pages with liberal anti-Communists. The political divisions were more blurred in some cases than others. *Awakening,* possibly the most radical of all, increasingly came under Communist influence and became a joint organ of Communists and the left Guomindang after the establishment of the United Front between the two parties in 1923. The *Weekend Review* seemed in 1919–1920 more a publication of senior radicals gathered in Shanghai than an organ of the Guomindang. One of its editors (in addition to Dai Jitao) was Shen Xuanlu, who was among the founders of the Party in 1921 (he left the Party later). Chen Duxiu himself was closely associated with the group after he moved to Shanghai in early 1920.

This eclecticism warns us against jumping to conclusions concerning these publications' political direction and contributors, and in turn calls into question the ideological meaning of what they published. Although these journals were important sources on Marxism and the Russian Revolution, and did pave the way for Communism, the meaning of what they published must be comprehended within a contemporary context. The only thread that unified them was their interest in promoting social change, which they associated with one or another of the many various socialisms that found their way into Chinese thinking in the immediate May Fourth period. Their interest in

Marxism and the Revolution was part of this broader interest and does not imply a political inclination to promote the Bolshevik model in China. As I observed earlier some anarchists were quite active in this period (more so even than Li Dazhao) in publishing on the Revolution, which obviously did not reflect a desire to promote allegiance to Bolshevism. Indeed, while these publications were associated with one political group or another, their tone was dominated by a vague anarchism that prevailed in Chinese thinking in the May Fourth period. These problems have been recognized by Chinese historians, if only in an elliptical way. Of *Awakening,* the most radical, one author has written:

> Among the youth who submitted articles to *Awakening* or corresponded with it, there were very few initially who were not influenced by anarchist thought. There were some among them who later became Marxist under the influence of Marxist propaganda or as a result of their direct encounters with the realities of China. There were some who, having left the hot-headedness of youth behind them, came to terms with contemporary realities, lost their spirit, and pushed to the back of their minds the limitless aspirations of their youth, or even degenerated to the point of becoming bureaucrats or politicians. There were still others who discussed Marxism but were not mature Marxists, who were bourgeois intellectuals in thought and feeling, and could not sustain their Marxism in the face of the difficulties of revolution. For these reasons, it is very difficult, when we examine the essays in *Awakening,* to analyze the threads that connected the process of development of their thinking as a whole; the best we can do is to subject to critical inquiry the thinking they reflect against their objective consequences.[48]

Interest in Marxism, in other words, did not point necessarily to a later Marxist political identity. I will say more on this subject later when I discuss Marxism in the May Fourth period. My point here is that in their eclecticism, these journals provided a variegated, and not altogether favorable, picture of the Soviet Union. While they combated the obscurantist notions about Bolshevism propagated by political and social authorities, their effectiveness must remain an open question. They remained dependent for their reporting on foreign sources, which more often than not did not favor Bolshevism. And their own messages concerning a Bolshevik future for China were at best mixed. They promoted the Soviet Union as *one* of the many revolutionary alternatives that Chinese should study and consider in planning for social change. More often than not, they concluded that the Soviet model was not the best suited to China's needs. Even Li Dazhao on occasion portrayed the Revolution as a "negative example" of what ought to be done to avoid a similar revolution in China.

On the basis of the reports in these publications in 1919, it is possible to observe that the Chinese radicals not of anarchist persuasion who were interested in the Revolution were more curious about the Bolsheviks' success in building a new political system than desirous of emulating the revolutionary strategy that had brought them to power. These reports consistently expressed admiration for the new Soviet leadership's ability to create a stable and reformist government in the face of adversity. Typical of these reports was one serialized in April 1919 in the *Nation Daily* (*Minguo ribao*), a Guomindang daily in Shanghai, entitled "The Real Visage of Socialist Communism in Russia: Russia Under the Worker/Peasant Government" ("Laonong zhengfuzhi xiadi Eguo—shixing shehui gongchan zhuyizhi Eguo zhenxiang"). The report discussed at length the policies of the new government on education, industry, agriculture, and women. The tone throughout was full of admiration. The report observed that the new Russian government had not only survived for a year and a half against all expectations, but had been able to put together successfully a new state structure. It pointed out that Chinese development since the 1911 revolution contrasted unfavorably with these accomplishments, and this was a cause of much shame for China. It was, however, noncommittal on whether Russia could serve as a model. Quoting Lenin on Bolshevism, it was satisfied to observe: "whether or not we approve of Lenin's ideology, there is no denying that he is a man in whom word and action are united."[49] Yet it expressed unqualified admiration for Lenin's ability to create a new government. The shift was under way from a stress on revolution to a stress on revolutionary construction, and Chinese of all persuasions were able to respond to the latter aspect much more positively. This appreciation combined over the next year with defense of the Soviet Union in the press against the unwarranted interference of foreign powers.

Not only was very little published at this time on the ideology and revolutionary methods of the Bolsheviks, but what references Chinese authors did make to Bolshevik revolutionary strategy were disapproving. While the reports before the May Fourth Movement had stressed the revolutionary dismantling of the system the Bolsheviks had inherited, reports from the May Fourth period stressed the new legal and governmental system being created. The vast majority of these publications, moreover, were translations; Chinese themselves wrote conspicuously little on the Revolution that was original, which makes it even more difficult to judge what they may have thought of it than before May Fourth. The choice of translation, and an occasional footnote added by the translator or the editor, are about the only guides.

Reports on the Soviet Union in this period may be divided into three categories. First were translations of official Soviet documents, which covered everything from the new Soviet constitution, to the new land and labor laws and the marriage law promulgated by the new state, to foreign policy documents. Most of these translations were published in *Awakening, Reconstruction,* and *Weekly Critic.*

The second category consisted of reports translated from the foreign press. In September 1919, *Awakening* published a piece by the Japanese Marxist Yamakawa Hitoshi entitled "The Direction of the World Thought Tide," which discussed the influence of the Russian Revolution on other countries. In April 1919, *The Light of Learning* (*Xuedeng*), supplement to *Current Affairs,* (*Shishi xinbao*) published brief biographies of Lenin and Trotsky. The same spring, *Morning News* serialized two books on the Revolution, one by a Russian populist, Stopniak, the other by an American government official surnamed Syke. Stopniak's book dealt with the populists and anarchists of the nineteenth century, Syke's with the revolutionary movement of 1914–1918. Later in the year the same paper published a number of eyewitness accounts of the Soviet Union, including an account by Arthur Ransome of the *Manchester Guardian* of six weeks' travel in Russia in 1919; an interview with Lenin by Lincoln Ayers (Steffens?) of *World Magazine* in New York; and a piece entitled "A Glimpse of Russia" by a Japanese journalist Fuse Katsuji.[50] In December, *The Citizen* published "An Analysis of Bolshevism" by Henry Emery. These reports were capped by the publication in the February 1920 *Weekend Review* of William Bullitt's "Report" on Russia, supplemented with copious notes by Dai Jitao. In May, the same journal published a translation from an American paper entitled "The Eye Opener."

Chinese commentators look with disfavor on these translation from the "bourgeois" press which, they believe, gave Chinese a distorted picture. The distortions were partially empirical. Many of these works, pioneering efforts to find out about the Soviet Union, reflected a prevailing uncertainty. But this was only part of the story. Fuse Katsuji was actually hostile to the Bolsheviks, and believed that the Marxist basis of the Revolution had long been abandoned by socialists in Europe.[51] While Syke, Ransome, and Bullitt were highly favorable to the Soviet regime, there was a profound ambivalence in their attitudes toward the Revolution. Syke, advocating American help for the Soviet Union, commented that "while the situation in Russia was dangerous, it was not hopeless."[52] Bullitt, whose influential "Report" was to predispose many in the United States to accepting peace with the Soviet Union, stated nevertheless that the Soviet form of government was "unquestionably . . . a form of government which lends itself to gross abuse and tyranny."[53] Reporters such as Ransome and Steffens, and government officials such as Syke and Bullitt, saw a great deal to admire in the accomplishments of the Bolsheviks' regime. ("These men who have made the Soviet government in Russia," Ransome wrote, "if they must fail, they will fail with clean shields and clean hearts, having striven for an ideal that will live beyond them.")[54] However, the common purpose in what they wrote at the time was to derevolutionize Bolshevism, and present the Bolsheviks as the creators of a new, more humane, kind of government, so as to put an end to the hostile actions of Western governments against the Soviet Union. Bullitt stated repeaedly that the "destructive phase" of the Revolution had come to an end, the "terror" was over, and the Soviet government was firmly established in Russia because of the "general support which is given the government by the people in spite of their starvation"—which, he observed, was blamed by the people not on the government but on foreign invasion and blockade of the country.[55] Hostilities should be ended, in other words, not because the Soviet government was revolutionary, but because it had become a new establishment.

This was a cause Chinese could sympathize with easily and, as Chinese historians have noted repeatedly, it was not so much the methods that had brought the Bolsheviks to power but sympathy with the plight of Russia that attracted the greatest attention at this time. To be sure, some supported the Revolution as a step forward in social revolution even though they did not agree with its methods or believe in the feasibility of a Bolshevik-style revolution in China; they included liberals, anarchists, Guomindang revolutionaries, and possibly even Li Dazhao. Their ambivalence underlined the implicit ambiguity of these reports, whose publication they sponsored. Liberals such as Luo Jialun, who hailed the Revolution as a new world tide, nevertheless thought it inappropriate to China where, given the backwardness of the people, it could only lead to disorder.[56] Anarchists, many of whom were active in the translation of these reports, believed that the Revolution had been at best incomplete, at worst a total failure. Dai Jitao, in the very same essay where he enjoined the Chinese public to find out the truth about the Revolution, observed nevertheless that Bolshevik methods imported to China would only play into the hands of warlords and vagabonds. Zhang Dongsun, under whose guidance *Current Affairs* and *Reconstruction* published many of the available reports, went even further. While Zhang would speak admiringly of Lenin later on in the year, he wrote repeatedly in early 1919 that the Chinese should study Bolshevism in order to prevent the "danger" of Bolshevism in China; he went so far as to compare government suppression of discussions of Bolshevism in China to the methods the Bolsheviks used in Russia to silence the opposition![57]

While Chinese publications in the May Fourth period disapproved of foreign intervention and sympathized with the Bolsheviks' intention to bring economic justice and political participation to the common people, their reports on the Soviet Union could be read easily as part of an effort to find out about Bolshevism in order to forestall it in China. These reports, moreover, included very little on the revolutionary ideology that had brought the Bolsheviks to power. As with the rest of the world, the Chinese knew little at this time about Lenin and Leninism, or the precise connection between Marx and Lenin. Lenin's name came up with increasing frequency, but reports on him and his ideas were scarce. In September 1919, *Weekend Review* published a translation of a talk in which Lenin discussed the necessity of denying freedom of speech to counterrevolutionaries. In March 1920, *Reconstruction* published a translation of Lenin's "Present Tasks of the Soviet Government." What the Chinese knew of Lenin as revolutionary did not go beyond what *Labor* had published in 1918. Brief biographies of leaders of "The Social Movement in the West," published in *Morning News Supplement* in August 1919, referred to Lenin as "the leader of Russian extremists" and mentioned him in the same breath as Marx, Lasalle, Bebel, Liebknecht, Rosa Luxemburg, and a number of labor leaders, including one who was a fervent opponent of the Bolsheviks, Samuel Gompers! The author gave the greatest prominence to Lasalle.

To the extent that Chinese publications discussed the revolutionary ideology of Bolshevism at this time, they did so within the context of a third kind of writing on Russia, discussions of socialism in general which took up the question of Russian socialism in passing, in comparison to other socialisms. These are best discussed later in the appropriate context. Here we need only note that in these discussions, too, the Revolution appeared in less than favorable light. More often than not, Russian socialism was portrayed as "centralized," either undesirable because it was inconsistent with democracy, or irrelevant because of the particularities of Chinese society. While the Revolution appeared as another manifestation of the decline of capitalism, whether it promised the best substitute was an open question.

Not until the second half of 1920 did Chinese publications turn to the systematic study of the Russian Revolution and its ideology. There were a number of reasons for this change, which may indeed be described as dramatic. In March 1920, the Soviet government declared its unilateral renunciation of the Unequal Treaties with China it had inherited from the czarist government. Even the most avid pursuers of early Russian influence have conceded that this declaration invoked immediate enthusiasm in China and provoked a dramatic interest.

There was, however, another side to this interest. A recent study by Xiang Qing, a noted Chinese student of this period, has suggested that the declaration eased the tensions between China and Russia, and led to a relaxing of the Chinese government's vigilance over the border which for the first time made possible sustained contact between Chinese radicals and the Soviet Union.[58] In the fall of 1920, the later Communist leader Qu Qiubai would go to the Soviet Union as a reporter for *Morning News,* sending back the first direct reports on the Soviet Union by a Chinese. More immediately, in the same month that the declaration was made public in China, the Comintern agent Gregory Voitinksy arrived in Beijing and initiated the founding of the Communist party of China. Voitinsky brought with him literature on the Soviet Union, including some of Lenin's important writings. If overall enthusiasm for the Soviet Union in China at this time might account for the proliferation of publications, it was in the course of efforts to establish the Party that the first systematic studies began to appear, especially in that part of the press controlled by those involved in those efforts. Nevertheless, the legacy of the previous three years of reporting was still alive. At this time, Yuan Zhenying has recalled, Chen Duxiu asked him to join the editorial board of *New Youth* as the editor on the Soviet Union.[59] In September 1920, a new section entitled "Examination of Russia" ("Elosi yanjiu") began to appear. Yuan, who edited the section, and contributed the majority of its articles, was an anarchist.

The point here is not only that the most qualified person Chen could find to do this job was an anarchist. Before the founding of the Communist party of China, or rather the initiation of activities that culminated in that founding, Chinese radicals who later founded the Party did not show a dramatic interest in or keen understanding of the complexities of the Revolution.

In 1917–1920, Chinese interest in the Russian Revolution was part of a general interest in the wave of revolutions and labor unrest around the world in the wake of the First World War. Ding Shouhe writes:

> In order to understand the influence of the October Revolution in China, it is necessary to include in that influence the chain of responses (around the world) invoked by the Russian Revolution. Turning over the pages of journals and newspapers published in 1918–1919, it is possible to see that every day there were detailed reports on the revolutions in Germany and Hungary, labor strikes in England, France, the United States and Japan, and national liberation movements in colonies such as the Philippines, India, Egypt, Korea, and so forth. This high tide of revolutions worldwide made evident to the Chinese people that capitalism was on the decline while socialism was on the rise and national liberation movements were growing, and naturally deepened the impact of the October Revolution.[60]

Initially, moreover, these radicals shared in the general impression of the Revolution as a social revolution, and conceived of it in terms that were highly colored by anarchist aspirations. Even the solitary exception, Li Dazhao, upon whose response to the Russian Revolution we have based our interpretations of its influence, was not a real exception. Li, like his contemporaries, saw the Revolution as the most dramatic example of social revolutions that seemed ready to engulf the capitalist world in the near future. In his case, as for others who joined him in founding the Party in 1921, a genuine appreciation of the Revolution would come after, not before, the initiation of the process out of which would emerge the Communist Party of China.

3

The October Revolution and Marxism
in China: The Case of Li Dazhao

In his essay "On New Democracy," published in early 1940, Mao Zedong remarked that the May Fourth Movement had been "called forth by the worldwide revolution at the time, by the Russian Revolution and Lenin, it was part of the world revolution of the proletariat."[1] The statement has long shaped Chinese Communist historiography. It has also compelled reorganization of the memories of those who, having come of political age at the time, became the founders of the Communist Party of China.

The problem lies not in Mao's claim that the May Fourth Movement was part of a worldwide wave of revolutions that surged forth from Europe in the aftermath of World War I, which it was, but rather in his suggestion that it was fashioned by Lenin's Marxism, which it was not.

As late as 1921, when the Party was formally established, the intellectuals who participated in its founding knew little about Marxism, and even less about the Marxism of Lenin than about the Marxism of Marx. A few could claim a rudimentary knowledge of Marxist theory, but no more. One recent study suggests that out of the forty-eight identifiable Communists represented by the twelve delegates who met in Shanghai only twenty-one were committed Communists, and they had only a rudimentary knowledge of Marxism.[2] Liu Renjing, a delegate to the first Congress and later Trotskyist, recalls that he became known as "little Marx" at Beida because he gave a lecture on Marxism for the Society for the Study of Marxist Theory (*Makesi xueshuo yanjiuhui*) sometime in 1921 on the basis of a couple of secondary works on Marxism. Cai Hesen, the Hunanese Marxist, did even better, basing a whole lecture on a dictionary.[3] Li Hanjun, at whose brother's house the Party was founded, and whom Zhang Guotao has described as "the Marxist theorist among us" (he would serve as Party secretary briefly during Chen Duxiu's absence from Shanghai), is said to have opposed the founding on the grounds that Chinese Communists should first find out more about Marxism and Communist politics.[4]

Historians have long recognized that Chinese became Communists before they were Marxists or even knew much about Marxism. Yet simultaneous claims have been made that knowledge of or identification with Marxism

43

significantly evolved in these early years. Meisner, who has questioned that the initial interest in the Russian Revolution implied a simultaneous interest in Marxist theory, nevertheless finds sufficiently unambiguous evidence of such evolution in the publication of such Marxist works as the *Communist Manifesto* and Karl Kautsky's *Class Struggle,* to conclude that "the dissemination of Marxist theory . . . increased rapidly in the wake of the May Fourth Movement," and that the publication of these works represented the establishment of "ideological foundations" for Communism in China.[5]

The literature on the origins of Marxism in China has further represented the establishment of these "foundations," at least implicitly, as a product of identification with Bolshevism and Marxism. In these accounts, the publication of the *Communist Manifesto* and *Class Struggle* culminates an accumulation of literature on Marxism that started in spring 1919, which itself is traced back to the first expression of interest in Marxism in 1918 when Li Dazhao established in Beida the Marxist Research Society (*Makesi zhuyi yanjiuhui*), the first society of its kind in China. This society has entitled Li Dazhao to the appellation "China's first Marxist." It is also evidence of the link between the Russian Revolution and the origins of Marxism in China.

Perhaps nothing illustrates better the problematic nature of our understanding of early Chinese Marxism than the historical status of this society, which sustains the seminal status of the Russian Revolution as the event that launched Chinese radicals on the Marxist path that would inexorably lead them to the founding of the Party in 1921. Whether such a society ever existed has long been questionable; yet historians have assigned it a landmark position. Their preference to err on the side of its affirmation is revealing of the power of the ground plan that has structured our thinking on the origins of Chinese Communism.

While some Chinese historians continue to affirm it, contemporary Chinese scholarship for the most part ignores this society's existence, when it does not deny it altogether. A recent study not only states that it existed, but claims that Li chose the name *Maergeshi xueshuo yanjiuhui* to throw off the authorities by confounding the transliterations of "Marx" and "Malthus."[6] Whatever the merits of this argument, which ignores that there was then no standard transliteration of Marx's name, most Chinese scholars ignore the existence of this society. For good reason: none of the later Communist recruits who were students at Beida (and participated in the indisputable Society for the Study of Marxist Theory established in 1920) can recall the existence of such a society in 1918—including some who supposedly through its meetings were converted to Marxism. Zhang Guotao, who has described the Beida library under Li Dazhao as "the cradle of the ideological trend toward the left," does not recall studying Marxism before 1920.[7] Nor does Liu Renjing, who recognizes that "some comrades" insist on the existence of such a society, but himself does not recall its existence.[8] But perhaps the most important evidence comes from Mao Zedong, for whose benefit the existence of such a society may have been invented. Mao spent some time in the Beida library in late 1918, when he is supposed to have been introduced to Marxism.[9] It is all the more curious, therefore, that in his discussions with Edgar Snow in 1936 he should not have mentioned participating in a Marxist study society, when he clearly recalled his participation in philosophy and journalism study societies.[10]

There may well have been a Marxist Research Society at Beida in 1918. Li was undoubtedly engaged in the study of Marxism by late 1918–early 1919, and there is no reason to think that he would not have discussed his studies with others close to him. There is no evidence, however, that those who may have participated were therefore converted to Marxism and Bolshevism. Their recollections of their interest in Marxism do not reach before 1920 and even then, as with Liu Renjing's confessed ignorance, the grasp of Marxism did not match the interest. The ambiguity of the evidence only dramatizes further the hold on historical imagination of a presumed link between the Russian Revolution and the conversion of Chinese intellectuals to Marxism.

Other evidence of this link, primarily the first writings on Marxism to appear in Chinese publications, is comparably ambiguous. Here again the case of "China's first Marxist," Li Dazhao, is crucial because we have assigned paradigmatic status to the progress of his Marxism.

Li's first important discussion of Marxism, "My Marxist Views" ("Wodi Makesi zhuyi guan"), was published in the May 1919 issue of *New Youth* magazine. The dating of the publication makes it the first important discussion of Marxism by any Chinese. We have conventionally read this article not only as a discussion of Marxism, but as Li's declaration of his new-found faith. It is on the basis of this article, also, that Li has been assigned his preeminent role as China's first Marxist. The article supposedly completes Li's progress to Marxism under the influence of the Russian Revolution: from his enthusiastic response to the Revolution, through a growing interest in Marxism provoked by it and concretized in his alleged founding of the Marxist Research Society, to his final declaration of his conversion in this article. It is not that this article eliminated all ambiguity from Li's thinking; rather, whatever ambiguities remained in his thinking must now be "read" in terms of his declared conversion. On this basis, for example, Meisner commented on Li's continued fascination with Kropotkin: "Li Ta-chao . . . looked with great favor upon Kropotkin's theory of 'mutual aid'; but the influence of Kropotkin was most strongly evident after Li had already declared himself a Marxist in 1919, and he then used the idea of 'mutual aid' for the explicit purpose of reinterpreting the Marxist theory of class struggle."

This text, which is crucial to our interpretation of the Marxism's origins in China, yields a significantly different reading when we take seriously an anarchist presence in Li's thinking. Indeed, the article did not constitute a declaration of faith in Marxism, but appears so only in light of prior assumptions concerning the impact of the Russian Revolution on Li's thinking, in particular his alleged founding of a Marxist Research Society in 1918. A textual examination of Li's article, and a reconsideration of the circumstances of its publication, reveal that we have endowed it with a significance out of all proportion to its contemporary importance, either in Li's thinking or, therefore, in the progress of Marxism in China. Especially important in this connection is another brief piece Li penned in mid-1919 entitled "Class Competition and Mutual Aid ("Jieji jingzheng yu huzhu").

"Wodi Makesi zhuyi guan" was published in two parts, starting with the May 1919 issue of *New Youth,* which was a special issue on Marxism (the "first" of its kind in China), edited by Li himself. The article offered one of the first lengthy discussions of Marxist theory in Chinese. Li stated that Marx's theories were important for understanding the "social revolutions" that had swept Russia, Germany, and Austria since the war, and went on to discuss Marx's economics, the materialist conception of history, and class struggle, drawing heavily on the translated works of the Japanese Marxist Kawakami Majime. Marx's economics, however, provided the framework for the discussion and dominated its tone. Li offered a lengthy exposition of Marx's discussion of value and the concentration of capital, replete with mathematical formulae, which must have mystified not a few of his readers.[11] All that renders the article unique among comparable discussions of Marxism at this time is our reading of it—as Li's declaration of faith. We have reaffirmed this reading in our literal translation of the article's title as "My Marxist Views."

Placed against the sheer bulk and theoretical density of this article, the second one, "Class Competition and Mutual Aid" seems a relatively marginal piece that merely footnoted Li's faith. The timing of this brief piece would seem to confirm this impression. In this second article, published in the July 1919 issue of *Weekly Critic,* Li expressed concern that Marx's ideas were insufficient for revolution. He argued that for revolution, both Marx's idea of class struggle and Kropotkin's idea of mutual aid were necessary. To the reader of the article, class struggle might well have seemed a necessary evil, the price humanity must pay to achieve a humane society. Li drew attention to Marx's distinction between "prehistory" and "history," which corresponded respectively to pre-Communist and Communist societies. He continued:

> The present-day world has reached the extremes of darkness. If we are to carry forward the history of humankind, we must undergo a great transformation. This transformation is the great flood after Noah's, one that will wash clean the former world of class competition, and bring about the glorious new world of mutual aid.

Class struggle, the characteristic of "prehistory," was the means to bring about the "real history" of humankind; but even as a means it seemed less fundamental than mutual aid. Class struggle was necessary to purge the legacy of the past, but mutual aid would bring about the new world: "This final class competition is the means to transform social organization. The principle of mutual aid is the creed to transform the human spirit. We advocate the transformation of both the material and the mental, the simultaneous transformation of body and soul."[12]

These lines prompted Meisner to observe that "Li Ta-chao . . . looked with great favor upon Kropotkin's theory of 'mutual aid.' " However, presumably because of the temporal relationship between the two articles, he has added that "the influence of Kropotkin was most strongly evident after Li had already declared himself a Marxist in 1919, and he then used the idea of 'mutual aid' for the explicit purpose of reinterpreting the Marxist theory of class struggle." The use of an anarchist idea to qualify a central premise of Marxism is problematic enough in itself; evidence has become available since Meisner's study that suggests the problem may go even deeper than has previously appeared.

This evidence pertains to the question of timing. Recently published research by Chinese scholars indicates that while the *New Youth* special issue on Marxism was dated May 1919, it was not actually published until September of that year, no doubt because of the confusion the May Fourth Movement created among its editors.[13] If this was indeed the case, the special issue of *New Youth* loses much of its specialness, since by September 1919 there was many a publication on Marxism (most of them translations from Marx and Japanese discussions of Marxism, as I will show later). And since much of what this issue said about Marxism was already available elsewhere, Li's "Wodi Makesi zhuyi guan" also loses much of its specialness as the first serious original treatise on Marxism in Chinese (upon which his reputation has rested as China's first Marxist) and it appears instead that much of its material was drawn from works already published elsewhere.

More to the point here, this new evidence suggests that Li's two articles were written at about the same time. It would be very surprising, therefore, if the issues raised in the one article did not overlap in the author's mind with those of the other. A textual comparison of the two shows more than a temporal coincidence. The two articles' discussions of class struggle are merely variations on the same theme; some statements appear verbatim in both. "Wodi Makesi zhuyi guan" does not refer to Kropotkin by name (or to William Morris, whom Li also mentioned in the shorter article), but otherwise Li presents the same argument in both, employing identical terminology. It is difficult not to speculate that Morris and Kropotkin were very much on his mind when he referred in "Wodi Makesi zhuyi guan" to recent idealist scholars who had placed more emphasis than Marx on the ethical dimensions of change.[14] It is not far-fetched, therefore, to view "Class Competition and Mutual Aid" as a statement in resume, or ground plan, sort of to speak, of the discussion in the longer article. Since (as Meisner has observed) Li viewed class struggle as the "golden thread" that tied together all aspects of Marxism, his discussion of class in "Class Competition and Mutual Aid" may be taken as the expression of the outlook that guided his attitude toward Marxism, as well as his understanding of it. Since the order of publication of the two articles has been reversed, moreover, it is not proper to suggest, as Meisner does, that "the influence of Kropotkin was most strongly evident after Li had already declared himself a Marxist in 1919." Kropotkin and anarchism were still very much relevant, in Li's mind, to the possible application of Marxism to the Chinese revolution.

There is more than one possible reading of "Class Competition and Mutual Aid." It could be read as an advocacy of class struggle, an expression of Li's new realization that mental and spiritual change, as represented in the idea of mutual aid, were insufficient to bring about the good society of his dreams. Or it could be read as a defense of mental and spiritual change against this realization. Chinese scholars, to the extent they have recognized the persistence in Li's thinking of pre-Marxist "petit-bourgeois" influences, have opted for the first reading.[15] Meisner has opted for the second. The two readings focus on two sides of the same coin, but their differences are not, therefore, any the less significant. The first reading yields the conclusion that the idea of mutual aid, and the anarchist influence it implied, was fast becoming residual in Li's thinking as he committed himself to Marxism. Meisner, on the other hand, sees a persisting preoccupation, even as Li became a Marxist, with consciousness and ethical questions; these had always characterized his thinking and now shaped his reading of Marxism, accounting for its peculiarities.

In spite of these differences, the two readings both suppress what is, perhaps, the most striking question this article raises: what place anarchism occupied in Li's thinking even as he proclaimed his Marxism. Meisner states from the beginning of his study that anarchism was inconsequential in China after 1911, and that Li opposed it because he did not approve of its advocacy of terror. He thus disassociates Li's attraction to Kropotkin, or his increasing references to "mutual aid" starting in 1918, from the question of anarchism. Chinese historians have recognized that anarchism was pervasive in May Fourth thinking, but still view it as a retrograde philosophy which quickly became marginal when Marxism appeared. In recent years some historians have gone so far as to suggest that the popularity of anarchism obstructed the progress of Marxism. Yet this interpretation has not included reconsideration of Li's Marxism, or a recognition that it raises far-reaching questions concerning the origins of Marxism in China.

These readings also both represent perspectives more interested in historical "tendency" than historical "context," even if one stresses the burden of the past while the other looks to future developments. In hindsight, it might be reasonable to read Li's qualification of a central Marxist premise by an anarchist idea as his final hurdle before becoming a full-fledged Marxist. But to contemporary readers, in an environment where anarchism clearly was more popular than Marxism, Li's article would have conveyed a different message, presenting class struggle as a necessary evil, a means to the higher goal of mutual aid. Indeed, given that articles by anarchists who were openly critical of Marxism were its context, the article could quite possibly have been read not as an affirmation but as a criticism of Marxism.

These comments are not meant to imply that Li was an anarchist. Rather, "Class Competition and Mutual Aid" tells us unequivocally that as late as the summer of 1919, anarchist ideas were important in his thinking on Marxism, as with many Chinese radicals at this time. The relationship of this article to

"Wodi Makesi zhuyi guan" offers insights on a number of puzzling questions associated with the latter, and the special issue that included it.

By September 1919, not much was "special" about the special issue Li edited. The contributions on Marx and Marxism duplicated what was already available in other publications; about half of them were simply reprints of essays from well-known publications. More significantly, this special issue is so problematic that one Chinese commentator has even suggested that we should not make too much of it as evidence of the progress of Marxism in the May Fourth period.[16] The issue included an essay on Bakunin, as well as an essay highly critical of Marxism by Li's anarchist colleague at Beida, Huang Lingshuang. The remainder, already published elsewhere, praised Marx for his revolutionary commitments and important contributions to socialism, but critized Marxist theory, suggesting that revision was required because many of its assumptions were no longer relevant. Li himself probably had authored these essays, which I will discuss in chapter 6.

This context only underlines Li's critical tone. It was Marx's economism that seems to have impressed him the most, yet it was on this account, which Li deemed central, that he was most critical. Li criticized the materialist conception of history for its materialism, he viewed class struggle as a necessary evil, and he even found problematic Marx's theory of value, which he described as "the foundation" of Marxism's validity. Marx's economism, in his view, was a reflection of the importance the economy had assumed in nineteenth-century Europe. He observed, along with his fellow contributors, that Marxism's value was circumscribed by its temporal and spatial limitations.

> We cannot utilize a theory that was the product of a certain time and a certain place to explain the whole of history, or apply it in its entirety to the present, but this does not negate its value, or its special discoveries.[17]

The article provides ample evidence that Li had been hard at work studying Marxism over the preceding months. It also states that Chinese should study Marxism because of its importance in the contemporary world. But Li does not say anywhere in the article that he has adopted Marxism as his political faith. For all its commendations, the article does not recommend Marxism any more definitely than the critical discussion offered by Li's fellow contributor Huang Lingshuang. To quote Meisner's eloquent evaluation of Li's treatment of Marxism in the article,

> Although Li's treatment of the materialist conception of history was rather ambiguous, he left no doubt that he found wholly unpalatable the Marxist de-emphasis on the role of ethical and spiritual factors in history. He noted that the Marxian conception of socialism had deep ethical roots, but he was critical of Marx for relegating the role of ethics to the post-revolutionary future when a "truly human history" will have replaced the "prehistory" of class struggles. On the contrary, Li argued, "in this period of transition, ethical and humane movements ought to redouble their efforts to eliminate the evils of the earlier periods in history.

. . . We cannot rely on material change alone." On this point he bluntly stated that Marxist theory should be revised so that Marxists would recognize that the reformation of the human spirit must accompany the transformation of the economic organization.[18]

Meisner also observes, correctly, "that the Marxism that Li discussed in 'My Marxist Views' was orthodox pre-Leninist Marxism."[19] Indeed, Li at one point identified Marxism with social democracy:

> Three components may be distinguished in Marx's theory of socialism: First is his theory of the past, his theory of history, which may also be called his theory of the progress of social organization; second, is his theory of the present, his economic theory, which may also be called his theory of the capitalist economy; third, is his theory of the future, his theory of policy, which may also be called his theory of the socialist movement, which is social democracy.[20]

To construe this article as a declaration of faith and, on that basis, to describe Li as a "committed Marxist" in 1919, is to overlook all the doubts Li himself expressed. It is possibly on account of the relationship between Marxism and the Russian Revolution (which he notes at the beginning of the article) that we have read the article as evidence of conversion, since Li had already expressed admiration for the Revolution. His response to it was actually quite vague, however, and insufficient to imply attraction to its Marxist ideological basis; the most that can be said is that the Revolution (and the other revolutions Li mentioned) aroused his curiosity about Marxism, which he did not at the time equate with Bolshevism. It is somewhat circular to read "Wodi Makesi zhuyi guan" as Li's declaration of faith in Marxism because he admired the Revolution, and then to propose that such admiration indicated Bolshevik inclination because he shortly "declared" his faith in Marxism.

I have refrained from using the English title for this article; the conventional translation, "My Marxist Views," which is not the only possible one, leads us to read it as a declaration of faith. This article tells us only that by mid-1919 Li was a socialist, an eclectic one at that, to whom Marxist theory was insufficent and in need of revision. Therefore, it is more appropriate to translate the title along the lines of "My Views on Marxism" which is more in keeping with what Li says about Marx and Marxism in the essay.

One could still argue that Li's qualifications of Marxism merely expressed his characteristic ethical and populist inclinations. Yet those inclinations only underline the anarchism in his thinking: he found in Kropotkin's mutual aid the ethical dimensions he thought were lacking in Marx's revolutionary theory. If an exclusive outlook embedded in the materialist conception of history, and a class-based perspective, are basic preconditions of a Marxist identity, Li was not a Marxist in 1919. He posited these elements as both essential to Marxism and inadequate either for historical explanation or revolutionary theory. He found that Marx's materialism neglected ethical considerations in history. While he accepted class struggle, he viewed it as a sign of humanity's fall from grace. A class-based perspective was a reprehensible feature of human "prehistory." Marxism showed the way to conclude human "prehistory," but "genuine" history would begin with the universalization of the ethical ideals of mutual aid.

Mutual aid as an ultimate goal could be quite consistent with an anti-economistic, anti-statist reading of Marx. This was not, however, Li's reading. He identified determinism and materialism with Marxism, as I shall discuss later, and in his writings over the next year, this aspect of Marxism held his attention. Li was critical of these ideas, but if he was indeed a "committed Marxist" when he wrote his first article on Marxism in 1919, it was because he came close to accepting at this time the necessity of confronting the economic dimension of society in dealing with the problem of change, as he came close to accepting class conflict as a necessary evil.

In other words, Li was attracted to Marxism not because of common points between it and anarchism, but in spite of them. For the same reason, he continued to believe throughout 1919 that anarchism was needed to supplement Marxism and guide it. Chinese anarchist criticisms of Marxism had informed him of the significant conflict between the two ideas, yet he declared mutual aid as the goal of revolution. Finally, mutual aid was not simply the goal but a means to it. Marxist economism could resolve problems of the flesh. Mutual aid would cure the soul.

This economistic reading of Marxism was commonplace among May Fourth radicals. This is not surprising. Chinese views of Marxism in the May Fourth period were shaped by Japanese writers, especially Kawakami Hajime who (according to Gail Bernstein) also subscribed to an economistic interpretation of Marxist historical and revolutionary theory.[21] When Li wrote his two articles, Kawakami's writings were widely available in Chinese. "My Views on Marxism" was almost entirely derivative of them.

It would be misleading, however, to attribute Li's attitude to the "influence" of an outside source. The attitude toward change that underlay his criticisms of Marx at this time reflected attitudes toward change that characterized May Fourth thinking. Attitudes like Li's shaped the initial Chinese reading of Marx. Others were showing an inclination to accept Marxist explanations, while continuing to look for anarchist or other solutions. Just a week after the publication of "Class Competition and Mutual Aid" in the *Weekly Critic* in Beijing, the *Weekend Review* in Shanghai published "Competition and Mutual Aid" ("Jingzheng yu huzhu") by Shen Xuanlu (one of its two editors, along with Dai Jitao).[22] He also argued for the necessity of tempering class conflict with mutual aid because while competition was a necessity of social progress, mutual aid was its condition and purpose. Shen's approach to the question was social Darwinian in inspiration; but the primacy of mutual aid was supported, he believed, by all learned scholars of the nineteenth century, including Marx, Ruskin, and Kropotkin.

Chinese writers in the immediate May Fourth period felt uneasy with materialism and class struggle, and found mutual aid a means to bypassing violent revolution. The prevalent culturalist attitude to change reinforced nationalistic fears of class struggle. Li Dazhao was unique in his acceptance of class struggle as a necessity of genuine revolutionary change. (He also identified class struggle more closely with Marx than did others; Shen Xuanlu, for example, who *did* place an anarchistic reading on Marxism, presented mutual aid as a common goal of Marx and Kropotkin.) However, Li did not give up on other means of changing China. As late as December 1919 he still advocated "social reorganization through small groups" (*xiao zuzhi da lianhe*). In 1920 he was a foremost supporter of the communal experiments that briefly held the attention of Chinese radicals as a means of achieving non-violent social transformation.

I will say more on the meaning of Marxism during this period in Chapter 6. Suffice it to say here that while curiosity about the Revolution generated Chinese interest in Marxism, Li (and others) discovered a meaning in Marxism separate from the role it had played in the Revolution. Li may have been more willing to view the Revolution and Marxism as one, and accept both; for others Marxism was undesirable to the extent it was identified with the Revolution. Even in his case, however, there was a question of meaning. That Marxism was the unequivocal message of the Revolution, or that the Russian model was the only legitimate expression of Marxist commitment, was an idea that would not find a receptive audience until 1920.

The basic question is whether the Chinese became Communists under the influence of the Russian Revolution which turned them to the study of Marxism which in turn established an ideological foundation for Communist politics, or whether they became Communists first, through direct Comintern intervention in 1920, and then discovered Marxism. I would like to argue the latter case. The former explanation is, in my opinion, based on a fundamental contradiction: that the ideology involved was one devoid of substance, a Marxism without theoretical content or social analysis. Before the Party's founding the Chinese knew very little about Marxist theory, and had an even shallower appreciation of its relevance to them.

Evidence indicates, moreover, that the publication in 1920 of important works such as the *Communist Manifesto* and *Class Struggle* is not to be taken *prima facie* as evidence of a spontaneous diffusion of interest in Marxism among Chinese intellectuals. These works were published *following* the initiation of activities to establish the Party in 1920, and were products of that interest, not its premise. One Chinese author has pointed out that between the Revolution in 1917 and the Party's founding in 1921, one-hundred and thirty-seven pieces related to Marxism were published in *New Youth* alone.[23] The author does not specify what might be covered under "Marxist-related works." A perusal of *New Youth* indicates readily that even with the inclusion of all writings pertaining to Marxism, socialism, the Revolution, and labor, only a fraction of "Marxist-related works" were published before 1920. The great majority were published after May 1920, when the founding of the Party had already gotten under way.

Epilogue

The disassociation of Marxism from the Russian Revolution helps us bring out the complexities of radical ideology in the May Fourth period. Did the interest in Marxism during the early May Fourth period have only one source; that is, the Russian Revolution? Was the interest in Marxism the only interest in radical ideologies spawned by the Russian Revolution? What was the relationship between Marxism and Communism? Is it possible to speak of an evolutionary growth of interest in Marxism during this period?

The burgeoning interest in Marxism must not be taken as evidence of a Marxist identity, let alone a Bolshevik-Communist one. The equation of interest with identity is simply a consequence of what I have already termed "teleological hindsight": the assumption that just because certain individuals eventually became Communists (or Marxists), any interest they showed in Marxism before that time points to their eventual conversion. As I shall undertake to demonstrate, those who possibly most clearly understood Marxism in 1919 did not eventually become Communists, while those who did become Communists for the most part had a poor appreciation of Marxism at this time or rejected it altogether. Indeed, many of them were inclined toward anarchism, or, at best, viewed Marxism through anarchist eyes, and lacked a clear sense of ideological identity.

The question of Marxism in the immediate May Fourth period is not merely a question of Chinese *knowledge* of Marxism or the Revolution. Most socialists who were actively interested in Marxism brought to it political and ideological predispositions that predated the Revolution and cast both it and, therefore, Marxism, in less than a favorable light as a model for China. The meaning of Marxism, moreover, was colored in 1919 by New Culture assumptions about change which anarchism had done much to fashion. Marxism, or rather Bolshevism, acquired greater credibility over the next two years; the credibility, however, derived more from developments within Chinese society than the Revolution's power of example. The assertion of a Marxist identity, on the other hand, would require the suppression of other socialisms which, while they had paved the way for Marxism by spreading the vocabulary of social change, had also obstructed the emergence of that Marxist identity, or even of a favorable attitude toward Marxism.

The immediate May Fourth period in China was a period not of ideological certainty (except perhaps for liberals such as Hu Shi), but of visionary quest, ideological fluctuation, and political self-searching. Marxism, as it appeared in 1919, was part of the inquiry. The identification of Marxism with Communism or the Russian Revolution obviates—even obfuscates—the need to address a more basic question: Why the appeal of socialism in general, or of the ideology of social revolution, in radical thinking of the immediate May Fourth period?

PART II
From Enlightenment to Socialism:
Radical Intellectuals, Labor, and Social
Radicalism in May Fourth Thought

Prologue

"There are moments in history," James Joll has written, "when ideas, long discussed by intellectuals, begin to acquire political reality, when new forces appear that are capable of upsetting the balance of power between classes, as between states, when old doctrines and practices have gradually to be abandoned, and existing society strains itself to come to terms with a new age."[1] The years immediately surrounding the turn of the decade in 1920 were such a moment in the history of socialism in China. In the earlier part of the century, socialism had been marginal politically and intellectually, taken even by its proponents to be more relevant to the future than the present. By 1920, the future had arrived.

Structural changes in Chinese economy and society, the effects of which became evident after 1919, endowed socialism with a new reality. While politics deteriorated after 1911, commercial and industrial growth brought important changes to Chinese society. During the two decades after 1905, Chinese cities grew rapidly. In 1919 Shanghai had a population in excess of one and a half million. Between 1919 and 1923 alone, the population of Beijing rose from around 600,000 to well over a million. Other cities such as Tianjin, Guangzhou, and the Wuhan urban complex grew into major urban centers.

Rapid economic growth during this period, especially during the "Golden Age" (in Marie Claire-Berger's words) of industrial development during World War I, produced a visible urban bourgeoisie and, with it, an urban proletariat. By 1919 there were more than a million and a half industrial workers in the country. Shanghai alone accounted for 300,000 workers, or about twenty percent of the city's total population. While small in proportion to China's total population, this working class had become starkly visible in the cities. The growth of urban population resulted largely from migration; most workers were of recent agrarian origin. Rapid urban growth and industrialization brought with them the kind of urban misery characteristic of the early stages of industrial society. Living conditions of the Chinese working class were reminiscent of working class life in mid-nineteenth-century Europe.[2]

The militancy of Chinese labor enhanced its visibility and, therefore, society's consciousness of class exploitation and conflict. Between 1919 and

1926, according to Chen Da, more than 1,200 strikes were reported for all of China, 469 of them in Shanghai.[3] Economic issues (wages and work conditions) led all other causes by a wide margin. Patriotism fueled this militancy; since foreigners held a large share of the new economy. More workers struck against foreign concerns than Chinese enterprises, but this was probably because the former were larger. In terms of number of strikes, Chinese enterprises were more often than not the targets of workers' grievances.[4]

Questions of class and class conflict were no longer abstract, as they had seemed only two decades earlier. In theory, perhaps, a working class that made up only a half percent of the population did not constitute a basis for socialism, but it has yet to be determined how large a working class is sufficient basis for a credible socialist movement. More importantly, the new working class and its conflict with capital provided the socialist argument with a concrete basis. Shanghai's working class in 1919 was comparable in size to that of Paris in 1848, when Marx and Engels published the *Communist Manifesto*.[5] The socialist movement in Europe also got under way during the initial stages of industrialization, when the majority had yet to shed their agrarian existence.

Along with industrial capitalism and the proletariat, a Chinese intelligentsia came of age with the New Culture Movement. The New Culture Movement was an ideological movement of intellectuals directed at a younger generation of intellectuals. The publication of *New Youth* in 1915 is the conventional originating date of the movement. It got under way in earnest in 1917 when reforms in Beijing University provided radicals with an institutional base in China's most prestigious university.

Initially, most of the leaders were old enough to have participated in the radical political fringes of the early 1900s. The New Culture movement brought them together with a younger generation who had experienced the anti-Qing Republican revolutionary movement in the course of its maturation. In spite of the age spread, certain characteristics distinguished both from the leaders of the earlier phase of revolution. Their greater familiarity with Western thought and culture implied a significantly more tenuous relationship to "received culture." They also felt a deep alienation from the society around them, which was reflected in the preoccupation in writings of the period with the relationship between self and society. If this alienation was a source of despair to some, it also reinforced their commitment to transforming society in accordance with their own newly acquired or formulated visions. A changed audience, which now included the roughly ten million youths who had received some "new" education between 1907 and 1917, gave force to their vision.

Chinese intellectuals had for generations been mortgaged to political service in a society that allowed little room for intellectual activity except in service to the state. The New Culture movement marked the ascendancy of an intelligentsia that sought in intellectual activity of one sort or another careers independent of politics. The unity of intellectual life and political activity that had characterized the Confucian elite of imperial China was broken with the abolition of the civil service examination system in 1905. The generation of the New Culture Movement was the first to celebrate the break. In this sense they were comparable to the Russian intelligentsia of the 1860s, or the intellectuals of the Enlightenment in Europe to which the movement has been compared.[6]

New Culture intellectuals rejected the venerable notion of the intellectual as political servant, and substituted for it a new notion of the intellectual as an autonomous creator of culture who could find fulfillment only in intellectual career and activity. This image expressed their new-found confidence in a rapidly changing society where their career choices were proliferating. And yet, in this flux, their role was problematic, and few could settle with comfortable resignation into the social niches for which their education had prepared them. What moved them, rather, was their fervent urge to participate in the fashioning of a society in the process of becoming. The crisis of intellectual life in China was also the source of their hope in the possibility of creating a new world.

The New Culture break with politics, therefore, did not signify obliviousness to politics and political problems, but rather a new attitude that intellectuals could best influence politics from outside formal political institutions. If anything, this reflected a heightened sense of the public obligations of the intellectual, as well as the belief that public service could no longer be identified with service to the state, but must be pursued in the realm of society. The need to define this new public, and the individual's relationship to it, informed much of the intellectuals' efforts at this time. The discovery of the "common people" was to go a long way towards resolving the predicament of an intelligentsia in search of its role.

The May Fourth Movement was the conjuncture that brought together these two new forces on the Chinese scene, the intelligentsia and the working class. The conjuncture provided the spark that lit the fuse of socialism. Before 1919, radicals' vision had been limited to educated youth, while the working class led, as far as intellectuals were concerned, a subterranean existence. The May Fourth Movement was itself motivated by patriotism (it was a protest against the anti-Chinese decisions of the Versailles Conference). But the movement brought the intelligentsia out of their universities and workers out of their factories. The encounter between these two new forces in the streets of Shanghai, Beijing, and other cities marked the beginning of a decade-long partnership between the intelligentsia and the working class, and the first and last attempt by China's socialists to achieve a social revolution in which the urban proletariat played a leading part.

It was with this encounter that a sense of the relevance of socialist solutions to China's problems took hold of radical political thinking. In 1919–1920 socialist ideas and politics spread rapidly among Chinese youth, and penetrated within a matter of years the most important social, political, and intellectual movements in China.

4

Social Consciousness and Socialism:
Class, Society, and Social Revolution
in May Fourth Thought

It was not quite accurate to say, as Zhang Dongsun did in late 1919, that "before the conclusion of the World War, not one person in China spoke of socialism; since the war ended, everyone has suddenly begun to discuss socialism."[1] The first discussions of socialism in China had preceded the May Fourth Movement by a decade and a half, when Sun Yatsen's Revolutionary Alliance, established in Tokyo in 1905, had incorporated a program of social revolution in its agenda.

Since then, socialism had been a perennial presence. Between 1907 and 1910, Chinese anarchists in Paris and Tokyo had taken up the cause of social revolution. In the first few years after the 1911 revolution, there had been a lively interest in socialism. The Revolutionary Alliance abandoned its socialist program when it became the Guomindang in 1912, but Sun Yatsen did not. In 1912, he still professed socialist beliefs, and the Chinese Revolutionary Party he established in Japan during his exile after the "second revolution" of 1913 continued to display interest in socialism. Meanwhile in 1911 Jiang Kanghu established the Chinese Socialist Party, the first political party in China to bear that name. Also in 1912, anarchists abroad returned to China, and a new anarchist group formed in Guangzhou under the charismatic leadership of Liu Sifu (better known under his adopted name of Shifu). In 1913–1914, Shifu criticized the socialism of Sun Yatsen and Jiang Kanghu, which led to the first debate among socialists to take place in China. This debate had done much to clarify differences among the various socialisms that Chinese had encountered in Europe and Japan. Jiang went into exile in 1913 when his party was proscribed, and Shifu's death in 1915 cramped anarchist activities, but socialism and the advocacy of social revolution were kept alive, primarily through the activities of Shifu's followers in China, and the continued activities of anarchists in Paris. Their contribution to the New Culture movement made for a significant socialist presence in Chinese thought in 1915–1919. Shifu's followers also had some success with labor organization. The return of Sun Yatsen and Jiang Kanghu to China after 1916 also initiated a new phase of activity, though the effects of such activity would not become visible until after 1919. Radicals who had been initiated into socialism before 1911 were active throughout these years and were crucial in the direction May Fourth socialism took in 1919.

Zhang's statement nevertheless pointed to an unprecedented development. Publications such as *New Youth,* on which intellectual attention had been riveted since 1915, had shown little interest in socialism; the term itself was rarely encountered in them before 1919. Starting around the time of the May Fourth Movement, however, socialism was quickly to become by later summer of 1919 the rage of intellectual inquiry and debate. While youth, women, and the family remained New Culture concerns, they were viewed increasingly from a socialist perspective. The sense of novelty was heightened by the amnesia writers displayed concerning earlier discussions; even the debate between Shifu and Jiang Kanghu seemed forgotten as radicals once again turned to sorting out the bewildering variety of socialisms confronting them. In 1919, socialism was no longer a remote future issue, it was *the* issue of the times. Feng Ziyu, a Guomindang advocate of socialism at the time, remarked caustically in late 1919 that socialist ideas had become fashionable to the point where even warlords established societies for their study.[2] Some conservatives sponsored the publication of books attacking socialism; others made efforts to assimilate it to native Confucian ideals.[3] Even the United States government was sufficiently concerned to instruct its consuls in early 1920 to ferret out "Bolshevists" in cooperation with Chinese authorities. For the first time in Chinese history, it was appropriate to speak of socialism as an idea in the air. But what was radically new was not the advocacy or novelty of socialism but the social and intellectual environment that provided the context for it.

Due to changes in Chinese society, and especially the increasingly national scope of intellectual activity with the New Culture Movement, socialism now had a broad audience. There were good reasons in 1919 for "amnesia" concerning earlier discussions: they had been regional in scope and parochial in audience. It is unlikely that most Chinese who were interested in socialism in 1919 had access to publications that had discussed it earlier. The sole exception may have been discussions of anarchism which, thanks to strenuous anarchist activity during the New Culture Movement, had been disseminated widely. While anarchists made a direct, significant contribution to the rise of interest in socialism in 1918–1919, however, they had kept a low profile ideologically during the early years of the New Culture movement, and their contributions were not always readily identifiable as distinctively anarchist.

This situation changed dramatically with the communications explosion around the May Fourth period. The national attention then focused on Beijing and Shanghai guaranteed that significant journals published in these cities found their way, by whatever means, even to remote provincial centers. But the flow was not necessarily one way. Intensified social activity, especially the student movement across the face of China, guaranteed a national hearing even to provincial publications. If people in the provinces avidly awaited copies of Shanghai publications, Mao Zedong could get his first article published in the premier intellectual organ of the day, *New Youth,* and attract the attention of national intellectual leaders when his "Great Union of the

Popular Masses," first published in *Xiang River Review* in Changsha, was reprinted in Shanghai's popular *Light of Learning.*[4] *Awakening* in Shanghai regularly reprinted articles from the anarchist journal *Fujian Star* in remote Changzhou. The reprinting of articles guaranteed them far greater circulation than otherwise, and heightened the impression of a spontaneous proliferation of interest. This was the case, as we shall see, with the first translations of Marxism in China.

Perhaps the most important change, however, was to be in the staying power of socialism. Parochialism had given the earlier activities of socialists a fleeting quality. In 1912–1913, Jiang Kanghu's Chinese Socialist Party had claimed a membership figure of about 400,000. While we have probably under-estimated the role of this party (and its anarchist opponents) in acquainting the Chinese with socialism, its socialism was not as resilient as those of the May Fourth period. Jiang's membership figures signified little; even if not exaggerated, they did not indicate seriousness of interest or commitment, and the huge following Jiang Kanghu had claimed dissolved with his exile in 1913. Marginal to Chinese political thinking, what socialists had said and written primarily interested small clusters around individual leaders, or circles of intellectual acquaintances, that pursued their own parochial interests. Only other socialists, similarly placed had taken note of them, besides government authorities, who displayed paranoia about socialism even before it was po-litically significant. Their vigilance in suppressing socialism had added to the fleeting quality to socialism in these years.

Socialism's new-found popularity had a good deal to do with the fecund New Culture intellectual predispositions which enthusiastically welcomed every new and progressive idea. By the time of the May Fourth Movement, China had become part of a world market of ideas, in which socialism was a very visible commodity. In this particular sense, Mao's claim that the Movement was called forth by the worldwide tide of revolutions was valid. A perusal of Chinese publications in 1918–1920 leaves a distinct impression that the world was being engulfed by a wave of revolutions and social unrest, of which the Russian Revolution was the most visible peak. The Chinese had initially greeted the end of World War I as a victory of "universal principle" (*gongli*) over "naked force" (*giangquan*).[5] In the course of 1919 this turned increasingly (no doubt with frustration with the Versailles Treaty and the betrayal of the Wilsonian principle of self-determination) to doubts about the future of a Western capitalist society. The question for those who doubted capitalism's future was no longer whether or not fundamental changes were the order of the day, but how they could be brought about: through the "extremist" meth-ods emanating from eastern Europe, or the more moderate, conciliatory means of western European social movements.

The advocates of socialism in China had from its earliest days been con-vinced of the imminent demise of capitalism. Most significant in 1919 was a novel sense that the fate of capitalism in Europe was immediately relevant to China, as a new question appeared on the scene: the question of class.

Earlier advocates of socialism had for the most part denied that class oppression and conflict were immediate problems for China. Consequently, discussions had been diverted easily in other directions. The Revolutionary Alliance had portrayed socialism as a component of a larger question of political integration; a means to *prevent* class struggle. The first debate over socialism that erupted in Tokyo between Revolutionary Alliance writers and Liang Qichao in 1905–1907, though it had started off with class oppression and conflict, had ended up discussing the relative economic virtues of capitalism and socialism for China. In 1913–1914 Shifu and Jiang Kanghu had debated the authenticity of their respective social revolutionary ideologies. Anarchists had done much to bring the question of labor to the intellectuals' attention, and had organized the first efforts toward class-based labor syndicates. But the cultural orientation of the anarchists had obviated the need for a clear articulation of the question of class.

In the May Fourth period this question quickly emerged as the focus of debate. Increasingly aware that changing their mentality would not change China, Chinese intellectuals began to see social transformation as not simply an adjunct to political or cultural revolution, but the point of departure for any significant change. Daily evidence of social oppression and conflict endowed with a concrete reality their earlier abstract awareness of the question of class. The idea and the reality reinforced one another. Socialism gave them a way to conceptualize and articulate the evidence—to comprehend it *as* evidence of class oppression and conflict. The evidence in turn nourished conviction in socialist interpretation.

In December 1919, Zhou Fohai, later a founder Communist Party and an important Guomindang Marxist theoretician, wrote:

> Class struggle! Class struggle! This idea and its sound waves have already reached China from western Europe in gusts and squalls. Placed in the midst of this tide, there is no way for China to withstand its power. Class struggle must soon become the reality of China.[6]

During the year following the May Fourth Movement issues of class gradually overshadowed others and, in the process, transformed the New Culture *problematic* on social change, making social revolution into the central question of changing China. The turning point was the political emergence of Chinese labor in June 1919. In early June 1919 laborers in Shanghai struck against foreign enterprises in support of the May Fourth movement. The strike was to have far-reaching implications for radical consciousness. As Deng Zhongxia, at the time a student at Beida and later an important Communist labor organizer, wrote in his *History of the Chinese Labor Movement,*

> The gentlemen of the upper classes had so far not bothered to take note of laborers. With this movement (the June Third movement), laborers demonstrated their power to bourgeois intellectuals who could not but be impressed with its manitude, and began to make efforts to influence laborers to secure their support.[7]

Deng should know; he was one of those so impressed.

If May 1919 may legitimately be described as the Month of the Intellectual in China, May 1920 was to be the Month of the Laborer. In early 1919, few Chinese intellectuals spoke of laborers except in the most abstract terms. In the course of the ensuing year, their encounter with labor in the flesh dispelled romantic notions that had emerged on the eve of the May Fourth Movement. These romantic notions had not disappeared altogether when the radical press celebrated May Day in 1920 with great fanfare; but the celebration revealed a much better understanding of the condition of laborers and a closer identification with them, than ever before. If socialism had profound consequences for Chinese intellectuals' conceptualization of society and their place in it, the awareness of laborers was to have profound consequences for the future of socialism.

The political emergence of labor in June 1919 had two consequences. First, it enhanced the urgency of the situation. Labor's emergence was traumatic for the intellectuals: confronted with a new force they were ill prepared to comprehend, they responded with ambivalence. While laborers added a significant force to the ranks of revolution, the hopes this aroused were accompanied by fear of what a movement of the uneducated masses might mean. Chinese intellectuals did not have a high opinion of the intellectual and political qualifications of Chinese laborers as a revolutionary force, and feared that a labor movement beyond their control, motivated by blind interests born of ignorant frustration, might have adverse consequences for the revolution over which they had hitherto made exclusive claims. There was a profound ambiguity in May Fourth socialism (as in Chinese socialism throughout the twentieth century—and, perhaps, all socialism) that reflected this ambivalence toward labor: socialism was intended as much to promote working-class interests as it was to ward off the possibility of class conflict. Whether motivated by hope or fear, however, a concern emerged in the immediate aftermath of the May Fourth Movement to close the gap between the culture of intellectuals and the culture of the oppressed masses. This new consciousness was also largely responsible for the diffusion among intellectuals of a conviction that socialism offered the only hope of overcoming problems created by class division and oppression.

The emergence of labor, secondly, provided seemingly incontrovertible proof that China's problems were rooted in the global forces of capitalism. The emergence of labor forced intellectuals to realize that capitalism was already a reality of Chinese society. In the postwar world, alive with the revolutionary ferment of labor against capital and of colonies against imperialist states, it seemed superfluous to distinguish social problems on the basis of national boundaries. The ideological cosmopolitanism of the New Culture Movement had predisposed intellectuals to think in universalist terms. Now socialism lost its remoteness and appeared as a universal solution as immediately relevant to China as to any other society.

Contrary to Deng Zhongxia, Chinese intellectuals had not been entirely oblivious of laborers before June 1919. The anarchist critique of the oppression of labor by the "idle rich" and their promotion of "laboring" as a fundamental social virtue had already introduced the question of labor into New Culture consciousness. To be sure, anarchist treatment of labor was highly abstract, possibly concerned more with improving intellectuals through labor, or at least the consciousness of the value of labor, than with laborers per se. Nevertheless, at least some took the question in a more concerete sense. Anarchists had been concerned all along with the education of laborers; the work-study program they initiated in France at this time was possibly inspired by earlier efforts in Paris to educate Chinese laborers who had been taken there to help out with the war effort. The intellectual laborer was on the other side of the laboring intellectual in the anarchist program for social revolution. In China, anarchists connected with Shifu had been among the first Chinese to organize labor syndicates. In Guangzhou in south and Hunan in central China, anarchists spearheaded the movement in 1919–1920 to organize and educate laborers. If the anarchist advocacy of "laborism" was abstract, as Communist historians suggest, it was not because they shied away from living laborers but because of their attitudes toward the relationship between labor and social class.

Anarchists approached the question of class as a question of distinctions between rich and poor, between those who labored and those who did not. When they did speak of classes, it was in order to reconcile class difference in society. As Wu Zhihui wrote in Labor magazine in March 1918:

> So the *Labor* magazine wishes to make clear the principles of class war and to research methods of pacifying it, so that along with the laboring people of the whole world, we can resolve this problem and seek a correct life.[8]

Already before 1919, Chinese publications reported widely on labor. After 1911, but especially after 1915, Chinese newspapers frequently reported on labor strikes. In the radical press, anarchist publications took the lead in discussing the problem of labor. Shifu's *People's Voice* (*Minsheng*) reported widely on labor in China and abroad. Some of the anarchist publications in France were directly concerned with labor and laborers, such as *The Journal of Chinese Laborers* (*Huagong zazhi*), published starting in January 1917. In 1918, anarchists started publication in China of the first journals devoted to labor, *Labor* and *Mirror to Labor*. This interest received further impetus from the Russian Revolution and the postwar movements in the West. In late 1918 and early 1919, the *Weekly Critic,* edited by Chen Duxiu and Li Dazhao, began to report on the condition of laborers in China, probably under the influence of Li Dazhao, who published here his article on Tangshan miners.

Already, moreover, Chinese radicals were beginning to express some impatience with abstract discussions of labor. In early 1919 Li Dazhao called upon Chinese youth to go to the villages.[9] In February 1919 Wang Guangqi, leader of the Young China Association and at the time influenced by anarchism, called on students to stop talking and "enter the world of labor in person."[10] Some were already doing just that, and Li Dazhao was successfully encouraging his students in Beida to do the same. *Morning News* in Beijing celebrated May Day in 1919 with contributions by Li, Wang, and a Yuan Quan, the translator of the first works on Marxism in China.[11] (See Chapter 6 for Yuan Quan.) Reports on labor in the press had not expanded dramatically over the previous few years, but now, under the influence of anarchism and Marxism, more Chinese radicals began to read them with a new perspective and sense of personal engagement.

What emerged following the June Third movement, as Deng Zhongxia correctly pointed out, was an awareness not of labor but of its power. Hitherto, radicals had praised the sanctity of labor but did not see an equal sanctity in laborers who, in their "ignorance," seemed more an obstacle to than force for change. An object of sympathy, they did not qualify in the eyes of intellectuals as subjects of their own destiny, let alone others'. The June Third Movement brought forth the power of laborers as a force to be reckoned with, and presented radical intellectuals with a challenge that had not existed so long as labor had remained an abstract question. As the question of labor assumed concreteness, the question of class and class conflict also assumed political immediacy. It did not necessarily change earlier assumptions about the "backwardness" of Chinese laborers, but that "backwardness" which had earlier been taken as evidence of the social and political inertness of Chinese laborers appeared now as a source of new social and political challenge. Concrete evidence of the potential for class conflict in Chinese society was to create a profound ambivalence in radical thinking: it substantiated radicals' belief in the inevitability of socialism, but it also challenged their assumptions concerning the means and the speed with which socialism could be brought about. The initial consequence of the political emergence of labor was to provoke fear that the Chinese revolution might be deflected from its proper path should laborers engage in "premature" activity. This in turn strengthened arguments for socialism, since the majority of Chinese radicals in the early May Fourth period perceived socialism as a means, not to foment, but to resolve class conflict. Zhou Fohai's enthusiastic welcome extended to the new "tide" of class struggle was a warning to his compatriots that class struggle was around the corner unless they moved immediately to ameliorate the condition of laborers.

This attitude set the tone for discussions of class and revolution in the wake of the May Fourth Movement. Even those who seemingly advocated class struggle often had no more in mind than a process of labor organization and education that would prevent violent social conflict. If they thought that conflict was already unavoidable, as Li Dazhao seemed to on occasion, they still believed that "spiritual change" must modify revolution if it was to reach its ideals of "mutual aid" and cooperation. These attitudes provide a substantial social context for understanding the ambivalence toward Marxism of the early May Fourth period, as well as the changes in that ambivalence starting in early 1920, by which time the possibility that had emerged in June 1919 of an alliance between intellectuals and labor in pursuit of class struggle had begun to appear to some as a necessity.

In 1919, Chinese intellectuals discovered Chinese society. Socialists had always pointed to society as the basis for political order; the preoccupation with social change as the means to changing China had been a hallmark of socialist thinking from its earliest appearance in China in the early 1900s. The May Fourth generation, in its frustration with politics, had turned to culture as the proper realm of change, only to discover that cultural change could not be fulfilled without a simultaneous change in social institutions. To this generation, in 1919, the question of society appeared in all its nakedness.

Chinese historians have long stressed the effects of labor's emergence in June 1919, but labor was not yet *the* social problem it would become by the mid-1920s. That honor still belonged to the problems of youth and the family, especially women. In 1919, writings on this question still far exceeded those on labor. The two questions were not mutually exclusive, however, least of all for socialists who had always been active in promoting women's causes. This was especially the case with the anarchists, who viewed the family, and the habits of authority it engendered, as a major source of gender and, therefore, social oppression. Attention was now once again focused on the relationship between socialism and feminism. Socialism appeared to some initially as a means of resolving the problems of the family and gender (reflected in popular images of socialism as an advocacy of the sharing of wives!).[12] This assimilation of socialism did, significantly, divert attention from questions of class. However, a parallel and opposite tendency arose to view gender oppression in terms of a paradigm provided by labor's oppression.[13] The awareness of class and socialism in other words, would have a transformative effect in this central area of New Culture thinking as well.

In the early May Fourth period, awareness of labor found expression in two ways. First was a new recognition of the plight of Chinese laborers. As early as March 1919, Li Dazhao's brief article on the Tangshan miners described the daily sufferings of these "hungry ghosts."[14] In ensuing months labor unrest brought further attention to their condition, culminated in extensive surveys of labor published in the radical press in the late spring of 1920.

Second, and equally important, was a new awareness of an autonomous political consciousness among laborers. Despite "the sanctity of labor," in its elitist intellectualism the New Culture Movement of the preceding few years had attributed to the laboring population all the ignorance and superstition which it blamed for China's problems. Laborers, even to the "populistically" inclined Li Dazhao, had appeared not as subjects of history but as objects of social activity awaiting the intellectuals' helping hand. This view persisted into the May Fourth period. It was challenged now, however, by another view which demanded that intellectuals not only teach laborers but learn from them. This new consciousness was to change the visage of Chinese thinking and politics during the ensuing decade and long thereafter.

The emergence of the "common people" into politics was the fulfillment of two decades of radical political aspiration, though not all radicals were happy about it when it finally came about. Intellectuals had to adjust: they could no longer speak "about" or "for" the common people but had to speak "with" them. Not all could, and even those who did remained fatally divided from the "masses" they aspired to lead. In this undertaking, New Culture intellectuals were handicapped even vis-a-vis earlier revolutionaries. It was one of the fundamental ironies of the New Culture Movement that while it advocated democratic rights for all, the language in which intellectuals expressed their aspirations alienated them not just from existing structures of authority but from the people they now wanted to lead; more so in the latter case, because the division was not just metaphorical but literal: even their discussions of socialism were laced with foreign terminology that (while intelligible to other members of the elite with access to foreign languages) would have meant little to the average Chinese. When Beida radicals made their first foray into Beijing suburbs in early 1920, armed with a dictionary of popular usage compiled by the anarchist Wu Zhihui, they found it inadequate for communicating with the people.[15]

Perhaps for this reason, the sobering effect of the political emergence of labor led to profoundly radical consequences. Romantic notions about labor were dispelled and intellectuals were eventually shocked out of their complacency. Within a year of the May Fourth Movement, ability to champion the cause of the masses and to promote mass participation in politics came to serve as a crucial test for correct radical politics—and radical political legitimacy in general. This turn had immediate and concrete implications for the self-image of radical intellectuals. Foreign students of Chinese politics, themselves members of an intellectual elite preoccupied with its relationship to social and political structures of power, have generally concentrated their attention on the relationship of Chinese intellectuals to the state and politics.[16] This was a major concern, but what was authentically radical at this point was the rise of a new concern: the relationship of intellectuals to the "common people" that constituted society. Socialism provided a necessary language for their reconceptualization of this relationship.

As an immediate effect, some became convinced that education alone could not ameliorate the condition of the common people, that only change in material existence and social relations could resolve China's problems. Changing the economic structure of society moved to the forefront of radical thought, gradually overshadowing concern with cultural transformation. New Culture intellectuals became especially interested in the social relations that constituted the economic basis. By late 1919, many would echo the lines that Chen Duxiu penned in December 1919: "I believe that measures concerning a society's economy should take up the greater part of politics. Moreover, if the economic problems of a society remain unresolved, then neither can any important political problem be solved. A society's economy is the foundation for its politics."[17] This new appreciation of politics had already, at the time of the writing, launched Chen on the way to socialism, and Communism.

Sun Yatsen or Jiang Kanghu, reading Chen's words, might well have muttered to themselves, "So, what's new?" And to some extent they would have been right. That good politics required a just and equitable economic system was not new to those who had been advocating socialism for nearly two decades. To the older generation of China's socialists, socialism was not a new, foreign idea to be transplanted in Chinese thought, but a long-familiar one whose time had come.

They would have been wrong, however, to think that May Fourth socialism was merely an extension of what they had known and advocated all along. In 1919, there was a new consciousness of socialism abroad. In China, socialism had new constituencies which endowed it with new social and cultural concerns. Consciousness of class within China had given socialism a new urgency that had not existed earlier. The world had changed since they had first begun to espouse socialism and, with it, socialism had changed. It had gained in complexity, as socialists in different societies had created political and organizational forms to cope with their particular problems. If socialism provided a common language for the discussion of social change, socialists did not speak with one voice. United in opposition to capitalism, they were deeply divided among themselves. Chinese socialists had to position themselves in a more complex field.

Most importantly, Chen's words were inspired by a newly emerging orientation on the question of social revolution. Earlier, socialists in China had two alternative ideas of social revolution. Advocates like Sun and Jiang had called for a "revolution" from above that would utilize the agency of the state to resolve the social problems created by economic inequality—'socialism' as a reformist social policy. Opposed to this was the anarchist call for a revolution from below that also sought to abolish the state, which anarchists held to be the ultimate bulwark of inequality and oppression, in society; a revolutionary anti-political mass mobilization, in other words, that would render social problems irrelevant by reconstituting society as community. In practice, social policy socialists gave priority to a political revolution that would create a new kind of state, which would then institute socialist measures to guarantee social justice. Anarchists looked to cultural revolution and social reorganization to achieve a social transformation that would render the state irrelevant. While each recognized a crucial relationship between state and society, neither conceived of social revolution as an integral part of the process of political revolution; the anarchists because they wished to dispense with politics altogether, the social policy socialists because they put social revolution after the task of establishing a new state.

The new orientation emerging in 1919 integrated social and political revolution. It made social revolution a *condition* of political revolution not a substitute for it (as the anarchists wished), or an extension of it (as social policy socialists wanted). Social revolution must be an integral part of the very process of political revolution. (It is important to note that, as earlier in Chinese socialism, "revolution" implied not necessarily violence but fundamental change. The issue of violence was separate, and confused and divided the advocates of social revolution.)

This idea of social revolution was not new as an idea; it had been ever-present as a possibility in the socialists' conceptualization of revolution as a process of both political *and* social transformation. Whether social change should be part of the process of political revolution or wait upon political victory had been an open question. The two alternatives were not mutually exclusive nor divisible by absolute lines, either with regard to the scope of social change or the nature of the social forces that would participate in the making of revolution.

Alternative ideas of social revolution overlapped, therefore, and retained a measure of fluidity (even in the case of anarchists); the distinctions were enunciated with clarity only when socialists sought to distinguish their various revolutionary strategies. Revolutionary opportunity played a significant part in the articulation of strategy, moreover, even if the different conceptions of social revolution were informed by different ideological premises concerning the nature and dimensions of social conflict.

This idea of social revolution had been present so far only as a "suppressed" possibility, however, since socialists had themselves rejected it for its "irrelevance" to preindustrial China. With the social ferment of 1919, "social revolution" became an immediate *reality* that had to be incorporated into the formulation of any strategy of political change. The world seemed, to Chinese radicals, poised on the threshold of a total transformation under the pressure of new social forces. It was meaningless to speak of state and society separately, especially in a society where the state had been reduced to mere political fiction, and revolutionaries needed all the social forces they could muster to overcome the militarists who made politics their plaything.

The new appreciation of social revolution appeared, in the aftermath of the May Fourth Movement, not so much as a clearly identifiable political position but more as a political orientation. It did not have a single, identifiable source, nor am I aware of any individual or group in 1919 who delineated it with the sharpness with which I have stated it here. As had been the case earlier with alternative ideas of social revolution in Chinese socialism, it would eventually be enunciated in the debates among socialists as they positioned themselves in 1920 around issues of class and revolution; now it was more a silent premise that gave socialist discourse its coherence. The idea that a new politics could only be created in the process of a thorough reorganization of Chinese society may not have seemed equally novel to all in 1919, but its emergence to the center of socialist discourse was to call forth a radical reconstitution of that discourse.

This was nowhere more evident than in the diffusion of Marxist vocabulary. The crucial difference between pre- and post-May Fourth socialism was Marxism—its almost total absence previously, and its rapid diffusion following the May Fourth Movement. Chinese socialists had long been familiar with the name of Karl Marx, but there had never been Marxists in China in any serious sense of the word. Those who had shown interest had known him only through the eyes of anti-Marxist social reformers, and assimilated his ideas to the reformist social policy "socialisms" of the kind prominent in Europe in the early 1900s. Marx had appeared in their writings as the long-deceased ancestor of socialism whose revolutionary ideas had been superseded by the very social reform ideas to which thy had given rise.

In 1919 Karl Marx was once again alive, not just among Chinese radicals who discovered for the first time that Marxism had been a living ideology of revolution all along, but among socialists everywhere, in whom the social movements of the postwar years rekindled hopes of imminent social revolution. To Chinese radicals, revolutionary Marxism as it emanated from eastern and central Europe carried most vibrantly the news of Marxism's resurrection as revolutionary ideology. This was not the only source. The resurgence appeared everywhere—in the guild socialism of England, the social democracy of Germany, the labor movements of the United States and Japan. Marxism appeared in many contemporary guises, which was a source of endless confusion, but all these movements, regardless of their conflicting appearances, pointed to the social revolutionary idea that was the hallmark of Marxism among all socialisms: the idea that the social reconstruction of the economic structure was the key to all revolutionary change.

The coincidence between the Marxist (though not necessarily Leninist) idea of social revolution, and the emergent orientation to social revolution in May Fourth socialism explains, I think, why the language of Marxism infused Chinese socialist thinking before there were any socialists in China to take up the Marxist-Communist revolutionary cause. It is a moot question whether this new orientation was acquired under the "influence" of external events or was a prior orientation that issued from social developments within China. The idea and the social experience coincided in time; they were not isolated from one another, but were dialectical moments in a single historical process that shaped socialist discourse: if social experience rendered the ideas relevant—and real—the ideas rendered the experience intelligible, and enhanced its reality.

By 1919, Chinese radicals had already begun to perceive the social problems of Chinese society as a local manifestation of a global capitalism that knew no boundaries, appearing not as a foreign intrusion but as an internal feature of Chinese society. The solutions might not be identical in every society, but the root explanations were the same. Socialism was a global discourse, in other words, and Chinese socialism was part of it—or should be.[18]

That no Chinese socialist in 1919 accepted the Marxist message in its totality underscores my argument that the new importance of Marxism was a consequence more of an emerging predisposition to social revolution in general than an attraction to the Marxist version of it. The dialectic between the idea and the social experience, moreover, was not teleological but historical. If the Marxist social revolutionary idea found a ready audience in China because it coincided with a new social revolutionary orientation in Chinese socialism, there was also a conflict between the Marxist and the Chinese socialist readings of socialism. The Marxist social revolutionary idea brought with it a message of which Chinese socialists were already uncomfortably aware in 1919: that Marxism was a class-based ideology that promoted the cause of the working class against other classes. It was an ideology not of statist social reform, or of a whole society against the state, but of a class. Marxism as social revolutionary idea was readily accepted, but Marxist class ideology was not. Other historical events would have to intervene before Chinese socialists, beginning in 1920, could begin to think of themselves in class terms, and of social revolution as class struggle for the conquest of political power. In the immediate May Fourth period, the effect of Marxism was restricted to clarifying, and enhancing the credibility of, socialist economic reasoning.

The reorientation in social revolutionary thinking did not carry an identical or unambiguous meaning for all constituencies. For the older generation of socialists, it presented a problem: how to reconcile it with long-standing commitments and positions. They felt quite at home with the new emphasis on social change (they had never been entirely happy with the anti-political New Culture movement) and played a crucial part now in the propagation of socialism, including Marxism (indeed, it is doubtful that without their publications, socialist ideas would have spread with such rapidity). While their politics remained unchanged on the whole, however, the language of their socialism became considerably more radical. Their efforts to assimilate this language to previous political positions (some that reached back to pre-Republican days) created severe strains for their socialism. They took up the new question of class with enthusiasm, but only in order to suppress the potential for class conflict in Chinese society. They did more than anyone else to introduce Marxist ideas into Chinese socialism, but remained suspicious of Marxist politics. Their advocacy of socialism helped improve their image among New Culture youth, who had become suspicious of their politics. But their continued loyalty to old political positions cast them in an unfavorable light in the eyes of many. The inconsistencies in their socialism came into sharp relief against the new social revolutionary orientation (which, ironically, they helped articulate). These ideological inconsistencies would be expressed in the contradictions in their politics over the ensuing decade. The same inconsistencies have led Communist historians to conclude that they "obstructed" the sperad of Marxist ideology.

For New Culture radicals, especially of the younger generation, the new orientation created different contradictions. Unlike the older socialists, when they turned to socialism and social change in 1919 their thinking shifted in a major way. Yet they were better placed to receive the message of social revolution as the precondition of all other change. With all their culturalism, their idea of cultural change presupposed a change in social institutions; this was especially evident in the wide diffusion of anarchist ideas among them. They were not burdened, moreover, by loyalty to old political ideas, since basic to the Movement was the rejection of politics. In their case, the problem was how to reconcile social to cultural change. Their initial response to the challenge in 1919 was to assimilate questions of social change to the *language* of culture and ideology. Their elitist conception of culture had to be overcome before they could grasp the social problems they confronted in their own right. There were problems, moreover, where Marxism was concerned. The political implications of Marxism were not readily welcomed by a generation that had renounced politics as the realm of selfishness and particularity. They conceived of society in holistic terms, which did not predispose them to class division and conflict. While they favored a thoroughgoing social revolution, they understood it in a non-Marxist sense, informed by anarchist ideas on politics and society.

These contradictions were evident from the beginning, however, and New Culture radicals only needed to overcome their anti-political bias to make the shift to socialism; this is in fact what happened with the May Fourth Movement in 1919. It is interesting that while the older generation of socialists did the most to propagate the new social revolutionary idea, when a Marxist-Communist political option appeared in 1920 its constituency was recruited mostly from among New Culture radicals who until the May Fourth Movement had shown little inclination to socialism or socialist ideas. The interaction of these two groups, and of their predispositions, help us disentangle the complex web of May Fourth socialism.

5

Radical Culture and Social Activism:
Anarchism in May Fourth Radicalism

If "social change was at the heart of what progressive May Fourth publications advocated and discussed" in 1919,[1] anarchism was the tongue in which
this advocacy found its expression. By the eve of the May Fourth Movement,
anarchists' vocabulary had already become integral to the language of radicalism in China.

Anarchist popularity, Chinese historians have observed, was a condition
of contemporary political circumstances and the social constitution of the
Chinese intelligentsia.

> Under the conditions of several thousands of years of feudal despotism,
> especially with the decline of government with constant warlord disaster
> and repeated but ineffective efforts at governmental reform, it was easy
> for the people at large to become disgusted with politics. On the other
> hand, the Chinese intelligentsia was mostly of petit-bourgeois origin; it
> had a personality that was subjective, superficial, evanescent and impa-
> tient. When they began to demand revolution, what best suited their taste
> was not scientific socialism but empty and highflown utopias, and anar-
> chism which flaunted existing customs.[2]

While there is probably a good deal to be said for this evaluation, it essentially misses the point. The liberationist and cosmopolitan thrust of May
Fourth thinking (which appears reprehensible from a perspective that would
make socialism into a tool of national liberation) was not inimical to "scientific socialism" but a precondition for its propagation. The democratic impulse it generated among Chinese youth extended New Culture aspirations
for a just and rational society beyond intellectuals to the population at large,
and prepared the intellectual grounds for the diffusion of socialism.

Eric Hobsbawn has observed that anarchism has proved most appealing
under circumstances of spontaneous social mobilization.[3] While the social
mobilization which accompanied the May Fourth Movement was no doubt
responsible for the diffusion of anarchist ideas among Chinese youth, the
mobilization was not entirely spontaneous but congealed around the numerous (albeit ideologically diffuse and disparate) organizational cores that had
taken shape over the preceding years, especially in China's colleges and uni-

versities, which in May 1919 spearheaded the first waves of protests. Likewise, the diffusion of anarchist ideas among Chinese youth was not the result of a spontaneous petit-bourgeois utopianism (however that may have helped to prepare a fecund ground for it) but of anarchists' persistent efforts over the preceding decade to spread their ideas.

Anarchists, the only socialists to participate actively in the New Culture movement, significantly contributed to its intellectual climate. Radical intellectuals in these years had become increasingly convinced that China's youth must be liberated from the crippling authority structure of Confucian tradition, with its foundation in the family, which precluded the nourishment of socially responsible individuals and obstructed the growth of public consciousness and social cohesiveness. Thus the anarchist message that a good society could be created only on the basis of free association among free individuals found a receptive audience. Anarchists, who had most consistently advocated this message over the previous decade, propagated it among Chinese youth as participants in the New Culture Movement. The central social problems identified in New Culture thinking, the family and the liberation of women, were as central to Chinese anarchist thinking as they have been to all anarchist critiques of society. This may help explain why, of all available socialisms, Chinese youth of the May Fourth period found anarchism most congenial to their concerns. It also explains why other socialists, with their predominantly political orientation, were at first suspicious of the New Culture Movement, and their suspicion was reciprocated.

To stop here, however, would be to ignore the revolutionary message embedded in the anarchist contribution to these main themes of the New Culture Movement. The anarchist concern with individual liberation may explain why anarchism found a receptive audience during the New Culture Movement; but this does not explain anarchism's role as a clearinghouse for socialism in the wake of the May Fourth Movement. What distinguished the anarchists' contribution to New Culture thinking was their insistence that the question of individual liberation was fundamentally a social question. The common tendency, not least of all among Marxists, to contrast anarchist "individualism" with Marxist "socialism" distorts not only Marx's fundamental concern with the individual but also portrays anarchism as a version of libertarianism. As Richard Saltman has observed of Bakunin's preoccupation with remaking the individual as a "free and dignified being," mainstream anarchist philosophy has "understood that man could accomplish this restoration of his human capacities only with and through his fundamental unity with his fellow man."[4] This is especially the case with Kropotkin's anarcho-communism which, of all versions of anarchism, exerted the greatest influence on Chinese anarchist thinking.

Chinese anarchists were neither liberals, who took the individual to be the end of social activity, nor libertarians, who placed the individual above society. While a few Stirnerian anarchists took absolute individual liberation to be the end of revolution (and some alienated youth exploited the anarchist argument), most anarchists' idea of revolution was informed by an uncompromisingly social vision of humanity characteristic of Kropotkin. A truly socialized humanity, they believed, could be achieved only through the creation of truly socialized individuals. This vision informed their views of the education necessary to the creation of anarchist morality, the single most important means to anarchism in the anarchist conception of revolution. The goal of education was to liberate the consciousness of individuals from authority, only to restore them, as it were, to their instinctive sociability.

Anarchists' sensitivity to the social basis of individual liberation enabled them to inject social concerns into New Culture thinking, otherwise preoccupied with ideas and culture. It was in this regard that anarchists had a radicalizing impact on the New Culture Movement. While anarchists were also prominent among New Culture radicals as the only ones to take up questions of labor, and the need for intellectuals to be cognizant of the problems of the common people, their social message was to have the most profound effect on the consciousness and behavior of radical intellectuals. Before socialism had become a visible feature of the Chinese intellectual scene, anarchists had already introduced the issues of socialism. While their impact on Chinese intellectuals was not without its ambiguities, especially where Marxism was concerned, anarchists played an important part in creating dispositions within New Culture thinking that would facilitate the growth of socialism following the May Fourth Movement, when social developments endowed their ideas with an immediate reality.

Among the ideologies contributing to the New Culture Movement, anarchism emerged early on as the ideology of the radical left that sought to steer the cultural revolution in the direction of a social revolution, saw in cultural transformation a means toward socialism, and desired, at least in theory, to expand the cultural revolution to encompass the common people *(pingmin)*. Yet studies of the Movement, including those by Communist scholars, leave the impression that socialism was not a significant component of the movement until after 1919 when, under the influence of the Russian Revolution, Chinese intellectuals began to show interest in it. This is misleading, valid only if we deny the socialism of the anarchists. It is true that the word "socialism" does not appear very often in New Culture literature before 1919. Chinese anarchists themselves did not advertise their anarchism in their contributions to mainstream journals such as *New Youth* or *Renaissance (Xin chao)*; the word "anarchism" appears rarely in their contributions, and then only in the description of the political philosophy of authors such as Tolstoy and Goldman, whose works they translated. What distinguished anarchist writings in these years was not their claim to socialism, but their advocacy of a social revolution, the hallmark of socialist ideologies in China since 1905. During the New Culture Movement, anarchists emerged as champions of a social revolution that went beyond changes in culture and ideology. They introduced not just socialist ideas and vocabulary but a socialist vision. This not only prepared the ground for the efflorescence of socialism after the May

Fourth Movement, but also helps explain why anarchism enjoyed an immense popularity among competing socialist ideologies in the early May Fourth period.

Social revolution to the anarchists had two meanings. First, it was a revolution to transform society root and branch. Second, it was a revolution of the whole society (*quantizhi geming,* as some anarchists described it).[5]

This broad idea of revolution was open to interpretation, and could be taken to condone—as it was over the years—anything from individual eremitism to class struggle. Nevertheless, it is possible, on the basis of anarchist writing and activity, to pinpoint a number of basic characteristics that distinguished the Chinese anarchist idea of social revolution.

This idea was, in the first place, consciously antipolitical. Competing ideas of social revolution in the pre-May Fourth period made social revolution part of a "broader" program of political revolution. Anarchists rejected the latter as "a revolution of the few," and viewed their own as the only authentically revolutionary alternative; a social revolution of the whole of society would be the only way to overcome particularistic interests and to establish public-mindedness (*gongdao*).[6]

The anarchists' rejection of politics, however, went much deeper than doubts about the limitations of political freedom. The fundamental goal of revolution, which underlay all its more specific objectives, was to eliminate "authority" (*qiangquan,* also translatable in this context as "naked force" because anarchists identified the two) from society. They saw in authority the fundamental cause of the distortion of the natural goodness of people, which would assert itself in the formation of an anarchist society once authority was eliminated. Authority was diffused throughout present society, embodied in its various institutions. "What we mean by authority is not merely the militarism of Germany and Austria, or the 'supermanism' of Nietzsche, but the politics, religion, law and capitalists of present society that obstruct the realization of freedom and happiness by humanity as a whole."[7]

The most conspicuous institution of authority was the state, not only itself the greatest source of oppression, but also the bulwark of all other authoritarian institutions. The elimination of the state, therefore, was the primary task of revolution, and the prerequisite to the abolition of all authority. Politics, and political activity of all kind, took the existence of the state as its premise; hence the anarchist rejection of politics.

Second, they saw tradition as a source of authority, and wanted to purge its hold on Chinese minds. Not the first Chinese to raise doubts about Confucianism, anarchists were possibly the first to call for a "Confucius revolution" (*Kongzi geming*).[8] To them, Confucius was the source of many a superstition. Superstition, served as a foundation for authority, and must be purged in order to abolish authority. In China, this required the abolition of Confucianism.

Confucianism was undesirable to them for a deeper reason. Confucian beliefs served as the foundation for the family which, next to the state (or even perhaps more important in China), was the major source of authority.

As one Paris anarchist had observed in the 1900s, "Today's society . . . is like a high tower in appearance. Marriage is its foundation."[9] The family did not merely perpetuate authority, however; it also served, in the words of a Hunanese anarchist manifesto of 1925, as "an instrument for the production of selfishness."[10] At any rate, the abolition of marriage and the family, a revolution in the Three Bonds (the bonds that tied together rulers and ministers, husbands and wives, and parents and children) and the Five Constants (in addition to the above, the bonds that tied together brothers and friends), was to the anarchists high on the agenda of social revolution. This required, they believed, a "thought revolution" (*sixiang geming*) to liberate the individual from the hold of familistic ideology, and an "economic revolution" (*jingi geming*) to provide individuals with the economic security that would guarantee their autonomy from the family.[11]

Finally, anarchists called for the abolition of class oppression, or the authority exercised by one class over another, which they viewed as another manifestation of the selfishness created by a social order based on the principle of authority. The anarchist position on the question of class was problematic. While their analysis of class oppression overlapped with Marxist explanations, they differed from Marxists (at least mainstream Marxists of the day) on the causes of class oppression and, therefore, on the solutions. Anarchists took account of the economic basis of class oppression, and placed the abolition of private property and production for profit high on the agenda of revolution. Shifu, more radical than most anarchists in this respect, pointed to capitalism as one of the twin evils of contemporary society, the other being the state.[12] Nevertheless, unlike the materialistic Marxist understanding of the problem in terms of the process of production, anarchists viewed the question of class moralistically. Although anarchist analyses often referred to the bourgeoisie and the proletariat, their descriptions of classes more often than not juxtaposed the rich against the poor, those who did not labor against those who did, and mental against manual labor. This was consistent with the anarchist view that ultimately power and authority, and the "selfishness" they generated, were the cause rather than the effect of economic inequality.

Indeed, beneath their radical class rhetoric, anarchists rejected class conflict as a means to resolve class oppression. This was articulated fully after the May Fourth Movement in the course of anarchists' critiques of Communism, but was already expressed in anarchist writing before 1919. They believed that class conflict was just another expression of societal selfishness that merely perpetuated social problems in another guise. Anarchism offered a means to resolving this problem peacefully. As Wu Zhihui stated, "The *Labor* magazine wishes to make clear the principles of class war and to research methods of pacifying it, so that along with the laboring people of the whole world, we can resolve this problem and seek a correct life."[13] Classes, the anarchists believed, could be abolished only with the abolition of authority the architechtonic principle of society.

The advocacy of social revolution was basic to anarchist philosophy, even if expressed in a Chinese idiom. The individual was the point of departure:

the goal of social revolution was ultimately to restore individuals, deformed by the burden of authority, to their true, natural selves. Anarchists believed that with the abolition of authority, the basic instinctive goodness of human beings would assert itself, and the tendency to selfishness, plunder, and oppression of individuals under present-day society would be eradicated. As a manifesto that issued from Changzhou put it, "the principle of anarchical communism" was "a truth hidden in every individual's mind." This truth ("anarchical morality"), the manifesto explained, was "nothing but labor and cooperation [*sic*], both of which are natural gifts to human beings and are not derived from the outside."[14] Moral transformation, or rather moral restitution, of the individual was, therefore, the key, and education the best means, to achieving social revolution.

Anarchists' writing and programs often displayed a penchant for violence that disguised the basically reformist and moderate measures they advocated. "Propaganda by the deed" was a regular feature of anarchist programs ("one bomb is better than a hundred thousand books").[15] But anarchists in their deeds placed peaceful propaganda and education ahead of violence. To what extent they practiced the violence they preached must await a different kind of research. Suffice it to say here that anarchism could also serve as a moderating influence. Most notably Shifu, the paradigmatic anarchist leader from Guangzhou, when he became an anarchist, foreswore the assassination activities he had engaged in before 1911 as a member of the China Assassination Corps.[16]

The anarchist emphasis on education as a strategy of social revolution was implicit: they saw revolution as a process, which they identified broadly with progress. An article in *New Era* (*Xin shiji*), the Paris anarchist organ, explained revolution as "re-evolution," portraying it as the motive force of evolution; this same explanation was repeated by Huang Lingshuang in 1919 in the Declaration of Evolution Society.[17] This conceptualization of revolution as a process, rather than as a discrete historical undertaking, had a fundamental implication: anarchists refused to distinguish the ends from the means of revolution. Revolution must in its progress create the institutions that contain, in embryo, the new society. These institutions, in turn, would secure the further progress of revolution. This revolutionary dialectic ruled out the utilization of any means that were in contradiction to the ultimate goals of revolution.

In this process, education was but the positive aspect of revolution, as violence was its negative aspect. The negative purpose of revolution was to clear away the institutional and material obstacles to the liberation of the human potential; but education, its positive aspect, would nurture the morality the anarchist ideal demanded, and make possible the creation of the embryonic anarchist institutions.[18] The dialectic was ultimately between the individual and social institutions: The diffusion of anarchist morality among individuals would lead to the substitution of embryonic anarchist institutions for authoritarian institutions that would, in turn, further promote the progress of anarchist morality until, eventually, anarchism came to encompass all aspects of life for all of humanity. Education was revolution: revolution was education.

Anarchists viewed learning, especially scientific learning, as an important component of the education they proposed. "There is no morality other than learning," proclaimed one article in *New Era* in 1908.[19] The Truth Society at Beida adopted as its basic guideline the slogan of "advancing morality and cultivating knowledge."[20] The Declaration of Evolution Society in 1919 stated, quoting Thomas Huxley:

> If the present advance of learning cannot fundamentally alter the decadent condition in which the great majority of humankind lives, then I can say only one thing; let us quickly call upon that merciful comet to wipe out this globe, and us with it.[21]

Anarchists commonly held, in good rationalist fashion, that the morality of a people was proportionate to their learning. This underlay their call for the "universalization of education" (*jiaoyu puji*), which they believed was the prerequisite to human progress.

Ultimately, however, the goal of education was the ethical transformation of the individual. The premises underlying the anarchist view of education and, therefore, social revolution, can be gleaned from their vision of good society. By vision here I do not mean utopian blueprints, so much as the vision of what human beings could be if allowed to develop in freedom. Chinese anarchists had produced a number of utopian blueprints before 1915. Of these, possibly the most popular was the description of future society by Shifu, whose ideas on anarchist society acquired the status of an "ism" (Shifuism, or *Shifu zhuyi*) by the May Fourth period. His description, which blended native utopias with Kropotkin's futurism, pointed to a future without national boundaries, state, private property, or family, without laws or institutions of coercion, without the superstition of religion.[22]

All the institutions anarchists wished to abolish were institutions that, in their eyes, divided people from one another, and obstructed the creation of an organic society that derived its cohesiveness not from coercion but from the "natural" tendency of humankind to voluntary association.[23] The anarchist belief in such a society was grounded in a vision of humanity that was at once natural, esthetic, and rational. "Anarchism is the means to (achieving) beauty, Communism is the means to (achieving) goodness," Huang Lingshuang wrote in his prefatory essay to *Records to Freedom*.[24] A letter in the same issue of the journal states: "The morality of anarchism is equality, universal love [*boai*] and freedom; there is not one among these that is not in accord with the spontaneous growth of human natural endowments."[25] "The principle of anarchism," as the manifesto from Changzhou had put it, was "a truth hidden in every individual's mind."

While some of this vocabulary sounds Mencian, and mystically Mencian at that, the anarchist idea of human goodness derived its language from Kropotkin and, to a lesser extent, Tolstoy. As the Changzhou manifesto (most probably penned by a disciple of Shifu) pointed out, this truth hidden in every individual's mind was "nothing but labor and cooperation" (the latter probably "mutual aid" in the original). Mutual aid was to the Chinese anarchists the cornerstone of anarchist morality, as it had been to Kropotkin, who had written:

> The ant, the bird, the marmot, the savage have read neither Kant nor the fathers of the church nor even Moses. And yet all have the same idea of good and evil. And if you reflect for a moment on what lies at the bottom of this idea, you will see directly that what is considered as *good* among ants, marmots, Christians or atheist moralists is that which is *useful* for the preservation of the race; and that which is considered *evil* is that which is *hurtful* for race preservation.[26]

Kropotkin viewed solidarity, therefore, as "a natural law of far greater importance than the struggle for existence," and concluded that the "law of mutual aid," not competition, was "the law of progress."

Chinese anarchists, following Kropotkin, took this natural tendency to mutual aid as the essential content of human goodness (*liangxin*). They endowed this tendency with the status of a universal scientific principle (*gongli*), and set it against Darwinian notions of conflict which, they believed, encouraged "men to eat men."[27] Hua Lin argued that nineteenth-century science had proven that man was a "social animal."[28] Cai Yuanpei, the chancellor of Beida during the May Fourth period, lectured to Chinese workers in Paris that division of labor and social interdependence were fundamental characteristics of human society.[29] Mutual aid was rational not only because it was natural to humankind (and the rational operation of the cosmos), but because it had the blessings, the anarchists believed, of modern science.

If mutual aid was one instinctive endowment of humanity, the imperative to labor was the other. "Anarchist morality," Shifu wrote in 1914, was "nothing but mutual aid and labor; the two are instinctive to humanity."[30] He went on to explain that "labor is humankind's natural duty and mutual aid its inherent virtue." Labor was not simply a necessity for the sustenance of life, but a moral imperative of human existence. What made labor unpleasant was its present coercive nature; with the liberation of humankind, labor would realize its true nature as a fundamental human endowment.

The stress on mutual aid as the motive force of progress in nature and society alike, present in Chinese anarchism from its origins in Paris before 1911, was spread by Li Shizeng, who had been trained as a biologist. Labor received scant attention in Chinese anarchist writings before 1911. In the hundred-odd issues of *New Era* published before 1911, only two articles dealt with labor, and those in the most general terms. Labor as a necessity of anarchist society had received greater attention from Liu Shipei, the leading light of the Tokyo anarchists, who had incorporated into his anarchist utopia that manual labor must be performed by every individual. Liu's anarchism, agrarian in orientation and deeply influenced by the "pan-laborism" (*fanlaodong zhuyi*) of Tolstoy, as well as native agrarian utopianism, was essentially antimodernist. He did not share the Paris anarchists faith that with the advance in technology, labor would become more pleasant, if not disappear altogether. The radical implication of his belief was that laboring by all would guarantee social equality.

The increasing attention Chinese anarchists devoted to labor after 1911 was possibly a consequence of their intensifying relationship with laborers: the syndicalist activities of the Cantonese anarchists, and in the education in Paris of the laborers they had helped import to France during the war. There was also a subtle, but most significant, change in these years in the attitudes toward labor. Even Shifu displayed an ambiguity on the question. He presented labor as an instinctive human endowment, but went on to explain that it would become more pleasant with help from technology. By the time of the New Culture Movement, however, anarchists presented labor not as a necessary burden, but a manifestation of the essential beauty of anarchist morality and human instinct. This was possibly due to increasing familiarity with those of Kropotkin's works extolling labor, namely *The Conquest of Bread* and *Fields, Factories and Workshops,* both of which were widely read in China in the latter part of 1910–1920. All one can say with certainty, however, is that labor as one of the twin natural endowments of humanity, a moral imperative that expressed the natural goodness and beauty of the human spirit, was more and more stressed as the anarchist involvement with labor gained momentum after 1915. By 1919, mutual aid and labor appeared to many as the cornerstones of anarchist philosophy, and the means to achieve the good society of the anarchist vision.

Anarchists, then, perceived two interrelated functions in education. First, an accumulation of learning was necessary to purge individuals of their "superstitions," which encompassed all the ideological beliefs that undergirded authoritarian society. More important, education must create social spaces where, freed from the authority of existing institutions, individuals would be able to realize their propensity to social existence. Especially important in this regard were institutions that promoted mutual aid and the free exercise of labor. The one prepared the ground for the other, in a dialectical interplay between consciousness and social institutions which was the essential content of anarchist social revolution.

Anarchist faith in education was such that it gave their idea of revolution a strongly cultural flavor. They expected education not only to transform individual consciousness but to resolve the most serious social problems. The Declaration of the World Society, established by the Paris anarchists in 1912 to promote educational activities, stated:

> Far-sighted men regard the fact that higher education is not yet universal as the reason why classes are born. They grieve about this and (think that) the way of remedying the situation is to make education equal (for all).[31]

It is important to note that not high culture, but culture in its most fundamental sense, quotidian culture, everyday habits and thinking, was what anarchists sought to transform; hence its importance as a means of transforming social relations.

This idea of social revolution, with its strong cultural content, was not far removed from the concerns that emerged to the forefront during the New Culture Movement. We are accustomed to thinking of the New Culture Movement in terms of its intellectual leaders, and the abstract ideas they unleashed upon the Chinese intellectual scene. While these ideas were significant "moments" in the unfolding consciousness of the movement, what rendered them significant was their relevance to the practical problems of a whole generation. Anarchist ideas as well derived their power not from their abstract value, or their instrumental appeal, but from the resonant chord they struck in the hearts and minds of young New Culture intellectuals.

To appreciate the appeal of anarchism, or for that matter any of the currents of thought that went into the making of the New Culture Movement, it is necessary, therefore, to view the movement not simply as intellectual, a "revolution" in the realm of ideas, but as a movement of real living people who sought in ideas solutions to concrete practical problems. The turn to culture as the arena of significant activity for change was itself provoked by the failure of the Republican experiment in China and the political degeneration that followed in its wake. As Chen Duxiu put it in 1917,

> If we desire to consolidate the Republic today, we must first wash clean the anti-Republican thinking that infuses the thinking of our countrymen, for the ethical basis that underlies the state organization and the social system of a republic is the diametrical opposite of the ethical basis that underlies the state organization and the social system of monarchical despotism; one is founded upon the spirit of equality; the other on a distinction between classes of high and low. The two cannot be reconciled.[32]

What China needed, Chen was to conclude, was reeducation in Republican ethics and literacy. Even the literary revolution, an important undertaking of New Culture leaders, was tied to this practical question. The reform of writing was not an end in itself (at least not to everyone) but rather a means to purge the hegemony of old ideas and make new ideas accessible to larger numbers of people.

It is significant that in his proposal for a new approach to the question of change, Chen cited in his support the anarchists, in particular a recent speech by Li Shizeng which had argued for the priority of ethical change. The corruption of Chinese politics at this time endowed this anarchist message with a new practical urgency. If revulsion with existing politics turned Chinese intellectuals to the realm of culture, moreover, the cultural revolution they sought to achieve was not simply a revolution in ideas, but a revolution in the ethical basis of society. The message of cultural revolution exerted the greatest power where it promised to transform existing social institutions, chief among them the family, because it licensed a struggle against the authority of the old where it impinged directly on everyday life. Chinese youth was no doubt dissatisfied with the old-fashioned leadership that ruled China, but it was the promise of the overthrow of authority in everyday life that drove it to the New Culture Movement, and provided it with the social substance that has given it historical significance. Ultimately, the motive force of the movement was to be provided by the new generation of intellectuals who came of age in 1915–1920; their idealism only exacerbated their alienation from a social system that, unlike their predecessors, they no longer took for granted. Perhaps the most important contribution of the older generation of intellectuals who initiated the movement was to provide Chinese youth with the confidence to create a social system of its own where it could breathe freely, and a vocabulary with which to articulate its unspoken yearnings. As one *New Youth* reader phrased it,

> This spring I read your magazine for the first time. As if woken by a blow on the head, I suddenly realized the value of youth. We should emulate the West, and abolish the old and welcome the new. I am like somebody who is sick, and who must breathe in fresh air and exhale the old. Although at present I am not what you might describe as a new youth, I am sure that I can sweep from my mind all the old thoughts of the past. The credit for all this goes to the save-the-youth work you have been doing.[33]

The struggle against the authority of the old was not some abstract struggle between the old and the new in the realm of ideas; it was a real life struggle in a society where the culture that intellectuals rebelled against was very much alive in the social structures of power and authority. The icons the "iconoclastic" New Culture youth sought to destroy were icons that watched over their everyday existence. The intellectual radicalism of New Culture leaders found its fulfillment in the social radicalism of a generation to whom the burden of the past was not an idea but a lived experience. This youth was to take over the leadership of the movement rapidly, and when it did, it escalated the radicalism of the movement beyond the anticipations of some of its original leaders, who discovered that they no longer controlled the pace of the events they had set in motion. When the New Culture Movement is viewed from this perspective, the increasingly ineffective efforts of those who took the movement as one of ideas pure and simple, and tried to keep it that way, appears not as the movement's essence, but as an ideological position within it that held forth intellectualism to keep in check the social radicalism their ideas had unleashed.

The call for cultural revolution did not necessarily reject all that was old, but focused on those aspects of the Chinese tradition that legitimized institutions that reproduced "social relations of domination and subordination" (the phrase is Raymond Williams'), especially where it related to youth and women. Wu Yu, the uncompromising critic of Confucianism, attacked tradition not because it was "old" (he did not extend the same attack to Daoism and Legalism but rather used them to attack Confucianism), but because it upheld the family system. His remark (note the similarity to the Hunanese anarchist manifesto) that "the effect of the idea of filial piety has been to turn China into a factory for the manufacturing of obedient subjects" is revealing of the material, because social, understanding of culture that infused the call for cultural revolution in these years.[34] It was not abstract issues of culture or ideas, but the call for the struggle against the hegemony of the old over the young, of men over women, of the rich over the poor, of state over society, in short, against authority, that in these years fashioned a social movement out of ideas.

The New Culture ideas of culture as it had emerged by the May Fourth period was, therefore, a social idea of culture; cultural revolution, in other words, required the revolutionization of basic social institutions.

There was a conjuncture between the social logic of this idea of cultural revolution and the cultural logic of the anarchist idea of social revolution. The distinction between culture and society lost its meaning in either idea of revolution that conceived of society as the institutional embodiment of a culture of authority, and of culture as the architectonic expression of social structures of domination and oppression. In their search for cultural liberation, New Culture youth sought out social spaces where they could live in freedom. More than any other group participating in the New Culture Movement, anarchists offered such spaces to youth. Anarchists promised that their idea of New Culture was not to change ideas but rather life at its most basic, everyday level. The work-study institutions they promoted, perhaps even the syndicates, represented those spaces. As Wang Guangqi (an important leader of the influential Young China Association) observed, work-study groups were not simply utilitarian institutions to promote education, but havens from the families youth sought to escape. (Runaways from home, as we shall see later, provided the Communists with some of their following in late 1920 in the Socialist Youth Corps!)

It is probably no accident that the social plight of Chinese youth, and the escape it discovered in the New Culture Movement, has been depicted most cogently in the autobiographical novel *Family,* written by an anarchist, Ba Jin, who came of age at this time. Anarchists by the very nature of their ideology were attuned to the most basic concerns of Chinese youth at this time. But anarchist ideology did not merely express general concerns; the ideas of "mutual aid" and "labor," basic to the social philosophy of anarchists, were specifically anarchist ideas that were to have a profoundly radicalizing effect on New Culture thinking. Before 1919, they were important primarily for pointing beyond the almost narcissistic preoccupation of intellectuals with their own liberation. But they also foreshadowed the concerns that would emerge in 1919 as central concerns of radical thinking, and resulted in the reorientation of New Culture thinking.

More eloquent than ideas, and much more effective in their propagation, were anarchists' efforts to translate their vision into the beginnings of reality in the womb of contemporary society. This social activity, which provides *us* with an ideological text in which their utopian vision assumes concrete form, enabled the anarchists to articulate the practical constitution of their vision.

This activity would culminate in the wave of communal experiments that swept Chinese youth in 1919, and revealed both the richness of the anarchist vision, and its social limitations. The ultimate expression of the cultural radicalism of the New Culture Movement, these experiments would in their failure mark a turning point in the thinking of Chinese youth—to the social radicalism of the post-May Fourth period.

Anarchists' activity ranged from the Diligent Work Frugal Study Program in France to the syndicalist activities of the anarchists in China, from the Promote Morality Society (*Jindehui*) at Beida to the New Village movement (*xincun yundong*), of which the writer Zhou Zuoren was the major proponent, but especially the labor-learning movement that, around the May Fourth Movement, assumed the proportions of a "thought tide" in the student world. Differing widely in scope and constituency, these activities had one purpose in common: to provide youth with an institutional environment in which to cultivate habits of mutual aid and labor. For some, at least, they were also the starting point of the reorganization of society as a large association of small-scale organizations.[35]

The syndicalist and work-study movements were the most significant. The anarchist syndicalist movement represented the emergence of the modern labor movement in China. Anarchists spearheaded the labor movement in Guangzhou and Hunan, and possibly in Shanghai. (With the exception of Guangzhou, this influence would be short-lived; anarchists began to lose ground to the Communists almost immediately after the establishment of the Party in 1921.)

Moreover, the organizing tactics they employed were to become common tactics of labor organization in China: the establishment of workers' schools and clubs to organize them in the process of education.[36] These tactics were partially a consequence of anarchist belief that Chinese labor was too backward culturally to permit immediate organization. As late as 1918, Wu Zhihui wrote in *Labor* that the establishment of a "labor party" (*gongdang*) in China must await the education of the working class.[37] Anarchists believed that if labor organization was to be effective, and in accordance with anarchist principles, laborers must do their own organizing; education would enable them to take charge of their own organizations.

These tactics also reflected the deep-seated anarchist belief in social revolution as a process of education. To the anarchists, syndicates were not merely organs for representing labor interests, but new social institutions in which to cultivate anarchist morality. When the time arrived for the final social revolution, these institutions would serve as the units of anarchist social organization.[37] This goal was possibly more important to some anarchists than the promotion of labor interests, which may have been a reason they found themselves unable to compete with the Communists in the 1920s.

Anarchist syndicalist activities brought Chinese labor and students together for the first time. What effect this had on laborers' consciousness is difficult to say; it certainly left its imprint on the consciousness of students.

The encounter would ultimately result in the explosive mixture that burst forth in the 1920s in urban social revolution.

More significant in immediate consequences was the work-study movement in France, which was also a product of anarchists' experiences with labor. It was their experiences with educating Chinese laborers in France that inspired the idea of laboring intellectuals that lay at the basis of the work-study program. Indeed, it was in such journals as the *Journal of Chinese Students in Europe* (*LuOu zazhi*), which started publication in 1916, and *Journal of Chinese Laborers* (*Huagong zazhi*), which started publication in 1917, both of them in Paris, that anarchists first started propagating the idea of combining labor and study.[38]

The basic reasoning was quite practical. As in the case of the laborers, whose education the anarchists had conducted as spare-time (*gongyu*) education in night schools, students who went to France on the program would work part-time to finance their education, and study part-time. To many in China, including participants, the appeal of the program was largely practical: one could acquire an education that might otherwise have been financially difficult or impossible. To some, such as Hu Shi and Wang Jingwei (who was himself involved in the program and was, for a while, editor of the *Journal of Chinese Students in Europe*), this practical feature was the most important. Hu Shi saw a parallel to the part-time work, part-time study programs he had encountered in the United States; he objected to the more idealistic aspects of the program as obstacles to its success.[39] Many participants seem not to have shared its sponsors' idealistic zeal; the latter often complained that students cared little about labor and were concerned mainly with "making it" by acquiring an education.[40]

To its anarchist initiators, the program carried a much more ambitious significance. Hua Lin remarked that if China were to change, the change would be accomplished by those who participated in work-study.[41] An article in *Labor* stated: "With work and study combined, workers will become scholars, scholars will become workers, to create a new society that will realize the goal of 'from each according to his ability, to each according to his need.' "[42] Possibly the most eloquent advocate of work-study was Cai Yuanpei, the chancellor of Beida, who saw in it the solution not only to "the problem of youth acquiring an education, but to the weightiest problems of China and the world."[43]

As the work-study movement gained momentum (as I noted earlier) anarchists' writings noticeably changed toward the glorification of labor. *Labor* in 1918 adopted as its guidelines "reverence for labor and the promotion of 'laborism' [*laodong zhuyi*]." Beyond its contribution to production, ethically labor was "the greatest obligation of human life" and "the source of civilization." Morally, labor was "the means to avoid moral degeneration and help moral growth, it was a means to forging spiritual willpower." Work, the guidelines stated, helped not only the individual but society as a whole. "Laborism" was to become a common term of New Culture vocabulary during the May Fourth period, comparable in its popularity to "mutual aid," but the phrase that caught contemporary imagination was provided by Cai Yuanpei in a speech he gave in later 1918.

> The world of the future is the world of labor! The labor we speak of is not the labor of metal workers, of carpenters, etc. The undertaking of all those who use their own labor power to benefit others is labor regardless as whether it is mental or manual. Farmers do the labor of cultivating crops, merchants do the labor of transporting commodities, writers and inventors do educational labor. We are all laborers. We must all recognize the value of labor. Labor is sacred [*laodong shensheng*].[44]

Anarchists in China, as Ghandi in India about the same time, viewed labor as "the great equalizer." As noted earlier, they differed from Marxists in their class analysis in the emphasis they placed on those who labored and those who did not. The economic problems of contemporary society, they believed, arose largely from the exploitation by a parasitic class of others' labor. The major distinction, as Cai's statement implies, was not between the proletariat and the bourgeoisie, but between those who labored and those who did not. The distinction had a special relevance in China, where Confucian tradition had for two thousand years distinguished the governors from the governed as mental and manual laborers. The combination of manual and mental labor was, to the anarchists, a means to overcoming economic exploitation. Cai's views are worth quoting at some length:

> In our ideal society, all people will live according to the principle "from each according to his ability, to each according to his need." "According to his ability" points to labor; whether it is manual or mental, all is labor that contributes to the existence of humankind and the advance of culture. Needs are of two kinds; physical needs such as clothing, food and shelter, and spiritual needs such as learning. Now there are some people who do not do any work, or do work that is not real work. Those who do real work cannot but work bitterly and work long hours. Aside from them, the rest use special privileges to take and waste in huge quantities what humankind needs. Consequently, the real workers do not get enough of what they need. Perhaps they get some of what they need physically, but they are totally deprived of what they need spiritually. Is this not a great obstacle to the advance of culture? If we want to eradicate this obstacle, we must first realize a life where labor and learning proceed together.[45]

We can only imagine how Cai's words rang in the ears of his Beijing audience, many of whom had hitherto thought their goal in life was to acquire an education so as to rule over laborers. They had an immediate impact on one intellectual, Li Dazhao, who in the following month would describe the October Revolution in Russia as the victory of "laborism" and, two months later, call upon youth to go to the villages. Over the ensuing year, the terms "laborism" and "the sanctity of labor" would become commonplace, bolstered by numerous discussions of Tolstoy's "pan-laborism" in the Chinese press. The May 1920 special issue on labor of *New Youth* carried the words "Labor is sacred" on its cover in Cai's own calligraphy.

By 1919, "mutual aid" and "laborism" had become among the most fundamental (and common) ideas of New Culture radicalism. Articles on Tolstoy's "pan-laborism" appeared not only in anarchist periodicals, but in the radical and liberal press in general, including influential publications such as the *Eastern Miscellany;* even conservative authors found it a directly relevant idea.[46] Even more widespread was the interest in "mutual aid" and its progenitor, Kropotkin, who in 1919 may have been the most revered European radical in Chinese eyes. Works by him such as *Mutual Aid, The Conquest of Bread,* and *Fields, Factories and Workshops* were readily available, and found their way into periodicals with a broad readership. In March 1919 *The Light of Learning* in Shanghai began to serialize his autobiography. In April *Eastern Miscellany* began to serialize Li Shizeng's translation of *Mutual Aid.* Later on in the year, *Weekend Review* serialized Kropotkin's *The State,* the only lengthy foreign work to appear in that periodical. In addition, articles on Kropotkin or translations from his works appeared in numerous publications; "mutual aid" became a cornerstone of May Fourth thinking. (This perhaps explains why rumors concerning Kropotkin's well-being in the Soviet Union created widespread anxiety among Chinese of different political persuasions.)

The idea of "mutual aid" may have found easy acceptance within the context of Chinese intellectual tradition, which had long held forth the essential goodness and sociability of human nature, even if, as New Culture intellectuals believed, that tradition had perpetuated practical "selfishness." The idea of "laborism," on the other hand, was authentically radical within the context of the very same tradition, which had made learning the condition of rulership. Within the context of the New Culture Movement, the idea not only radically affected the self-images of Chinese intellectuals, it was an important preparation for their encounter with labor in the flesh in the immediate aftermath of the May Fourth Movement.

Communist historians often point out that these ideas of labor and "laborism" were meaningless in their abstraction, and played a negative role in the May Fourth period, obstructing the emergence of a genuine class consciousness. The latter charge is, I think, valid. Most anarchists' advocacy of "laborism" was a means to avoid a bloody social revolution. Their interpretation of class division as between those who labored and those who did not certainly blurred Marxist ideas of class division as embedded in the process of production. Some of them went so far as to portray class struggle as an obstacle to the realization of good society because it perpetuated selfishness. The spread of these ideas would almost certainly create some resistance during the May Fourth period to the Marxist message; after 1921, these same ideas would provide ammunition for anti-Communist arguments.

Ironically, the spread of these ideas was aided by the October Revolution, which appeared initially as the victory of labor and principles of "laborism" over parasitic classes in Russia. Partially an anarchist misinterpretation, this idea was also implicit in the mixed messages that emanated from Russia. Anarchists were not the only ones to misinterpret the Revolution, moreover; the same attitudes pervaded the response to the October Revolution of later Marxists, chief among them Li Dazhao.

Most significant historically is that anarchists brought laborers to the attention of intellectuals who were blissfully oblivious to distinctions between elitist liberal and anarchist-socialist ideals of individual cultural liberation. The impact extended beyond intellectuals; anarchists were the first to engage in labor organization and education. While most anarchists adopted a disdainful attitude toward laborers for their ignorance and backwardness, they believed that the goals of the New Culture Movement must be extended beyond intellectuals. The physical and spiritual plight of the Chinese laborer (urban or rural) became through their advocacy, an important concern. Finally, anarchists raised the troubling question of intellectuals' relationship to society; if Chinese intellectuals had hitherto been concerned mainly with their relationship to politics or to culture, what concerned them most in the aftermath of the May Fourth Movement was their relationship to other groups in society. Even though anarchist ideas blended easily with New Culture goals in 1918–1919, they also introduced a discordant note, an implicit challenge to liberal individualism and elitist intellectualism. These ideas did obstruct acceptance of Marxist ideas, in other words, but they were also crucial to the spread of socialist ideas in Chinese thought in 1919, which provided the context for the implantation of Marxism.

To appreciate the significance of anarchism in New Culture thinking, it is necessary to think of anarchism not simply in ideological terms but, even more importantly, in cultural terms; that is, as an ensemble of ideas, sentiments, and practices that constituted a culture of radicalism. That anarchist ideas of "mutual aid" and "laborism" were widely diffused in Chinese radical thinking in 1919 does not imply, therefore, that Chinese radicals wholesale became proponents of a coherent and articulate ideology of anarchism, or even thought of themselves explicitly as anarchists. Rather, these ideas were most important in serving to inspire social practices in which radicals, especially young radicals, expressed their yearnings for a new life. In these social practices was inscribed an ideological text which reveals most cogently the impact of anarchism on Chinese radical culture. And in this form, as an essential ingredient of May Fourth radical culture, anarchism made a lasting impression on the evolving culture of radicalism, which embodied the diverse, even contradictory, aspirations that went into the making of the Chinese revolution as it unfolded historically.

Anarchist ideas of "mutual aid" and "laborism" must be comprehended within the context of the anarchist vision of good society. Conviction that a good society could be built only on free association had led anarchists all along to look to a social reorganization emanating from relations between individuals. The immediate group, "small group," provided the most viable space for individual participation as well as the cultivation of habits of sociability. Accordingly, anarchists conceived of a good society as a federation of small groups, associated democratically on the basis of voluntary choice, rather than a hierarchical organization based on coercion. Within this context, "mutual aid" and "laborism" appeared not as utopian values but as basic values functional to social cohesion.

A communal movement among Chinese youth around the idea of labor-learning had by late 1919 assumed the proportions of a "new tide" in the guise of the New Life Movement. Communal experiments went by different names. The most famous was the Labor-learning Mutual Aid Corps (*Gongdu huzhu tuan*), established in Beijing at the end of 1919, sponsored by Wang Guangqi, the preeminent leader of the Young China Association, who himself had participated in the work-study program in France and went through an anarchist phase at this time. Almost equally famous was the Labor-learning Association (*Gongxuehui*), established on May 3, 1919, by students at Beijing Higher Normal College. The following day, a member of this group, Kuang Husheng (a Hunanese anarchist) led the attack on the home of the pro-Japanese minister Cao Rulin that turned the student demonstration on May 4, 1919 into a confrontation with the government. Also part of the New Life Movement was the "New Village" Movement in which the writer Zhou Zuoren played a leading part. These experiments in turn inspired similar experiments in 1919–1920 in other major urban centers, including Tianjin, Shanghai, Wuhan, Nanjing, and Guangzhou.

These labor-learning groups were not identical, but they shared certain characteristics that point to their anarchist inspiration. Mutual aid and labor were essential to their functioning. They were expected to finance their members' educational activities through income from group enterprises or individual labor. In either case, the pooled income provided the economic basis for a "communal" (*gongtong*) life. The division of labor was to enhance interdependence among the members. The guiding principle in most cases was "from each according to his ability, to each according to his need."[47]

The "New Village" Movement had some notable peculiarities. The major goal of "new villages" as conceived by Zhou Zuoren was not study but the promotion of labor (except for those members with special talents!). Most interesting, however, was the underlying agrarian impulse (even though the "new villages" were not necessarily agrarian). New Villages were conceived as communes that would carry the anarchist message into the countryside. (The New Village Movement was inspired by a similar movement in Japan, in particular the movement initiated by Mushakoji Saneatsu, which itself had taken its inspiration from Tolstoy and Kropotkin.[48]) Nevertheless, before the May Fourth period, both the socialists of Jiang Kanghu and the anarchists of Shifu had experimented with "new villages" of their own; the Shifu group had for a while even resided in the countryside in a rural communal experiment.[49] During the May Fourth period, the "New Village" Movement was not as influential as other such experiments, except in Beijing, where in a number of schools students organized their own "new villages" and engaged in agricultural cultivation to meet their subsistence needs.[50] More often than not, however, "new village" served merely as another metaphor for communal existence.

All these experiments were quick failures. The Beijing Labor-learning Mutual Aid Corps lasted only about four months before foundering on economis difficulties. This was the common fate of all May Fourth communal experiments. In a situation that made economic enterprise and employment difficult, the groups rapidly fell victim to financial difficulties. Some were to conclude from these experiences that labor-learning groups did not offer a solution to problems that went deep into the economic structure of the society. The consequences of failure were to be radical in turning intellectuals to social activities that reached beyond educated youth.

As long as they lasted, however, the labor-learning groups seemed to offer a glimpse of the good society. Though the movement was restricted to intellectual youth, its proponents included many prominent progressives who saw in it the potential reorganization of Chinese society on the basis of the "small group" (*xiao zuzhi*). Wang Guangqi, who led the Young China Association's close attention to "small groups," enthusiastically sponsored the Labor-learning Mutual Aid Corps in Beijing. His ecstasy was shared by some of China's most prominent intellectuals at the time.

> Labor-learning mutual aid groups are the embryo of a new society, the first step to the fulfillment of our ideals. . . . If the labor-learning mutual aid groups succeed, the ideal of "from each according to his ability, to each according to his need" will be gradually realized. The present labor-learning mutual aid movement may well be described as a peaceful economic revolution.[51]

No one, however, equaled in ecstasy a contributor to *Labor-learning* (*Gongxue*), the magazine of the Labor-learning Association in Beijing, who saw in labor and learning the two tracks of "the railroad to Heaven!"[52]

Enthusiasm was not restricted to those directly involved. As I shall discuss in Part 3, even after the first Marxist groups were founded in the spring of 1920, Li Dazhao and Chen Duxiu expressed hope in these revolutionary possibilities. In late 1919, the socialist press reported widely and enthusiastically on these experiments. One author wrote, in *Reconstruction,* "The principle of labor-learning marks a new stage in the evolution of human life, it is a beautiful product nurtured by the new thought tide of the twentieth century, and the foundation for a new society of the future."[53] Shen Xuanlu, himself a landlord with Tolstoyan pretensions, went so far as to assert in the *Weekend Review* that labor-learning groups fulfilled Marx's premise that cultural change must be dependent on social change; he believed that this premise was shared by anarchists and social democrats as well. He believed that labor-learning experiments would succeed as long as they received public support, and called upon intellectuals to provide it.[54] For Shen, and many others in late 1919 and early 1920, even Marx appeared at the service of ideals defined by anarchism!

Many socialists already believed that small groups, based on free association, offered the best means toward a new future. Wang's promise of a bloodless revolution explains their enthusiasm. Though the experiments were restricted to educated youth, some socialists were quick to see their implications for other groups; a contributor to *Light of Learning* called these groups "vanguards in the organization of labor that would realize the liberation and reform of laborers."[55]

Why anyone invested so much in these idealistic experiments is a moot point. In the heady atmosphere of May Fourth China, where every new movement pointed to a "new era," almost anything seemed possible, at least as long as it lasted. For Chinese youth the experiments expressed real physical and emotional needs, havens from the homes they were alienated from, as Wang Guangqi was quick to perceive. For their older supporters, the experiments offered a means not only to reform youth but to rebuild from the bottom up a disintegrating society. Chinese socialists possibly understood much better than others the consequences of the failure of peaceful methods. Indeed, the visible failure of the labor-learning movement by late spring 1920 was crucially significant in forcing some of them to reconsider the premises that had guided efforts toward social change during the May Fourth period. Ironically, the labor-learning associations would provide the basis for the creation of a new kind of organization that stood in direct contradiction to their premises of free and voluntary association.

The labor-learning movement represented a turning point in the fortunes of both anarchism and Marxism in China. It represented the apogee of the belief among youthful radicals, and their older supporters, in the possibility of converting anarchist aspirations into reality. Within its context, anarchist ideals of "mutual aid" and "laborism" appeared not as utopian aspirations but highly functional values of social cohesion of immediate relevance to building a new society. Failure caused some to despair of the anarchist dream that a good society could be willed into existence. As will foundered before social necessity, Marxism's implicit message of social conflict gained for them a new meaning. The movement radicalized Chinese youth into action; its failure was to change the direction of Chinese radicalism. But the ideal of labor-learning was firmly implanted in the emerging culture of radicalism as one of its most radical social aspirations.

In June 1919, Chen Duxiu wrote in the *Weekly Critic* that, recently, government authorities accused everyone who was politically suspect of being an anarchist, despite the fact that there were very few anarchists in China.[56] He was probably right about the numbers; there were indeed few committed anarchists, even if there were more of them than other socialists. He was wrong in his implication that anarchism was, therefore, a negligible element in Chinese radicalism. In 1919, anarchist ideas were everywhere in Chinese radicalism. More significantly, the anarchist vision had come to dominate radical culture. But already by June 1919, a new challenger to anarchism had appeared on the Chinese radical scene. The Marxist message of conflict seemed to point to a dismal future compared to the anarchist message of mutual aid and cooperation, but its explanation of social problems was compelling in its coherence. Chinese socialism in 1919 was to be shaped by efforts to reconcile the means offered by one with the vision of the other.

6

The Language of Class:
Marxism in May Fourth Socialism

Were there Marxists in China in 1919? In a vague sense, there were. There were those who were sufficiently drawn to Marxism to translate Marxist works into Chinese and even, toward the end of the year, to apply Marxist ideas to the analysis of Chinese society. Some of them were motivated by intellectual curiosity; others, it would turn out, had more than a passing interest. They found Marxism intellectually significant and sought seriously to propagate it among Chinese intellectuals. During the year following May 1919, this interest found its way into the thinking of most socialists.

Attraction to Marxist explanations, however, did not imply a simultaneous attraction to Marxist political solutions—to Communism. Chinese intellectuals did not agree, of course, on what political solutions were best in keeping with the spirit of Marxism, which in 1919 they only dimly perceived. Aware by this time of a definite connection between Marxism and the Russian Revolution, they were wary of Marxism to the extent that it was associated with the Revolution. Many of those who were interested in Marxism in 1919, and did the most to propagate it, refused to join the Communist movement as it emerged in 1920. Some of them turned against Marxism when faced with the prospect of Communism in China, others used Marxism to argue against Communism. Marxism and Communism were distinguished in the socialism of May Fourth intellectuals.

In this particular sense, Marxism shared a basic feature with anarchism: a wide diffusion of its vocabulary in the thinking of radical intellectuals who otherwise had no systematic commitment to its solutions. Marx's name and Marxist concepts appeared with increasing frequency in radical writing, Marxist ideas became issues of debate, and there was a growing feeling that the ideological tradition originated by Marx offered the best way to understand the problems of Chinese society. "Class" and "class conflict" were on the lips of many—as common, or almost as common, as "mutual aid" and "laborism," though without the positive connotations of the latter.

Yet there was also a fundamental difference in the receptions given to these two ideologies. Unlike with anarchism, there was no organized group or publication before 1920 devoted to the systematic propagation of Marxist ideology; Marxism, thus, was even more diffuse than anarchism. This was a factor, probably more than the novelty of Marxism or difficulty of access to Marxist sources, in the haphazard quality of Marxism's propagation. Anarchism in 1919 enjoyed a systematic accumulation of literature, the product of more than a decade of sustained activity. The available Marxist literature in 1919 seems ridiculously shallow in comparison. Marxism, too, had been discussed in China earlier, namely in the Revolutionary Alliance debates with Liang Qichao in 1905–1907. But the Revolutionary Alliance had taken up Marxism only to declare it largely irrelevant to China; Marx had taken the back seat to Henry George. Marx's name had come up again in the debate between Shifu and Jiang Kanghu in 1913–1914; but nobody had seriously defended Marx or Marxism.

In 1919, Marxism had to be discovered anew. Those who participated in the discovery presented what they found from their own diverse perspectives. Marxism, in other words, did not define the meaning of revolution for any political or social group. The pre-May Fourth legacy of Chinese socialism is crucial to understanding the guise in which Marxism appeared in 1919. If any single organized group in China at this time engaged in the propagation of Marxist ideas, it was the Guomindang socialists, the very same people who had first discussed Marxism fifteen years earlier as Revolutionary Alliance socialists. Their presentation of Marxism was stamped with Guomindang views of revolution.

Unlike with anarchism, in other words, there was not a single proponent of Marxism in 1919 who did not express some fundamental ambivalence toward it. Those who presented it favorably felt constrained to qualify it one way or another. Marxism pointed to the problem; it did not offer an acceptable solution. The solution, more often than not, came from anarchism, or anarchist-inspired qualifications of the most basic ideas of Marxism, including the idea of class. Li Dazhao, China's "first" Marxist, was no exception.

These attitudes were largely a product of the prevailing May Fourth social and political mentality. Marxism's essentially political thrust was not very appealing to the antipolitical New Culture generation; the Marxist idea of class in particular seemed subversive of the broad social unity they envisioned. Moreover, as an ideology of political action, Marxism, unlike anarchism, did not seem to offer the kind of radical activity this generation favored: social activity geared to achieving individual and collective cultural transformation. Indeed, the failure of apolitical or antipolitical social activity played a significant part in turning activists from anarchism to Marxism in the spring of 1920. The social utopianism of the early May Fourth period had to be crushed before the social movement in China once again turned to politics.

Finally, we must take into account the very real intellectual difficulties presented by the complex theoretical structure of Marxism. This is especially the case when Marxism is placed against anarchism, with its elegantly simple message. One radical from Zhejiang recalled years later that when faced with the choice, he had favored anarchism because he found Marxism difficult to

1. Chen Duxiu, founder of the Communist party and its first secretary.

2. Li Dazhao, China's "First Marxist."

3. Portraits of participants in the First Congress in 1921. *Top, left to right:* Dong Biwu, He Shuheng, Mao Zedong. *Bottom, left to right:* Li Da, Deng Enming, Wang Jinmei, Chen Tanqiu.

4. Zhang Guotao in later years.

5. Cai Hesen, who may have converted Mao Zedong to Marxism.

6. Deng Zhongxia, leader in the Common Peoples Education Lecturing Corps, founder of the Morning Garden commune, and later a prominent labor leader.

8. Goumindang Marxist Dai Jitao.

7. Zhou Enlai, about the time of his departure for France.

9. Zhou Fohai, participant in the First Congress in 1921 and later Goumindang theoretician.

10. Members of the New Citizens Society in France. On the extreme right is the prominent revolutionary leader, Xiang Jingyu.

11. The Awakening Society in Tianjin.

12. The first issue of *The Communist* (November, 1920) and the vol. 8, no. 1 issue (September, 1920) of *New Youth,* when it became a communist organ.

understand.[1] In introducing his essay "My Views on Marxism," Li Dazhao cited a German scholar's comment that anyone who claimed to have understood Marx before he or she was fifty deceived people. Similar sentiments have been expressed by others among China's earliest Communists, who recall that they had difficulty understanding Marxist concepts such as the "dialectic" even after they became Communists.

Marxism is very simple; it is also very difficult. As a holistic philosophy, it incorporates diverse ideas that stand in uneasy, if not contradictory, relationships to one another as well as to the whole. As an ideology of action Marxism may seem quite simple and straightforward, at least once a commitment has been made to its basic premises. The justification for action, however, rests on a complex theoretical structure that is open to more than one interpretation. In its conversion into an ideology of action, which is the ultimate goal of Marxism, the theory must inevitably be interpreted and instrumentalized, since otherwise the multiple possibilities for action implicit in the theory must undercut its aspirations to political practice. Political movements which claim Marxist inspiration have always simplified the theory to legitimize their particular political strategy, and the common understanding of Marxism rests on these various reductionist interpretations. Marxism is easily comprehended when reduced to one or another of its various aspects, while it takes considerable effort to understand these aspects in their integration into a whole.

Chinese intellectuals faced this problem in their first serious encounter with Marxism in 1919. They apprehended Marxism as an ideology of action before they had a firm grasp of its theoretical basis. In 1919 different political movements around the world claimed Marx as their source. The problem that attracted greatest attention was not how a common ideology had given rise to such diverse political forms, but rather to sort out the differences among them and determine which, if any, might be of relevance to China. They perceived Marxism, in other words, in its various reductionist manifestations.

Ignorance, in this case, may have been bliss. Gail Bernstein has observed that the Japanese Marxists at this time, from whom Chinese learned their Marxism originally, were so preoccupied with its philosophical underpinnings that they paid little attention to questions of political practice.[2] In the Chinese case the opposite was true; and theory was instrumentalized in the cause of practice. This instrumentalization, clearly evident earlier in Lenin's interpretation, had even more dramatic effects in China. As one Chinese historian has observed recently, Chinese Marxism did not benefit in its origins from an original thinker, similar to Lenin or Trotsky, who integrated theory into practice. Russian Marxists had gone through a prolonged process of theoretical consideration of Marxism before they came around to devising a revolutionary strategy of their own: Lenin himself had written *The Development of Capitalism in Russia* to demonstrate the relevance of Marxist theory there. Marxism in China was converted into a political movement too rapidly to allow time to find out about the theory, let alone apply it to the analysis of

Chinese society. While this may have delivered Chinese Marxists from a "dogmatic" preoccupation with philosophical questions, as Bernstein suggests, it also left them at the mercy of theoretical problems they only dimly perceived. In some ways, one could say that they walked backwards into Marxism; and decisions concerning revolution were made for them by others, who claimed political superiority because they commanded theoretical superiority. More of this in Part 3. Suffice it to say here that while the Marxist social revolutionary idea, and Marxist concepts of social analysis, emerged quickly in 1919 as fundamental components of the language of radicalism in China, it is wrong to deduce from that that there existed at this time an ideological commitment to or theoretical grasp of Marxism that pointed the way to a strategy of revolution that Chinese radicals could call their own.

These comments are best illustrated through a comprehensive review of Chinese writings on Marxism in the May Fourth period, which has not previously been undertaken (see Table 1). This review reveals the very serious questions of meaning that pervaded the Chinese encounter with Marxism in 1919, and their implications for the Communist movement that emerged in 1920.

A number of observations may be made on the basis of this table. In the first place, interest in Marxism predated the May Fourth Movement. The first publications on Marxism did not appear until April 1919, but given the time that would have had to elapse between the preparation of manuscripts and their appearance in print, we may observe safely that some Chinese intellectuals were already engaged in the study and translation of Marxist works by early 1919, if not earlier.

Secondly, while the list of writings in the table is fairly long, much of it consists of reprints of the same works. Until Liebknecht's biography of Marx appeared in the *Weekend Review* in January 1920, Yuan Quan's brief biography of Marx, reprinted numerous times, represented the extent of Chinese knowledge of Marx, the man. Kawakami Hajime's "Marx's Materialist Conception of History" was the major source on Marxist theory. And Kautsky's *Oekonomische Lehren,* in its two different translations, provided a major source for Marxist economics.

Thirdly, the same names appear repeatedly—both publications, and writers and translators. The most prominent publications are the Research Clique papers *Light of Learning* and *Morning News,* and the Guomindang publications *Awakening, Construction,* and *Weekend Review.* Li Dazhao was involved in the editorial work of *Morning News,* and may have exerted some influence there; otherwise, publications associated directly with later Communists played only a small part in the propagation of Marxism. The only significant exception was *New Youth* with its special issue (whose problems I have noted in Chapter 3), which included mostly material already published elsewhere, some of it more than once.

Significantly, while only a few publications were involved, they com-

Table 1. Biographies of Marx, translations from Marx's works, and other publications directly related to Marxist theory in the early May Fourth period (early 1919–May 1920)[a]

Title	Author (translator)	Publication
"Socialism and China"	(Ke) Yiceng	*Light of Learning* (April 1–2, 1919)
"Marx's Life of Struggle"	Yuan Quan	*Morning News* (April 1–4, 1919)
"The Life of Struggle of Marx, the Founder of Modern Socialism"	Yuan Quan	*Citizens' Daily* (*Guomin gongbao*, (Sichuan) (April 1919)
The Communist Manifesto (paraphrased selections)	Karl Marx (She)	*Weekly Critic* 16 (April 6, 1919)
"Anarcho-Communism and State Socialism"	Ruoyu (Wang Guangqi)	*Weekly Critic* 18 (April 20, 1919)
"Marx's Materialist Conception of History"	Kawakami Hajime (Yuan Quan)	*Morning News* (May 5–8, 1919)
"The Life of Struggle of Marx, the Founder of Modern Socialism"	Yuan Quan	*Light of Learning* (May 6–7, 1919)
Labor and Capital (*Wage Labor and Capital*)	Karl Marx (Shili)	*Morning News* (May 9–June 1, 1919)
"The Theory of Marx, the Luminary of the Socialist Party"	Liu Nangai	*Light of Learning* (May 12–14, 1919)
"Marx's Materialist Conception of History"	Kawakami Hajime (Yuan Quan)	*Light of Learning* (May 19–21, 26–27, 1919)
Explanation of Capital (*The Economic Theories of Karl Marx*)	Karl Kautsky (Yuan Quan)	*Morning News* (June 2–November 11, 1919)
"What is Socialism"	Hou (Li Da)	*Awakening* (June 18, 1919)
"The Goal of Socialism"	Hou (Li Da)	*Awakening* (June 19, 1919)
"Two Schools of Socialism"	Liu Nangai	*Light of Learning* (June 23–24, 28, 1919)

Table 1 (Continued)

Title	Author (translator)	Publication
"Social Reform and Socialism"	Liu Nangai	*Light of Learning* (July 7–8, 1919)
"Marx's Materialist Conception of History"	Kawakami Hajime (Yuan Quan)	*Awakening* (July 21–31, 1919)
"An Outline of Marx's Materialist Conception of History"	No author (from Japanese)	*Awakening* (July 21–31, 1919)
"A Critique of Marx's Materialist Conception of History"	No author (from Japanese)	*Morning News* (July 25–August 5, 1919)
Labor and Capital (see above)	Karl Marx (Kawakami Hajime) (Shili)	*Light of Learning* (July 25–August 4, 1919)
"A Critique of Marx's Materialist Conception of History" (from *Morning News*. Original title in Japanese: "A Criticism of Socialism.")	No author	*Awakening* (August 1–9, 1919)
"The Political Program of the German Social Democratic Party" (Erfurt Program)	tr. Dai Jitao	*Weekend Review* 10 (August 10, 1919)
"The Theoretical System of Marxist Socialism"	Kawakami Hajime (Luo Zhuozhang)	*Light of Learning* (August 5–December 24, 1919. Scattered, translator changes)
"The Condition of Various Socialist Parties and a General Discussion of Socialism"	Ensor (Jingren)	*Morning News* (August 13–17, 1919)
"Marx" (in "Western Advocates of the Social Movement")	No author (from Japanese)	*Morning News* (August 21–23, 1919)
"Social Problems" (included the ten-point program of the *Communist Manifesto*)	Zhang Wentian	*Daily of the Nanjing Student Federation (Nanjing xuesheng lianhehui)* (August 1919)

100

Title	Author	Source
"My Views on Marxism"	Li Dazhao	New Youth, 6, 5–6 (dated May 1919, but published September. 6, 5 special issue ed. Li Dazhao)
"Marx's Theory"	Gu Zhaoxiong (Mengyu)	New Youth, 6, 5
"A Critique of Marx's Theory"	(Huang) Lingshuang	Ibid.
"Marx's Materialist Conception of History and the Question of Moral Purity" (originally published as "The Monetary Value of Women's Moral Purity" in New China, Xin Zhongguo)b	Chen Qixiu	Ibid.
"Marx's Materialist Conception of History"	Yuan Quan	Ibid.
"Marx's Life of Struggle"	Yuan Quan	Ibid.
"Marx's Biography"	Liu Binglin (Nangai)	Ibid.
"Examining the Origins of Disorder in China from an Economic Perspective"	Dai Jitao	Construction 1, 2 (September 1919)
"A Materialist Examination of the History of Chinese Philosophy"	Hu Hanmin	Construction 1, 3–4 (October–November 1919)
"Explanation of the Materialist Conception of History"	Lin Yungai	Weekend Review (special October 10 issue)
"The Communist Manifesto of Marx and Engels" (selections)	Li Zezhang	The Citizen 2, 1 (November 1919)
"The Nature of Commodity Production"	from Karl Kautsky (Dai Jitao)	Awakening (November 2–7, 1919)
Explanation of Marx's Capital (The Economic Theories of Karl Marx)	Karl Kautsky (Dai Jitao)	Construction 1, 4–6, 2, 2–3 and 5 (November 1919–June 1920)
"Marxism; Scientific Socialism"	Yang Baoan	Guangdong New China (Guangdong xin Zhonghua bao) (November 1919)
"Why Must We Discuss Socialism?"	Zhang Dongsun	Reconstruction 1, 1

Table 1 (Continued)

Title	Author (translator)	Publication
"China's Class Struggle"	Zhou Fohai	*Ibid.*
"Material Change and Moral Change"	Li Dazhao	*Renaissance (Xinchao)* 2, 2 (December 1919)
"A Criticism of a Criticism of the Materialist Conception of History"	Hu Hanmin	*Construction* 1, 5 (December 1919)
"A Chronology of Marx"	Shaoyu	*Morning News* (December 1, 1919)
"Marx's Philosophy of History"	Li Dazhao	"Lectures in the History of Historical Thought," 1920
"An Economic Explanation of Changes in Modern Chinese Thought"	Li Dazhao	*New Youth* 7, 2 (January 1920)
"Ethics and the Materialist Conception of History"	Karl Kautsky (Boyang)	*Fujian Star* 1, 4–2, 6 (December 1919–January 1920)
"Classes and Moral Theory"	Hu Hanmin	*Construction* 1, 6 (January 1920)
"Classes and Evolution Theory"	Hu Hanmin	*Ibid.*
"Classes and Evolution Theory"	Hu Hanmin	
"Idle Words on Marx"	tr. Hengshi (from Japanese)	*Awakening* (January 5–6, 1920)
	tr. Hengshi	*Awakening* (January 1 and 3, 1920)
"Scientific Socialism"		*Awakening* (January 5–8, 1920)
"A Paragraph from Idle Words on Marx"	T.T.S. (Shi Contong?)ᶜ	*Weekend Review* (special New Year issue)
"Biography of Marx"	Wilhelm Liebknecht (Dia Jitao, selections)	*Weekend Review* (special New Year issue)

"An Explanation of the Materialist Conception of History"	Yoshino Sakuzo (tr. Chen Wangdao)	*Journal of Friends of the Zhejiang Provincial Normal School (Zhejiang shengli shifan xuexiao xiaoyouhui shirikan)*, 10 (January 10, 1920)
"An Outline of State Formation under Socialism"	Lin Yungai	*Construction* 2, 1 (February 1920)
"The Thought Tide of Modern Socialism"	Lin Yungai	*Construction* 2, 3 (April 1920)
"Two Currents in Social Renovation"	Li Shizeng	*Ibid.*
"Historical Development of the Economy"	Dai Jitao	*Awakening* (April 11, 1920)
"From AA to AD"	Zhu Qianzhi	*Struggle* (April 30, 1920)
"An Examination of Kinship from an Economic Perspective"	Hu Hanmin	*Construction* 2, 4 (May 1920)
"The Economic Basis of Morality"	A. Loria (Li Hanjun)	*Construction* 2, 4–5 (May–June 1920)

a Works related to Marxist theory here involve some ambiguity. I have tried to restrict the list to works that sought to come to terms with the ideas of Marx and Engels, though I have also included important works by later Marxists that served as sources for Marxist theory, such as the works of Kautsky (it might also be worth underlining here the absence of works by Lenin). Moreover, references to Marx were on the increase during this period in many different contexts. I have had to use some judgment in choosing from among these works; but throughout, I have preferred to err on the side of inclusiveness. The items included represent works that, in my opinion, had something of significance to say about Marx or Marxism. The table was compiled on the basis of the following works: *Wusi shiqi qikan jieshao* (Introduction to periodicals of the May Fourth period); *Makesi Engesi zhuzuo zai Zhongguodi chuanpo* (The propagation of Marx and Engels' works in China); *Yanjiu Makesi Engesi zhuzuo he shengping lunzhu mulu* (An index of writings relevant to research on Marx and Engels' writings and lives); *Makesi zhuyi zai Zhongguo* (Marxism in China); *Wusi yundong zai Shanghai* (The May Fourth Movement in Shanghai); *Li Dazhao xuanji* (Selections from the works of Li Dazhao); *Li Da wenji* (Collection of Li Da's Writings).

b See *Yanjiu Makesi Engesi zhuzuo he shengping lunzhu mulu*, p. 71.

c T.T.S. was possibly Shi Contong. His name in the Wade-Giles transliteration (Shih Ts'un-t'ung) would have yielded these initials, though it is difficult to be certain that he would have chosen these initials. Others at the time sometimes used initials for pseudonyms, such as T.S. for Chen Duxiu. Shi Contong, a radical from Zhejiang, was at this time involved with *Weekend Review*. Prof. Lu Zhe has suggested that he could also read Japanese before he went to Japan in the summer of 1920.

manded wide respect and circulation—especially *Morning News, Light of Learning,* and *Awakening,* all newspaper supplements. That newspapers, rather than specialized periodicals, published this kind of material tells us much about the general interest in these questions and the intellectual scene. These papers, of course, were not devoted to the propagation of Marxism per se; if anything, they published more on other socialisms, especially anarchism. It is not clear, in light of their association with political groups of long standing, what their publication of Marxist-related materials meant to their readership; what is clear (as Chinese historians have pointed out) is that they did not always portray Marxism in a favorable light. Yet Marxist discussions reached a readership of impressive breadth through them.

With the exception of Li Dazhao, future Communists are not particularly prominent among these authors. There is some difficulty in determining the ideological orientation of the first translators of Marxist works. A case in point is Yuan Quan, who was responsible for translating the first significant works: Marx's biography and Kawakami's "Marx's Materialist Conception of History." We cannot conclude, on the basis of his translation work, that he was a Marxist. In the May Day 1919 issue of *Morning News* he stated that laborers must be made into the heart of Chinese society; but laborers to him included both physical and mental laborers. If he was a Marxist, his Marxism, this statement implies, was infused with the prevailing anarchist-inspired ideas of labor.* On the basis of authors whose names are familiar, it is evident that the most important part was played by Guomindang radicals. Given the preponderance of Japanese works, it is also safe to say that Japan-returned students also played an important part.

Of future Communists, the ones whose names appear on the list are (in addition to Li Dazhao) Li Da, Chen Wangdao (later translator of the first complete edition of the *Communist Manifesto*), and Zhang Wentian. Of these, the only one to make a significant contribution in this discussion was

---

* Since this study was written, it has come to my attention that in a new work published internally (*neibu*), Yuan Quan is given as the pseudonym for Li Dazhao. See Chen Yutang, ed., *Zhonggong dangshi renwu bieminglu* [Pseudonyms of Chinese Communists] (Beijing: Hongqi chubanshe, 1985), p. 57 (In the absence of confirming evidence, I have hesitated to incorporate this information in the main body of the discussion, but some comments are necessary here.) This would suggest that Li's contribution to the propagation of Marxism was more extensive than I thought, but only in such a way as to confirm the argument presented in Chapter 3 and the present chapter. He was at work on the study of Marx and Marxism from early 1919, and making available his findings as an editor of *Morning News*. The brief biographies of Marx are most impressive for their emphasis on the moral integrity of Marx the individual, paralleling Li's moralistic interpretation of the October Revolution. These, as well as the translation from Kautsky, also emphasized Marx as an economist, and Marxism as an economism. Most important, however, this would make Li the translator of Kawakami's important article, "Marx's Materialist Conception of History," which is the first direct evidence of the link between Kawakami's Marxism and Li's thinking on Marxism. It is also noteworthy that, in light of this evidence, Li was responsible for half of the articles in the special issue of *New Youth* on Marxism. I am indebted to Prof. Lu Zhe for this information, and to Dianne Scherer for the citation.

Li Dazhao. Otherwise, the major contributors were Guomindang socialists such as Dai Jitao, Hu Hanmin, and Lin Yungai (an associate of Hu's), and the Research Clique-related Liu Nangai.

Fourthly, the table indicates that only a few original sources were available. *Wage Labor and Capital* and parts of the *Communist Manifesto* were the only works of Marx and Engels. Besides these, Chinese had access only to the brief translations of passages from the *Poverty of Philosophy* and the "preface" to *A Contribution to the Critique of Political Economy* which were included in secondary discussions, such as Li Dazhao's "My Views on Marxism." The most systematic work of European Marxism available was Kautsky's *Oekonomische Lehren,* an elucidation of the first volume of *Capital.*

Fifthly, all of these works, as well as their understanding of Marxism, Chinese intellectuals owed to Kawakami Hajime. He provided the translations, as well as their elucidation; it may not be an exaggeration that Chinese thinking on Marxism in the immediate May Fourth period was shaped by Kawakami. His emphases became theirs, his doubts appeared as theirs. Some other Japanese authors were translated; Kawakami was the furthest left. The others for the most part were even more severely critical of Marxism. Kawakami's critics from the left did not find their way into Chinese before 1920.

Finally, it is quite evident that by far the greatest emphasis was on economics. While these writings also discussed class struggle and Marx's theory of history, their contents seem to reveal that Marxism made the greatest impression as an economic interpretation. This is ironic, for it was about Marx's alleged economism that intellectuals of this period (and their Japanese mentors) expressed the most serious reservations. This irony provides us with a clue to the reasons for the Chinese interest in and attraction to Marxism.

Most writings on socialism in the May Fourth period portrayed Marx as the founder (literally, "first ancestor") of scientific socialism, whose time, nevertheless, was past. Marx the man was depicted in glowing terms, as an example for Chinese revolutionaries. Yuan Quan, whose brief biography of Marx was widely circulated at the time, described his goal as "to provoke interest in the study of socialism"; but the "life of struggle" he described was an entirely personal one. His main emphasis was on the existential adversities Marx had to overcome in order to write his crowning achievement, *Capital.* Yuan described in some detail Marx's poverty, quoting from Liebknecht's description of the Marx family's sufferings at the sickness of their young son, Marx's own subsequent illness and, in the midst of all this, his determination in writing *Capital.* The biography described *Capital* as having "opened a new era of scholarship." But the basic point of the rather melodramatic account was moral: Marx's tenacity.[3]

The subject of "Idle Words on Marx," published a few months later, was similarly his personal integrity as a journalist! The brief selection in *Weekend Review* described his resistance to Bismarck's temptations when other socialists had given in. The comment by the translator, T.T.S., pointedly compared Chinese radicals to Marx, unfavorably, and held him out as an example for Chinese journalists.[4]

More important were the biographies by Liu Nangai, published in *New Youth,* and Liebknecht, published in *Weekend Review* in January 1920. Liu discussed Marx's activities in the International, and provided some information on his major writings, including the *Communist Manifesto, A Contribution to the Critique of Political Economy,* and *Capital.* Liebknecht's biography was the richest in these respects, especially as it was supplemented with informative notes by Dai Jitao, the translator. Liebknecht's description of the *Communist Manifesto* "as the basis of and the program for the modern labor movement" in this selection may have been responsible for prompting Dai and Chen Duxiu to seek a complete translation of this work into Chinese in the spring of 1920.

Most importantly, however, these two biographies, for the first time in the May Fourth period, placed Marx within the context of the European socialist movement. Liu Nangai described him as an advocate of "centralized authority" and associated him with social democracy. This was also the basic thrust of Liebknecht's biography, which discussed at some length Marx's struggles with Bakunin in the International, and placed Marx on the side of centralized authority against the anarchists. Unlike Liu, however, Liebknecht portrayed Marx as a revolutionary nevertheless. A note added by Dai also described contemporary social democracy as "revisionist" Marxism, and remarked somewhat cryptically that though the Bolshevik government described itself as "Communist," it was in fact "centralist" (*jichan zhuyi*), with the state at the center. The remark was presumably intended to correct the contemporary identification of Bolshevism with anarchism.[5]

Anarchists and socialists had debated the issue of Marx's centralism a few years earlier; it emerged as an important issue once again in the May Fourth period. Liebknecht's biography added an authoritative voice to the discussion of this important distinction between Marxism and anarchism. Anarchists had insisted on this distinction all along. Li Da's June 1919 essay "What is Socialism?" (though it did not refer to Marx by name) clearly drew the same distinction. This was also the point of Dai Jitao's translation of the 1891 Erfurt Program of the German Social Democratic Party, which was published in August in *Weekend Review.* Dai's note observed that the program was in keeping with Marx's ideas, since Engels had guided its writing.[6] Liebknecht's biography confirmed the distinction by tracing it back to struggles within the International, which was new in the May Fourth period (it had come up in 1913–1914 in the debates between Shifu and Jiang Kanghu). Liebknecht, however, also represented Marx as a revolutionary, against the identification of centralism with reformist social democracy.

Where Marx's contribution to socialism was concerned, he appeared in these writings primarily as an economist who had initiated a new era in economic science, and provided a scientific basis for socialism. As early as November 1918, Li Dazhao (in his "Victory of Bolshevism") had stated that the Bolsheviks upheld "the ideas of the German socialist economist Marx."[7]

Yuan Quan's biography, with its emphasis on *Capital,* lent support to this view. Another biography, by Liu Nangai in *New Youth,* quoted Friedrich Lange to describe Marx as "an economist without peer." "According to the French economist Gide's evaluation of Marx," Liu wrote, "even though Marx as the founder and the leader of the Workers' International had engaged in severe criticism of European governments, he was in actuality not a revolutionary like Bakunin. From the perspective of his writings, he was a thorough scholar; his later fame . . . rests on *Capital* which . . . opened a new era in modern economics." Liu went on to observe (citing Richard Ely): "it is no wonder that *Capital* is the holy book of social democracy."[8] This evaluation was accepted even by those who saw a close connection between Marxism and the Russian Revolution. In the *Weekend Review* in late June 1919, Dai Jitao noted the connection between Marx and the Bolshevik revolution and went on to discuss Bolshevism, with the remark that the study of Marx was best left to economists.[9]

This view of Marx was extended to a view of Marxism as an economistic theory of history and society. Chinese intellectuals were well aware, of course, that it was possible to interpret Marxism differently, as a social theory with class conflict at its core. The *Communist Manifesto* would not be translated in whole until 1920, but enough of it was available already to give a clear idea of the importance of class struggle in Marx's thinking. The author of one translation stated: "We hope that the first step in the revolution of labor [*laogong geming*] is to elevate the proletariat, place them in power, and secure victory in the war for democracy. These proletarian common people [*wuchan jiejidi pingmin*] will achieve political power, overthrow all classes, confiscate the capital of the middle class [*zhongchan jieji*], will return all production organs to the hands of the government, and organize a new organ of rule."[10] The terminology may be confusing, but it leaves no doubt about the importance of class struggle. This was recognized at the theoretical level as well. Li Dazhao, who was among the few people at this time who had possibly come to accept the inevitability of class struggle in China, followed Kawakami Hajime in describing class struggle as "the golden thread" that tied together the three aspects of Marxism: economic analysis, the materialist conception of history, and socialism.

In the current literature, however, "the golden thread" would have been more identified with Marx's economic analysis. The only complete text of Marx available at this time, *Wage Labor and Capital,* was basically economic. Originally a product of Marx's political activities—of lectures he had given to the German Workers' Association in Brussels—this work dealt mainly with economic issues pertinent to the determination of wages, the division of labor, and the accumulation of capital. It was criticized within the International for not having discussed "the economic relationships which constitute the material foundation of the present class struggle and national struggles."[11] Within the Chinese context, the text would have appeared all the more as an economic treatise. This was also true of the other major European Marxist text available—and enjoying obvious popularity at this time—Kautsky' *Oeko-*

nomische Lehren, which, in Kolakowski's words, served for the first few decades after its publication as "a handbook of Marxist economic theory for beginners."[12]

While what was available of the *Communist Manifesto* raised the question of class, there is no reason for us to assume, therefore, that it militated against an economistic reading of Marx. The most prominent selection from the *Manifesto* available was Marx's ten-point program for a socialist society, which in many ways stands in contrast to the emphasis on class struggle in the rest of the text. This program, essentially social democratic and reformist, outlines the economic changes the state must undertake to bring about socialism. This section had always enjoyed popularity in China; it was first translated in the early 1900s, and appeared repeatedly during the May Fourth period in discussions of Marx and Marxism.

The point here is not that Chinese readers misunderstood Marx because they were most struck by his economic analysis. His economic analysis is obviously of fundamental significance. The point rather is that a one-sided emphasis, divorced from the analysis of classes, could create a misunderstanding of Marxism as an evolutionist economic determinism.

This is indeed the way Marxism appeared in the discussion of the May Fourth period, as well as in the initial efforts by Hu Hanmin, Dai Jitao, and Li Dazhao to apply Marxist theory to Chinese society. These were simply efforts to find economic explanations for various phenomena of modern and premodern Chinese history, with special emphasis on changes in ideology and in kinship relations. What they all shared was an economic deterministic appreciation, with no sense of a dialectic between economic change and changes in society, politics, or ideology.[13] There is considerable irony in the appreciation of Marxist theory that informed these analyses: Chinese authors seemed to be most fascinated by that aspect of Marxist theory of which they were the most critical: its materialistic economism.

This same tendency was evident in Li Dazhao's seminal essay, "My Views on Marxism," the only thorough discussion of Marxist theory penned by a Chinese author in the May Fourth period. An ambitious essay, in its nearly forty pages it discussed the "three components" Li considered essential to Marx's theory: the materialist conception of history, class struggle, and Marx's economics. Whatever its merits in interpretation, the essay displayed remarkable critical acumen on the part of its author who had only recently begun to grapple with Marxist theory.

Li structured the essay around Marx's place not in socialism, but in the development of economic thought. Of the nearly forty pages of the essay, about half were devoted to Marx's economic ideas, especially of surplus value and the concentration of capital. This provided the context for the materialist conception of history and class struggle. Li observed at one point that while many people recognized the importance in Marx's thinking of *Capital,* few realized the equal importance of the materialist conception of history, which, though not discussed in *Capital,* appeared on every page of that work as its premise. Yet Li did not evaluate Marx's economic ideas in light of the materialist conception of history: he did the reverse, and interpreted history and class struggle in highly economistic terms.[14]

To Li, the outstanding feature of Marx's materialist conception of history was not his historical appreciation of materialism but his materialistic appreciation of history. Li viewed Marx not as the creator of the materialist conception of history but rather as one in a series of historical materialists from Condorcet to Proudhon. They all, he observed, interpreted history in terms of economic structure and class conflict. What distinguished Marx was his emphasis on the "forces of production" as the determinant of all social relations and ideological structures. His selections from Marx (*The Poverty of Philosophy, The Communist Manifesto,* and the preface to *A Contribution to the Critique of Political Economy*) were chosen with this thesis in mind, or interpreted in accordance with it. While Li's discussion of classes, which he deemed essential to understanding the materialist conception of history, observed that "economic structure was shaped by class opposition," he viewed this not as an exclusive feature of Marx's materialism but rather an assumption of all materialistic conceptions of history.[15]

Li's economistic interpretation became even more evident in his criticisms. There were a number of those, some political, others theoretical. Politically, he believed that Marx's economic determinism had had a baneful influence on socialists who chose to await "the natural maturation of the collective system" rather than to act. Theoretically, he observed that the materialist conception of history ignored the ways the superstructure (especially laws and ethics) could affect the course of history. The superstructure may not be able to contradict economic tendencies, he conceded; however, it could not only speed up historical change, as recent labor struggles demonstrated, but even change the course of history, as the differential effect of laws on English and French history had proven. Li's most important criticism, though, was of the apparent contradictions in Marx's analysis of the economic basis of society. Marx in places found the motive force of history in production, in other places in class struggle; he would suggest that class struggle determined the evolution of society, but argued at other times that class struggle could have no effect on the historical development of the economy.

To Li, who had not read enough Marx to be personally cognizant of them, these contradictions obviously undermined the validity of the materialist conception of history. These criticisms, which Li with frankness credited to "others," pointed to fundamental problems of Marxist theory. What is interesting is that he chose not to reject the theory but to resolve the contradictions by choosing one interpretation over others. The view he opted for portrayed Marxism as an economic determinism with the forces of production as its dynamic motive force. He suggested, accordingly, that it was more proper to describe Marx's historical theory as "the economic view of history" than as the materialist conception of history. This did not lead him to give up on Marx. Marx's "exaggeration" of the role of the economy in history, he observed, had served a useful function in dramatizing the place of the economy in society, which had been ignored until Marx's time. In what may have been the first use of a

Marxist insight in historical analysis in China, Li proceeded to explain Marx's limitations in terms of the intellectual constraints of his material environment: the nineteenth century, a period of economic revolution, had brought the economy to the forefront of consciousness; other important factors in history such as religion and politics had been driven to the background. Marx's consciousness, in other words, had been shaped by the consciousness of his age. New ideas were needed, Li argued, to update Marx's theory. Yet his comments later in his discussion that Marx's economic theories had themselves been subjected to acute economic criticism, which called into question Marx's whole theory, may well have left his readers wondering why anybody should expend the effort to update it.[16]

Li almost certainly based most of his discussion on the work of Kawakami Hajime. The essay drew upon Kawakami's translations. Li's view that the materialist conception of history should properly be called an "economic view of history" was also possibly derivative of Kawakami, who himself had derived the idea from the American economist Seligman. In his "Marx's Materialist Conception of History" (which was circulated widely in Chinese publications, starting with *Morning News* in early May), Kawakami had pointed to the economic explanation of history as the most basic feature of Marxist theory. Gail Bernstein has observed that it was Marx's economic determinism that most impressed and, as in the case of Li, bothered Kawakami.[17] Kawakami stated that "among all the economic phenomena, the one Marx viewed as the most central were the social forces of production [*shehuidi shengchanli*]."[18] To the extent that Kawakami stressed economic causation, moreover, he identified Marxism with an evolutionary view of history. Kawakami's views of Marxism had been shaped largely by his readings of Engels and Kautsky. Kolakowski has said of Kautsky that "he opposed all attempts to enrich or supplement Marxist theory by elements from any other source, except Darwinism. . . . It was thanks to his interpretive work that the stereotype known as scientific socialism—the evolutionist, determinist, and scientific form of Marxism—became universally accepted in its main lines."[19] Probably through the agency of Japanese Marxism, Kautsky was one of the first European Marxists whose interpretation was familiar to the Chinese; his writings on the economy and ethics were the most complete works by a European Marxist available in the early May Fourth period, and his *Class Struggle* was published shortly thereafter, close in the footsteps of the *Communist Manifesto*. The Guomindang socialists Dai Jitao and Hu Hanmin were interested enough in Kautsky to introduce his works to China. Li Dazhao without question was familiar with Kautsky, since the first translation of the *Oekonomische Lehren* appeared in *Morning News,* with which he was closely involved (and if he was Yuan Quan, he was the translator). When in "My Views on Marxism" he described the materialist conception of history as being comparable to recent discoveries in biology, therefore, he was merely echoing Kawakami and, through him, Kautsky and Engels.

Chinese ambivalence at this time, therefore, reflected Kawakami's ambivalence. Kawakami (according to Bernstein) never felt at home with what he perceived to be Marx's determinism and materialism, and sought to supplement Marxism with what he believed to be universal ethical truths derived from non-Marxist sources. Marxism, therefore, provided only part of his larger world view, an eclectic blend of materialism and idealism. He believed "in the existence of two truths, a scientific truth and a moral truth," which needed to be reconciled. "He did not recognize the total intellectual commitment demanded of him as an adherent to Marxism. Unwilling to choose between an idealist and a materialist view of history, he accepted both, straddling two mutually exclusive philosophies." Marxism to Kawakami was scientific truth and, for that very reason, limited truth. To the extent that Kawakami associated Marxism with moral truth, furthermore, he felt uncomfortable with it since to him the moral truths of Marxism, limited as they were by class interests, perpetuated a social selfishness inconsistent with his idealistic ethical universalism.[20]

The writings of Kawakami which served as sources for Marxism in China were infused by this idealism. And it is more than likely that Chinese intellectuals were directly familiar with Kawakami's pre-Marxist writings, which were not only anti-Marxist but anti-socialist. In his *Critique of Socialism* (*Shakaishugi hyoron*), first published in 1905, Kawakami had not only questioned that economic motives determined human activity, but even challenged the socialist assumption that economic motives were products of selfish human desires (probably responding to anarchists, who were popular in Japan at the time). This work, which had created quite a stir in Japan, criticized contemporary Japanese socialists for failing to understand the need for moral as well as institutional reform. Motivated by religious yearnings, Kawakami had recognized in the book the importance of economic forces while reaffirming, "we cannot fully explain history by studying only economic relations, since human history has been influenced by spiritual forces." Particularly relevant here is this observation on the materialist conception of history:

> When we reach a better world, where science controls population, where men do not compete, where goods are available, and so on, then economic conditions will lose their importance. Until that time, we must place more weight on economic conditions than on any others. . . . The economic explanation is relative, not absolute. Its theory best suits the past; in the future it will gradually lose its importance. It does not explain all progress; it just emphasizes the fact that economic circumstances seem most related to the rise of nations and peoples.[21]

It would seem, however, that Li went even beyond his mentor Kawakami. Having described the importance of the economy in Marx's thinking, Kawakami went on to suggest that Marx had not denied the influence of noneconomic superstructural elements. Li's view of Marx's determinism was more uncompromising.[22] It is possible that Li was indebted to another influential essay published in *Morning News* about the same time that he was writing "My Views on Marxism" (was Li the translator of this as well?). This was "A Critique of Marx's Materialist Conception of History," published originally in the Japanese socialist journal *Reform* (*Kaizo*) as "A Criticism of Socialism." Chinese historians have described this essay as a "counterrevolutionary" interpretation that had a pernicious influence on May Fourth thinking. This author criticized the materialist conception of history for ignoring the role of human ideals and motivations. As did Li, he presented Marxism as a product of the nineteenth century, reflecting the tendency of its times "to bow before machines." The author viewed the social movement of the nineteenth century as a "materialist movement," that of the twentieth century as "an ethical movement." He also argued, citing Ramsay McDonald, that socialism was not a dogma; it was also not limited to Marx's materialism, but was infused with "idealism."[23]

While the Japanese influence on Li is evident, what it means is another matter. By 1919 there were Marxist critics in Japan who disagreed with Kawakami's interpretations, especially his juxtaposition of ethical considerations with the materialist conception of history.[24] Chinese intellectuals, who quite obviously listened closely to developments in Japanese Marxism, were almost certainly aware of these criticisms. Another essay, "An Explanation of the Materialistic Conception of History," published in *Weekend Review* in October, points conclusively to this awareness. In this essay Lin Yungai, a Guomindang writer closely associated with Hu Hanmin, offered the most sophisticated understanding of the materialist conception of history of all in the immediate May Fourth period.

Lin rejected outright that Marxism was an economic determinism, or even a determinism. Unlike Li, he disagreed with Seligman's suggestion that the materialist conception of history was best described as an economic explanation of history. He pointed out instead that according to Marx, the economy was not so much a determinant of history as a condition of human activity which was history's basic motive force. Drawing on Marx's introduction to *The Eighteenth Brumaire of Louis Bonaparte* and Engels' 1890 letter to Joseph Bloch, Lin argued that while people could not make history as they pleased, according to Marx, they nevertheless did make their own history. The economy was only the ultimate determining factor, not a substitute for all others. Most interestingly, Lin pointed to Marx's own activities as proof.

> Marx himself understood that the idealism of the individual was more powerful than material interest or all other conditions. It was his indomitable will that made Marx a great socialist [*shehuizhe!*]. This is proof enough that materialist theory does not claim that economic forces shape history. But in the evolution of humankind, most important are social forces. And where do these come from? From economic conditions.[25]

Not Lin's complex understanding, which suggested a grasp of the dialectic between human activity and social conditions, but Li's monistic appreciation won the day in May Fourth China. This is quite evident in the first applications of the materialist conception of history to the analysis of Chinese society by Dai Jitao, Hu Hanmin, and Li Dazhao in fall 1919 and spring 1920. I have already referred to the "economistic evolutionism" that pervaded these analyses. Suffice it to reiterate here that these works' theoretical assumptions displayed the strong influence of Seligman and Kautsky via, above all, Kawakami Hajime. While they addressed different questions, these works all sought to relate changes in Chinese thought and society to economic changes. Class, and class-based human activity, played no significant part.

The question here is not whether the economistic appreciation of Marxism was a misinterpretation, which is open to debate, but rather why Chinese intellectuals of this period opted for the interpretation of Marxism as an economic determinism that denied to Marx his recognition of the role consciousness played in history, or even the centrality he had assigned to the social relations of production (against the forces of production). Why did they fail to see, as in Lin Yungai's essay, that the "contradictions" in Marx need not be viewed as a clash between mutually exclusive "moments" in historical development, but could be regarded instead as the articulation of the dialectics of history? Why, in their ethical concern, did they not seek to uncover Marx's ethical elements instead of concluding that the materialist conception of history was deficient? Why, instead of utilizing Marxism's possibilities as a legitimation of political voluntarism, did they choose to view it as a determinism with negative implications for political action?

There are no ready-made answers, especially since the problems involved are perennial and have long occupied Marxists. Chinese radicals might well be forgiven for not raising questions of which they were only dimly aware, concerning a social theory with which they were newly acquainted—in the most haphazard fashion—and which was the product of a philosophical discourse about which they were still in the dark. Besides, evolutionism, which had left a deep impression on Chinese thinking since the turn of the century, still held sway over May Fourth thinking; economistic Marxism, with its social evolutionary implications, had a familiar ring which they could appreciate readily.

There were too many anomalies in their discussions, however, to be dismissed with such ease. One is the incongruence between prevailing images of Marx the man as a paradigmatic revolutionary, and the anti-revolutionary determinism ascribed to his thinking (an incongruence that only Lin Yungai addressed). Even more important was the ironic duality already noted: they seemed most fascinated by that aspect of Marxism of which they were critical—its economic determinism. If they found Marxism wanting as a theory of history and revolution on account of its materialism, in other words, it was the same materialism that seemed to attract them the most. This was quite evident in the initial efforts to apply Marxist theory to the analysis of Chinese society, which were most conspicuous for their economic evolutionism and vulgar materialism. This fundamental ambivalence raises questions concerning the meaning of Marxism to May Fourth intellectuals, as well as their initial perceptions of the relevance of Marxism to the problem of revolution.

We will discuss in the next chapter how Marxist concepts appeared in socialist political thinking in the immediate May Fourth period. Here we need to elucidate the sources of the contradictory attitudes embedded in New Culture thinking on revolution or, in some cases, political dispositions that predated the New Culture movement. The contradictory attitudes toward Marxism among May Fourth radicals appear puzzling if we assume that Marxism had an immediate transformative effect on their thinking. Yet (as noted earlier of Kawakami) Marxism appeared in their writings as part of larger world views that predated their discovery of it. To view them as Marxists is misleading, if by that we understand that Marxism shaped their revolutionary outlook, or that they consciously assumed, on account of their interest in Marxism, a Marxist ideological identity. Marxism provided them with certain explanations of the problems they confronted; it was found wanting as a solution. The explanations themselves were found to be limited, in that the solutions they pointed to appeared to be circumscribed by the philosophical premises of Marxist theory.

Li Dazhao's critique of classical economy in "My Views on Marxism" is worth quoting at some length, as it offers insights into what he found appealing in Marxism, and where he thought it needed amendment.

> There are two important features to individualistic economics. First, it affirms the contemporary economy. Second, it affirms the individual pursuit of self-interest [*liji*] within the context of this economic organization. Socialist economics opposes the first. Humanist economics [*rendaozhuyi jingjixue*] opposes the second. Humanist economists believe that no matter what improvements are made in the economic structure, if the human spirit [literally "human heart," *renxin*] is not changed but retains its present limitless avariciousness, social reform will offer no hope; therefore, they reject the economic pursuit of self-interest, and desire to replace self-seeking motivations by altruistic motivations. They not only stress change in economic structure but also stress change in the motivations of individuals active within that structure. Socialist economists believe that present-day economic and social ills are consequences of deficiencies in the present economic organization, and that if the economic organization is changed, all spiritual phenomena will change accordingly; therefore, they reject present-day economic organization, and advocate its total reform. Humanist economists uphold spiritual change [*renxin gaizaolun*], hence their goal is a moral revolution [*daodedi geming*]. Socialist economists uphold organizational change, hence their goal is a social revolution [*shehuidi geming*]. They are both opposed to individualist economics, but among humanists there are also socialists.
>
> The movement to change the world has already opened up a brilliant path from Russia and Germany. Earlier, economic orthodoxy rested on individualism. Now socialist and humanist economics are on the way to becoming orthodoxies, replacing individualism. Earlier, economics was rooted in capital and capitalists. From now on economics will be rooted in labor and laborers. This is indeed a time of transition from individualism to socialism, to humanism.
>
> Marx was the founding father of socialist economics. . . .[26]

Li would conclude later on in his essay that socialism was a cure for the body, humanism for the soul. After pointing out that the present economic organization, based on class opposition, extinguished both "the ideal of mutual aid" and "the concept of ethics," he stated:

> We advocate that humanism be used to transform the spirit of humanity, and at the same time that socialism be used to transform economic organization. If we seek to transform the human spirit without also transforming economic organization, there will be no significant change; if we seek to transform economic organization without also transforming the human spirit, we will not succeed. We advocate the transformation of both material and mental [*wuxin*] existence, of both body and soul.[27]

The kind of change Marx had advocated, in Li's view, was a necessary but not sufficient condition of human transformation. It needed to be supplemented by change in the human spirit, which Marxism rendered epiphenomenal and secondary, but which humanist economists since the time of Marx had stressed as a primary goal of change. Li did not say in this essay who the humanist economists might be; but (as we have discussed earlier) in "Class Competition and Mutual Aid," which he penned about the same time as "My Views on Marxism," Kropotkin and William Morris were prominent (see Chapter 3).

Li's essay articulated with unusual clarity where he found Marxism relevant, and where deficient. He was not alone in this evaluation. His thinking on Marxism, if it is taken as a paradigm of May Fourth thinking on Marxism, was so only because it revealed with clarity the contradictions born out of the confrontation between two modes of thinking on revolutionary change; the materialist mode, represented by Marxism, with its highly "disciplined sense of time" (in Meisner's words), which stressed necessity, and an ethical mode characteristic of New Culture thinking, with a rather weak sense of the burden of history, which stressed the freedom of conscious revolutionaries to define the future. The two were as yet not integrated in the early May Fourth period into a coherent account of revolution in history; rather, the initial response to Marxism was to place it in the service of revolutionary goals not of its making.

This is suggested by the functions Li and others assigned to Marxism in their conceptualization of revolution. Marxism was most important for offering means to clear away obstacles to revolution; the revolution itself would derive its inspiration from other sources.

Marxism did have a sobering effect on May Fourth radical thinking. When Li acknowledged that socialism was necessary to clear away obstacles, he was expressing a new sense of the burden of history. At a time when the social effects of economic change were becoming evident daily, moreover, Marxism offered a means to explain and resolve them. Marxism did not transform the May Fourth vision of revolution, but introduced to it a significant new dimension.

Marx's determinism also provided a welcome "scientific" support for New Culture radicals' rejection of the past, hitherto based on tenuous ideological grounds. As Zhang Dongsun was to remark in December 1919, there was no longer any need to struggle against old culture, because it was destined to extinction under the force of economic change.[28] Li expressed this same assurance toward the problem of inherited culture.[29] Whatever their reservations, Li and the Guomindang writers such as Dai Jitao and Hu Hanmin, who were the first to apply Marxist theory to analysis of Chinese society, had no qualms about explaining the past away in terms of the working out of economic forces. This use of Marx goes a long way toward explaining their attraction to his allegedly deterministic materialism, of which they were otherwise critical.

The present and future were another matter, however. No one in 1919 was willing to relinquish to the forces of history the prerogative of creating the future, as they did the extinction of the past. Marx's "determinism" was rejected to the extent that it suggested that economic forces conditioned their own revolutionary consciousness, or the future they sought to create. To be sure, Li Dazhao criticized the materialist conception of history for denying a significant role to ideology throughout history, but he was clearly most uncomfortable with it when it came to the future. Whether it was class struggle or "socialist economics" he spoke of, the task he assigned to Marxism was the purging of the past, not the creation of the future.

It might be illuminating here to juxtapose Marxism with anarchism. Unlike anarchism, Marxism did not resonate with the dominant values of this radical culture, which further contributed to the image of Marxism as an important but incomplete economistic ideology that did not match Anarchism or Humanism in its comprehensiveness.

Anarchism, as we have discussed earlier, made a radical contribution to New Culture thinking by pointing to the necessity of social transformation as a condition of cultural change. If New Culture radicals were receptive to this message, however, it was because anarchists themselves conceived of social revolution in predominantly cultural terms. Marxism clashed with the current culturalism in the seemingly unequivocal priority it assigned to material over cultural change. Li's statement indicates a willingness to recognize the essential importance of material change; he was not equally willing, however, to privilege it over cultural change, or to accept the claim that cultural change would follow automatically on its heels. If anything, he perceived in Marxism's failure to address culture a basic "incompleteness" in its theory of revolution.

Marxist historicism, moreover, clashed with the ethical voluntarism and the ideological rationalism that characterized New Culture culturalism. New Culture thinking was not particularly prominent for a strong sense of the burden of history; on the contrary, it was largely premised on the possibility of a rupture in time, a new beginning free of the dead weight of the past. The present was not a medium for translating past into future, but a moment when the past would be extinguished and the future created by those who had remade themselves intellectually and ethically. Li Dazhao, in his 1917 essay "Now," called upon Chinese youth to "kill" their selves of yesterday that they might create their selves of tomorrow.[30] This "pathos of novelty," as Hannah Arendt has called it, was by the May Fourth period integral to radical culture, which sought for the new in every realm of life—and displayed immense confidence in immanent cultural metamorphosis. A movement of intellectuals, the New Culture Movement expressed the faith of intellectuals to remake the world in their own self-image.

It is not surprising at such a historical moment that anarchism, with its faith in immanent social and cultural transformation, should have struck a responsive chord, or that Marx's "determinism" should have been the most fascinating, yet disturbing, aspect of Marxism. With its emphasis on society's subterranean forces in shaping the course of history, Marxism challenged their faith in their ability to remake society through the agency of consciousness. The "disciplined sense of time" of Marxist historicism, on the other hand, raised immediate doubts about a break in time, a new beginning free of the hold of the past. Ready to employ Marxist "determinism" to declare the pastness of the past, May Fourth radicals were not prepared to see their own consciousness as subject to the subterranean forces of history.

Neither were they prepared to think about history and revolution in "class ways." May Fourth radicals' attitude on class goes a long way toward explaining their economistic reading of Marxism. Still affected by New Culture assumptions about the good society, they were wary of the implications of the idea of social revolution which Marxism introduced. There is little evidence that anyone in 1919 felt comfortable with the notion of class struggle, which conflicted with ethical universalism. Li Dazhao may have gone beyond his contemporaries in thinking class struggle inevitable, but even he continued to view it as a necessary evil society had to go through to achieve the realization of mutual aid and "universal love" (*boai*). Marx's advocacy of class struggle seemed to May Fourth intellectuals to perpetuate one of the basic assumptions of capitalist society that they sought to abolish: that the pursuit of economic interest determined human behavior and social activity. Such "selfishness" contradicted the altruism that they thought was essential to the establishment of a good society. While by late 1919 Chinese radicals had become acutely aware of the working class, they did not yet perceive anything "utopian" about the working class, or identify with it; and they felt uncomfortable with Marxism to the extent that they perceived it as the ideological expression of the interests of a single class.

This suspicion of class and class struggle had crucial implications for initial Chinese reading of Marxism; namely, their ready acceptance of the interpretation of Marxism as an economistic evolutionism. There is no need here to inquire into the highly complex, and controversial, issue of the status in Marxist theory of the social relations of production, to which class and class struggle are crucial. It is not very controversial, however, to observe that whether or not we recognize centrality to class relations has important consequences in the interpretation of Marxism. The dialectic of history in

Marxism is preeminently social in conceptualization, premised upon the placing of the forces of production within the context of the relations of production. While denial of centrality to class relations in social dynamics may not necessarily abolish the dialectic, as Cohen has suggested,[31] it does open the possibility of rendering Marxist theory into an economic monism, which at best yields an evolutionary, undialectical, deterministic view that makes social change into a function of development in the forces of production. Such monism suggests a deterministic portrayal of social formation since it renders social relations functional to the organization of production. For the same reasons, it suggests an evolutionary rather than a revolutionary view of social change because it renders human activity into a function, rather than a determinant, of a productive activity which follows its own rules of development.

Obviously, the economistic reading also renders consciousness epiphenomenal, a function of the very same productive organization that fashions social relations in general. It is not true, as Chinese radicals seemed to think, that Marxism is lacking in ethical considerations or that it denies a significant role to consciousness in history. But these questions appear in Marxism in class terms; to the extent that classes are rendered secondary in theory, so are consciousness and ethics. Furthermore, Marx's notion of class was a utopian one. Whatever the merits of the conception, Marx thought of the proletariat as a "universal" class because he considered its oppression as a class to be absolute; its liberation, therefore, would signify the liberation of society as a whole. Proletarian consciousness was not merely pertinent to a single class but was pregnant with significance for the whole society. The universalistic claims of Marxism as a revolutionary ideology are very much contingent upon this utopian conceptualization.

This is not how May Fourth radicals perceived working-class consciousness, however, and they rejected, therefore, a class-based view of consciousness as a guide to revolution. Lin Yungai's discussion of the materialist conception of history, which pointed to the dialectic in the relationship between human activity and history, was an exception. Suspicion of class and class struggle obviated the need to challenge the economistic reading of Marxism.

Marxism had a sobering effect on May Fourth ideas; it introduced a new consciousness of the social dimensions of change. Its notion of social space, much more complex than New Culture conceptions, pointed to limits on what could be achieved through culture and the transformation of consciousness. Its "disciplined sense of time" reminded revolutionaries that they had to come to terms with the legacy of the past, even if they might not be bound by it themselves. The impact of Marxism was not, however, only on the revolutionary voluntarism of New Culture radicals. As we shall see in the next chapter, even the older generation of socialists, who had remained largely skeptical of the new generation's culturalism, found in Marxism a reminder of the social dimensions of change. The notion of "saving the country through industrialization" (*shiye jiuguo*) gave way in 1919 to a demand that social reorganization must precede, or at least accompany, industrialization.

This new consciousness was absorbed into radical culture immediately but did not immediately transform it. Indeed, the initial uses made of Marxism indicate that it did not provoke May Fourth radicals to locate themselves in history more carefully than hitherto; rather, they applied Marxism to their sense of revolutionary time to strengthen their own argument for change. This, I think, helps explain the aforementioned ironic ambivalence in their attitudes toward the question of Marx's determinism: their attraction to Marx's determinism even as they found in determinism the Achilles' heel of Marxism. It also explains why they might have found Kawakami's interpretation more appealing than those of his critics from the left. Aside from the authority commanded by his reputation as a learned Marxist (which appealed to the still academically oriented Chinese radicals), they found it quite congenial to follow him in placing Marxism within a broader world view dominated by universalist ethical concerns.

Toward the end of the 1920s, when Chinese radicals would truly discover Marxism after their first attempt at social revolution failed, they urgently needed to locate Chinese society in history in order to formulate a "correct" revolutionary strategy. In the May Fourth period, when they first encountered Marxism, they used it to delineate that moment in history when "the realm of necessity" gave way to "the realm of freedom." The concern with whether or not Chinese society, on the basis of its historical development, was ready for a socialist revolution was in no way as significant as it would be later. The concern was, rather, with Marxism's implications for the freedom of the revolutionary to set the course for the future.

The suspicion of class and class struggle weakened (if it did not preclude) the possibility of a dialectical resolution of the theoretical problems created by the juxtaposition of a past, that was readily consigned to the realm of necessity, against a future which was to be free of all necessity. The response to this theoretical dilemma was to historicize the theory itself. Marxism, George Lukacs once stated, is the "self-criticism of bourgeois society." Li Dazhao might have been anticipating Lukacs when he assigned Marxism the task of purging past evils (including class struggle) but denied it the prerogative of defining the revolutionary future. His juxtaposition of the various metaphors of prehistory and history, material and spiritual, body and soul, all expressed what he believed were the limitations of Marxism as historical and revolutionary theory. Particularly revealing was his juxtaposition of prehistory and history. The Marx that seemed to draw him was the Marx who had, quite uncharacteristically, pointed to the possibility of a rupture in time—drawn a distinction between a "prehistory" when humanity was subject to the unconscious forces of nature and society, and "history," when human consciousness would establish its control and the "laws" of social development in "prehistory" would no longer apply. Li, however, herein diverged from Marx in an interesting way. Where Marx had drawn it to distinguish

Communist from pre-Communist society, in Li's usage the distinction pointed to a division between a past subject to necessity and a revolutionary present (regardless of what social formation it might be) where revolutionaries freely defined the course of the future. Unlike Lukacs, Li believed the future thus defined was no longer subject to Marx's theoretical postulates and revolutionary vision; on the contrary, it would draw its inspiration from sources extraneous or even hostile to Marxism: anarchism, and the "humanist economists" who had transcended Marx in their appreciation of revolution.

It goes without saying that Li's revolutionary voluntarism needs to be distinguished from Lenin's or Lukacs'. Marxist voluntarism finds its legitimization in a reading of theory that minimizes deterministic implications, seeking to rest itself in the class-oriented reading. Li's reading of Marxism did not point to a Leninist reading; on the contrary, it was much closer to Kautsky's more deterministic reading of Marx. His revolutionary voluntarism, therefore, was anti-theoretical—not justified by the theory, but possible only with the relegation of the theory to "prehistory." Li, in effect, separated theory from practice, and justified the practice by calling on revolutionary authority that was extraneous to Marxism. Among the May Fourth radicals who were drawn to Marxism, Li came closest to acknowledging its relevance to the Chinese revolution; but if he was indeed a Marxist at the time, his Marxism still did not point to a Leninist reading. The tenuous appreciation of the relationship between theory and practice, which would always characterize Chinese Marxism, was already present in the earliest Chinese response.

To the extent that Chinese socialists made an effort to incorporate Marxist ideas into a political strategy of revolution in 1919, their attitudes were conditioned by thinking which was most clearly expressed by Li Dazhao. These efforts were undertaken not by the New Culture generation, but by the older generation of socialists who had a more explicitly political orientation. Their suspicion of class and class conflict, which rested in sources other than New Culture ethical universalism and reached back to the beginnings of socialism in China, was, if anything, even more pronounced than that of the New Culture generation. In 1919, their ideas of socialism dominated socialist *political* thinking. In 1919 they too, however, came under the sway of the emerging culture of radicalism in which the ideas that have been discussed in the last two chapters played a formative part. In the various revolutionary strategies they formulated, we find the articulation at the level of politics of this culture. Their socialism brings into even clearer relief the uncertainties and the contradictions of May Fourth socialist thinking.

7

Corporatist Resolutions:
Class Politics Without Class Struggle

Starting in June 1919, the question of class quickly emerged as a central one in May Fourth cultural and political thinking. The radicals who expressed this with the greatest sharpness were those of the older generation, more sensitive to the political emergence of Chinese labor than the younger generation of New Culture radicals, who were still most interested in cultural change. It was also these older radicals who most feared the imminent appearance of class conflict in China, and believed it would threaten the Chinese revolution. In 1919 they displayed the greatest urgency in seeking ways to incorporate labor into politics so as to forestall violent social upheaval. They discovered their answer in a variety of corporatist socialisms.

The term corporatism, like socialism has been applied to movements that run the gamut of the political spectrum. I use it here as it has been employed in studies of European politics in recent years: a means of transcending capitalism through the use of class reconciliation rather than conflict.[1] The sense in which the term has been absorbed into Chinese political vocabulary supports this use. A recent Chinese dictionary defines the term corporatism as "class reconciliationism" (*jieji tiaohe zhuyi*).[2] I shall use it to describe those currents in Chinese socialism that accepted class as a fundamental fact of contemporary social organization but rejected political solutions premised on the inevitability of class struggle. The intention was not to abolish classes, but to reorganize the articulation of social interest so as to render class struggle unnecessary. To the extent that socialism assumed political form in May Fourth thinking, it appeared in a number of guises that promised this kind of peaceful social revolution.

Guomindang Socialism in the May Fourth Period

The new consciousness of labor and its implications, with all the contradictions it brought out, was nowhere more evident than in the writings of Dai Jitao and his coeditors in the *Weekend Review,* which with the other Guomindang-related publications, *Awakening* and *Construction,* emerged between

121

May 1919 and May 1920 as the foremost publications to discuss the problem of labor. *Weekend Review* started publication only a few days after labor's emergence with the participation of laborers in the growing mass movement in Shanghai in early June 1919. Shen Xuanlu in its second issue (June 15) took immediate note of the significance of the "June Fifth Movement."[3] The event was discussed again in subsequent issues, but it was not until March 1920 that Dai, in a piece entitled "The Origins and Causes of the Labor Movement," offered his analysis of the meaning of the "June Fifth Movement" for China. His is the most cogent analysis I know of, from this period, of the impact on radical consciousness of the political emergence of labor. It also illustrates the contradictions in the consciousness of class and class conflict that shaped the meaning of socialism.

The most revealing aspect of Dai's analysis was his reinterpretation of the May Fourth Movement in light of the emergence of labor. He re-presented the May Fourth Movement, as the context for the events of June, as the first stirring of class consciousness among the bourgeoisie and laborers alike.

> It was in the area of changing the lives of common people that the May Fourth and the June Fifth movements were a turning point. . . . The result of this movement to change the lives of the common people was, moreover, to stimulate the emergence of class consciousness among both the laboring and the capitalist classes. It stimulated, at once, the movement for industrial revolution—the large-scale industry of the capitalists—and the organization of labor in new forms. These two movements each provided the core for two forces that are antithetical to one another, that will be in ceaseless conflict until the one force has eliminated the other.[4]

Dai explained that capitalists had at first thought the May Fourth Movement was in their favor, as the boycott of foreign goods had stimulated Chinese-owned production; hence they had joined the movement willingly. The emergence of labor with the "June Fifth Movement," and the labor organization that movement spawned, no matter how meager, rudely shocked the capitalists and awakened them to their class interests. Their awareness of the consequences of labor organization, argued Dai, made them even more keenly conscious of their class interests than were laborers, who had just become aware of themselves as a class.

These events' radical effect on Dai became apparent in his discussion of the developmental trajectory of Chinese society. Guomindang socialists had long held (and still held, as we shall see) that given China's backwardness, questions of class and class conflict were irrelevant to revolution, and even that the bourgeoisie had an important role to play in China's development. Dai now argued, against those who claimed a special "national essence" for China, that all societies followed the same course of development in history. Those who argued otherwise, including those who held that China was too backward, were either lacking in consciousness or out to protect their own class interests. Those who argued this position most fervently, he added, were those who had already become "Manchester-style" capitalists!

Not only did Dai affirm the relevance of class to the Chinese revolution, he went on to repudiate the notion that the bourgeoisie had a role to play in China's development. As far as he was concerned, China's industrial development did not need capitalists any more than the cultivation of land needed landlords. He pointed to the plight of the Soviet Union, oppressed by world capitalism. Russia needed foreign trade to acquire commodities it lacked, but imperialist powers withheld it to bring socialism to heel and restore capitalism in Russia. China was in an even worse position: if as a country it was an "industrial slave" (*gongnu*) and an "agricultural serf" (*nongnu*), it was all on account of capitalism. "What a society needs is provided in common by the society," he observed, "therefore what the society provided was meant to meet the needs of the whole society"; there was no reason to create "gross inequalities in production or distribution" by "man-made limitations."[5]

Dai did not say how the question of class was to be resolved. At this point his analysis turned into a "dialogue" to explain basic economic concepts and phenomena, using socialist sources on economic theory, most prominent among which were the works of Marx and G. D. H. Cole. The "dialogue," like the rest of the article, stressed the use of coercion by the ruling class (the wealthy) to protect its interests. The promised second part of the article never appeared in *Weekend Review,* and the issue of what the working class might do for itself remained unanswered.

Other discussions of the question of labor in *Weekend Review* help us guess at what Dai's answer might have been, or at least suggest that it would have been problematic. He wrote this article when he was at his most radical—in the spring of 1920, when the question of labor had moved to the forefront, and radicals of his circle had already initiated activities to establish a Communist party. Dai himself participated in these, until he was sharply recalled to the Guomindang fold by Sun Yatsen, after which he moved progressively to the right. His later anti-Marxist stance might have been anticipated, however, from his negative attitude toward questions of class and class conflict even during the period when he appeared as possibly the best-informed (and maybe even the most radical) propagator of Marxism. At no point was his appraisal of class relations in Chinese society accompanied by an affirmation of a leading role for the working class. And when others adopted that line after 1920, he was to turn against the idea even of classes, as did other major Guomindang theoreticians who had favored Marxist social analysis in 1919–1920.

Dai (and others in *Weekend Review*) wished to educate laborers to raise their class consciousness, but with the professed objective of preventing, not fomenting, class struggle: an educated working class, they believed, was the best guarantee against class conflict. In his piece in the June 15, 1919 issue of the journal, which first referred to the "June Fifth Movement," Shen Xuanlu, Dai's coeditor, perceived in the movement an opportunity for laborers to organize according to "universal principle," "morality," and "public will." Dai himself took up similar themes in his "The Question of the Education of Laborers," published in the third issue in late June. Dai often bemoaned the intellectual backwardness of Chinese workers which facilitated their oppression. This article presented two means of worker education: unions, and the help of intellectuals. Unions he deemed irrelevant in China where the workers were too ignorant to organize. The task, therefore, devolved on intellectuals.

The goal of workers' education to Dai was "to prevent a thoroughgoing social revolution" of the kind that had taken place in Russia. The thought of such a revolution in China, placed as it was under conditions of backwardness and imperialist oppression, made his "whole frame tremble with fear."[6] He recommended instead that Chinese laborers follow "social democracy" of the kind practiced in England. Dai called upon "capitalists and educators" to help laborers, and thus fulfill their own obligations of "mutual aid."

Dai's article was addressed not to laborers but to capitalists and educators, and especially those who felt that educating laborers would open the gates to "flood waters." As with his efforts to promote the study of the Russian Revolution, his goal here was to warn against ignoring labor. The organization of labor unions or workers' education could help avoid a "bloody" revolution by cultivating "the morality of citizenship" and habits of "mutual aid" which would help workers become participants in national development. Despite his criticism of those who, on the grounds of "national essence," rejected socialist solutions for China, Dai himself argued on occasion that Chinese socialism must fit the special circumstances of Chinese society.[7] He believed that guild socialism of the English type might be a suitable model; he also expressed admiration for the liberal-oriented Meireikai in Japan, which provided an example for intellectuals to carry out their social responsibilities.[8] On more than one occasion, he called upon capitalists to help with the education of laborers. To him, the greatest danger to peaceful development in China was presented not by laborers, but the bureaucrats, militarists, "national essence" scholars, and "financiers who believed in the omnipotence of money," all of whom stood in the way of incorporating laborers in the national enterprise. With all its radical class rhetoric, Dai's socialism was intended not to bring about a revolution, but to promote an enlightened capitalism that would open the doors of culture and politics to the working class. Of the necessity of this opening he had no doubts. To him, the ultimate meaning of socialism resided in its insistence on the necessity of recognizing laborers as rightful participants in social and political life.

Socialism was also a means, so to speak, of socializing laborers, because Dai also perceived a grave threat to China in unsocialized workers, and "ignoramuses" who incited them to premature activity. In a revealing discussion with Sun Yatsen, which he reported in the same issue as "The Question of the Education of Laborers," Dai quoted himself as saying to Sun,

> Chinese workers have no education; many of them cannot even write their names. Hence they do not have the slightest trace of class consciousness. . . . In Shanghai, there are 300,000–400,000 workers, and frequent strikes. The recent boycott also stimulated labor strikes. Fortunately, the proclamation arrived from the Beijing government dismissing

Cao, Lu, and Zhang [the three "villains" of the May Fourth Movement]. If it had been a day or two late, I am afraid that there might have been a city-wide general strike. Everybody who had any knowledge was extremely concerned, and tried to exhort workers not to go on strike. Why? Because there was extreme danger in a strike by workers who have no organization, no education, no training and no preparation. Besides, it would have been of no benefit to the workers themselves.[9]

Dai also complained of half-baked intellectuals who, not seeing the danger of inciting ignorant masses, spread revolutionary propaganda among them. He mentioned specifically a recent report concerning a leaflet entitled "What Soldiers Ought to Know," which, he seemed not to realize, was an anarchist pamphlet calling on workers and soldiers to rise up in revolution. It caused Chinese authorities great consternation, and apparently Dai also.[10] It was to Sun's credit as a revolutionary that he seems to have soothed Dai's fears, observing that such things happened in times of intellectual transition and should not be taken overly seriously.

Not all contributors to Guomindang journals shared Dai's fears of the working class, although they all agreed that class struggle should be conducted without violence, most commonly under the aegis of the revolutionary state to be founded. Lin Yungai (whose views on the materialist conception of history we have discussed in the last chapter), a prolific Guomindang writer on socialism in 1919, also found in "social democracy" the answer to China's problems. In a piece entitled "An Examination of Class Struggle" he refuted the suggestion that socialists were fomenting class struggle, and instead explained the emergence of class struggle in classical Marxist terms: as a consequence of the division of society into two hostile camps with the concentration of capital in ever fewer hands. The solution he offered was the socialization of production through a social revolution. As he explained it,

the necessity of social revolution does not imply violent bloodshed, but only a thoroughgoing social transformation. This fundamental transformation means that laborers must be given the power to manage not only the instruments of labor but also its products. In other words, the goal of the laboring class is the socialization of all organs of production. . . . The socialist movement enhances the power of laborers to realize this goal of socializing the organs of production. . . . Once this has been realized, it will be possible to establish with the spirit of social democracy a life where the benefits of society are shared in common by all.[11]

Lin's understanding of socialism extended socialist ideas over a broad historical range, from Confucius to St. Paul to Karl Marx. In modern socialism, he perceived two important trends, the "idealist" trend going back to Robert Owen, and the "scientific" trend going back to Marx. The idealists advocated free association and mutual aid; the scientists wished to use the power of the state to transform the economy. The goal of socialism in every case was to restore to society an organic cohesion that would extend from the individual through the family, the city and the country, and the nation, all the way to the entire globe. His own choice lay with "scientific socialism" in its most recent tendency, which he equated with social democracy of one kind or another. He observed that Marx's *Communist Manifesto,* in spite of its various defects, had guided socialist movements since the middle of the nineteenth century and continued to do so. While some criticized social democrats for deviating from its revolutionary ideas, there was nothing in the *Communist Manifesto* that social democracy either had not achieved or could not achieve. The tendency toward peaceful, legislative means to achieve socialism was itself grounded in the labor movement, which tended toward peace, the more laborers became aware of themselves as a class and organized themselves accordingly for struggle with capital. This development, Lin concluded, had made the more violent anarchist advocacy of revolution irrelevant where socialism had succeeded, as in contemporary Russia and Germany![12]

Guomindang writers followed Marx in taking classes as a fundamental premise of politics. They stood Marx on his head, however, in arguing that class consciousness and organization were the means not to class conflict but to class reconciliation. They viewed socialism, accordingly, as a preventative against revolution. One can perceive here the sources of the ideological schizophrenia that plagued the Guomindang in the mid-1920s, when class struggle had emerged as a reality. This contradiction was much more evident in the contributions to *Weekend Review* and *Construction,* with their unmistakable Guomindang affiliation, than in *Awakening,* which served in 1919 as a general forum on socialism. The contradiction was ultimately between the sharpening awareness of class and loyalty to a political formulation that went back to Revolutionary Alliance days. More than a decade ago, when these writers had first discussed social revolution as young followers of Sun Yatsen, they had justified socialism as the means to "social revolution" that would forestall the kind of bloody revolution they thought European society was headed for; a revolution, in other words, to prevent revolution. The revolutionary state should institute social policies to counteract the trend toward class cleavage that would emerge in China inevitably with economic modernization, as it had already in Europe. The contradictions became even more evident in the May Fourth period when they recognized the existence of classes as the reality of Chinese society, without, however, abandoning hopes in the possibility of avoiding class conflict. Their rhetoric was quite radical; the political solution they clung to was that of a bygone age. Besides, while the policies they suggested might have been instituted under a revolutionary state, in 1919 that state was yet to be created. The policies they offered ignored the question of how the Guomindang was to deal with the question of classes in the process of revolution. These contradictions would be articulated further in Guomindang politics in the mid-1920s, and would divide the Party deeply.

While both *Weekend Review* and *Construction* promoted Marxist social analysis at this time, the political ideology they promoted was that of Sun Yatsen. Neither journal openly advocated Sun's socialism, but the ideological premises that guided his Three People's Principles were clearly visible in their discussions. *Construction* was openly a Guomindang organ, *Weekend* sibility of reorganizing Chinese society from the bottom up, without resort to either class struggle or a moribund state.

To the extent that *Reconstruction* pieces advocated class struggle, it was a class struggle that directed attention away from conflict between labor and capital. We have referred in Chapter 4 to Zhou Fohai's December 1919 discussion welcoming class struggle to China. His "welcome," however, was intended in fact to show that the struggle between labor and capital was still irrelevant. Zhou presented class struggle as the expression of conflicting class interests but he held that, thanks to China's industrial backwardness, it might still be able to escape class conflict and revolution of the kind that awaited European society. His was a moralistic, anarchist-inspired notion of classes. According to him, China did not yet have a "middle class"; there was no need, therefore, to even speak of conflict between labor and the middle class. The major division in Chinese society was between a "parasitic" class that did not engage in productive activity (which included not only vagabonds but militarists and bureaucrats as well), and a producing class exploited by the parasites. The task in China was, therefore, to unify the "self-sufficient" (*ziji*) classes to overthrow the parasitic classes.

> Is there a way to overthrow the parasitic class by the power of the working class? Of course not. Therefore it is necessary to form a self-sufficient class to struggle with the parasites. . . . To reform society, it is necessary to get rid of obstacles to reform. The obstacle in China is the parasitic class; therefore, it is necessary first to overthrow the parasitic class. To overthrow the parasitic class, it is necessary to unify the self-sufficient class, and to engage in class struggle against the parasites. This is China's class struggle.[18]

In China, therefore, class struggle was against the elite that lived off the labor of others. The idea was as much moral as social structural.

Zhou Fohai's views may explain why, after a brief flirtation with the Communist party (as one of its founding members), he emerged in the mid-1920s as a foremost Guomindang theoretician of revolution. In the May Fourth period, when Marxist and anarchist ideas of class were not yet clearly distinguished but superimposed one upon the other, his notion expressed a widespread, profound ambiguity over the question of class as structural and moral concept. Guild socialism's solution addressed both aspects of the question: eliminating class as *structural* determinant of society, while creating the conditions for the realization of a social morality that class society precluded. The anarchist inspiration in guild socialism was evident in its strategy of change: education grounded in the reorganization of society from the bottom up.

In 1919, others writing for *Reconstruction*, notably Zhang Dongsun, agreed with Zhou's diagnosis of the major line of class division in China. The great majority of them, however, saw the task of social reorganization as construction, not destruction: rather than concentrate on analysis of this relationship, and ways to overthrow the parasitic class, they devoted their atten-

Review more of a private undertaking in which Guomindang writers participated extensively. In October, *Weekend Review* followed the lead of *Construction* in publishing in its "Double Ten" issue Sun's plan for national industrial development. A program outlining "The Future of National Construction" published in the June 15 issue (probably written by Dai himself) followed Sun's idea of "people's livelihood" almost to the letter. If neither journal named the Guomindang's particular brand of socialism, its premises were inscribed on every page of their discussions.

The outstanding characteristic of that socialism, going back to Revolutionary Alliance days, had been its insistence that the problem of inequality in contemporary society rested not in capital but landownership. This premise remained central even as Guomindang writers recognized in 1919 the consequences of China's burgeoning industrial development. The Double Ten issue published a lengthy discussion by the important Guomindang leader Liao Zhongkai, entitled "The Task of Continuing the Revolution." Liao elaborated on Sun's idea of "people's livelihood," and argued that the land question was the key to resolving China's economic problems. As earlier in the Revolutionary Alliance journal *People's Journal* (*Minbao*), where he had first discussed the issue, Liao placed the burden for social inequality on the owners of land. They benefited from the increase of land value with economic development but did not contribute themselves to the production of value. (Sun Yatsen had first gotten this idea from Henry George.) "Peasants, workers, merchants, and capitalists all produce," Liao stated, "but it is the owners of land who take the largest portion of the profits as if the rest of society consisted of horses and cows working for them."[13] He pointed to the Russian Revolution to warn that the worse the land problem got, the more drastic must be the solution. Solving it at the present, before Chinese society had experienced significant development and inequality, would make the task considerably easier. Liao's analysis confirmed a belief shared by most Guomindang writers, that socialism did not preclude alliance with "merchants and capitalists" who, with peasants and the working class, suffered at the hands of the landowning classes.

In 1905 Revolutionary Alliance theoreticians could argue with some plausibility that China did not yet suffer from the severe inequalities of industrial society. Such arguments appeared less convincing in 1919, when they recognized the existence of conflict betwen workers and capitalists. The strategy they had advocated earlier, moreover, had meant social change coming from above, through the agency of the state. The appearance of class-based people's movements in 1919 challenged this belief, and some of the Guomindang came close to accepting the necessity of taking up the leadership of these movements. Nevertheless, they perceived the tasks of this leadership to be as much to keep movements from below under control as to promote the class interests of the oppressed. In 1919, many among radical intellectuals shared in this belief. Only when a more clear-cut class orientation to socialism emerged over the next two years did Guomindang socialism come under suspicion, placing strains upon Guomindang theoreticians themselves. In this process, the new Communist intellectuals would also gradually "forget" the very significant contribution of Guomindang writers in 1919 to the propagation of Marxism in China in its initial phase.

Among the revolutionary leaders of the Guomindang, perhaps the lone exception to this assessment at this time was Zhu Zhixin, whom Martin Bernal has described as the most radical among Guomindang socialists as far back as Revolutionary Alliance days. Among May Fourth socialists, Zhu and Li Dazhao came closest to concluding that class struggle must be an integral part of the Chinese revolution. When in 1920 Zhu wrote, "class struggle is not an imaginary method, it is a fact of contemporary society; all you need to do is look at the facts of history to see that they are all expressions of class struggle," it may be significant that he made this statement in the anarchist periodical *Fujian Star,* sponsored by Chen Jiongming, with whom he served as the Guomindang liaison at the time.[14] Zhu's death in 1920 deprived the Guomindang of one of its most revolutionary socialist leaders.[15]

The Guomindang conception of politics, as it began to assume visible form in 1919, was a corporatist one, what Philip Schnitter has described as "state corporatism."[16] While writers such as Dai Jitao pointed to guild socialism, with its implications of decentralized political power, as the form that might be most appropriate for China, the state was essential to the Guomindang conception. This conception recognized the existence of class and class oppression as a fundamental social given, but rejected class conflict as a means of resolving class oppression, attempting instead to devise ways of reconciling conflicting class interests through the agency of the state. No one class could—or should—rule society; the working class should be educated so as to establish labor unions to represent its interests in a political process that included other classes. The Guomindang's conception of the state as a clearing-house for conflicting social interests went back to Revolutionary Alliance days.

Dai's attitude was typical of May Fourth socialist thinking, which rejected capitalism but remained highly dubious of the transfer of power to the laboring classes, especially the idea that class struggle and "the dictatorship of the proletariat" were the means to effect such a transfer. Even those who wrote passionately about the plight of the Chinese working class could not yet see in its liberation the key to the liberation of all humanity.

The Guild Socialists of the Research Clique

Similar premises guided the socialism propagated in various publications associated with the Research Clique, chief among them *Reconstruction.*[17] The guiding spirit behind these in the early May Fourth period was Zhang Dongsun, an Anglophile intellectual and admirer of Bertrand Russell. Without a clear ideology such as the Three People's Principles to direct them, these publications were even more eclectic in their socialism than the Guomindang journals. In their pages the ideological positions range from the class advo-

cacy of Li Dazhao, to the state socialism of Zhang Junmai (who was attracted to German socialism), to syndicalism and anarchism. It was Zhang Dongsun's socialism that set the tone for *Reconstruction,* however, and made guild socialism its trademark.

Chinese historians have predictably been quite harsh on the socialism Zhang Dongsun, and other contributors to *Reconstruction,* whose writings often leave the impression that they were intended as much to undercut class struggle as promote it. This impression is enhanced by the opposition to Bolshevism and the pervasive liberal tone. Above all, however, it is the political activities of the Research Clique that render suspect its members' socialism. Members of the Research Clique, then the Progressive Party (*Jinbu dang*), had been involved with the *bête noire* of the Republic, Yuan Shikai (after 1911), and continued to flirt with warlord governments into the twenties. Their leader, Liang Qichao, had been opposed to socialism since his debates with the Revolutionary Alliance in 1905–1907, and, rightly or wrongly, was perceived as a conservative opponent of revolution. In 1919, when modern labor unions did not yet form a significant social force, Zhang's guild socialism easily looked like an abstract intellectual exercise, whose only aim could be to defuse conflict between labor and capital.

Guild socialism commands our attention, however, not only because of its intrinsic interest, but even more so because, of all those that appeared in China in the May Fourth period, it was in some ways the socialism most deeply imbued with the hues of May Fourth thinking. Uncertainty over the question of classes or the Soviet Union was pervasive in the May Fourth period, and does not cast sufficient doubt on the seriousness of the guild socialists, any more than on the socialism of the Guomindang socialists, Chen Duxiu, or even Li Dazhao. Zhang Dongsun continued to advocate socialism in later years and in the 1940s threw his valuable support behind Mao's New Democracy. His association with the Research Clique, moreover, does not imply that his socialism was merely a disguise for their anti-revolutionary tendencies; it only reveals, as with the Guomindang writers, the complexities in the relationship between ideological attraction and political affiliation in these years. He was himself chastised by Liang Qichao for his advocacy of socialism; indeed, in late 1920 Liang moved in to take over the editorship of *Reconstruction* in person to put an end to its advocacy of socialism (an unnecessary move since by that time Zhang, faced with the establishment of the Communist party, had already begun to retreat from his position).

In 1919 guild socialism seemed to offer a means of social reorganization whose appeals extended beyond Zhang Dongsun and his followers and for awhile held the attention of most radicals, ranging from Dai Jitao to Chen Duxiu and Li Dazhao. This appeal was twofold. First, in the May Fourth intellectual atmosphere, when anarchist ideals remained coupled to Marxist social analysis, guild socialism seemed to combine the best of what anarchism and Marxism had to offer. This appeal was supported, secondly, by the simultaneous suspicion of class struggle and lack of faith in the Chinese state, an existing cause of political disorder. Guild socialism offered the po-tion to alternative possibilities of social reconstruction that would render parasitism irrelevant, and liberate the whole society in the process. This was reflected in the full title of *Reconstruction, Jiefang yu gaizao,* literally *Liberation and Reform* (it was changed simply to *Gaizao* [*Reform*] when Liang took over in 1920).

Zhang Dongsun, like Dai Jitao, perceived socialism not as a revolutionary ideology, but as a means to bring labor and capital together in a new kind of social organization. His complexity as a socialist easily matched Dai's. Like Dai, Zhang was responsible during the May Fourth period for the dissemination of information on Marxism as well as the Russian Revolution. The publications he had a hand in included, in addition to *Reconstruction, Morning News* in Beijing, and *Current Affairs* and *Light of Learning* in Shanghai—all major sources on the Russian Revolution, Marxism, and socialism. Zhang had a complex attitude toward Marxism, and on occasion spoke approvingly of the Revolution, but was highly suspicious of both violent revolution and the idea of class struggle. Much of the material in these publications concerning the Revolution was intended as a warning. Zhang himself believed that the Revolution had been a consequence of the Czarist government's suppression of free speech and its inability to meet the most basic needs of the people. Suppression of discussion of the Revolution, or of socialism, in China, would only fuel the fires of revolution. To him, as to many of his contemporaries, the Russian Revolution offered much that Chinese could learn from, if only by way of negative example. Similarly, the discussion of socialism should not be suppressed because it showed the way to improving people's livelihood and, thereby, forestalling the possibility of revolution.[19]

This attitude toward socialism shaped these publications' discussions of class. Even before the May Fourth Movement, an article in *Light of Learning* by Ke Yiceng, "Socialism and China," described the goal of social reform as "the elimination of the ingredients for social revolution."[20] Liu Nangai, a prolific writer on socialism in these publications, argued in July 1919 that the best way to control "extremism" was to apply selectively the rational elements in socialism. The fear of extremism, moreover, was not simply ideological, but displayed a suspicion of the Chinese working class similar to that of Dai Jitao. In May 1919, *Light of Learning* warned students against inciting laborers to action.

> Our national salvation movement should not ignore laborers. But Chinese laborers are unorganized and, for the most part, ignorant. . . . Their patriotism is fervent to the point of stupidity, and can easily lead to violence with great harm to everyone. Efforts to unify laborers require much, much caution.[21]

This wariness of labor fashioned *Light of Learning*'s response to the June Third movement. An article published almost immediately on June 10, "1919 and Labor," hailed the strike in Shanghai as the beginning of a "new era" for Chinese labor, and predicted, with precocity, that 1919 would be "the year of labor." At the same time, however, the author urged "learned laborers" to educate "ignorant laborers," and called upon students and educators in Shanghai to take advantage of the boycott of classes to establish "labor support groups" which could enter factories to lecture to laborers and educate them. He also voiced fears of the strike taking a violent turn, and called upon Chinese capitalists to continue to pay laborers so as to support the anti-foreign strikes, since these strikes were aimed not at capital, but foreigners.[22]

These writers, while their attitudes were similar to Guomindang writers' on labor and class, even more explicitly called on capital to cooperate in the education of laborers. In January 1920, Zhang Dongsun's *Current Affairs* would start to publish a new supplement, *Friend of Industry and Commerce* (*Gongshangzhi yu*), intended to awaken capital to this obligation. The new supplement was edited by Ke Yiceng, who was also at this time the editor of *Light of Learning*. While the new supplement on occasion published articles intended to stimulate greater class consciousness among laborers, its goal was to promote conciliation. Like the Guomindang writers, these contributors believed that greater class consciousness among laborers was necessary to the organization of labor, which in turn would enhance the possibilities of reconciliation between labor and capital. The anti-revolutionary intention of *Friend of Industry and Commerce* was quite evident in its use of the revolutionary idea of "the sanctity of labor" to persuade laborers that one of their sacred obligations was the labor they owed their employers![23]

While these contributors bore a remarkable similarity to Guomindang socialists, they differed in their evaluation of the agency of a peaceful social transformation. While some Guomindang writers such as Dai also flirted with the idea of change from below in 1919, to the extent that their political formulations were shaped by Sun's Three Principles, the state was essential to their conception of socialism. Similarly, some Research Clique contributors, most prominent among them Zhang Junmai, rested their hopes on the agency of the state. The majority, however, including Zhang Dongsun, were as suspicious of the state as of class struggle. They discovered their models in decentralized forms of socialism, chief among them syndicalism and guild socialism. The discussion of these, and advocacy of guild socialism, was the most distinctive feature of *Reconstruction,* which started publication in September 1919 under Zhang Dongsun's editorship.

An article by Liu Nangai in the first issue of the journal sounded a note similar to Dai's. Liu welcomed the rise of labor consciousness and expressed hopes in the establishment of a labor federation that would represent workers' interests. He was not too optimistic about the future of labor; the basis for unity among laborers was weak, in his opinion, because Chinese industry was yet underdeveloped. Only in Shanghai was there sufficiently large industry to form the basis for unions, and even there laborers lay prostrate before the power of capitalists and labor bosses, too ignorant and unorganized to engage capital in a genuine struggle. The situation was even worse for nonproletarian laborers, who worked under the "sweating system" (*sic*).[24]

Under the circumstances, Liu believed, the only way out was syndicalism of the type practiced in France and England. According to him, in spite of all their differences over method, all socialisms shared one goal: to relieve the plight of the working class by abolishing the private ownership of land and capital. Syndicalism contained the best of socialism. "Socialism" (meaning social democracy) relied on the state for its success, which was not only unwise, but impractical in China. Others of a more radical persuasion (anarchists?) advocated revolutionary methods such as the general strike, which presupposed a kind of education Chinese workers did not have. Syndicalism, on the other hand, steered clear of the government, and also offered the means to education. Syndicates would not only guarantee the equal distribution of the fruits of labor, but also provide spaces for the cultivation of habits of self-management and cooperation. The advantage of syndicalism over state-oriented socialism was that it required self-reliance, instead of reliance on unreliable governments; state socialism, Liu believed, had always accrued to the advantage of capital, not labor. Unlike anarchism, on the other hand, syndicalism allowed for a positive attitude toward government, refusing to call for its immediate overthrow, which was impractical. The key to liberation was not destruction but education in self-government. Perhaps the greatest advantage of syndicalism, however, was in its organizational methods. "Its immediate goal is to bring together workers in one trade in one large organization; these organizations federate to form a state, and states federate to form one large international organization."[25] This mode would not only secure the organizational basis of society, but would also nourish recognition of the common good.

Liu's discussion is significant not for its advocacy of syndicalism, which not everyone shared, but his underlying reasoning, which was typical of *Reconstruction* socialism. His argument was echoed in an article in the third issue by an Yu Shang who criticized syndicalism for downplaying the importance of the state, and instead proposed guild socialism as "the only way to liberate the worker."[26] To Yu, guild socialism had one distinct advantage over syndicalism: it recognized the rights not only of producers, but also of consumers. Under guild socialism, the guilds would represent the rights of the producers, the state those of the consumers. Cooperation would guarantee a harmonious relationship between the two that was essential to a good socialist order.

> Guild socialism represents a kind of social system that makes the trade association of producers into the basis of economic organization. It does not merely seek to revive the guilds of the medieval period, but takes as its ideal the national guild organizations of the modern economy; in other words, to organize national guilds from workers in each trade, including manual and mental workers. Each trade is then regulated democratically by the guild representing the trade, which makes possible the abolition of the present wage system. Its most important aspect is, on the one hand, to realize industrial democracy—the producers managing their own production—and, on the other hand, to manage all other questions in cooperation with the state, in order to avoid the danger of sacrificing the rights of consumers to those of the producers.[27]

To avoid misunderstanding, Yu added that the recognition of the state did not simply superiority of politics over economic organization. He viewed guild socialism as a compromise between state socialism and syndicalism, a compromise that leaned heavily toward syndicalism. His objection to syndicalism was that it ignored the rights of consumers. State socialism, on the other hand, he viewed as merely a modified form of capitalism, a "state capitalism" which perpetuated anarchy in production, while increasing the despotism of consumer over producer. But his primary objection to state socialism was its undemocratic nature. "State capitalism is contrary to democracy, it is in reality nothing but a kind of bureaucratism [*guanliao zhuyi*]." He elaborated:

> The common point between guild socialism and state socialism is that they both advocate the reversion of the means of production, such as land, mines, factories, machinery, and so forth, to the state which represents the whole of society. Their greatest difference is in the management of production. Under collectivism [*jichan zhuyi*], the state manages all production, replacing dispersion with unity, the will of the individual with the will of the collectivity; it does not wish to allow others to manage production, but desires to accumulate all power in the state. In other words, collectivism wishes to utilize the state to establish socialism; hence it is called state socialism. Guild socialism, on the other hand, wishes to realize democracy of production, to abolish the wage system, and to make guilds into the foundation of the economy.[28]

These discussions help us understand the methods *Reconstruction* writers suggested. Education and cultural transformation were fundamental, but both were conceived in a specific organizational context. Whether the guild or the syndicate, *Reconstruction* writers discovered in the "small group" the means to reorganize society and to create spaces for the education (in its most basic sense) necessary to the creation of a "new civilization." The dialectic between cultural transformation and social reorganization from below had informed much speculation during the May Fourth period. Guild socialism now introduced this dialectic into socialist thinking. To socialists who feared class conflict, guilds offered the possibility of achieving socialism nonviolently. Guilds also offered the means toward social equality without giving up on democracy, dear to the hearts of many during this period.

These ideas were articulated in all their breadth in an essay published in December by Zhang Dongsun, entitled "Why Must We Discuss Socialism?" Written in dialogue form, which enjoyed considerable vogue at this time, the essay overruled objections to socialism and explained Zhang's conception of it.

Zhang gave a number of reasons for the importance of socialism to China; most prominent were socialism's spiritual, moral strengths. The origins of socialism, he pointed out, lay in the demands of the proletariat for equality with capital. The development of modern "material civilization" had given rise to a situation where "the rich got richer and the poor, poorer." Socialism, which had arisen in response to this situation, appeared, therefore, as an "economic question," a "class question." This had been the case especially

Review more of a private undertaking in which Guomindang writers participated extensively. In October, *Weekend Review* followed the lead of *Construction* in publishing in its "Double Ten" issue Sun's plan for national industrial development. A program outlining "The Future of National Construction" published in the June 15 issue (probably written by Dai himself) followed Sun's idea of "people's livelihood" almost to the letter. If neither journal named the Guomindang's particular brand of socialism, its premises were inscribed on every page of their discussions.

The outstanding characteristic of that socialism, going back to Revolutionary Alliance days, had been its insistence that the problem of inequality in contemporary society rested not in capital but landownership. This premise remained central even as Guomindang writers recognized in 1919 the consequences of China's burgeoning industrial development. The Double Ten issue published a lengthy discussion by the important Guomindang leader Liao Zhongkai, entitled "The Task of Continuing the Revolution." Liao elaborated on Sun's idea of "people's livelihood," and argued that the land question was the key to resolving China's economic problems. As earlier in the Revolutionary Alliance journal *People's Journal (Minbao)*, where he had first discussed the issue, Liao placed the burden for social inequality on the owners of land. They benefited from the increase of land value with economic development but did not contribute themselves to the production of value. (Sun Yatsen had first gotten this idea from Henry George.) "Peasants, workers, merchants, and capitalists all produce," Liao stated, "but it is the owners of land who take the largest portion of the profits as if the rest of society consisted of horses and cows working for them."[13] He pointed to the Russian Revolution to warn that the worse the land problem got, the more drastic must be the solution. Solving it at the present, before Chinese society had experienced significant development and inequality, would make the task considerably easier. Liao's analysis confirmed a belief shared by most Guomindang writers, that socialism did not preclude alliance with "merchants and capitalists" who, with peasants and the working class, suffered at the hands of the landowning classes.

In 1905 Revolutionary Alliance theoreticians could argue with some plausibility that China did not yet suffer from the severe inequalities of industrial society. Such arguments appeared less convincing in 1919, when they recognized the existence of conflict betwen workers and capitalists. The strategy they had advocated earlier, moreover, had meant social change coming from above, through the agency of the state. The appearance of class-based people's movements in 1919 challenged this belief, and some of the Guomindang came close to accepting the necessity of taking up the leadership of these movements. Nevertheless, they perceived the tasks of this leadership to be as much to keep movements from below under control as to promote the class interests of the oppressed. In 1919, many among radical intellectuals shared in this belief. Only when a more clear-cut class orientation to socialism emerged over the next two years did Guomindang socialism come under suspicion, placing strains upon Guomindang theoreticians themselves. In this process, the new Communist intellectuals would also gradually "forget" the very significant contribution of Guomindang writers in 1919 to the propagation of Marxism in China in its initial phase.

Among the revolutionary leaders of the Guomindang, perhaps the lone exception to this assessment at this time was Zhu Zhixin, whom Martin Bernal has described as the most radical among Guomindang socialists as far back as Revolutionary Alliance days. Among May Fourth socialists, Zhu and Li Dazhao came closest to concluding that class struggle must be an integral part of the Chinese revolution. When in 1920 Zhu wrote, "class struggle is not an imaginary method, it is a fact of contemporary society; all you need to do is look at the facts of history to see that they are all expressions of class struggle," it may be significant that he made this statement in the anarchist periodical *Fujian Star,* sponsored by Chen Jiongming, with whom he served as the Guomindang liaison at the time.[14] Zhu's death in 1920 deprived the Guomindang of one of its most revolutionary socialist leaders.[15]

The Guomindang conception of politics, as it began to assume visible form in 1919, was a corporatist one, what Philip Schnitter has described as "state corporatism."[16] While writers such as Dai Jitao pointed to guild socialism, with its implications of decentralized political power, as the form that might be most appropriate for China, the state was essential to the Guomindang conception. This conception recognized the existence of class and class oppression as a fundamental social given, but rejected class conflict as a means of resolving class oppression, attempting instead to devise ways of reconciling conflicting class interests through the agency of the state. No one class could—or should—rule society; the working class should be educated so as to establish labor unions to represent its interests in a political process that included other classes. The Guomindang's conception of the state as a clearing-house for conflicting social interests went back to Revolutionary Alliance days.

Dai's attitude was typical of May Fourth socialist thinking, which rejected capitalism but remained highly dubious of the transfer of power to the laboring classes, especially the idea that class struggle and "the dictatorship of the proletariat" were the means to effect such a transfer. Even those who wrote passionately about the plight of the Chinese working class could not yet see in its liberation the key to the liberation of all humanity.

The Guild Socialists of the Research Clique

Similar premises guided the socialism propagated in various publications associated with the Research Clique, chief among them *Reconstruction.*[17] The guiding spirit behind these in the early May Fourth period was Zhang Dongsun, an Anglophile intellectual and admirer of Bertrand Russell. Without a clear ideology such as the Three People's Principles to direct them, these publications were even more eclectic in their socialism than the Guomindang journals. In their pages the ideological positions range from the class advocacy of Li Dazhao, to the state socialism of Zhang Junmai (who was most attracted to German socialism), to syndicalism and anarchism. It was Zhang Dongsun's socialism that set the tone for *Reconstruction,* however, and made guild socialism its trademark.

Chinese historians have predictably been quite harsh on the socialism of Zhang Dongsun, and other contributors to *Reconstruction,* whose writings often leave the impression that they were intended as much to undercut class struggle as promote it. This impression is enhanced by the opposition to Bolshevism and the pervasive liberal tone. Above all, however, it is the political activities of the Research Clique that render suspect its members' socialism. Members of the Research Clique, then the Progressive Party (*Jinbudang*), had been involved with the *bête noire* of the Republic, Yuan Shikai (after 1911), and continued to flirt with warlord governments into the twenties. Their leader, Liang Qichao, had been opposed to socialism since his debates with the Revolutionary Alliance in 1905–1907, and, rightly or wrongly, was perceived as a conservative opponent of revolution. In 1919, when modern labor unions did not yet form a significant social force, Zhang's guild socialism easily looked like an abstract intellectual exercise, whose only aim could be to defuse conflict between labor and capital.

Guild socialism commands our attention, however, not only because of its intrinsic interest, but even more so because, of all those that appeared in China in the May Fourth period, it was in some ways the socialism most deeply imbued with the hues of May Fourth thinking. Uncertainty over the question of classes or the Soviet Union was pervasive in the May Fourth period, and does not cast sufficient doubt on the seriousness of the guild socialists, any more than on the socialism of the Guomindang socialists, Chen Duxiu, or even Li Dazhao. Zhang Dongsun continued to advocate socialism in later years and in the 1940s threw his valuable support behind Mao's New Democracy. His association with the Research Clique, moreover, does not imply that his socialism was merely a disguise for their anti-revolutionary tendencies; it only reveals, as with the Guomindang writers, the complexities in the relationship between ideological attraction and political affiliation in these years. He was himself chastised by Liang Qichao for his advocacy of socialism; indeed, in late 1920 Liang moved in to take over the editorship of *Reconstruction* in person to put an end to its advocacy of socialism (an unnecessary move since by that time Zhang, faced with the establishment of the Communist party, had already begun to retreat from his position).

In 1919 guild socialism seemed to offer a means of social reorganization whose appeals extended beyond Zhang Dongsun and his followers and for awhile held the attention of most radicals, ranging from Dai Jitao to Chen Duxiu and Li Dazhao. This appeal was twofold. First, in the May Fourth intellectual atmosphere, when anarchist ideals remained coupled to Marxist social analysis, guild socialism seemed to combine the best of what anarchism and Marxism had to offer. This appeal was supported, secondly, by the simultaneous suspicion of class struggle and lack of faith in the Chinese state, an existing cause of political disorder. Guild socialism offered the possibility of reorganizing Chinese society from the bottom up, without resort to either class struggle or a moribund state.

To the extent that *Reconstruction* pieces advocated class struggle, it was a class struggle that directed attention away from conflict between labor and capital. We have referred in Chapter 4 to Zhou Fohai's December 1919 discussion welcoming class struggle to China. His "welcome," however, was intended in fact to show that the struggle between labor and capital was still irrelevant. Zhou presented class struggle as the expression of conflicting class interests but he held that, thanks to China's industrial backwardness, it might still be able to escape class conflict and revolution of the kind that awaited European society. His was a moralistic, anarchist-inspired notion of classes. According to him, China did not yet have a "middle class"; there was no need, therefore, to even speak of conflict between labor and the middle class. The major division in Chinese society was between a "parasitic" class that did not engage in productive activity (which included not only vagabonds but militarists and bureaucrats as well), and a producing class exploited by the parasites. The task in China was, therefore, to unify the "self-sufficient" (*ziji*) classes to overthrow the parasitic classes.

> Is there a way to overthrow the parasitic class by the power of the working class? Of course not. Therefore it is necessary to form a self-sufficient class to struggle with the parasites. . . . To reform society, it is necessary to get rid of obstacles to reform. The obstacle in China is the parasitic class; therefore, it is necessary first to overthrow the parasitic class. To overthrow the parasitic class, it is necessary to unify the self-sufficient class, and to engage in class struggle against the parasites. This is China's class struggle.[18]

In China, therefore, class struggle was against the elite that lived off the labor of others. The idea was as much moral as social structural.

Zhou Fohai's views may explain why, after a brief flirtation with the Communist party (as one of its founding members), he emerged in the mid-1920s as a foremost Guomindang theoretician of revolution. In the May Fourth period, when Marxist and anarchist ideas of class were not yet clearly distinguished but superimposed one upon the other, his notion expressed a widespread, profound ambiguity over the question of class as structural and moral concept. Guild socialism's solution addressed both aspects of the question: eliminating class as *structural* determinant of society, while creating the conditions for the realization of a social morality that class society precluded. The anarchist inspiration in guild socialism was evident in its strategy of change: education grounded in the reorganization of society from the bottom up.

In 1919, others writing for *Reconstruction*, notably Zhang Dongsun, agreed with Zhou's diagnosis of the major line of class division in China. The great majority of them, however, saw the task of social reorganization as construction, not destruction: rather than concentrate on analysis of this relationship, and ways to overthrow the parasitic class, they devoted their attention to alternative possibilities of social reconstruction that would render parasitism irrelevant, and liberate the whole society in the process. This was reflected in the full title of *Reconstruction, Jiefang yu gaizao*, literally *Liberation and Reform* (it was changed simply to *Gaizao* [*Reform*] when Liang took over in 1920).

Zhang Dongsun, like Dai Jitao, perceived socialism not as a revolutionary ideology, but as a means to bring labor and capital together in a new kind of social organization. His complexity as a socialist easily matched Dai's. Like Dai, Zhang was responsible during the May Fourth period for the dissemination of information on Marxism as well as the Russian Revolution. The publications he had a hand in included, in addition to *Reconstruction, Morning News* in Beijing, and *Current Affairs* and *Light of Learning* in Shanghai—all major sources on the Russian Revolution, Marxism, and socialism. Zhang had a complex attitude toward Marxism, and on occasion spoke approvingly of the Revolution, but was highly suspicious of both violent revolution and the idea of class struggle. Much of the material in these publications concerning the Revolution was intended as a warning. Zhang himself believed that the Revolution had been a consequence of the Czarist government's suppression of free speech and its inability to meet the most basic needs of the people. Suppression of discussion of the Revolution, or of socialism, in China, would only fuel the fires of revolution. To him, as to many of his contemporaries, the Russian Revolution offered much that Chinese could learn from, if only by way of negative example. Similarly, the discussion of socialism should not be suppressed because it showed the way to improving people's livelihood and, thereby, forestalling the possibility of revolution.[19]

This attitude toward socialism shaped these publications' discussions of class. Even before the May Fourth Movement, an article in *Light of Learning* by Ke Yiceng, "Socialism and China," described the goal of social reform as "the elimination of the ingredients for social revolution."[20] Liu Nangai, a prolific writer on socialism in these publications, argued in July 1919 that the best way to control "extremism" was to apply selectively the rational elements in socialism. The fear of extremism, moreover, was not simply ideological, but displayed a suspicion of the Chinese working class similar to that of Dai Jitao. In May 1919, *Light of Learning* warned students against inciting laborers to action.

> Our national salvation movement should not ignore laborers. But Chinese laborers are unorganized and, for the most part, ignorant. . . . Their patriotism is fervent to the point of stupidity, and can easily lead to violence with great harm to everyone. Efforts to unify laborers require much, much caution.[21]

This wariness of labor fashioned *Light of Learning*'s response to the June Third movement. An article published almost immediately on June 10, "1919 and Labor," hailed the strike in Shanghai as the beginning of a "new era" for Chinese labor, and predicted, with precocity, that 1919 would be "the year of labor." At the same time, however, the author urged "learned laborers" to educate "ignorant laborers," and called upon students and educators in Shanghai to take advantage of the boycott of classes to establish "labor support groups" which could enter factories to lecture to laborers and educate them. He also voiced fears of the strike taking a violent turn, and called upon Chinese capitalists to continue to pay laborers so as to support the anti-foreign strikes, since these strikes were aimed not at capital, but foreigners.[22]

These writers, while their attitudes were similar to Guomindang writers' on labor and class, even more explicitly called on capital to cooperate in the education of laborers. In January 1920, Zhang Dongsun's *Current Affairs* would start to publish a new supplement, *Friend of Industry and Commerce* (*Gongshangzhi yu*), intended to awaken capital to this obligation. The new supplement was edited by Ke Yiceng, who was also at this time the editor of *Light of Learning*. While the new supplement on occasion published articles intended to stimulate greater class consciousness among laborers, its goal was to promote conciliation. Like the Guomindang writers, these contributors believed that greater class consciousness among laborers was necessary to the organization of labor, which in turn would enhance the possibilities of reconciliation between labor and capital. The anti-revolutionary intention of *Friend of Industry and Commerce* was quite evident in its use of the revolutionary idea of "the sanctity of labor" to persuade laborers that one of their sacred obligations was the labor they owed their employers![23]

While these contributors bore a remarkable similarity to Guomindang socialists, they differed in their evaluation of the agency of a peaceful social transformation. While some Guomindang writers such as Dai also flirted with the idea of change from below in 1919, to the extent that their political formulations were shaped by Sun's Three Principles, the state was essential to their conception of socialism. Similarly, some Research Clique contributors, most prominent among them Zhang Junmai, rested their hopes on the agency of the state. The majority, however, including Zhang Dongsun, were as suspicious of the state as of class struggle. They discovered their models in decentralized forms of socialism, chief among them syndicalism and guild socialism. The discussion of these, and advocacy of guild socialism, was the most distinctive feature of *Reconstruction,* which started publication in September 1919 under Zhang Dongsun's editorship.

An article by Liu Nangai in the first issue of the journal sounded a note similar to Dai's. Liu welcomed the rise of labor consciousness and expressed hopes in the establishment of a labor federation that would represent workers' interests. He was not too optimistic about the future of labor; the basis for unity among laborers was weak, in his opinion, because Chinese industry was yet underdeveloped. Only in Shanghai was there sufficiently large industry to form the basis for unions, and even there laborers lay prostrate before the power of capitalists and labor bosses, too ignorant and unorganized to engage capital in a genuine struggle. The situation was even worse for nonproletarian laborers, who worked under the "sweating system" (*sic*).[24]

Under the circumstances, Liu believed, the only way out was syndicalism of the type practiced in France and England. According to him, in spite of all their differences over method, all socialisms shared one goal: to relieve the plight of the working class by abolishing the private ownership of land and capital. Syndicalism contained the best of socialism. "Socialism" (meaning social democracy) relied on the state for its success, which was not only unwise, but impractical in China. Others of a more radical persuasion (anarchists?) advocated revolutionary methods such as the general strike, which presupposed a kind of education Chinese workers did not have. Syndicalism, on the other hand, steered clear of the government, and also offered the means to education. Syndicates would not only guarantee the equal distribution of the fruits of labor, but also provide spaces for the cultivation of habits of self-management and cooperation. The advantage of syndicalism over state-oriented socialism was that it required self-reliance, instead of reliance on unreliable governments; state socialism, Liu believed, had always accrued to the advantage of capital, not labor. Unlike anarchism, on the other hand, syndicalism allowed for a positive attitude toward government, refusing to call for its immediate overthrow, which was impractical. The key to liberation was not destruction but education in self-government. Perhaps the greatest advantage of syndicalism, however, was in its organizational methods. "Its immediate goal is to bring together workers in one trade in one large organization; these organizations federate to form a state, and states federate to form one large international organization."[25] This mode would not only secure the organizational basis of society, but would also nourish recognition of the common good.

Liu's discussion is significant not for its advocacy of syndicalism, which not everyone shared, but his underlying reasoning, which was typical of *Reconstruction* socialism. His argument was echoed in an article in the third issue by an Yu Shang who criticized syndicalism for downplaying the importance of the state, and instead proposed guild socialism as "the only way to liberate the worker."[26] To Yu, guild socialism had one distinct advantage over syndicalism: it recognized the rights not only of producers, but also of consumers. Under guild socialism, the guilds would represent the rights of the producers, the state those of the consumers. Cooperation would guarantee a harmonious relationship between the two that was essential to a good socialist order.

> Guild socialism represents a kind of social system that makes the trade association of producers into the basis of economic organization. It does not merely seek to revive the guilds of the medieval period, but takes as its ideal the national guild organizations of the modern economy; in other words, to organize national guilds from workers in each trade, including manual and mental workers. Each trade is then regulated democratically by the guild representing the trade, which makes possible the abolition of the present wage system. Its most important aspect is, on the one hand, to realize industrial democracy—the producers managing their own production—and, on the other hand, to manage all other questions in cooperation with the state, in order to avoid the danger of sacrificing the rights of consumers to those of the producers.[27]

To avoid misunderstanding, Yu added that the recognition of the state did not simply superiority of politics over economic organization. He viewed guild socialism as a compromise between state socialism and syndicalism, a compromise that leaned heavily toward syndicalism. His objection to syndicalism was that it ignored the rights of consumers. State socialism, on the other hand, he viewed as merely a modified form of capitalism, a "state capitalism" which perpetuated anarchy in production, while increasing the despotism of consumer over producer. But his primary objection to state socialism was its undemocratic nature. "State capitalism is contrary to democracy, it is in reality nothing but a kind of bureaucratism [*guanliao zhuyi*]." He elaborated:

> The common point between guild socialism and state socialism is that they both advocate the reversion of the means of production, such as land, mines, factories, machinery, and so forth, to the state which represents the whole of society. Their greatest difference is in the management of production. Under collectivism [*jichan zhuyi*], the state manages all production, replacing dispersion with unity, the will of the individual with the will of the collectivity; it does not wish to allow others to manage production, but desires to accumulate all power in the state. In other words, collectivism wishes to utilize the state to establish socialism; hence it is called state socialism. Guild socialism, on the other hand, wishes to realize democracy of production, to abolish the wage system, and to make guilds into the foundation of the economy.[28]

These discussions help us understand the methods *Reconstruction* writers suggested. Education and cultural transformation were fundamental, but both were conceived in a specific organizational context. Whether the guild or the syndicate, *Reconstruction* writers discovered in the "small group" the means to reorganize society and to create spaces for the education (in its most basic sense) necessary to the creation of a "new civilization." The dialectic between cultural transformation and social reorganization from below had informed much speculation during the May Fourth period. Guild socialism now introduced this dialectic into socialist thinking. To socialists who feared class conflict, guilds offered the possibility of achieving socialism nonviolently. Guilds also offered the means toward social equality without giving up on democracy, dear to the hearts of many during this period.

These ideas were articulated in all their breadth in an essay published in December by Zhang Dongsun, entitled "Why Must We Discuss Socialism?" Written in dialogue form, which enjoyed considerable vogue at this time, the essay overruled objections to socialism and explained Zhang's conception of it.

Zhang gave a number of reasons for the importance of socialism to China; most prominent were socialism's spiritual, moral strengths. The origins of socialism, he pointed out, lay in the demands of the proletariat for equality with capital. The development of modern "material civilization" had given rise to a situation where "the rich got richer and the poor, poorer." Socialism, which had arisen in response to this situation, appeared, therefore, as an "economic question," a "class question." This had been the case especially

since Marx, the founder of "scientific socialism," who had presented socialism primarily as an economic question. Nevertheless, argued Zhang, Marx's
socialism was not sufficiently comprehensive, and there was no reason to
restrict socialism to the meaning he had attached to it. Since his time, socialism had been transformed from a class concern (that of the proletariat) into
a general concern of the whole society; at the present, even aristocrats were
studying socialism. Socialism had changed accordingly: "Materialism" (*weiwu
zhuyi*) had given way to "spiritualism" (*jingshen zhuyi*), and "single-class-
ism" (*yijieji zhuyi*) had given way to "whole-worldism" (*quanshijie zhuyi*).[29]

Socialism, in other words, was no longer simply an economic or class
matter but, even more fundamentally, a matter of "life outlook and world
outlook" (*rensheng guan*). It required for its realization the transformation
not only of all existing structures, but of the human spirit itself—in other
words, the creation of a new morality. The difficulties of modern society,
Zhang conceded, lay in the rapacity of capitalism; but that itself could be
traced to what Bertrand Russell called "the possessive impulse." Ultimately,
the eradication of this possessive impulse was a prerequisite to the creation
of socialism, which was not merely a new economic system but a "new
civilization," what Zhang on occasion termed "the Third Civilization." This
civilization required the transcending of old morality as a whole, that of the
bourgeoisie as well as the proletariat. As long as the old morality persisted,
socialism would merely lead to new forms of rapacity.[30]

In China the old morality was on the decline with the transformation of
the old economic system. The new material civilization, however, could not
be counted on to bring about the kind of morality appropriate to the creation
of socialism. In the first place, industrial development would only bring about
further absorption by foreign imperialism. Even material development faced
serious obstacles in internal disorder. Development, moreover, created capitalists, and added the rapacity of capitalism to the parasitism of existing
social forces, in particular the family. "I often say that China does not have
a society, just a collection of families. Now to that has been added capitalism, which only sees money, but ignores people. How can we have humane-
ness [*rendao*] in this kind of nation which has only families but no society,
which only sees money but ignores people?"[31] Spiritual transformation was
necessary not only to the establishment of socialism, but to China's economic
development and integration as well. Indeed, at this point in the argument,
Zhang's remarks were addressed not to materialist socialists, but to those who
held that "industrialization would save the country" (*shiye jiuguo*). Socialism was a prerequisite to China's development, in other words, and socialism
itself presupposed the spiritual transformation of the people.

Zhang pointed to the many socialisms in the West as examples Chinese
could choose from. As far as he was concerned, China differed from other societies not in "nature" but in level of development. He would not at this time
specify what socialism might be best. The immediate task, he asserted rather
uncharacteristically, was destruction; not by the few, but by the many, to
purge old society of its ills. If there was to be construction, he reaffirmed, it

should be in the direction of socialism. There is some evidence, however, that Zhang thought socialism was more than just a historical tendency. In an essay in mid-1920, he described socialism as the expression of a "natural" desire among human beings for "equality, freedom, and 'reaching-upward' [*xiangshang*]," which encompassed the spheres in human life respectively of economics, politics, and culture.[32] If people rejected socialism, in other words, it was because they were out of touch with their own innermost inclinations.

When Zhang asked himself rhetorically what the steps were to a socialist society, his answer was that there was none—only a direction, and spiritual at that. The closest he came to specifying a method at this time was when he said:

> When we discuss socialism, it is not in order to start with the task of destroying the material basis of the present system; it is to propagate new thought, new morality, a new life outlook, a new life so as to destroy the habits of capitalism [*zibenzhuyidi xiguan*] in present-day society.[33]

Education and cultural transformation in their most basic sense, in other words, were to provide the answer to a problem that was profoundly spiritual and cultural in nature.

Zhang did not declare himself a guild socialist until 1920, but his tendencies were implicit earlier. While he more than once lauded revolutionary methods, his appreciation of socialism was basically cultural, and so were the methods he proposed. Among all the radicals prominent in the discussion of socialism in 1919–1920, Zhang was possibly the most "intellectual," consumed by constant doubt about his own advocacy, or the efficacy of the ideas he propagated. That he may have felt something of a black sheep within the Research Clique did not help.

In 1920, when Zhang engaged his Research Clique colleague Zhang Junmai in a debate over socialism, he concluded ominously, predicting "revolution, several revolutions which no one had the power to forestall."[34] Earlier in the discussion, he expressed admiration for Lenin's revolution, but he deemed it irrelevant as a model because Chinese were too backward: "This is not the time to establish a dictatorship in China of the poor [*pinmin*]; we can only try to change the personalities of the poor. If this personality is not improved, all talk of social revolution will be empty. If China is to undergo social reform, it will take another fifty years."[35]

Zhang wrote these lines at a difficult time in his life. He was under pressure from Liang Qichao to abandon his socialism, and had just broken with his erstwhile radical associates in Shanghai, such as Chen Duxiu, who had already turned to the establishment of a Bolshevik party in China. He declared at the end of his discussion that in the future he would stay out of all political activity and devote himself to the study of culture. His concluding lines—that he "had neither the power to make revolution nor a means to stop it"—were those of a resigned man who could commit himself to no more than cultural activity that might serve to "bring reason" to the inevitable revolution that he perceived on the horizon. It is fair to say, however, that his difficulties only brought to the surface the cultural orientation which had been present in his thinking since 1919. His break with radical socialists only strengthened this tendency. Within a few months, when he would engage his former radical colleagues, now turned Communists, in a debate over socialism, cultural change would almost totally overshadow his earlier concern with material change. Although he never renounced socialism (he turned again to it in the 1930s), his socialism, highly abstract to start with, would become even more abstract and intellectualized to the point of political irrelevance as he sought to distance himself from Bolshevism.

It was during his debate with Zhang Junmai that Zhang first expressed clearly his attraction to guild socialism. The reasons he gave for this attraction are revealing of the considerations that had guided *Reconstruction* socialism since September 1919.

> My views of late have been leaning toward guild socialism. The principles of guild socialism combine the advantages of anarchism and syndicalism. Anarchism tells me that state and society are two different things. The state is an organization of coercion; society is an organization that follows the inclinations of human nature. The power of the coercive organization gets broader in scope with statism and parliamentarism. The goal of statism is to expand the power of the state abroad; parliamentarism seeks to absorb all within its legislative organs. The more this power expands, the less equality there is, and the more the legislative organs expand, the less freedom there is. The reason for the rise of anarchism is opposition to these two tendencies. . . . I believe that we must restrict political power within the smallest possible unit, and not allow it to expand, in order to allow for free development outside of politics. . . . In short, I have absorbed the spirit of anarchism, but have not become an anarchist, because I want to restrict politics within the smallest possible scope without abolishing it. Because within a restricted scope, politics can be useful. . . . Hence I oppose only state ownership of property which concentrates economic power, and parliamentarism which concentrates political power.[36]

Zhang's statement may explain why, under his editorship, *Reconstruction* was a major publisher of discussions of anarchist social and economic theory. While he was more explicit than other contributors to *Reconstruction* in acknowledging his anarchist inspiration, they shared his suspicion of the state as an obstacle to democracy and freedom, an important motive in their choice of guild socialism as a form that promised both equality *and* democracy.

Zhang's choice was not based simply on ideological considerations, however, for he also saw in the small-scale organization of guilds and syndicates an answer to practical problems. As already noted, Zhang frequently stated that China "does not have a society but is simply an aggregate of countless families." The reorganization of China through guilds, or rather "small groups" (*xiao zuzhi*), of which guilds were one, would provide the means not only to the realization of socialism but to the creation of a society. This society would be cohesive, but also egalitarian and democratic or, as a translation from Japanese put it, "the democracy of society."[37]

Guild socialists did not put political ahead of economic questions, as their preoccupation with the state, or with democracy and freedom, might imply; indeed, their insistence on the priority of economic over political reorganization was their hallmark. But they did insist that economic reorganization to bring about equality must also resolve the political question of democracy.

Theirs, too, was a corporatist solution, this time a "societal corporatism." They sought to avoid class warfare not through the intermediation of the state, as Guomindang socialism presupposed, but through a reorganization of society from the bottom up in a hierarchy of associations that guaranteed the harmonizing of conflict and the supremacy of the public interest. They never quite addressed how this reorganization was to be brought about in a class society where labor itself, by their own acknowledgment, had little power. That question was not posed sharply until sometime in the spring of 1920. Up till that point, their ideal of social reorganization through the "small group" (as we shall discuss further) carried considerable appeal among the radical intelligentsia beyond their own circle.

"Jiang Kanghu Socialism"

The name of Jiang Kanghu, the erstwhile founder of the Chinese Socialist Party, was not highly visible in 1919, but his ideas further illustrate May Fourth socialism. In 1922–1923, Jiang would reemerge on the scene, on the socialist lecturing circuit (after a trip to Moscow), advocating what he called "new democracy" and "new socialism," ideas he probably acquired in the United States around 1915.[38] According to his later recollections, he also published at this time a newspaper called *The New Land* (*Xin dalu*) which propagated socialism.[39] He had been active in spreading socialist ideas since his return from the United States in 1917. An announcement in the *Nation Daily* in June 1917 called on former members of the Chinese Socialist Party and the Society for the Discussion of Socialism to get in touch with Xie Yingbo in Shanghai.[40] Xie, the pro-Guomindang labor leader from Guangzhou, had also recently returned from the United States after a period of study at the Rand School in New York. He was anarchist in inclination. In 1919, he and the Guomindang socialist Feng Ziyu established a "Nine/Nine Club" in Guangzhou that advocated anarchism. Nevertheless, in 1918 he collaborated with Jiang Kanghu in the establishment of a Center for the Study of Socialism and a Socialist Party Preparatory Center in Guangzhou to propagate Marxist social democracy.[41] According to another reference, Jiang Kanghu was in Jinan (Shandong) in 1919, where he started a girl's school. In this school some of the first women Communists in Shandong were first introduced to socialism.[42]

Jiang's "new democracy" referred to the political aspects of the social re-organization that he proposed, "new socialism" to its economic aspects. It is noteworthy that he was the first in China to use the term "new democracy," later a crucial concept in Mao's Communism. The two usages were similar but not identical. Jiang, by his own admission, had his own peculiar social-ism; he noted at one point that people described it as "Jiang Kanghu social-ism."[43] He referred his socialism to the "scientific socialism" of Marx, but added that things had changed a great deal since Marx, and his socialism was no longer appropriate.

Jiang, too, rejected the idea of class struggle as a means to achieving so-cialism, and proposed a strategy of change both from the bottom up and the top down. His "new democracy" would be a simultaneous transformation of politics at the local and state levels. Like the guild socialists, he proposed that socialist political institutions be built from the bottom up through a hierarchy of representative institutions founded on trade associations. These would cul-minate in a parliament at the state level. "Popular" elections (restricted to "superior elements," to be determined through educational criteria and ex-aminations) would add "popular" representatives, to the parliament, guar-anteeing representation to all the different interests in society.[44]

The economic measures of Jiang's "new socialism" consisted of the so-cialization of the means of production, remuneration according to labor, and the universalization of education. The first would take the form of state and local ownership according to the particular realm of production. The second drew the most marked distinction between mental and manual labor; the for-mer was to be rewarded in excess of the latter. Finally, education would pro-pel society toward greater equality.[45] As he had from his earliest advocacy of socialism, Jiang regarded difference in education as the cornerstone of all inequality, its abolition as the key to the creation of a socialist society.[46]

Jiang's socialism was in some ways a compromise between the Guomin-dang statist orientation and guild socialism, which stressed reorganization through trade associations. Jiang's approach had always been eclectic and the various socialisms he proposed in the course of his career were always theo-retical hybrids of one kind or another. For this reason his socialism, better than any that appeared during the May Fourth period, illustrates the com-plexity of May Fourth socialist thinking and the range of problems it con-fronted. The problem was not simply economic inequality, but social, politi-cal, and cultural reconstruction. Inasmuch as socialism brought a new focus, concerns that had emerged independently of it were now also imposed upon it.

What were, finally, the salient features of May Fourth socialism? The one common to all interpretations was the rejection of capitalism; all agreed on the abolition of private property as a *sine qua non*. Believing that capitalism was on its way out in the postwar world, Chinese socialists were particularly anxious that China move toward a non-capitalist future rather than play into imperialist hands. Belief in the necessity of economic change, as the prereq-uisite of all other change, was the feature that most distinguished their thinking from the New Culture movement. In August 1918, Li Dazhao wrote that "in Russia, before the Romanovs were overthrown, and the economic system changed, no problem could be solved. Now everything has been resolved."[47] Few among China's contemporary socialists would have disputed that statement, the major lesson they had learned from the Russian Revolution, even if they did not wish to follow the Russian example.

The assurance with which May Fourth socialists predicted the demise of capitalism was not matched by a comparable assurance about the direction social revolution should take in China. While quite cognizant of socialism as an ideology of revolution, they believed that with proper foresight it could accomplish revolutionary change without violence. They welcomed the emergence of labor and class consciousness in Chinese politics, but saw in it the opportunity for not class conflict but class conciliation. Their socialism was propagated for the benefit more of the Chinese government, or the social and intellectual elite, than the working class: its underlying intention was to persuade the government, such as it was, to ameliorate the condition of the working class so as to avoid the eventuality of class struggle. The radical note they sounded on occasion belied their basic intention (and caused those in power to misunderstand it). Indeed, one of the remarkable features of May Fourth socialism was that while it derived its plausibility from the political emergence of the working class, it was motivated as much by fear of that class as sympathy for it.

This sympathy was motivated more by ethical considerations than any sense of identification. The inclusion of the working class would make politics not only more stable, but more humane. As long as the interests of the working class were excluded from politics, its sense of public interest remained deficient, which presented a threat to the political system. Beyond that, however, simple humanitarian considerations demanded the inclusion of the working class. Socialists did not conceive of the working class merely in terms of the proletariat, but included within the term all producers whose activities contributed to social existence. The exclusion of producers could only be motivated by parasitic selfish interests, which perpetuated selfishness for all. They did not view the working class, in a Marxist sense, as one that, in its universality, promised the liberation of the whole society; rather, the liberation of the working class from the oppression which kept it backward was the precondition for the creation of a humane society of mutual aid.

Accordingly, education appeared the most efficacious means. Chinese socialists in 1919 agreed that Chinese workers lacked political maturity and the intellectual qualifications for leadership. Their task was not merely to nurture the class consciousness of laborers but also to educate, even civilize them. In early 1919 Li Dazhao called on Chinese youth to go "to enlighten benighted villages so that the despotic village could be converted into a constitutional one."[48] Zhang Dongsun advocated socialism "to revolutionize the spirit of the Chinese people."[49] Dia Jitao, ironically, sounded the most populist of all when he found in socialism the means to revitalize a Chinese spirit that was being crushed by capitalism:

> Since ancient times, we Chinese have rejected "self-aggrandizement" [*zili*] in favor of "altruism" [*lita*] in "social organization." If we now revive this spirit of "altruism," and fertilize it with the "spirit of science" . . . we should have no difficulty creating "a nation of equality and peace" [*pinghe guojia*] and "a society of mutual aid" [*huzhu shehui*].[50]

Finally, given that many felt Chinese society lacked any social organization to speak of, socialism provided a means to establish a viable society. Socialist ethical ideals were not divorced from organizational considerations; indeed, the education of the working class was the obverse of its political organization. But the goal of organization, for most socialists, was not to divide but to unite society. Hence the organizational forms they advocated, be they labor unions or trade associations, had as their ultimate goal the creation of spaces for the cultivation of habits of citizenship and mutual aid. The most desirable form of organization was not by class but by trade, which would bring members together regardless of their economic place, thus providing the building blocks of a new, unified society.

May Fourth thinking shared widely in a feeling expressed early in the century by Liang Qichao and popularized in Sun Yatsen's description of China as a "pan of loose sand": that due to the subversive legacy of traditional Chinese morality, and its institutional base in the family, Chinese lacked the cohesiveness required for a viable society. Zhang Dongsun never seemed to tire of reiterating this concern, and put it most bluntly in 1920: "China has hitherto had no organization."[51] New Culture leaders had expended considerable effort to cultivate habits of organization and cooperation among youth. Socialism now extended this concern to the whole of Chinese society.

This may help explain why May Fourth socialists did not find it easy to advocate conflict. The concern for unity, a byproduct of New Culture universalism, was bolstered by a concern for the consequences of conflict for China as a nation. In its very origins, the New Culture Movement had been inspired by concern for China's plight, which—as the new intellectuals viewed it—was a consequence of the selfish pursuit of partial interest by those who controlled politics. To pursue the cause of another partial interest, that of class, was not very appealing when China was already torn by the pull of such interests. In 1919, Chinese were yet to discover Lenin, and learn to articulate an argument that class conflict, rather than dividing, might instead serve the cause of national integration.

Epilogue

The dissemination of socialism in May Fourth thinking is inseparable from the social and political phenomena that impinged upon the consciousness of Chinese intellectuals. Socialism already appeared to them as a rising world tide in the aftermath of World War I, as was dramatized in the worldwide proliferation of revolutionary social movements of which the Russian Revolution was the most prominent. The political emergence of labor in June 1919 rendered this world tide immediately relevant to China, and created a sense of urgency to resolve the problem of class before violent class struggle erupted. The significance of socialism to Chinese intellectuals rested in its promise of a peaceful resolution of this question. One of the most significant features of May Fourth socialism was its eclecticism.[1] Even socialists who identified themselves with one or another current in contemporary socialism did so for eclectic reasons. This was true of Guomindang socialists and Jiang Kanghu, who fashioned their own socialisms out of available socialist ideas. It was true of *Reconstruction* socialists who drew upon Marxism, anarchism, and syndicalism in articulating their socialism. It was true of China's "first Marxist," Li Dazhao, who found in anarchism the solution to the social problems to which Marxism pointed—and even to the problems of Marxism itself. It was true even of the anarchists, the most purist of all, some of whom were unwilling to reject out-of-hand Marxist ideas of class struggle or even Bolshevik approaches to the problems of revolution.

This prevailing eclecticism points to more than one inspiration, and more than one future direction. In other words, it was not simply a product of the inspiration or model provided by the Russian Revolution; nor did it point to a Bolshevik future. Many of the ideas socialists advocated at this time predated the Russian Revolution in China. Others were inspired by contemporary socialist currents in Europe and North America. The Russian Revolution unmistakably intensified Chinese radicals' attraction to socialism as a "world tide," but its role as a model was quite dubious; for many it was a warning.

It is also clear that Chinese socialism in 1919 was not written in a Marxist code. By the end of the year, Marxism had acquired an important place in radical thinking as a "scientific" mode of social analysis. It also provided a vocabulary for the new awareness of class conflict. On the other hand, Chinese socialists of the May Fourth period did not share Marx's views of the proletariat, or Marxist solutions to the problems Marxist analysis revealed. Since most of the literature on Marxism was published within the context of socialist publications that rejected class struggle or violent revolution, Marxism appeared as a social philosophy whose truths were partial and politics reformist. To the extent that Marxism was accepted as a revolutionary social philosophy, it was rejected on practical grounds as a source more of division than of future promise, and on ethical grounds as an extension of some of the most basic, and undesirable, premises of capitalist society.

Marxism and anarchism held a comparable place in May Fourth socialist thinking as the grounds for socialist discourse in general: the vocabulary of Marxist social analysis was as much a part of the language of radicalism as was the vocabulary of the anarchist vision. Marxism appeared in a cerebral guise, as a scientific explanation of social change. Anarchism appeared in a quotidian cultural guise, as an ethical guide to the realization of the socialist vision. By late 1919 this mixed vocabulary was common to all Chinese socialism; for the same reason, the mere presence of the vocabulary serves as a poor guide to ideological loyalty or exclusive commitment to one or the other strategy of political change. Anarchism and Marxism appeared as antinomic principles of social change, each of which had something to contribute to the process of social revolution.

The opposition between the two philosophies became clear early on, mainly through anarchist or anarchist-inspired critiques of Marxism. The most important division was over the issue of the state. Marxism's association with the Russian Revolution or with German-style social democracy made it, in anarchist eyes, a philosophy founded on the reprehensible concept of authority. Anarchists' publications were at one in this criticism. And the issue spilled over to other publications. As early as April 1919, letters in *Morning News* engaged in a debate over the relative virtues of Marxism and anarchism. This debate, in which Wang Guangqi defended the anarchists' position, divided socialism into two currents, state socialism or "collectivism" (*jichan zhuyi*) and anarchism or "communism" (*gongchan zhuyi*). Advocates of the latter argued that it was important to overthrow the state in order to establish a society of "mutual aid" guided by the principle, "from each according to his ability, to each according to his need." "State socialists" rejected the need for social revolution, and argued that state policies aimed at socializing the means of production and educating the people would be sufficient to establish socialism.[2] In other words they accepted the charge of authoritarianism and used it as a plea for a reformist socialism. This contrasts interestingly with a debate in *Awakening* a year later where similar issues were raised, this time in connection with the Soviet Union. Anarchists still counterposed authority or might (*giangquan*) and "universal principle" (*gongli*), and argued that after social revolution there should be no need to revive authority as the Bolsheviks had. Their opponents' position revealed the enhanced appeal of Bolshevism in China, and changing attitudes toward authority, no longer associated with an anti-revolutionary socialism. They argued that authority was not good or bad in itself, but must be measured by the uses to which it was put. It could be employed in the service of naked might, or of universal principle (*giangquan wei gongli*). This was what the Bolsheviks had done.[3] The relative status in socialism of the two philosophies had changed; the issues were the same.

As over the role of the state, Chinese radicals were also divided over the nature of the revolutionary movement to which Marxism and anarchism pointed.[4] The Marxist idea of revolution was, in their eyes, a political conception, seeking to use political means to achieve economic transformation. The anarchist conception of revolution was social, relying on social reorganization and cultural change not only to transform the economic structure but also to abolish politics. The role of class struggle was more ambiguous. "Class struggle" did not necessarily mean violent conflict, even for those inspired by Marxism. Indeed, the frequent association of Marxism with social democracy implies that Marxism was seen as a means for avoiding class conflict. And some anarchists did advocate class struggle, but anarchist inspiration more often than not called for social reorganization and education, to abolish distinctions between classes, promising a bloodless revolution. For anarchists communal experimentation took the place of class conflict. Education to transform cultural habits was essential to this experimentation.

Finally, May Fourth radicals associated Marxism with class interest and anarchism with a broad "humanism" (*rendao zhuyi*) that transcended all particular interests including class. This perception colored both the goals and the means of revolution they associated with anarchism and Marxism. In this area they found Marxism most deficient. Before they could decide that Marxism provided all the legitimacy they needed, they would have to learn to identify the working class with "humanity" and themselves with that class.

Until then, however, the preeminent tendency in May Fourth social thought was to abolish the distinctions between Marxism and anarchism by presenting them as different means to the same goal, or to set them up as complementary, if antinomic, philosophies. Already in the May Fourth period Chinese radicals believed that Marxism offered a better explanation of the social phenomena of poverty and oppression than anarchism, and even an essential point of departure of social change. By fall 1919 Chinese socialists believed that economic transformation was crucial to social change, and that the transformation of class relations must be an essential component of economic transformation. But this transformation must be of limited value if not supplemented by the transformation of both material and spiritual culture; altruism must replace selfish interest, and free association must replace coercive social relations. Hence anarchism, which took these goals as its ideological cornerstone, represented to them the ultimate solution. Even those who came closest to advocating Marxist solutions sought to reconcile Marxism to these ideals. There was sufficient overlap between the two to justify such reconciliation, but their assimilation of Marxist means to anarchist ends compromised profoundly their barely audible Marxist professions.

Already in May Fourth thinking on Marxism, there were hints of the transformation in Chinese socialism that would take place between the May Fourth Movement and the spring of 1920. Two social developments especially gave this transformation substance. The initiation and rapid failure of the New Life Movement (*xin shenghuo yundong*)—anarchist-inspired communal experiments to transform Chinese society—which raised serious questions concerning the viability of anarchist ideas of social change. Second, Chinese labor emerged on the political scene. Over the year following the May Fourth Movement, the working class increasingly impinged on the consciousness of Chinese intellectuals, forcing a choice they had not confronted earlier. The choice was simple; its intellectual, emotional, and political implications were momentous. One alternative was to continue to speak for the working class in the name of humanity; the other was to act with the working class because its interests represented those of humanity. An article Wang Guangqi (at the time of anarchist inclination) published in *Morning News* in February 1919, "Students and Labor," stated that "To just talk loudly about labor outside the world of labor is not the same thing as entering the world of labor to change it. Those who stand outside the world of labor and talk about the interests of labor do not necessarily represent the interests of labor. One understands the misery of labor only if one enters that world in person."[5] Over the next year, some among Chinese youth tried to do just that. Anarchism was a major stimulant; Marxism helped them read what they saw. In the process, some of them discovered that Marxism not only pointed the way to material change, but also supplied the ethical values they had looked for in anarchism. They did not shed their ethical universalism, therefore, but began to think about it in "class ways." This ideological reinterpretation of New Culture humanism in light of the new consciousnes of labor would also recast as ideology the supra-class humanism which—in denying an exclusive claim to humanity of the working class—now seemed an ideological negation of working-class interests, or even a pernicious cover for the interests of the bourgeoisie. It is not surprising that as Marxism came of age in China with the assumption by some Chinese radicals of a Communist identity that permitted no compromise with alternative social philosophies (not because they understood Marxism any better), anarchism, which they had viewed earlier as complementary to Marxism, would come to appear as the foremost threat to the new identity.

PART III
From Study Society to Political Cell:
Ideology and Organization in the
Origins of Chinese Communism

Prologue

In March 1920, Gregory Voitinsky, chief of the Far Eastern Bureau of the Comintern in Irkutsk, arrived in Beijing, accompanied by his wife and several secretaries, among them a Russian Chinese Communist named Yang Mingzhai who served as his interpreter. Sergei Polevoy, a professor of Russian at Beijing University (Beida), introduced Voitinksy to Li Dazhao, and possibly the anarchist Huang Lingshuang, probably the two most prominent radical professors then at Beida. Voitinsky held several meetings there with Li and his radical students, discussing the nature of the Russian Revolution and inquiring after the conditions in China. Upon Li's recommendation, and with a letter of introduction from him, Voitinsky proceeded the following month to Shanghai to meet with Chen Duxiu. Chen was, in early 1920, still the most prominent of May Fourth intellectual leaders and, unlike Li Dazhao, whose influence was restricted to Beijing, commanded a nationwide reputation as a radical. Voitinsky held extensive meetings in Shanghai with Chen Duxiu and the group of elder radicals congregated there, including Dai Jitao and Zhang Dongsun, with whom Chen had associated closely since he had moved there from Beijing in January. Shortly thereafter Voitinsky was in southern Fujian, this time armed with a letter of introduction from the anarchists in Beijing, to confer with General Chen Jiongming and his anarchist coterie where, among other things, he presented the general with a personally autographed photograph of Lenin.[1]

In March, Li Dazhao and his radical students at Beida secretly established the Society for the Study of Marxist Theory (*Makesi xueshuo yanjiuhui*). Following Voitinsky's visit to Shanghai, a similar society came into existence there in May under Chen Duxiu's leadership, this time named Society for the Study of Marxism (*Makesi zhuyi yanjiuhui*). Over the next few months, four more such societies were established in Changsha (Hunan), Wuhan (Hubei), Jinan (Shandong) and Guangzhou (Guangdong). Another came into existence in Tokyo in the summer of 1920, followed in 1921 by one in Paris. In the summer of 1920, the society in Shanghai was converted into a Communist cell (*Gongchanzhuyi xiaozu,* literally, Communist Small Group). The others followed suit during the fall. The founding of the Communist party was under way.[2]

The rapid emergence of Communist groups, which would serve as the building blocks for the party established the following year, seemingly provides *prima facie* evidence of the maturing of Marxism over the year following the May Fourth Movement. Voitinsky's visit was obviously crucial in triggering the organization, but the very coincidence of his visit with the founding of the societies in Beijing and Shanghai suggests that it was more a catalyst than a cause; without prior preparation, his visit would probably not have had such rapid results. Where the ideological situation was not propitious, as with the anarchists in Fujian, moreover, no Communist group issued from his visit.

Voitinsky's was not the first visit to China by a representative of the Comintern. The previous summer two Bolsheviks had shown up in Tianjin. Li had reportedly established contact with them, and been "introduced" through them to Lenin's *Imperialism: The Highest Stage of Capitalism*.[3] This earlier contact had, however, barely created a ripple among Chinese radicals. Now, in the spring of 1920, the response to Voitinsky was immediate and far-reaching. For all practical purposes, the establishment of the Communist cell in Shanghai in August 1920 constituted a nucleus for the party that would be established formally under the leadership of Li and Chen a year later. By fall 1920, *New Youth,* the former organ of the New Culture movement, had been moved from Beijing to Shanghai and converted to the dissemination of information on Marxism and the Soviet Union. In November, Communists established *The Communist (Gongchandang)*, the first publication in China devoted to the propagation of Communism. A number of periodicals were established at about the same time to spread Communism among laborers. Already in May 1920, China's Communists had celebrated May Day with great fanfare in Shanghai and Beijing, as well as in provincial cities. The history of May Day, which Li penned for the occasion, was reprinted widely in periodicals and newspapers in Chinese cities, possibly bringing him the national reputation he had hitherto lacked.

The changes that got under way in late spring 1920 were extremely significant in the founding of the Party; yet where the Marxism of Chinese radicals is concerned, these changes appear much more ambiguous if we look beneath their surface. One Chinese scholar has suggested that "from the eve of the May Fourth period all the way to the first half of 1921 . . . Communist intellectuals were in transition from democracy to Communism."[4] Even after the initiation of party-building, "when they propagated Marxism, they used democracy to explain it; when they discussed materialism, they confounded it with idealism. . . . The labor organs *World of Labor, Voice of Labor,* and *Laborers,* published by the Communist groups in Shanghai, Beijing, and Guangdong respectively, explained to laborers the cause of their oppression and exploitation, and urged them to organize labor unions, but when it came to action, they stopped with economic struggles."[5] Interestingly, Zhang Jingru bases these observations on a distinction between Marxist influence and Communist identity; the former was everywhere, the latter was highly problematic: "That a person has begun to accept Marxism does not mean that he has, therefore, become a Communist; conversely, if a person does not complete his conversion from the one to the other, or ends up in error, it does not mean that he never went through the process."[6] The former part of the statement might have been meant for Li Dazhao, the latter for Chen Duxiu. In either case, as far as Zhang is concerned, the summer and fall period of 1920 was as transitional as the immediate May Fourth period, with unpredictable results for individual Communists. The organizing activities of spring 1920 were not simply the culmination of May Fourth ideological developments, finally bearing political fruit; the uncertainties concerning Marxist politics had not evaporated.

It is quite misleading, I think, to collapse the distinction between the immediate May Fourth period and the period of party-building in 1920 because the new activities of spring 1920 had profound consequences for the dynamics of Chinese socialism. Nevertheless, Zhang Jingru points us in the right direction in arguing that Marxism does not explain these activities: the appreciation of Marxism remained rudimentary past spring 1920, and those who participated in these activities remained unsure of their ideological identity. Zhou Fohai, who participated in some of Voitinsky's meetings with Shanghai radicals, recalled later that well into summer 1920, Voitinsky told them that there were two major problems with "the tides of new thought rolling into China now."

> In the first place, it is too complex. There is anarchism, there is syndicalism, there is social democracy, there is guild socialism, all kinds of thinking without a dominant current, which makes for a great deal of confusion. Secondly, there is no organization. There are many people who write essays, and spout empty words, but there is no practical activity at all. You cannot make revolution like this. He concluded with the hope that we would establish a "Chinese Communist party."[7]

Luo Zhanglong has recalled that Voitinsky sounded a similar note in Beijing, telling Li's group that what they needed most was "an organization similar to the Communist party in Russia."[8] According to Zhang Guotao, Li was unaware of Voitinsky's real mission, taking him at his word that he was a journalist. This seems unlikely, since the first Marxist organization at Beida was established during Voitinsky's first visit there when Zhang Guotao himself was away from Beijing. He was closer to the mark when he remembered that during summer 1920 Li still resisted the idea of establishing a Communist party on the grounds that Chinese still did not know enough about Marxism.[9] Indeed, it was not Li, as Chinese historiography has long claimed, but Chen Duxiu in Shanghai who took the lead in establishing the Communist cells in China during summer and fall 1920.

The continued uncertainty about Marxism, and its relationship to Communism, was evident in the Marxist study societies that were established in Voitinsky's wake. They did not have a clear ideological identity, since initially a commitment to Marxism was not a condition of membership. Socialists of various shades, and especially anarchists, participated widely in their founding; the one in Guangzhou consisted entirely of anarchists (those who had returned to Guangzhou with Chen Jiongming), with two Russian advisors.[10] Anarchists and Marxists cooperated closely in the May Day celebrations in 1920; participants recall a tone dominated by anarchism, which is corroborated by the contemporary press.[11] This cooperation continued into fall 1920, when anarchists were still responsible for publishing the periodicals sponsored by the new Communist groups. Not until late fall 1920, as Marxist study groups began their transformation into Communist cells, did the question of identity emerge as important. And not until early 1921 did an exclusive Communist identity emerge. Ideologically, 1920 was still a period of transition.

The Chinese Communist Party was not to achieve organizational coherence until its second congress in 1922, and ideological ambiguities persisted well past its formal establishment. Nevertheless, Voitinsky's visit marks at once a conclusion and a new beginning. It concluded the May Fourth phase of Marxism, during which Chinese radicals had understood Marxism eclectically; and it initiated a new process, which culminated in the definition of a Marxist identity which brooked no eclecticism, and which took Marxist social and philosophical postulates, as defined by Bolshevism, as the premise of a total social outlook. To be sure, the uncertainties persisted well into 1920 and beyond. But Marxism's new meaning in the context of Communist organizational activity forced new choices on May Fourth socialists, and brought a new clarity to the debate over social revolution, which had so far managed to subsume conflicting ideas within vaguely conceived visions of social liberation. For the same reasons, the relationship of Marxism after spring 1920 to May Fourth Marxism was not evolutionary but dialectical. While May Fourth developments were the indispensable precondition of the activity in 1920, the latter was not simply an evolution, or historical extension, of the former, but rather required for its emergence the suppression of its own legacy.

Organization was the key to this rupture. It disciplined the interpretation of Marxism, and separated out those who were willing to make a total commitment to a Marxist political outlook. The immediate expression of this break was the parting of the ways in late 1920 of socialists who had worked jointly until then to propagate Marxism. The establishment of an exclusive identity for those who made the commitment would take even longer. For some, this would not happen until after the formal establishment of the Party in 1921. Others, who played key roles in that founding, nevertheless dropped out shortly thereafter to pursue their own independent Marxism. Even to those who persisted to the end, the organizationally established identity would appear, under different historical circumstances, intolerably exclusive.

With the appearance of an organizationally defined Marxism, some of those who had played the most prominent roles in the propagation of Marxism in the May Fourth period quickly turned anti-Marxist. For those who chose not to do so, it became important to distinguish Marxism from Communism. Those who submitted to the new organizationally defined Marxism, most of whom had in fact not been prominent in May Fourth discussions, or done much hitherto to spread Marxism, adopted a Marxist identity that was a product not so much of any serious understanding of Marxism as of Bolshevik organizational prerogatives. The Communist identity that emerged, in other words, was shaped by organizational ideology, not an autonomous appreciation of Marxist theory. Few may have achieved this identity completely, which required total surrender to organizational norms; but certainly organizational norms now provided the counterpoint, if not the boundary, to theory, in the dialectics of political identity.

In this part, I will trace the organizational emergence of the Communist party and its conseqeunces for relationships and ideology among May Fourth socialists. The salient points may be summarized briefly. In the first place, the founding was not an overnight accomplishment but a process that took nearly two years. It got under way in March 1920, but not until 1922, with the second congress, did the membership stabilize and the Party assume the organizational and ideological visage that distinguished it in the 1920s. Nevertheless, "the organizational and ideological foundations of the Party," as Meisner has observed, were established between March and November of 1920. By November 1920 the new Communist organization had assumed the core features that would serve as the basis for formal organization the following July.

Communist organization assumed such rapid coherence, secondly, largely because of the efforts of the Comintern advisors. The Comintern did not merely "catalyze" the organization of Communism in China. Circumstantial evidence indicates that Voitinsky and his assistants participated directly in all phases and aspects of party organization. He may justifiably be viewed as the architect of the Communist party of China in the initial phase. He initiated the first organizational activities in March 1920. In November he left behind not only a core organization but a preliminary program as well.

This Communist organization thirdly, was not created out of thin air, but out of the radical movement that had its origins in the May Fourth Movement. The Communist Party of China as it emerged in 1920–1921 was the creation of May Fourth radicals. Most socialists who had participated in the propagation of Marxism during the early May Fourth period now reaffirmed their pre-May Fourth political affiliations, in response to the emergence of the Party. The new party, on the other hand, recruited its membership from among May Fourth youth, and its leadership was provided by two intellectuals, Chen Duxiu and Li Dazhao, who had renounced their "old politics" during the New Culture Movement and acquired their distinctive political personae during the May Fourth period.

These points are important for understanding the characteristics of the Communist movement in its emergence. The appearance of Communist organizations in the summer and fall of 1920 was not a spontaneous development out of May Fourth radicalism, but represented a process whereby radical societies that had formed over the previous two years were converted into political organizations. Chen Duxiu, and to a lesser extent Li Dazhao, and the personal relationships they had established with young radicals during the May Fourth period, played a key role in this reorganization. The Communist party represented a confederation of a variety of organizational forms now brought together through a personal network emanating from Shanghai and Beijing. The existence of these organizations facilitated the construction of the party. The process of organization, on the other hand, introduced two new tendencies into radical associations. One was to replace personal relationships with abstract organizational relationships. The second was to establish centrally defined ideological criteria, and organizational rules based on them, as a condition of membership. While personal relationships or local autonomy were not abolished in the Party (then or later) as basic features of its organizational dynamics, these tendencies clearly distinguished it from the previous organizational forms and imposed unprecedented demands upon them. Personal relationships, the basis for much of the previous cooperation, broke down under the pressure of these new demands. May Fourth socialists were split by the new organizational demands before they got around to enunciating their ideological basis. The debates over ideology—in particular over the relative virtues of Marxism, anarchism and guild socialism—that flared up in fall 1920 coincided with the conversion of study societies (or other intellectual clusters) into Communist cells. Central party organs that had already come into being (however inappropriate that title in terms of actual power) were to play a crucial role in the ideological and organizational reconstitution of these various associations.

The accumulating contradictions in May Fourth radicalism, as experienced by these associations, are important for understanding their receptivity to Voitinsky's message. This may be most important in the cases of Chen Duxiu and Li Dazhao because of their key roles; but I suggest that the contradictions motivating them were only more dramatic manifestations of those their younger followers also experienced—if anything, with sharper severity. The coincidence of several historical events makes it difficult to sort out the relative significance of the various factors that went into the conversion of May Fourth radicals into Communists in the spring of 1920. Rather than engage in a fruitless effort to decide which factor may have been the ultimately determining one, it is best. I think, to acquire as thorough a picture as possible. The historical trends that were becoming visible in radical thinking served as "moments" in the emergence of Communism as an organized movement ("moments" in the Marxist sense of elements, possibly interrelated but each with a momentum of its own). The relationship between these moments is best conceived in terms of the structuralist concept of "overdetermination," a conjuncture in history of autonomous, if not unrelated, moments.[12] The associations that had come into existence during the May Fourth Movement, it may be noted here, provided spaces in which the contradictions of May Fourth radicalism were articulated. These contradictions, rather than any identifiable ideological predispositions, provided the May Fourth contribution to, and the immediate precondition for, the establishment of Communism in China. The goal of organization was to resolve these contradictions. Unlike Guomindang or Research Clique socialists, who could look to their already existing affiliations to resolve these contradictions, those who established the Communist party had no organized political outlet for their radical strivings. The Party provided one.

The description of the process of party formation that follows is based for the most part on the memoirs of participants. Predictably, they do not always agree on details. The process, however, is clear enough, and its general trend is confirmed by contemporary materials. Where details are concerned, mostly involving the role of particular individuals, I have based my judgments on general agreement in the available sources, and the plausibility of their authors' claims.

8

May Fourth Radicalism at a Crossroads:
Study Societies, Communes, and
the Search for Social Revolution

In July 1921, thirteen Communists met in Shanghai, under the supervision of two Comintern advisors, to formally establish the Communist party of China. The Comintern advisors were the Dutch Communist Maring (H. Sneevliet) and a Russian named Nicolaevsky from the secretariat of the Far Eastern Bureau of the Comintern. Neither Chen Duxiu (who was in Guangzhou) nor Li Dazhao attended, although Chen was represented by Bao Huiseng. The other twelve participants represented the fifty-three members of seven local Communist groups in China and abroad. They were:

Shanghai: Li Da, Li Hanjun
Beijing: Zhang Guotao, Liu Renjing
Hunan (Changsha): Mao Zedong, He Shuheng
Hubei (Wuhan): Dong Biwu, Chen Tanqiu
Shandong (Jinan): Wang Jinmei, Deng Enming
Guangdong (Guangzhou): Chen Gongbo
Tokyo: Zhou Fohai

In the activities that brought these individuals together in July 1921 is written the history of the founding of the Communist party of China. Each had followed his own path to Shanghai, but their paths had crossed repeatedly over the previous two years, and commonly shared hopes and frustrations brought them together. It would become clear in the aftermath of this first congress, when about half left the Party they had helped found, that they did not necessarily share a common set of reasons for being in Shanghai. But when they met there, they were already part of a radical network that shared a common orientation, if not a common program; what endowed their participation with significance was their membership in groups across the face of China which, though small in numbers, exerted considerable influence in their various localities, where they had been active since May Fourth or earlier. The first congress created neither a strong organization nor a well-defined program; rather, its power then rested largely on these groups' mobilization of support in their localities. The congress formalized the existing network of Communist groups at a national level, and created an organization unprecedented in its ability to coordinate radical activities across China.

The Party was built out of informal associations of young radicals that had sprouted in major Chinese cities around the time of the May Fourth Movement. Radical associations would proliferate with the May Fourth Movement, but in places such as Beijing, Changsha, and Wuhan, they had been established before May 1919 and played a crucial part in the organization of the Movement. Some were anarchist, others were products of the New Culture Movement influenced by anarchist ideas, still others were patriotic. Once in existence, however, they became vehicles for ideology formation and propagation, in which anarchist ideas were formative. Beida played a particularly important part in the formation of this network of activists. Student groups organized there in 1918–1919 played a significant role in initiating the May Fourth Movement, and thereafter served as nuclei for the organization of students there and elsewhere (as far as Guangzhou). In these groups later Communists played key roles, though at the time little in their thinking pointed to their eventual conversion.

These associations had certain features in common. Their membership was based for the most part on personal relations, more often than not from common schooling. Membership was inclusive rather than exclusive, open to all who wanted to pursue common intellectual interests; so it tended to be fluid, and changed as interests changed. While the associations frequently changed names and membership, the few individuals who played key roles in them gave them continuity, especially in the publication activities which more than anything gave them their identity. Government suppression was a constant threat to their existence, and these persistent individuals even more important in providing continuity. Finally, these same individuals had some personal relationship or other to leaders at the national level, in particular Chen Duxiu and Li Dazhao, which made them part of an informal national radical network, and enhanced the significance of their local activities.

Brief histories follow of the seven groups represented in the first congress, plus a brief account of the one group in Paris which, though founded in 1921 (after the establishment of the Party) had its roots in these same radical activities, and contributed significantly to the initial development of Communism in China.

Beijing

In Beijing, the Communist group was recruited in 1920 from students associated with Li Dazhao, most of them from Beida. These students had a long history of common activity. When the Society for the Study of Marxist Theory (*Makesi xueshuo yanjiuhui*) was established in March 1920, its most prominent members, such as Deng Zhongxia, Luo Zhanglong, Huang Rikuei, Zhang Guotao, Liu Renjing, and Gao Shangde, were already tied by personal bonds forged in the course of radical activities that originated before the May

Fourth Movement. Their names regularly appear in the prominent organizations of the May Fourth period, and some, like Zhang Guotao, played leadership roles then. By early 1920, before Voitinsky arrived, they already constituted a radical core which was all dressed up for revolution.

The Society for the Study of Marxist Theory, according to Luo Zhanglong, benefited from the prior existence of study societies at Beida. "If we examine the process of fermentation, preparation, and organization of the Society for the Study of Marxist Theory, we will see that the radical elements represented by Li Dazhao had already on the eve of the May Fourth Movement formed an organized power which was the antecedent for the Society for Study of Marxist Theory; they initiated and led the May Fourth Movement intellectually and organizationally."[1] We have paid insufficient attention hitherto to the organized power that went into the making of the "spontaneous" outburst of student resentment at Beida on May 4, 1919. Its presence in Beijing and elsewhere lends some support to the claim that "Communists" were instrumental in the making of the May Fourth Movement—as long as we remember that Communism, Marxist Communism, was the farthest thing from their minds at the time.

The organized power at Beida had several sources. Perhaps the most important were the organizations that had come into being in the course of student protests against Japan, especially against the Mutual Assistance Agreement of 1917, which had led Chinese students to leave Japan *en masse* in protest in May 1918. Also important were the various study societies encouraged at Beida by its chancellor, Cai Yuanpei, who believed they were important instruments for the cultivation of habits of cooperation. Finally, there were the anarchist or anarchist-inspired organizations. A member of the anarchist-inspired Labor-learning Association (*gongxuehui*), established in Beijing Higher Normal College in February, played an important part in escalating the student protests of May 4, 1919, into a major confrontation between the students and the government.

Among the patriotic societies formed in protest of warlord collusion with Japan, the most important were the Young China Association (*Shaonian Zhongguo xuehui*) and the Student National Salvation Association (*Xuesheng jiuguohui*), in both of which Japan-returned students played key roles. The Young China Association, founded in June 1918, was a national organization which counted among its members in the provinces Mao Zedong, Yun Daiying, and Zhang Wentian. Its members in Beijing included, in addition to Li Dazhao, Deng Zhongxia, Gao Shangde, Shao Shiyan, Huang Rikuei, and Zhang Guotao, who all became key members of the Beijing Communist group in 1920. The Young China Association would split into two camps after 1920, with one group opting for Marxism and politics and the other group developing into the anti-revolutionary Chinese Youth Party (*Zhongguo qingnian dang*); but during the May Fourth period, its members agreed on a broad patriotic struggle for national salvation. The association's journal, *Young China (Shaonian Zhongguo)*, promoted social reform. Its leader, Wang Guangqi, was influenced by anarchism, and was a prominent promoter of anarchist ideas of social revolution in the May Fourth period. In *Young China,* he and his cohorts promoted the "small group" (*xiao zuzhi*) as the best means for reorganizing China. He was the foremost advocate and patron of the labor-learning societies in Beijing, part of the communal movement of the latter half of 1919.[2]

Similar in origins but somewhat more restricted in scope (to Beijing and Shanghai) was the Citizens' Magazine Society (*Guomin zazhishe*) which was founded in Beijing in October 1918. *Citizens' Magazine,* which we have already encountered as a prominent propagator of Marxist works in the May Fourth period, was closely associated with the Student National Salvation Association. This society counted among its members Deng Zhongxia, Zhang Guotao, Gao Shangde, Huang Rikuei, Wu Tianfang, and Yi Keyi, all of them later Communists (and some of them also members in the Young China Association). Zhang Guotao has claimed that he was responsible for founding this society; it is more likely that (as in the case of the Young China Association) students returned from Japan took the initiative in its founding and played the most important part in its activities, especially its publications, because its publications on Marxism probably were authored by Japanese or by Chinese students in Japan. Among the major publications to issue from Beida, the *Citizens' Magazine* was the most radical. There was a noticeable shift to the left in its contents in the wake of the May Fourth Movement, but it remained ideologically diffuse, counting among its members not only later Communists but anarchists and guild socialists as well.[3]

Of the specifically Beida societies, the Journalism Society seems to have been the most important in 1918 in bringing together later Communists. Two Cantonese members, Chen Gongbo and Tan Pingshan, were later instrumental in establishing the Communist group in Guangzhou. Others were Luo Zhanglong and Gao Shangde. In late 1918, when in Beijing for a short while, Mao Zedong himself participated in this society's meetings, possibly through the introduction of his fellow-Hunanese, Luo Zhanglong.[4]

Most important in the May Fourth "fermentation" was the Beijing University Common People's Education Lecturing Corps (*Beijing daxue pingmin jiaoyu jiangyantuan*). In 1920, members of this society provided the immediate "pool" for the recruitment of Communists. Zhang Guotao has claimed responsibility for founding this society as well. Whether or not he did, this society clearly recruited its members from participants in the activities of the societies just enumerated. Deng Zhongxia and Huang Rikuei were among its founding members; Deng may have played the most significant part in providing direction. As in the other societies, the lecture corps' membership and ideology were diffuse; what distinguished it was the nature of its activities, which created an immediate potential for social radicalism. While its immediate motivation was patriotic, its patriotism desired to reach beyond students to society at large. It was founded in March 1919 under the inspiration of the slogan "Go to the Masses," which was popularized in Beijing by Li Dazhao but may have originated with the anarchists. Its immediate goal in the May Fourth period was to make the population of Beijing aware of national issues.

To this end, the students organized themselves into lecture corps which held public meetings around the city to instruct the "common people" on issues of the day. In the lectures, patriotic goals were coupled with a desire to spread the new learning the New Culture movement and university education had brought to intellectuals; subjects ranged from the Shandong question, to modern philosophy, to the laws of modern physics![5]

In bringing them face to face with the common people, the lecture corps had a radicalizing effect on its participants. Zhu Wushan, who joined in early 1920, has suggested that the corps not only served as a recruiting ground for Communists but, once the Communist group in Beijing was established, became a Communist front that enabled the Party to reach out to the population.[6] By early 1920, members had extended their activities to Beijing's agrarian suburbs. At one of these locations, Zhangxindian, the Communists would launch their successful organization of labor in northern China, aided by the experiences gained and connections secured through the corps. Their initial experiences in Zhangxindian offer clues to the radicalizing process of confrontation between the students and their popular constituency.

Quite clearly, these societies at Beida, all founded before May 1919, were motivated originally by patriotic considerations. They were also expressions of the ferment of the New Culture Movement's intellectual and social concerns. Once founded, they not only promoted patriotic causes but became vehicles for the propagation of New Culture concerns. Their publications freely blended national with cosmopolitan aspirations, nationalism and anarchism, narrowly intellectual and broadly social concerns. They were active in the organization of the May Fourth Movement: their members were prominent among the students who met on May 3 at Beida to plan the next day's protest. Once the movement was under way, they were able to sustain it as organized cores. And, finally, they helped keep its broader aspirations alive after others dropped out in late June 1919 with the achievement of immediate goals. In other words, they provided the locus for continued radical activity from before the May Fourth Movement through the founding of the Party. In the process, they also served as the training ground for a group of radical activists whose names appeared on the rosters of many societies and who had already by late 1919 come to identify themselves as a cohesive group. By early 1920, on the eve of the founding of the Communist group in Beijing, they were gathered together in the Common People's Education Lecturing Corps, which had pointed to new departures in social activism that it itself was not fully equipped to sustain.

Shanghai

The organizational context for Communism in Shanghai was more complicated. Shanghai had no single commanding figure comparable to Li Dazhao at Beida. When Chen Duxiu put together the Society for the Study of Marxism (*Makesi zhuyi yanjiuhui*) in May 1920, he was a relative newcomer to the Shanghai radical scene, having arrived there from Beijing only in January. While he commanded wide respect as a nationally known intellectual, and a vast network of radical associations, he was not the only prominent figure in radical circles in Shanghai, and he lacked the organizational affiliations of other important figures such as Dai Jitao and Zhang Dongsun. Until *New Youth* was moved from Beijing to Shanghai sometime in the summer of 1920, moreover, Chen did not even have a publication organ that he controlled directly; his own influence rested largely on his association with the elder statesmen of radical politics in Shanghai who were connected with the Guomindang and the Research Clique.

Shanghai had more than one organizational center, thus radicals there were not as tightly knit as in Beijing (or certain other areas such as Changsha, Wuhan, or Jinan). This lent a certain instability to the organization of Communism and the loyalties of radicals. With the establishment of Communism under Chen's leadership, Shanghai would emerge as the nerve center for the Communist movement in China, but the center would not achieve the same coherence as its branches.

According to Shao Lizi, Fudan University professor and editor of the influential *Nation Daily* (and its supplement, *Awakening*), who joined the Communist party in the early 1920s while still a member of the Guomindang, there were three sources for the organization of Communism in Shanghai: the Guomindang-related publication associations that published *Weekend Review, Construction,* and his own *Nation Daily;* students from Zhejiang, especially Hangzhou; and Japan-returned students such as Li Hanjun and Li Da.[7]

If there was a center in Shanghai, it was the Guomindang-related *Weekend Review,* edited by Dai Jitao and Shen Xuanlu. By the end of 1919, students from Zhejiang and Japan had also congregated around the journal. When Yang Zhihua, a radical woman student from Hangzhou Women's Normal School, went to Shanghai in the summer of 1919, she found working at the Weekend Review Association, in addition to Dai and Shen, Li Hanjun, Chen Wangdao, Shao Lizi, Yu Xiosong, Liu Dabai, Shen Zhongjiu, and a woman teacher from Shaoxing Women's Normal, Ding Baoling—many of whom would join the Communist party when it was founded.[8] Radical youth looking for a home in Shanghai often ended up with *Weekend Review.* Dai's house at No. 6 Yuyang Lane in the French concession served as headquarters for radicals and, after it had been taken over by Chen Duxiu in the late summer of 1920, for the Communist organization.

The moving force behind the journal ideologically was Dai Jitao, the most important promoter of Marxism in the May Fourth period. By early 1920, the name of Li Hanjun, the Japan-returned student from Hubei, recognized at the time as one of China's most learned Marxists, also began to appear more and more often. Shen Xuanlu, who financed the journal, was a wealthy landowner from Zhejiang, a member of its provincial assembly as a Guomindang representative. His activities indicate he may have had Tolstoyan pretensions. He provided the journal's connection with Zhejiang students. He supplied radical students with radical literature, and even financed activities in Zhejiang—

not just among his own tenants—to educate and mobilize peasants and workers there.[9]

Zhejiang offers another glimpse of the process of student radicalization during the May Fourth period. Hangzhou was a major center of radical activity in the aftermath of the May Fourth Movement; besides student activity, it had the beginnings of an anarchist-inspired labor and peasant movement.[10] Chen Wangdao, the translator in 1920 of the first complete Chinese edition of the *Communist Manifesto* and later a professor at Fudan University, recalls that at the time First Normal at Hangzhou matched Mao's First Normal in Changsha in radicalism. Chen himself played a major part in these activities. He had only recently returned from Japan, where he had been studying Marxism, and brought back materials on Marxism that proved quite useful to Shanghai radicals. His radicalism, however, was still the diffuse radicalism of the May Fourth period.[11]

In October 1919, teachers and students from First Normal, First Middle School, and the Industrial School in Hangzhou established a journal, *The New Tide of Zhejiang* (*Zhejiang xinchao*), whose first issue appeared in November. The "New Tide" was strongly anarchist in coloration. It advocated "freedom, mutual aid and labor" as the "natural" endowments of humanity. Its opening manifesto divided society into four classes: the political, the capitalist, the intellectual, and the laboring. The hope for social change, it declared, rested with the working class. The political and the capitalist classes were the enemies of the working class; the intellectual class often served the interests of the first two. The condition for change was "self-awareness" and organization of the working class, which required the help of intellectuals. The journal's ultimate goal was to promote this alliance.[12]

In the second issue an article appeared by Shi Contong, at that time Chen Wangdao's student at First Normal. Shi was, by his own admission, influenced at the time by Kropotkin, and the Beijing anarchist periodical *Evolution* (*Jinhua*), published in the first half of 1919. His article, "Against Filial Piety" ("Fei xiao"), was not unusual within the New Culture context: it attacked the family as the root of all social evil, and looked to its overthrow as the key to all social change. Yet within provincial Hangzhou it created quite a stir, possibly because its tone was so strident that even the radical if prudish-sounding Yang Zhihua recalls that at Women's Normal, they did not approve of it.[13] The authorities confiscated the issue, shut down the journal, and (against student protest) dismissed the four professors connected with it: Chen Wangdao, Xia Yanjun, Liu Dabai, and Li Cijiu. They were charged with "opposition to filial piety and Confucius, and advocacy of common property and common wives."[14] In the third and the last issue published in Shanghai, they recalled their "sin" as "the advocacy of social reform and family revolution, the sanctity of labor, and the evilness of filial piety and loyalty."[15]

Shi Contong, the eye of the storm, was according to contemporaries a very filial son, and his article was written not to reject filial piety, but in protest of dogmatic familism—which he had experienced personally in the mistreatment of his mother by his father. He apparently intended initially to write a second part to explain his ideas of a good family, but was unable to.[16] Some have suggested that the article became a *cause célèbre* because conservatives in Zhejiang used it to attack the progressive head of Zhejiang First Normal, against whom they had long born a grudge. Whatever the politics, the radical group responsible ended up as a consequence with the *Weekend Review* in Shanghai, with which it already had close connections. It was at this time that Chen Wangdao, dismissed from his teaching duties and with time on his hands, retired to his native village to translate the *Communist Manifesto,* under contract from *Weekend Review* and Chen Duxiu.

The institutional context for radicalism in Shanghai reveals both why it served as the headquarters of Communism in 1920, and the instabilities in organization there. Aside from all Shanghai's attributes as a "free" city and China's industrial center, Shanghai radicalism was preeminent for bringing together major radical leaders, who (especially those of the *Weekend Review*) were also foremost in the propagation of socialism and Marxism. It was "natural," therefore, that Voitinsky put his greatest effort into organization in Shanghai. Established two months after its counterpart in Beijing, the Marxist group in Shanghai quickly took the lead in the summer of 1920 in the organization of Communism.

Yet Shanghai radicals lacked the cohesiveness of the radical groups elsewhere. Because it had so many prominent leaders, Shanghai radicalism did not have a clear center. And these leaders' various political affiliations conditioned their participation. Especially interesting was the role played by Guomindang radicals. Their activities served as a focal point for radical activity in Shanghai, and they were crucial in the organization of Communism there. Before a united front was established between the Communist party and the Guomindang after 1922, there was already a basis for a united front in Shanghai radicalism. The participation of Guomindang or Guomindang-related activists facilitated the establishment of Communism in Shanghai; it also rendered Communist loyalties ambivalent. Many who participated in the founding of Communism in Shanghai would drop out of the Party shortly afterward, some to become major Marxist, but anti-Communist, theoreticians for the Guomindang. Unlike in Beijing and elsewhere, common ideological inclinations among Shanghai radicals did not necessarily coincide with personal bonds forged during the course of common struggles, or even with political loyalties. Even the radicals who established the Party remained uncertain of their loyalties, as their careers after 1921 would testify.

Shandong

Shandong had two major centers for radical activity in the May Fourth period, Tianjin and Jinan; only radicals in Jinan would participate in the founding of Communism in 1920–1921. Nevertheless, Tianjin was important not only because Zhou Enlai was there, but also because Tianjin radicals would participate in the founding of the Party branch in France in 1921–1922, and many of them would in later years become important party members. Their radicalism, too, was rooted in May Fourth activism.

The organizational basis for Communism in Tianjin was laid by Awakening Society (*Juewu she,* to be distinguished from the Guomindang publication in Shanghai discussed earlier), founded in September 1919. In early 1920 the society began to publish *Awakening,* which had only one issue, as most of the members, including Zhou Enlai, went to jail in early spring 1920 for their struggle against local warlords.

Awakening Society itself arose from the experiences of Tianjin radicals in two student societies born during the May Fourth struggles, the Federation of Tianjin Students (*Tianjin xuesheng lianhehui*) and the Organization of Patriotic Women Comrades (*Nujie aiguo tongzhihui*). These organizations of men and women students cooperated in student struggles. While many groups emerged from these struggles in Tianjin, Awakening Society distinguished itself to the point where the *Morning News* in Beijing called it as the "purest" of all the radical groups in Tianjin.[17]

Of the twenty initial founders, (divided equally between men and women), the majority of the men came from Nankai University or Nankai Middle School, while the women all came from the Beiyang Women's Normal School in Tianjin. Depending on their gender, they had all played major roles in either the Federation of Tianjin Students or the Patriotic Women Comrades. Of the males, Ma Jun (a fiery Moslem radical) had served as a vice-president of the Federation while Zhou Enlai had edited its paper. Among the women, Liu Qingyang (also a Moslem) had served as the president of the Comrades, Guo Longzhen had been among its founders and organizers, and Deng Yingchao (later Mme. Zhou Enlai), at the age of sixteen, came to serve as the head of the speakers' bureau when the two organizations merged. Their experiences in these two societies had a radicalizing effect on them. It was after a demonstration in Beijing, in which both groups participated through representatives (and Ma Jun was arrested), that they decided on the train back to Tianjin to establish a society that would be more tightly organized for unified action than either student society had been. Although Awakening Society, when it came into being in September, repudiated hierarchy, the previous leaders of the student organizations assumed informal leadership roles in it.[18]

Tianjin students frequently participated in demonstrations in Beijing, and came to establish a close relationship with Beijing radicals, in particular Li Dazhao. Just a few days after the Awakening Society was formally established, Li came to speak to them. He discussed his views on Marxism and the Russian Revolution, and drew their attention to his writings on these questions, as a consequence of which they turned to the study of Li's writings on the Russian Revolution from later 1918 as well as his more recent "My Views on Marxism." In August 1920, members of the society would hear Li once again when they participated in a joint meeting of radical student societies in Beijing, including the Young China Association, the Youth Labor-learning

Mutual Aid Corps (*Qingnian gongdu huzhutuan*), the Humanity Society (*Rendao she*), and the Light of Dawn Society (*Shuguang she*). Although Li was at this time already involved in the founding of Communism in Beijing, the members of these societies were mostly anarchist in orientation. Li may have been trying to convert them to the cause; it was at this meeting that he made his often-quoted statement, "Every organization must have a clear ideology [*zhuyi*]," though it is not clear whether or not he associated this with Marxism explicitly.[19]

Li was not the society's only contact with socialism. Zhang Shenfu, a Beida professor and close associate of Li Dazhao and Chen Duxiu, was close to the society's members (he later married Liu Qingyang). Members were acquainted with the work of the prominent anarchist Hua Lin who, according to Liu Qingyang, published an anarchist paper in Tianjin at this time.[20] The perennial socialist Jiang Kanghu was also in Tianjin, operating a Common Peoples' School (*Pingmin xuexiao*) staffed by members of his Socialist Party. Deng Yingchao's mother was a teacher at this school, which taught the ideal, "from each according to his ability, to each according to his need."[21] (In spite of its Marxist origins, this idea, it will be remembered, was associated in the May Fourth period with anarcho-communism.)

The ideological variety of these sources gave Awakening Society, as other student societies of the time, a complex ideological visage. As far as one can tell from the evidence, Zhou was the most sophisticated. He had been radicalized as a student in 1917–1919 in Japan, where he had begun to read publications related to Marxism, including those of Kawakami Hajime. As early as July 1919, in his opening piece for the Federation's paper, he praised the Russian Revolution, mass movements in Japan, and the Korean independence movement, and called upon students "to do real mass movement work" and "to get close to the working class."[22] While in jail in spring 1920, he not only studied Marx's *Capital* but lectured on it to his fellow inmates.[23] Nevertheless, as other members of Awakening Society recollect, the society was at this time quite diffuse ideologically.

Possibly because the Awakening Society was dispersed (mainly to France) just as the Communist organization was getting under way, the initiative for organizing Communism in Shandong passed to Jinan from Tianjin, and to Wang Jinmei and Deng Enming, two radical activists who had also distinguished themselves during this same period. In April 1920, when Voitinsky left Beijing for Shanghai, he stopped briefly in Jinan to discuss the matter of founding a Communist party with those two and Wang Xiangqian, whom Li Dazhao had already forewarned of Voitinsky's visit. Soon after, Wang Jinmei and Deng Enming would join in the organization of Communism.

In Jinan, as in most other provincial towns where Communism was established in 1920, students in the Normal School were the most active. Wang Jinmei had entered Jinan First Normal in late 1918. Deng Enming, the other founding member of the Communist organization, was a couple of years younger than Wang, and met him while a student at the First Middle School attached to First Normal. Deng was an activist in his own right, organizing a "self-government society" in his middle school; but in terms of ideas, he seems to have followed the older Wang's lead.[24]

Radical activity in Jinan got under way in the immediate aftermath of the May Fourth Movement in Beijing. The source of radical ideas was at first the Jinan Correspondence Society (*Jilu tongxunshe*) founded by a Guomindang member, Wang Leping. This society was reorganized in early 1920 as the Jilu Book Society (*Jilu shushe*), which began to publish a journal, *Ten Days* (*Shiri*). The society not only brought to Jinan the radical literature of the New Culture and May Fourth movements, but itself propagated, in addition to Sun Yatsen's Three Peoples' Principles, ideas of "the sanctity of labor," women's liberation, freedom of marriage, and so forth.[25]

Under this society's influence, students at First Normal organized in the latter half of 1919 the Promote the New Study Society (*Lixin xuehui*) which was to serve in 1920 as the immediate basis for Communist organization. Wang Xiangqian, Wang Jinmei, and Deng Enming participated in founding this society, with an initial membership of thirty which gradually grew to about sixty. Wang Jinmei was the person responsible for the organization, and when it began to publish *Promote the New* (*Lixin*) in December 1920 (after the Communist group in Jinan had already come into existence), served as the editor of that journal. Judging by the extraordinary number of Wangs in this society, kinship ties may have been important in recruitment. Wang Jinmei had gone to visit Li Dazhao in Beijing during the May Fourth Movement, and the Promote the New Society had connections from the beginning with radicals in Beijing and Tianjin.[26]

In early 1920, Wang Jinmei was dismissed from school for writing an article, "The Problem of the Rice Bowl" ("Fanwan wenti"), in which he criticized the teachers at First Normal for not participating in political activity for fear of losing their "rice bowls." The experience (according to one source) radicalized him, and he turned to the pursuit of revolution on a full-time basis.[27] Soon after the incident, Voitinsky stopped by at Jinan.

Hubei

The Communist group in Hubei came out of a conglomeration of local radical groups, and did not assume final form until 1922, when Yun Daiying and his followers joined the Party. Nevertheless, in Hubei, too, the Party was a product of relationships that predated the May Fourth Movement.

The institution in Wuhan that played the key role was the Wuhan Middle School (*Wuhan zhongxue*), founded by Dong Biwu and others in spring 1920. Dong was a veteran Guomindang member. He had spent the previous few years studying in Japan, where he had met Li Hanjun, a fellow student from Hubei, whom he later described as "my Marxism teacher."[28] During the May Fourth Movement he was in Shanghai. Though by his own admission he did not participate in the movement, it influenced him to the point of dissatisfaction with his work in the Guomindang.

In Shanghai in later summer 1919 Dong met Chen Tanqiu, who had just graduated from Wuchan Higher Normal School (*Gaodeng shifan,* later Wuhan University). Chen had played a leadership role in the May Fourth Movement in Wuhan, where he had cooperated with Yun Daiying and Lin Yunan (both of China University [*Zhonghua daxue*]; the latter the elder brother of Lin Biao, and from Huanggang County like Chen) and Li Shiqui of the Higher Commercial Institute (*Gaodeng shangye xuexiao*) in establishing the Wuhan Student Association (*Wuhan xuesheng lianhehui*).[29]

Dong and Chen struck it off right away personally, and decided the best course of action in Wuhan was to start schools and publish newspapers. Upon his return to Wuhan, Chen initiated the Wuhan Peoples' Correspondence Society (*Wuhan renmin tongxunshe*) where he encouraged factory surveys of workers' conditions. Dong, returning at the same time, prepared for the Wuhan Middle School in cooperation with Chen, Zhang Guoen, and Ni Jirui. The school opened in the spring. Also involved with the Middle School through personal relationships was Bao Huiseng, who was at Wuhan First Normal, where Chen was a teacher. These four schools served as the bases for the establishment of Communism in Wuhan.[30]

Perhaps more important in the long run, however, were the Benefit the Masses Book Society (*Liqun shushe*) and its companion Benefit the Masses Cotton Weaving Factory (*Liqun zhibuchan*), established in the fall of 1919 by Yun Daiying, Lin Yunan, Liao Huanxing, and others. (Chow Tse-tsung has also included Lin Biao as a founder.)[31] Yun was regarded by many at this time as the preeminent student leader in the central Yangzi region. His radical activities dated back to 1915 when in response to Japan's Twenty-one Demands he had organized, with Lin Yunan and Liao Huanxing (his fellow students in the Hubei Foreign Languages Institute), the Student Army for National Salvation (*Xuesheng jiuguojun*). In late 1918, he had called a meeting of students from various Wuhan institutions to discuss methods of self-cultivation and self-education, out of which had been born many small groups devoted to moral self-improvement. These activities made him a natural candidate for the leadership of the student movement in May 1919. The Benefit the Masses Society was an alliance of progressive student societies that had long recognized him as a leader.[32]

Yun had close personal relationships with the founders of the Communist group established by Dong Biwu and Chen Tanqiu, but he refused to join it on the grounds that self-cultivation should take precedence over political activity. His own Society was a labor-learning one established under the influence of the labor-learning and "new village" movements which, starting in Beijing, swept Chinese youth in the latter half of 1919. Participants, who included one worker, worked part-time in the factory and devoted the rest of their time to study. Yun and Lin Yunan both taught in China University, yet Yun was suspicious of formal education and believed self-study was a better means for acquiring an education. He acquired some fame at the time as the translator of Engels' *Origins of the Family, Private Property and the State* (published in the *Eastern Miscellany*) and Karl Kautsky's *Class Struggle.* This seems odd, not only because his activities point to strong anarchist influence but because, unlike many who were influenced by anarchist ideas without acknowledging them as such, he was a self-professed anarchist, a major reason for his refusal to join the Communist group in 1920. Yet the translation of Engels' work was not inconsistent with his anarchist beliefs; indeed, anarchists had been the first Chinese radicals to draw attention to the importance of that text (in 1907). As for Kautsky's *Class Struggle,* it has become known recently that Yun undertook the translation at the suggestion of Chen Duxiu, possibly when Chen was in central China in early 1920—about the same time he suggested to Chen Wangdao in Zhejiang the translation of the *Communist Manifesto.*[33]

Yun, and members of the Benefit the Masses Society, would join the Communist party only after 1921, and become some of its most active members in central China. Because of Yun's prestige, and the connections of the society, this group would also play an important part in the spread of Communism in Anhui and Sichuan (where Yun would serve as a teacher for a while after 1920). Benefit the Masses Society may also have served as a model for the Culture Book Society (*Wenhua shushe*) that Mao established in Changsha in the summer of 1920. Early that summer Mao stopped briefly in Wuhan, where he not only inquired into the workings of Yun's society, but took back with him to Changsha one of its few working-class members.[34]

Hunan

In the interlocking directorate of radical politics in China in the May Fourth period, Hunanese radicals played a part matching Beijing's in importance. The organizational context for Communism in Hunan was provided by the New Citizen's Study Society (*Xinmin xuehui*) founded in April 1918 by Mao Zedong, Cai Hesen, Xia Zisheng, He Shuheng, and others, with fourteen members initially, mostly students in Hunan First Normal in Changsha. The origins of the society went back to personal relationships formed as early as fall 1915 when Mao, along with Zhang Kundi, had posted a circular in several Changsha schools advertising for patriotic youth to join him in discussing common interests. The response had not been overwhelming, but the relationships established played some part in the group in 1918. Xiao Zisheng headed the society originally, but Mao was its outstanding activist.[35]

By the eve of the May Fourth Movement, this society already counted nearly seventy members. One of its remarkable features, as with the Awakening Society in Tianjin, was the high number of women participants who played central roles in the Communist movement in later years. Here personal relationship to male members seems to have played a more important part than in the Awakening Society in bringing the women in. The society was established at a meeting in the home of Cai Hesen, whose sister Cai Chang was one of the first to join. Through her women students from the Zhounan Women's School were recruited. Recruitment gathered momentum after the school's progressive principal, Zhu Jianfan, allowed the society to hold one of its meetings there in 1918. Other important women members included Xiang Jingyu, Tao Yi, and Fang Qirong.[36]

Members conceived of this society, among other things, as a vehicle of its members' education in China or abroad. In the fall of 1918, about twenty members, including Mao, Cai, and Xiao, headed for Beijing to look into the Diligent Work Frugal Study Program in France that the anarchists Li Shizeng and Wu Zhihui had initiated. At the end of 1919, many members including many of the women, would go to France. Luo Zhanglong, whose own hopes of study in Japan were frustrated by Chinese student exodus from Japan in 1918, ended up in Beida. Other members headed for Singapore. They did not consider Russia, Luo later recalled, because at the time they did not know much about it. Mao Zedong stayed in Hunan.[37]

The dispersal of this society's members across China and abroad made it almost as important as the Beida radicals in the establishment of Communism. While the Communist group in Europe was in the end established by northerners, society members in France played a central role in the radical activities of Chinese students and paved the way for Communism there by struggling against anarchist domination. Indeed, even at Beida, Hunanese students were among the central group who were to found the Communist group there. Luo Zhanglong was a member of the New Citizens' Society. Deng Zhongxia, while not a member, knew Mao Zedong from First Normal in Changsha and also as a student of Yang Changji, the progressive First Normal professor who had been responsible for opening up the minds of his pupils to new ideas.[38]

In spite of their physical dispersal, moreover, members of the New Citizens' Society were remarkably able to sustain a cohesive relationship. Correspondence was compiled and distributed for discussion by the membership as a whole as the *Compendium of New Citizens' Study Society Correspondence* (*Xinmin xuehui tongxinji*). Through his correspondence with Cai Hesen, who became a Marxist in France in 1920, Mao turned to Marxism and carried the rest of the society in Changsha with him (for details see Chapter 9). And when he established the Culture Book Society in Changsha in the summer of 1920, members of the society in France participated through correspondence in drawing up its chapter.[39]

While Maoist hagiography has certainly exaggerated his ideological perspicacity at this time, there seems little doubt that he played a crucial role in holding the society together and was, by the time of the May Fourth Movement, its most prominent member in Hunan. His activities in the student movement brought him close to Peng Huang (an anarchist), who became the head of the Hunan Association of Students (*Hunan xuesheng lianhehui*) when it was established in the aftermath of the May Fourth Movement. Mao himself became editor of the association's paper, *Xiang River Review* (Xiang-

jiang pinglun) and, when the authorities shut that paper down, of the *New Hunan* (*Xin Hunan*), a publication connected with the Yale-in-China medical school in Changsha. These activities, and the pieces he published in these papers, had already brought him national attention by mid-1919.

In the fall of 1919, when many members of the New Citizens' Study Society left for France, Mao and others were engaged meanwhile in Changsha in the popular movement to oust the warlord Zhang Jingyao. His participation in this movement took Mao out of Hunan for a second time, in the spring and summer of 1920 on a petition drive to Beijing, Shanghai, and Wuhan, just as the Marxist groups were being formed in those cities.

Guangzhou, Tokyo and Paris

The organizations that provided the context for Communism in Guangzhou, Tokyo, and Paris do not need extensive commentary here because they came into being rather late, when Party organization was already under way. They were a consequence, rather than a precondition, of the founding. Yet the same tendencies were at work there as elsewhere.

In Guangzhou, the Communist group would be established on the basis of the *Guangzhou Masses* (*Guangzhou qunbao*), founded in October 1920 under the joint editorship of Chen Gongbo, Tan Pingshan, and Tan Zhitang, whom we have already encountered at Beida during the May Fourth Movement as members of the Journalism Society there. Upon graduating in 1920, they returned to their native Guangdong to teach, and engaged in activities to spread their ideas of the New Culture Movement. The *Masses* was published with this goal in mind.[40] Collaborating with them in it were a number of anarchists who had been their fellow students at Beida (among them Ou Shengbai, Yuan Zhenying, and Huang Lingshuang), as well as other anarchists such as Liang Bingxian (editor of *Fujian Star*) who had only recently returned from Changzhou, following Chen Jiongming's triumphal return to Guangzhou in August 1920. Also associated in the publication's work were a number of student leaders who had distinguished themselves during the May Fourth Movement in Guangzhou, among them Peng Pai, later the organizer of the first Communist peasant movement in Haifeng.[41] In this complex situation, there was considerable organizational incoherence in Guangzhou (even more so than in Shanghai), and not until Chen Duxiu arrived in late 1920 did party work get under way in earnest there.

In Tokyo, when the Communist party was established in July 1921, there were only two members—Shi Contong, who had gone to Japan to study in June 1920, and Zhou Fohai. Zhou, originally from Hunan, had been close friends with Li Da, and it was possibly with Li's introduction that Shi Contong initiated him into the party. Also in Tokyo in 1922 Peng Pai joined the party. While Japan played an extremely important part in the ideological formation of the Party, the relationships in Tokyo seem to have been purely personal, and there was no organization to speak of there on the eve of the Party's establishment.

The situation in France was possibly the most complex of all. The Communist cell in Paris was formed sometime in 1921, and adopted its own name in 1922 as the Chinese Communist Youth Party (*Zhongguo shaonian gongchandang*), with its own publication, *Youth* (*Shaonian,* with the French subtitle *La Jeunesse*). This cell, however, was a direct offshoot of party organization in China. It was organized by the Beida philosophy professor, Zhang Shenfu, who had been a close associate of Chen Duxiu and Li Dazhao in Beijing, and participated in initial party organization back in China; he was personally requested by Chen to establish a party branch in Paris before he left for France in late 1920 to teach there. When he organized the party cell in Paris in 1921, he recruited two acquaintances from Beijing, Zhao Shiyan and Chen Gongpei, and two from the Awakening Society in Tianjin, Liu Qingyang and Zhou Enlai. Zhang and Liu had become lovers meantime, and it was possibly through Liu that Zhou Enlai was recruited.

Radical activity in France was to have consequences for the Communist movement in China beyond that implied by this group. By 1920 a large number of Chinese students in France, with connections to groups back home, were intensely active in political struggles, as well as among Chinese laborers in France. Being in a foreign environment intensified their radical sentiments. So did their problematic relationship with the sponsors of the Diligent Work Frugal Study Program who, for all their anarchism, took an authoritarian attitude toward them.

Of numerous student organizations in France, only two were to be of crucial importance to the spread of Communism. First was the Labor-learning World Association (*Gongxue shijie*), established in August 1920, on the basis of an earlier society formed in February 1920, the Labor-learning Promotion Association (*Gongxue lijinhui*). The society was formed by work-study students in Montargis, and the members of the New Citizens' Society (in Changsha) among them took the lead. When they were split in July 1920 over politicial issues, the radical faction led by Cai Hesen reorganized itself as the Labor-learning World Association. This split marked the turn of Cai and his followers to Communism.[42]

The other organization was the Labor Study Association (*Laodong xuehui*), established in Paris in early 1921 by Li Lisan and Zhao Shiyan. Unlike the Labor-learning World Association, which drew its force from students' dissatisfaction with their conditions, the Labor Study Association represented its members' commitment to hard work against all difficulties. This society was also interested in establishing contact with Chinese laborers in France, and engaged in extensive organizational and educational work among them (no doubt an important factor in Li Lisan's emergence as one of the Party's most effective labor organizers in China after his return). The founders had originally intended to name it the Communist Alliance (*Gonchan zhuyi tongmenghui*), but dropped the idea when it provoked dissension.[43]

These two societies merged on the eve of the founding of the Communist group in France, following the February Twenty-eight Movement of 1921, when around four hundred Chinese students demonstrated at the Chinese legation in Paris over the issue of government support for students. Led by the Labor-learning World Association, students protested against being forced to work "as running dogs of the capitalist factory system."[44] While the Labor Study Association had not approved of the Montargis faction's earlier activities, the two were able in the aftermath of this protest to reconcile their differences and join together in a new society, The Diligent Work Frugal Study Student Association (*Qingong jianxue xuehui*).

Student dissatisfaction with the operation of the Diligent Work Frugal Study Program was to erupt most extremely in the occupation of the Institute Franco-Chinoise in Lyon in September 1921, in which members of this association, and representatives of the new Communist cell, participated. Shortly afterward, radical leaders, including Cai Hesen, Li Lisan, and Chen Gongpei, were shipped back to China by French authorities. They were to emerge in the 1920s as important Communist leaders. Their organizations in France served as important recruiting grounds for Communism in Europe, and their members continued to play important roles there in the ensuing struggles between anarchists and the newly converted Marxists.

The Organizational and Ideological Dynamics of Radical Associations

By early 1920 there was in China a network of radical intellectuals, organized in small groups, who had been active for over a year in connection with the May Fourth Movement. The bonds between these groups were personal rather than ideological, usually formed in the course of common schooling in the new radical educational institutions. In the aftermath of the May Fourth Movement these associations tended toward a greater coherence, and abstract ideas and rules began to take precedence over personal relationships, but as of early 1920 this was still a tendency, and the groups retained many of the characteristics of their May Fourth legacy.

The May Fourth Movement was a turning point in the radicalization of Chinese youth, but organized activity was the product of a complex process of radicalization which had originated earlier. The New Citizens' Society in Changsha and the Benefit the Masses Society at Wuhan went back to activities initiated in 1915. Student societies at Beida had their origins in the reorganization of that university under Cai Yuanpei's leadership starting in 1917, or in the anti-Japanese activities that got under way in earnest in 1918. The May Fourth Movement was organized by these societies, which had diverse origins.

The roots of radicalism lay for the most part in two sources. One was anti-Japanese patriotism; the other was a diffuse radicalism associated with intellectual changes that had been at work since the turn of the century, but gathered speed around 1915–19. The latter arose from intellectuals' search for a new place in society. The new educational institutions gave them only a vague guidance. In some cases, as with Yun Daiying, students quickly came to view with suspicion the very educational institutions through which they had become radicalized in the first place. As Mao's case illustrates most dramatically they were in search of social spaces wherein they could discuss the new ideas and questions that intrigued and attracted them. Student societies provided one important means for sorting out their ideas in communion with others of a like mind.

The profoundly radicalizing effect of the May Fourth Movement on students lay partly in bringing them into politics. Even more significant was its turning of students from self-absorption to a concern with social questions. Initially, the agenda of study societies was dominated by a question that was the common point of departure for New Culture thinking that of the intellectual's place in society; the uneasy search of a whole generation for a new identity. The New Citizens' Society originated because Mao advertised for like-minded students. When he first met Luo Zhanglong, one of the first to respond, they discussed together questions of a "cosmic" nature. Members of the society initially spent most of their time on "questions of life"; only with the May Fourth Movement did politics begin to take precedence.[45] It was not that questions of life disappeared as a concern; but they were no longer alienated abstractions, appearing now within the context of immediate social and political problems. The outburst of patriotic fervor during the May Fourth Movement gave birth to numerous student associations, starting in 1918 with sharpening student protest against Japan, and turned them to popular mobilization activities which brought them into contact with the public at large. The most prominent of these was public education to extend to the people the cultural revolution hitherto restricted to intellectuals. It is important to remember that unlike the leaders of the New Culture Movement, whose activities were intellectual and removed from the population, students operated at the local, grass-roots level, which quickened their impulse for change, and enhanced their potential for social radicalism.

In the patriotic struggles of the May Fourth Movement, then, the cultural radicalism of the New Culture Movement was transmuted into May Fourth social radicalism. Zhang Guotao's progress was replicated by many radicals who were to end up in the Marxist camp in 1920.

> In the very beginning, I was a passionate patriot; and like the ambitious youths of the time, I looked forward wholeheartedly to China's becoming rich and powerful. Then I became more radical by supporting the New Culture movement, opposing the old influences, and advocating social reform and national salvation through revolution. Finally I became enthusiastic about the Communist movement, studied Marxism and looked up to the example of the Russian Revolution, believing it to be the panacea for national salvation and the guide to revolution. The majority of the radical youths of the time were generally similar to me in pursuing such a course of development.[46]

We have tended on occasion to overstress the distinction between New Culture cosmopolitanism and May Fourth patriotism, the intellectuals' anti-nativism and the masses' nationalism. While the distinction is useful, it must be approached with care. The radicalization of Chinese youth as they searched for new ideas was crucial to the escalation of patriotic radicalism in May 1919, and the associations formed during that search were significant in organizing the movement. As Zhang Guotao's case illustrates, in the minds of contemporaries the individual search for a new life was not distinguished from the collective search for new alternatives for China. In the culture of May Fourth radicalism, radical patriotism coalesced with cultural radicalism around the search for new social forms and for new principles of social organization. Even anarchism, with all its radical anti-nationalism, could serve patriotic ends, as in the case of Yun Daiying, who found in anarchism the means to establish a new kind of social organization which would both nourish a new kind of moral and socially committed individual and provide a model for national social reorganization. Again, Zhang Guotao's recollections of his progress in radicalism provide us with a revealing illustration.

> Although as a major figure in the National Magazine group [*Guomin zazhishe*] I served it enthusiastically, the divergent views of its members left me feeling dissatisfied. At the close of the European War, I developed a close relationship with Li Ta-chao, who was then director of the library at Beida. My interest in socialism increased as a result of his influence. At the same time, I began to have a close association with two anarchist schoolmates, Huang Lingshuang and Au [*sic*] Sheng-pai, and I began to read in Chinese such anarchist works as the writings of Kropotkin, Bakunin, and others. Such concepts as social reform and going to the masses were added to my thinking. Apart from patriotic zeal, it seemed, I developed some sense of social revolution.
>
> Prompted by such ideals, I gathered together Teng Chung-hsia, Lo Chang-lung, and other schoolmates and organized the *Society for Mass Education* [*P'ing-min Chiao-yu Hui*] [*sic*]. It advocated social reform through the education of the common man. The charter participants in this organization included more than sixty Peita students who came from the National Magazine group. Bent on social reform work, some of them were dissatisfied with National Magazine's purely patriotic stand.
>
> Such small organizations devoted to the promotion of social reform were coming into vogue in Peking at the time. A leading one among them was the Work-Study Mutual Aid group which hoisted the slogan "Experiment in New Living" in its quest for a utopian way of life.
>
> Though anarchists did not join the Society for Mass Education, it was established under the influence of their slogan, "Go into the Masses." Similar groups were formed in other Peking educational institutions also. . . . Our speeches attracted considerable notice and our audiences grew markedly. Since few Chinese intellectuals had ever thought of trying to communicate with the masses, ours was a very exceptional activity. It was there that I began to gain experience in effective public speaking and to grasp the dramatic possibilities of appealing directly to the masses.
>
> Each week we also sent teams into the slum areas to investigate the plight of the poor and to carry on limited amount of relief work. Members of our society, or people sympathetic to it, wrote accounts for the

Peking press of the conditions under which the average man lived. Such reporting was quite an innovation, and it attracted widespread attention. In addition, the organization called upon members to develop similar groups in their home villages throughout the provinces when they returned there for Summer and Winter vacations. In this way, we hoped to spread social reform throughout the country.[47]

This account is remarkable as a "sociology" of May Fourth radical culture: the formation, splintering, and regrouping of radical associations as new experiences created new orientations; the transmutation of vague ideas "in the air" into ideologies of social activity, as the groups defined themselves; the transformations that came about as intellectuals encountered the general public in the course of their social activities; the changes in social consciousness that were a product of radical activity, which revealed aspects of society that had so far remained beyond the intellectual horizon of radical consciousness; and the overall process of radicalization as intellectuals tried to resolve the contradictions between their ideas and social realities. If there is a teleology here, it is the teleology of radical activism, a historicized teleology, which separated out those who were willing to pursue the consequences of their radicalism from those who were not. The groups became vehicles to the transformations of which they were products.

For those involved in student associations, cultural radicalism was already, before the May Fourth Movement, being expressed in the search for alternative social relationships. Contact with the people at large, as with the Lecturing Corps at Beida and activities elsewhere, led to a heightened awareness of questions of social mobilization and reorganization. Cultural issues, such as the movement for a colloquial language, which continued to occupy the students (as with the New Citizens' Society and the Awakening Society),[48] were increasingly perceived in terms of their social functions. Questions of social change, the search for alternative forms of social organization, and interest in socialism emerged in the aftermath of the May Fourth Movement as central preoccupations, pointing to a new kind of radicalism among youth, shifting the earlier foundations.

Student associations, themselves products of intellectual and social radicalism, played crucial roles, by their very existence, in the radicalization of youth. How they came into being may be a moot question. The atmosphere was one of intellectual ferment, "heated arguments . . . in classrooms, dormitories, and elsewhere."[49] In the course of such arguments Chinese students discovered their radicalism, as well as other radicals of like mind in search of a way, and thus arose the many small group activities that served as nodes of a diffuse radicalism that swept the country in ensuing months. Any principle of organization is to be found in the personal relationships that already existed or were forged in the "storm centers of argument." From that point on it was a matter of "I tell my friends, my friends tell their friends, their friends . . ." and so on.[50] This principle would be visible in ensuing months during the social mobilization of the May Fourth Movement and, a year later, in the organization of Communism.

Once the groups had been formed, a process of institutionalization trans-formed, divided, and reformed them. Not everyone kept pace, or desired to keep pace, with these changes. Some dropped out, unwilling to abide by changes not in keeping with a group's initial motives, and new members were recruited whose ideas and activities were more in keeping with the group's changing identity. As the groups were institutionalized, in other words, they were transformed from havens for intellectual youth into initiators of social activity that expected loyalty to group norms. For those who remained in them, the groups came to serve at once as points of departure for radical social activity and support against the adversities that inevitably accompanied it. The group, rather than abstract ideology, served as the reference point for activists' emerging radical identities.

While changes in groups' constitution reflected changes in their ideologi-cal and political context, they had their own internal dynamics. Changes in context induced changes within radical concerns and activities, but individual attitudes toward larger social and political questions were intermediated by the consciousness of the group; it served as the reference for individual iden-tity once it was established.[51] Products of a diffuse radicalism that expressed itself in the radical rejection of existing social institutions, student associations became the vehicles for the establishment of a new radical identity which sought to fulfill, through social transformation, the goals defined by the new-found collective experience. The New Citizens' Society in Changsha, the Morning Garden Society (*Xiyuan she*) of Beida radicals, Awakening Society in Tian-jin all held regular meetings to consolidate group solidarity. The widely dis-persed New Citizens' Society kept its remarkable unity through correspon-dence. In some cases, as with the Morning Garden Society, common interests were put on a firmer basis through communal living. And Yun Daiying's Benefit the Masses Society in Wuhan institutionalized criticism-self-criticism sessions to ensure group unity.[52]

While the groups formally repudiated hierarchy, in the course of their institutionalization they gave rise to an informal hierarchy of certain indi-viduals. As far as is discernible from available accounts, there was no single criterion for leadership. In some cases whose who had taken the initiative in forming the group emerged as leaders (Yun Daiying); in others, activists who distinguished themselves emerged gradually (Mao Zedong). Age, ideological acumen, and greater knowledge were factors. Continued leadership required the ability to direct, or keep up with, changes in the groups' constitution. Whatever the source, there were leaders, and they played an important part in swaying the group's orientation. When the Communist party was founded in 1920, one of the first questions raised was how to identify leaders in vari-ous areas who could be recruited, bringing with them the groups over which they held sway.[53]

The study societies' role in shaping their members' attitudes draws attention to them as the social context for ideology formation in May Fourth China.

Frederic Jameson has described ideological activity as "strategies of containment"; that is, activity to close out the totality of consciousness by establishing boundaries to interpretation.[54] Study societies performed this function in a literal sense by establishing a social-institutional boundary for ideological activity. They helped to bring coherence to diffuse ideological dissatisfaction with existing social norms, to consolidate ideological loyalties, and to provide social spaces within which initial attempts were made to convert ideology into practice; in other words, they served as social institutions in which vague and abstract ideological yearnings were reformed into coherent ideological identification, which was articulated in the May Fourth period not so much through formal commitment as through collective social practice. Already, however, a search was under way for an ideological means to articulate the premises of this practice and its consequences for the group. In some cases a division of labor was established whereby members reported to the group on assigned topics, and the more knowledgeable shared what they knew. Through the discussions, abstract ideas were translated into a form accessible to the concrete experiences of the group. During the New Culture movement, Chinese youth were exposed to a wide selection of disparate ideas and ideologies. In these groups these ideas were filtered through students' needs and perceptions, and selections were made that gave some coherence to the groups' attitudes on the social and political problems of the day. This was the process through which many later Marxists were first exposed to Marxism.

In the aftermath of the May Fourth Movement there was a perceptible interest in Marxism, revealed in some of the radical associations' search for Marxist materials to discuss. It does not follow therefore that student radicals already had a preference for Marxism or assumed a Marxist identity. The groups' persistent organizational looseness militates against any assumption of an exclusive ideological identity. This includes anarchism, which in 1919 was still the most visible among all radical ideologies. Many anarchist societies at this time were active in the very same locations as these radical groups. While the student societies included anarchists and cooperated closely with their anarchist counterparts, they retained their own separate organizational identity.

As might be expected from the organizational fluidity of these associations, their ideological orientation tended to be fluid and eclectic. Liu Qingyang, the radical woman leader from the Awakening Society in Tianjin, recalled later that by early 1920, "the majority of them definitely inclined toward socialism, but were very fuzzy in their understanding of socialism."[55] Mao Zedong, the key leader in the New Citizens' Society, reminisced in 1936 that "at this time, my mind was a curious mixture of ideas of liberalism, democratic reformism and utopian socialism."[56] Perhaps the most cogent evidence of this "fuzziness" has been provided by Deng Yingchao, also of the Awakening Society:

> The members of the society often got together to discuss new tides of thought. I was the youngest among them, and did not participate much in

the discussions, but I listened to the older members discuss Socialism, anarchism, guild socialism, etc. We did not have any firm beliefs, and did not understand what Communism was; we only knew that the most ideal society was a society of "from each according to his ability, to each according to his need," we only knew that the October Revolution had succeeded thanks to Lenin, we only knew that their revolution had liberated the majority of the oppressed and had created a classless society, which aroused our sympathy. . . .[57]

If there was any unity to the ideological orientation of these groups, it was in a generalized kind of anarchism which members found "easier" to understand than other social philosophies. As I have argued earlier, of all the competing socialisms of the May Fourth period, anarchism appealed most to Chinese radicals. Its significance rested not in any formal commitment to it as an ideological system, but rather in its diffusion in May Fourth radical culture. The role anarchist ideas played in radical associations helps explain this should have been the case.

Association with anarchists was crucial, as Zhang Guatao's recollections reveal, in inspiring social radicalism among Beida students. Such inspiration was not restricted to Beida. Yun Daiying in Wuhan professed anarchist convictions. Wang Jinmei in Jinan "worshipped" Kropotkin.[58] Zhejiang radicals were inspired to activism by reading about Kropotkin in *Evolution*. Deng Yingchao recalled the Awakening Society's ideological vagueness:

At the time we craved for new learning but we had no books, so we asked famous people like Li Dazhao, Chen Duxiu, Zhang Shenfu, Liu Bannong to speak to us. We absorbed their lectures, but were very fuzzy about the content of the different ideologies. We were indeed closer to anarchism than to Communism.[59]

Li Dazhao, when he lectured to this society in September 1919, just a few days after its founding, drew their attention to his writings on Marxism and the Russian Revolution. These writings, themselves fuzzy in their ideological message (as I have argued earlier), did not represent members' only intellectual fare. They read widely in the works of Kropotkin, including his *Conquest of Bread*. The single issue of *Awakening* (the society's journal) published in January 1920 gave no hint of Marxist inclination but displayed a preoccupation with individual self-cultivation, women's liberation, and work-study, all of which were common May Fourth themes, inspired by anarchism.[60]

It was much the same with the other societies I have discussed. Yun Daiying, by the evidence of his contemporary diary, was an anarchist in 1919–1920, and so was the Benefit the Masses Society whose orientation he shaped. The New Citizens' Society was more complex ideologically; but Scalapino, among others, has made a convincing case for the anarchist orientation of its key member, Mao Zedong. Indeed, in the essay that brought him national attention in 1919, "The Great Union of the Popular Masses," Mao gave some indication of his inclinations, calling Kropotkin's ideas "broader and more far-reaching" than those of the "party of Marx." Kropotkin's party, he continued, was more moderate than that of Marx. It does not expect rapid results, but begins by understanding the common people. Men should all have a morality of mutual aid, and work voluntarily. As for the aristocrats and capitalists, it suffices that they repent and turn towards the good, and that they be able to help people rather than harming them; it is not necessary to kill them. . . . They want to unite the whole globe into a single family, and attain together in peace, happiness, and friendship—not friendship as understood by the Japanese—an age of prosperity.[61]

There is no reason to think other members did not share these sentiments. No member of this society declared himself a Marxist until mid-1920. The Labor-learning Promotion Association they established in France in early 1920 was inspired by "the morality of mutual aid."[62]

Anarchist ideas were also clearly visible in the Weekend Review Society in Shanghai. How anarchism entered the socialism of Dai Jitao has been discussed (in Chapter 7). The other editor, Shen Xuanlu, had unmistakably anarchist tendencies. Li Hanjun, who joined them in early 1920, has been described by Li Da as a "legal Marxist" with anarchist tendencies.[63] Anarchist influence was most evident with the Zhejiang group, many of whom drew their inspiration from Kropotkin's "An Appeal to Youth" (*Gao qingnian*), then being circulated in Zhejiang.[64] Shi Contong, by his own admission, was an anarchist at this time; so were Shen Zhongjiu and Liu Dabai.[65] Shao Lizi also, and his paper *The Nation Daily* was strongly tinted with anarchism in the May Fourth period. The paper's supplement, *Awakening,* had a regular column by the prominent anarchist Hua Lin, and frequently reprinted articles from the anarchist *Fujian Star.*

Almost all of the later Communists, with possibly the single exception of Chen Duxiu, in other words, were introduced to social radicalism through anarchist ideas (this included other major figures in early Chinese Communism, such as Qu Qiubai and Li Lisan, who were only remotely associated with these groups).[66] An anarchist identity is no more implied thereby than a Marxist identity; that these groups sought an identity of their own rather than joining anarchist societies is *prima facie* evidence against such a claim. Yet anarchism was everywhere in the radical culture of the time, in language no less than practice. This alone raises questions: The fact that anarchist literature abounded and anarchists actively spread their ideas, does not in itself explain the appeal of anarchism. Neither does the anarchist critique of the family and the oppression of women, which (while of great concern to members, especially of the Awakening and New Citizens' societies, with their large contingent of women) was not peculiar to anarchists at the time, whatever their influence in raising it. Finally, while anarchist advocacy of social revolution, with its attention to labor and the common people, was responsible for drawing attention to social change, in the aftermath of the May Fourth Movement anarchists were not the only ones to discuss such questions. If these facts explain the initial appeal of anarchism, they do not explain its continued hold on social radicals.

The popularity of anarchism had much to do with the very existence of the student associations in post-May Fourth, and their role in shaping their members' consciousness. As with the propagators of socialism discussed earlier, members of these groups perceived social change in the immediate May Fourth period not in term of classes and conflict, but in terms of alternative forms of social organization. The perception had an even greater immediacy because they themselves formed small, communal groups which, they believed, represented paradigms and initiations of social change. The radical associations, to the extent that they were conceived of as paradigmatic, served as vehicles for the diffusion of the anarchism that had originally inspired and shaped them. As faith in the efficacy of the "small group" as a means to social transformation advocated most fervently by the Young China Association, spread among May Fourth radicals, so did the anarchist values embedded in this conception, especially mutual aid and labor. As Mao Zedong was to state (in the article just cited),

> I have already discussed the possibility and the necessity of the "great union of the popular masses." In the present issue, I shall consider what method we should employ for carrying out this great union. The method is that of "small democratic unions."
>
> If we truly want to achieve a great union, in order to resist the powerful people confronting us who harm their fellow men, and in order to pursue our own interests, we must necessarily have all sorts of small unions to serve as its foundation. The human race has an innate talent for uniting together, that is to say, a talent for organizing societies. "Groups" and "societies" are precisely the "unions" I am talking about.[67]

This essay brought Mao to national attention precisely because the problem of group organization occupied many at the time; it also represented (as we have already seen) the basic thrust of May Fourth socialism.

The appeal of anarchist ideas lay not in their abstract, utopian promise, but in their direct, concrete relevance to group organization and life. Anarchism was seen as the source of values that would go into the forming of social bonds for a new kind of social organization: it was the anarchist promise of a new quotidian culture that left the deepest imprint on May Fourth radical culture.

We have underestimated the role of the communal experiments of the New Life Movement, in which youth experimented with new forms of association in China's educational institutions. While of little consequence in historical hindsight, these experiments were to their constituency an earnestly serious means to social transformation. Taking a variety of forms, they were usually called "new villages" after the New Village Movement in Japan. By the end of 1919 they were to culminate in the "tide" of experimentation with labor-learning mutual aid groups. Whatever their particular form or appellation, they represented a widespread faith in the possibility of transforming society through the agency of "small groups." Radical activity was shaped in late 1919, as was socialist writing, by this faith in the principle of "from small groups to a great alliance *(xiao zuzhi da lianhe)*. As long as this faith persisted, Marxist notions of conflict were viewed with suspicion, and yielded in appeal to anarchist values of mutual aid and cooperation.

Within this context, anarchist assumptions about the "innate talent" of humanity to cooperate—the ideal of mutual aid—appeared not as a remote utopianism but as an immediate, concretely functional, ingredient of group cohesion. The anarchist premise that individual and collective goals could be mutually reinforcing within the context of small associations had enormous appeal among a youth that sought individual identity in collective forms of organization based on voluntary association. Small groups became tests of the anarchist claim that if only individuals could overcome the distortion of their personalities by authority, their natural propensity to mutual aid would provide a new source of social cohesion. Youth who escaped, or sought to escape, existing institutions of authority, found in mutual aid their only hope, and in small groups the means to its realization. The idea not only shaped their lives for a brief while, but instilled optimism about the possibility of reorganizing society along similar lines. The idea was infectious; it even touched the lives of other radicals who perceived the possibility of a new life for youth in the small groups and portrayed them as paradigms of social change: communes for youth, labor unions for workers. It is no accident that when practitioners were confronted with the failure of their communal experiments, this faith gave way to a pessimistic recognition of the limits society imposed on individual activity, and conflict appeared as a necessary step toward the dream of unity.

The radical associations under discussion here were swayed by the same hopes as all the others. They viewed their activities as part of the "new village" movement and assumed the principles of communal living in their internal organization. If they did not subscribe to a formally anarchist ideology, they constituted their associations with values anarchism provided.

In August 1919, the social reformists of the Lecture Corps in Beijing organized themselves into a commune, the Morning Garden Society *(Xiyuan she)*, under the initiative of Deng Zhongxia. Deng, concerned about the future of the lecture corps, also wanted to establish a peaceful environment, away from Beida's crowded dormitories, where he and his radical friends and associates could pursue their study of radical theories, cultivate habits of communal life, and establish a basis for their social reform activities.[68] Zhang Guotao, who joined this Society sometime in October, has given us a brief account of its origins and nature.

> In October 1919 . . . I joined the Morning Garden Society [*Hsi Yuan*] which Teng Chung-hsia and some other schoolmates organized. Morning Garden was inspired by the New Life movement then popular among Peking students. Promoted chiefly by the anarchists, the New Life movement encouraged students to live communally, to assist one another in their studies, and to dirty their hands with manual labor. A group would band together and rent a house, in which they did all the housework themselves, including the cooking. These houses were usually called "new villages."[69]

Morning Garden Society had sixteen members, most of them from Hunan, including Luo Zhanglong and Yi Keyi. One of their goals was to study Marxism, in which Deng Zhongxia, and Luo with his knowledge of German, played a central role. The society drew up roles for sharing household duties, subscribed to journals and bought reading materials from a communal fund, and conducted regular discussion sessions on issues of the day. Sometime in October Deng received a letter from Mao Zedong (whom he had known in Changsha) outlining a series of questions Mao thought demanded the attention of radicals. The society incorporated these questions in its discussion agenda.[70]

Anarchism was also consonant with the organizational goals of the Awakening Society in Tianjin, which may best be described, like almost every student society of the early May Fourth period, as a collective association for individual improvement. The society derived its name from the aspiration of its members to achieve, in their own punning expression, "self awakening" *(zijue)* and "self-determination" *(zijue)* through the spirit of "renovation" *(gexin)* and "mental transformation" *(gexin)*. In the spirit of labor-learning, its members sought to combine mental and manual labor. Though the society had tight admission requirements, which were tightened even further in late 1919 as it geared itself for action, it repudiated hierarchy. In order to guarantee equality, members gave up their surnames (in good anarchist fashion) and assumed numbers for identification (Zhou Enlai's pseudonym in these years, Wu Hao, was derived from his appellation, Number Five, in the society).[71]

Even the more loosely organized Weekend Review Society adopted a radical life style in keeping with its radical philosophy. Yang Zhihua has recalled that in the work of the *Weekend Review* "everyone labored, everyone was equal." Members were on a first name basis to ensure equality. Most of the women working on the journal shaved their heads like "Buddhist nuns." They also engaged in labor activity, and laborers often stopped by the journal's headquarters.[72]

There is little need here to elaborate further on Yun Daiying's Benefit the Masses Society and the New Citizens' Society. In keeping with Yun's professed anarchist beliefs, members of Benefit the Masses Society were expected to combine labor and study, live a tightly organized communal life, and engage in criticism-self-criticism sessions on a regular basis. While members of the New Citizens' Society in Changsha, given their dispersal, do not seem to have engaged in significant communal activity, the members in France did. Mao himself, it will be remembered, was sufficiently interested in communal experimentation to visit Yun Daiying's society in Wuhan and inquire after its workings.

In the early May Fourth period, then, anarchism played a significant part in the ideology of the radical student associations that would in 1920 serve as the basis for the establishment of the Communist party. Besides their intellectual appeal, anarchist ideas contributed most importantly in everyday activity, especially as organizing principles in the highly communal experiments.

An important precondition for the turn to Communism among these radicals in 1920 was the disillusionment with anarchism that set in as communal experiments foundered upon the realities of power in Chinese society. Faith in anarchism declined; the alternative organization offered by Bolshevism acquired a new credibility. In the meantime, anarchism had done much to create the organizational units that facilitated the organization of Communism.

In order to evaluate properly the role Voitinsky played, we must place his arrival within the perspective of Chinese radicalism in the spring and summer of 1920. By early 1920, the optimism of the early May Fourth period had given way to a pessimism; the attempted social mobilization had revealed the fundamental differences within the middle-class alliance that had made possible the May Fourth political success.

Radical associations that had come into being and played an important part in this success now found themselves afloat in a sea of uncertainty as the Movement waned, having failed to fulfill the radical aspirations it had birthed. The Movement had radicalized intellectuals by making them aware of the contradictions in Chinese society; now these same contradictions seemed to stand in the way of further progress. May Fourth radicalism had been born out of the temporary, and tenuous, social radicalism of the May Fourth Movement, a social mobilization with limited goals. The intellectual associations which had been created to voice this social radicalism had served as vehicles for the further radicalization of an uncertain youth by providing them with social spaces for radical activity. Now these associations found themselves isolated from the population as social mobilization receded. By early 1920, they were in search of a means to make permanent the radicalism that seemed to be waning before their eyes.

As these societies expressed May Fourth radicalism, they were also the place where the contradictions of that radicalism appeared most sharply. The May Fourth Movement had achieved its immediate patriotic goals when the Chinese delegation to the Versailles Conference in Paris was prevented from signing the peace treaty in late June 1919. The new social radicalism, however, remained dissatisfied with its limited accomplishments. As we have seen, the attraction to socialism gained in intensity in fall 1919, even as the social mobilization which had provoked it had begun to wane. By late 1919 social radicals faced the problems of how to keep a social movement alive in order to promote the goals of social change to which they had become committed.

This problem was especially acute for the radical groups which had come to view themselves as embodiments of social radicalism, not only because of their attraction to socialist ideology, however vague, but even more so because they were themselves experiments in social change meant to serve as models for society at large. The contradiction between their own institutionalized radicalism and the deradicalized social context impinged upon their consciousness with increasing intensity: the models, in other words, found themselves without a public to emulate them. There appeared to be some realization at the time that if there was to be such a public, it would have to be created, since spontaneous mass mobilization could not be expected to fulfill the hopes it had created. In December 1919, the Awakening Society in Tianjin tightened its rules of membership in order to be able to act with greater coherence. Others, as we shall see below, were coming to a similar realization by late 1919.

There were other reasons for frustration and depression. Perhaps most important was the reactionary backlash to the May Fourth Movement. Chinese historians have played down the importance of oppression as a reason for the turn to Communism, presumably because they think this compromises positive attraction to Communism's obvious truth. Almost all the groups and individuals involved in the founding of Communism, however, suffered some repression in late 1919 and early 1920. In June 1919 Chen Duxiu was incarcerated for his activities during the May Fourth Movement and was not released until September. Mao Zedong and New Citizens' Society members found the *Xiang River Review* shut down by the authorities in July, after which they devoted their energies to the popular movement to get rid of the warlord Zhang Jingyao. Repression intensified as the year progressed. May Fourth radicals in Zhejiang lost their publication, and their jobs, toward the end of the year, on account of Shi Contong's criticism of filial piety. Wang Jinmei in Jinan lost his job for criticizing school authorities. In January the government dissolved the Beijing Federation of Students. On January 29, authorities in Tianjin reacted with violence to a student demonstration and jailed its leaders, including Zhou Enlai, most of whom were from the Awakening Society. About the same time, it will be recalled, foreign consuls in China joined in the hunt for radicals, even persuading Chinese magistrates to issue proclamations making radicals subject to arrest on the spot. Radicals, however innocuous their radicalism, were forced more and more into secrecy; radical literature was smuggled through the mail in false covers to avoid confiscation. There was every reason to think, under the circumstances, that not only had the May Fourth Movement fallen short of the very goals it had produced, it had failed even to nourish an atmosphere of freedom and democracy. "The January 29 tragedy in Tianjin," Liu Qingyang later recalled, "revealed to all the hideous visage of the reactionary government, and helped them recognize that patriotic freedom and democratic sovereignty could not be achieved without the shedding of blood."[73] The fears of the anti-revolutionary socialists were coming true.

Socialism as it appeared in China at the end of 1919 did not offer relief to radical frustration but instead underlined its contradictions. The basic contradiction was between the peculiar features of May Fourth socialism: the socialist promise of social transformation, and the reified intellectualism of May Fourth socialists. They seemed unable to convert their ideology into any kind of concrete action and even, in the face of increasing government suppression of even the most innocent radicalism, continued to advocate peaceful ways—the education of the oppressed and the charity of the oppressors. The contradiction was especially evident to younger radicals who, unlike Dai

Jitao or Zhang Dongsun, had little faith in the ability of existing social and political organizations (including the Guomindang) to bring about meaningful social change. Zhang Guotao, who encountered Sun Yatsen, Dai Jitao, and Zhang Dongsun in Shanghai, expressed deep disappointment that their socialist professions did not include any clear plan for action.

Members of intellectual associations were particularly, profoundly aware of the ambivalence in their radical identity. Already by the time of the May Fourth Movement, radical intellectual leaders such as Li Dazhao and Wang Guangqi, not to speak of the anarchists, had voiced concerns for a closer relationship between intellectuals and laboring people. Radical associations, however, continued to be associations of intellectuals, with only an occasional mention of workers' participation. The idea of intellectuals' responsibility to the working class had already taken root in the immediate aftermath of the May Fourth Movement; by late 1919 and early 1920, there were signs that this sense of responsibility, somewhat patronizing at first, was turning into something akin to adulation of the working class.

The reasons were twofold. First was the continued growth of labor activism, which contrasted sharply with the waning movements of students and urban bourgeoisie. Labor activism continued to grow after June 1919 and culminated in several successful strikes in early 1920 in Shanghai and south China. Among radical intellectuals, as consciousness of labor continued to intensify, so did a sense of the gap that separated them from labor, and the desire to bridge it.

This was accompanied, second, by the alienation of radical intellectuals from their own environment. Post–May Fourth radicalism had brought out the differences between social radicals and their more intellectually oriented liberal colleagues, with whom they had cooperated during the New Culture Movement. This was felt even more strongly by younger radicals, who clashed with and became alienated from the educational institutions where their radicalism had been born. This sense of alienation sharpened as the May Fourth Movement waned, with a consequent disillusionment in intellectuals' effectiveness, or even seriousness, in pursuing their own radical causes. This disillusionment would turn into a disillusionment with the aspirations of the New Culture Movement itself, as young radicals faced their own associations' failure to fulfill the promise of their first heady days. The failure of the communal movement, which reached its apogee in late 1919 and early 1920; played an important part in May Fourth radicals' disillusionment with utopian radicalism, and the anarchist philosophy that had inspired it. This disillusionment was a precondition for the break radicals made in spring 1920 with their own radical sources in the May Fourth and New Culture movements.

In May 1920 intellectuals in Beijing, Shanghai, Guangzhou, and other areas celebrated May Day with great fanfare. This was not the first celebration of May Day in China, but it was the first large and possibly coordinated one. The article on the history of May Day that Li Dazhao wrote for the occasion (based for the most part of the work of the American socialist Morris Hill-quit, who seemed to be Li's main source on socialist history at the time)[74] was reprinted widely in Beijing and Shanghai newspapers. Voitinsky may have had something to do with the celebration; the Soviet Union earlier had called upon sympathizers around the world to celebrate it to demonstrate solidarity against the invasion of Russia. The celebration was led by socialist and anarchist intellectuals in China's cities. As Zhang Guotao remarked caustically later, few workers participated. Only in Guangzhou, where anarchist had led the first May Day celebration in China two years earlier, did workers come out in large numbers.[75]

Communist historians have argued that the establishment of the Party starting in spring 1920 signaled the fulfillment of an alliance between the working class and the intellectuals, who had finally overcome their petit-bourgeois propensities. The paucity of working-class participation on May Day in 1920 indicates that it was not yet proper to speak of more than embryonic beginnings toward alliance. There is no question, however, of a new propensity on the part of intellectuals; consciousness of the working class was already an integral part of radical consciousness.

This consciousness is evident both in radical publications and in the activities of radical groups. In May 1920 *New Youth* published a special issue on labor to which most of China's major radical intellectuals contributed, if not their thoughts, at least their calligraphy![76] The issue was the first of its kind in China and reported extensively on labor conditions around the country. Its contents reveal that it had been in preparation for the few months *before* Voitinsky arrived in the country. The reports on Hubei, for instance, were prepared by local radicals who, it will be recalled, had been engaged in labor surveys since late 1919. Chen Duxiu's own long piece on Shanghai women workers from Hunan represented materials accumulated from Hunanese newspapers since February 1920.[77] It is possible to surmise, given the time required to collect, write up, and publish the reports, that much the same was the case for the other surveys included. Even before this special issue, moreover, radical publications in Shanghai and Beijing (discussed in Part II) had since early 1920 shown increasing interest in labor, which reflected both increasing labor activity and that labor was becoming increasingly important to radical intellectuals. What emerged in May 1920 was the culmination of a consciousness of labor that had been sharpening for the previous year. It was also a new beginning, the first public manifestation of the need radical intellectuals felt for an alliance with the working class.

This burgeoning consciousness was also evident in the initial efforts to link up with laborers. During 1919, the radical groups discussed made some effort, above all, to recruit laborers. Members of the *Weekend Review* had some contact with laborers. So did Mao in Changsha, mainly through his association with the anarchists there, who had been most active in labor organization in the May Fourth period.[78] Chinese students in France, who were thrown together with laborers in the work-study program in ways unparalleled in China, were intensely interested in the question of labor. Yun Daiying had at least one laborer in his commune. As early as June 1919, Zhou Enlai in Shandong had called upon intellectuals to unite with labor; Liu Qingyang recalls that there was some contact with laborers there.[79] Zhang Guotao even served briefly in March 1920 as general secretary of the All-China Federation of Industries connected with the Sun Yatsen.[80]

It is difficult, for lack of evidence, to estimate the significance of these contacts in practical terms, though they do offer unequivocal evidence of the importance of labor in radical consicousness. There is some indication that initial efforts to link up with labor were inconsequential, and frustrating, which may only have made radical intellectuals more cognizant of the contradictions in their radicalism.

The first well-documented instance of a serious effort to link up with laborers is from spring 1920, and is indicative of the problems this new-found constituency presented. In April 1920, Deng Zhongxia, with the aid of members of the Morning Garden Society, initiated the effort to carry the work of the Common Peoples' Education Lecturing Corps outside Beijing to suburban towns and villages. The failure of the previous patriotic mercantile undertakings of the group in Beijing had already convinced Deng of the futility of trying to "save the country through industrialization" (*shiye jiugo*), and the necessity of a social revolution through the masses.[81] The initial efforts at popular mobilization in Fengtai and Zhangxindian in April 1920 were equally disheartening. The villagers and townspeople were at best indifferent, at worst hostile. The curiosity of the onlookers, children and elder people, was provoked by the students' flags and the songs; when they embarked on their long-winded lectures they almost immediately lost their audience.[82]

One lesson the students learned by their experiences was the need to find a more effective means of communicating with the masses—in other words, to learn their language. The other was to look to better organized activity that would gain them a foothold with the masses. With these experiences, they would return to Zhangxindian in late 1920 to launch there one of the most successful Communist efforts at labor organization. For the time being, the experience only added to their sense of ineffectiveness.

For those individuals who would ultimately discover in Communism the solution to the problems they encountered, this kind of experience, rather than turning them away from laborers, reminded them of the gap, and sharpened their dissatisfaction with their own intellectualism. This is perceptible in the changing meaning attached to that anarchist-inspired slogan which had not only infused radical thinking in the early May Fourth period, but played an important part in bringing "labor" into the language of radicalism: "Labor is sacred." The slogan was still important; it was displayed prominently in Cai Yuanpei's own calligraphy on the inside cover of the *New Youth* special issue of May 1920. But it now carried a more exclusive meaning. In Cai's original presentation, and in its May Fourth reading, the slogan had pointed to the anarchist distinction between those who labored and those who did not, between those who produced and were therefore useful, and those who were parasites on others' labor: all labor was sacred that produced something for human civilization, including the labor of intellectuals and capitalists.

In a talk he gave before boat stewards and warehouse workers, "The Awakening of Labor" ("Laodongzhedi jeuwu"), which was printed in the May 1920 issue of *New Youth,* however, Chen Duxiu placed a more literal and exclusive reading on the slogan:

> Who are the most useful, the most important people in the world? People who are confused say it is the Emperor, or those who become officials or read books. I say they are wrong. I say only those who labor are the most useful and the most important. Why? Because the food we eat comes from those who till the fields . . . the clothes we wear come from those who weave . . . the houses we live in come from carpenters, tile-makers, common laborers . . . the cars and boats we ride in. . . . None of it comes from the labor of emperors, presidents, officials, or those who read books.[83]

"The sanctity of labor" had hitherto been a means for improving intellectuals; hereafter, it would appear reactionary to apply it to any but those who worked with their hands. The laborer was now perceived by some as the model for intellectuals. In an open letter to *Awakening,* the supplement to *The Nation Daily,* in April 1920, Shi Contong (who had earlier penned "Against Filial Piety") declared his "belief" that "the factory must be the battlefield for the social revolution. . . . What we must investigate is the method of gaining entry to factories." His concluding words were "I am deeply ashamed that I am still not a worker."[84]

This adulation of the laborer presupposed intellectuals' break with the New Culture assumptions that had hitherto guided them. Before the factory could emerge as the "battlefield" for social revolution, radical intellectuals had to lose their faith in the communal and labor-learning experiments of the May Fourth period. In March 1920, the first labor-learning group in Beijing, which had been supported by major intellectuals at Beida including Chen Duxiu and Li Dazhao, conceded defeat in the face of economic difficulties after only a four-month existence. The following month, in the April issue of *New Youth,* its sponsors discussed the cause of the group's failure.[85] Opinions varied. On the "right" were Hu Shi and Wang Guangqi (the foremost promoter of the group and architect of its program), who blamed the students' lack of commitment; Hu Shi added that idealism had been a major factor in failure. On the "left," Dai Jitao argued that labor-learning groups did not address fundamental social problems, which were rooted deep in the economic structure of society; such utopian idealism was doomed to failure within the context of capitalist society. Surprisingly, Li Dazhao agreed with Hu Shi in blaming the group for its excessive idealism, its efforts to achieve a utopian communal existence when it should have concentrated on the work-study needs of its members. Chen Duxiu positioned himself between two alternatives, conceding that the economic problems of the group had been beyond its control. He concluded with a quotation from a letter he had received from one of the group's members stating that while work-study remained a possibility, mutual aid was unworkable.

The disappointment of the group's sponsors did not match in intensity the disillusionment of the student participants, suggesting that against their older teachers, young radicals had invested enormous hope in the group as a vehicle for social change. Shi Contong once again provides a glimpse of their frustrations. He responded almost immediately with a long piece in *Weekend Review,* in which he could barely conceal his resentment of the patronizing attitude of the *New Youth* discussants.[86] He had gone to Beijing in early 1920 to join the group; his resentment was provoked by what he felt was the sponsors' lack of understanding of the group's workings. His discussion offers many insights into the working of these groups: their communal constitution; the divisions between the idealists who saw in the group a means to achieve "communism" and the more practical who saw in it only a means to acquiring an education; the many group discussions of family and gender equality; the disagreements over the group's relationship to the university, the institution in which they had discovered their radicalism but which many had come to view with suspicion as a breading ground for elitism, shaped by the demands of capitalist society. Of immediate relevance here is Shi's refutation of those who blamed the failure on individuals. While the group had been divided over the issue of Communism, and some had left for that reason, Shi argued, those remaining had shared the belief that "labor was manual labor, study was mental labor, mutual aid was progress; labor-learning mutual aid was the life of humanity; labor-learning mutual aid corps were vehicles for creating true human beings."[87] Describing the group's economic functioning, he laid the blame squarely on economic problems over which the group had no control. His conclusion echoed Dai's: the group had not failed; capitalism had failed the group. He predicted, accurately as it turned out, that the failure of other groups would soon follow. The lessons he drew from the experience are revealing:

> 1. In order to change society, it is necessary to change it in its totality, starting from the roots; it is no use to try and engage in piecemeal change; 2. Before society has been changed in its totality, it is pointless to engage in experiments with new village or the labor-learning mutual aid corps.[88]

In his open letter of about the same time, Shi affirmed that rather than shake up his faith in Communism, the labor-learning experience had strengthened his resolve to work toward it; he just no longer believed that social revolution could be achieved in isolation from society. (This was when he declared that he was ashamed not to be a worker, and that factories must be the next battleground.)

The labor-learning experimentation did not end in March 1920. Even though one group after another declared failure, the experiment continued to attract youth all the way into 1921. Chen Duxiu himself supported one group in Shanghai as late as June 1920. But the failure of the group in Beijing brought a loss of innocence among radical youth. It made them cognizant, as in the case of Shi, of the overwhelming social forces beyond their control, and called into question the anarchist-inspired optimism about the innate human propensity to mutual aid in the reorganization of society. The experience was one final blow in an accumulation of frustrations. Some radicals were sufficiently disheartened to retreat from radical activity: if social radicalism was one byproduct of this failure, the other was cynicism. Those who retained their commitment, in their newly acquired awareness of the social forces arraigned against them, concluded in the spring of 1920 that to overcome them they must look for new kinds of social alignments and organization. With whom they should ally themselves was a foregone conclusion by late spring 1920. The organizational possibilities were more problematic. As Zhang Guotao recalled of spring 1920, when he returned from Shanghai to Beijing,

> By that time the Peking Student Federation and other peoples' organizations had been sealed up. Although the students still carried out activities in secret, in comparison with the time around May 4 the tides had clearly receded. It seemed that the students generally had felt that use of the mass movement to express public opinion had become inadequate, and they were groping after new techniques. . . . So, for people who would not stay melancholy and wanted to grope for a way out, the road of Marxist victory offered a strong attraction.[89]

Radical intellectuals, at least those who still sustained their radical will, were all dressed up with nowhere to go. At this moment Gregory Voitinsky arrived in China.

9

The Comintern and the Organization
of Communism in China

To the extent that we emphasize organization over spontaneity, the role played by the organizers of the Party in the establishment of Communism assumes significance. Stress on organization underlines the part Voitinsky played as architect of the Party, and draws attention to the fact that Chen Duxiu, not Li Dazhao, played the key role in the founding of the Communist party of China.

Gregory Voitinsky and the Comintern Contribution

Voitinsky's mission in China was to provide Chinese radicals with their first real insight into the Russian Revolution. He did not merely bring a message; he also participated in the founding of the Party. While in Beijing he promised his Beida audience that should they decide to establish a Communist party, he would secure its affiliation with the Comintern—a source of hope for his listeners.[1] In Shanghai, he was not only a frequent visitor at Chen Duxiu's house, but guided the organization of the Communist group there in the summer of 1920.[2] The materials he brought (which included a copy of John Reed's *Ten Days that Shook the World*), as well as his conversations, aroused great interest, and young radicals avidly studied them. Surprisingly, he seems to have neglected to bring with him a copy of the constitution of the Russian Communist party; when the organizers in Shanghai got around to establishing a program for the Communist group, they had to rely on Marxist books and Comintern pamphlets.[3] Nevertheless, Voitinsky's materials, and his personal presence, served as essential sources for Communist organization and provided the first direct contact with Bolshevism.

Voitinsky himself seems to have stressed for his audiences the similarities between the Russian and Chinese revolutions. In a brief article he published under his Chinese name, Wu Tingkang, on the third anniversary of the October Revolution, he portrayed the revolution as one that had overthrown the power not only of foreigners but of "bankers, warlords, and bureaucrats."[4] We may only speculate that what he conveyed to his radical audiences was similar. The message, if not an accurate description of the Revolution's goals, could not have failed to strike a responsive chord. After listening to him several times, Li Da recalled, "the Marxist-Leninists of the time understood even better the conditions of the Soviet Union, and could reach but one conclusion: 'follow the Russian way.' "[5]

Voitinsky's role in launching the Party has been summarized cogently by a Chinese historian.

> (1) In the spring and summer of 1920, Voitinsky held many meetings in Beijing, Shanghai, Jinan and Wuhan, where he introduced his audiences to the October Revolution and current conditions in the Soviet Union, explained the revolutionary program and the organizational principles of the Comintern and the Russian Communist party. He presented revolutionary intellectuals with the many propaganda materials that he had brought with him, and started progressive intellectuals off in establishing a Bolshevik-style party. (2) Voitinsky and Mamanev helped Li Dazhao in Beijing and Chen Duxiu in Shanghai in establishing the Communist Party. They also helped with the task of organizing the Party in Jinan and Wuhan. After the organization of the Party, they helped with the determination of party work, and initiated propaganda activities and the labor movement. (3) Voitinsky and Yang Mingzhai helped organize the Socialist Youth Corps in Shanghai. . . . Yang Mingzhai also assumed responsibility for the Foreign Language Institute established to train cadres, and started the Russo-Chinese Correspondence Society.[6]

This evidence of direct Comintern participation has prompted one preeminent student of early Chinese-Soviet relations, Xiang Qing, to observe that "the founding of the Communist party of China was a direct consequence of Comintern intervention to establish a Chinese branch of the Communist International."[7] Xiang has unequivocally rejected any significant Soviet influence on China before Voitinsky's visit. Commenting on Mao's statement that "the roar of the October Revolution carried Marxism-Leninism to China," he writes:

> Speaking truthfully, "the roar of the October Revolution carried Marxism-Leninism to China" not after the October Revolution but after Russian revolutionaries came to China, and personally placed the works of Marx and Lenin in the hands of progressive elements. Neither did it lead to any relations between progressive Chinese and the Russian Revolution before this time.[8]

Xiang believes that as long as the Russian-Chinese border remained closed, neither the October Revolution nor the Comintern (first congress in 1919) had any appreciable influence on Chinese radicals. This situation changed drastically with Voitinsky's arrival.

> The history of the genuine transmission of Marxism to China by the Russian Revolution starts in March 1920, with the Comintern organization of Chinese radicals. The Comintern emissary Voitinsky was not a

theoretician (and did not become an expert on Chinese history until the 1930s) but a practical organizer. He was, however, quite helpful in the propagation of Marxism in China. He made sure of the establishment in China of the Marxist theory of the dictatorship of the proletariat, he made sure that Chinese Marxists went among the workers to propagate Marxism, he made sure that Marxists struggled against false socialism and anarchism.[9]

Voitinsky, in other words, was responsible not only for initiating Communist organization in China, but saw it through its infancy, keeping Communists on the straight and narrow path of Bolshevism. Communist organization, moreover, from its very beginnings came under Comintern guidance, which was to set its course through the 1920s. And, finally, it was under direct Comintern guidance that Marxism took root in China; Marxists began to distinguish themselves from the other socialists they had cooperated closely with before Voitinsky's arrival.

Voitinsky was no doubt helped in his mission by the very favorable impression he made on Chinese radicals. Luo Zhanglong recalls that at Beida, Voitinsky approached Li Dazhao with great respect, and was solicitous of the concerns even of his younger listeners. He impressed them not only with his concerns and experiences, but with his "grasp" of China's problems. Almost immediately they came to look upon him as "teacher and friend." In Luo's experience, he was the first foreigner who did not patronize the Chinese.[10] When Voitinsky met Chen in Shanghai, according to another report, the two hit it off right away, "as if they had been old friends."[11] Unlike his authoritarian successor Maring, Voitinsky seems to have chosen to guide and instruct rather than command. As the first Russian Communist whom Chinese came to know extensively in the flesh, he provided them with a better example than other foreigners, and a "glimpse" of the new kind of revolutionary Bolshevism had created.

Voitinsky's visit, moreover, seems to have been planned so as to elicit the most favorable response. By early 1920, Chinese radicals already felt considerable sympathy for the Soviet Union's suffering from the capitalist powers' aggression, and respect for the Bolshevik regime's ability to resist while proceeding with the business of internal reconstruction. Their nationalistically inspired sympathy for the Soviet Union received a tremendous boost in March 1920 when the Karakhan Declaration of the previous year was finally made public in China in March 1920. The declaration, which renounced the unequal treaties that had been signed between the Czarist government and the imperial Qing Dynasty, aroused widespread enthusiasm in the Chinese press, including the radical press. In April *Weekend Review* published a translation of the document with an enthusiastic endorsement by Dai Jitao. The following month *New Youth* followed suit. More than one Chinese historian has pointed to the publication of this document as a turning point in Chinese interest in the Russian Revolution. Li Da notes its implications for Voitinsky's visit: "Because the first declaration of the Soviet government on China had just been published, and was welcomed with great enthusiasm among many social groups, people were particularly happy when they heard that a Russian had just arrived in Beijing."[12]

It was the relay of this document to the Chinese government, ironically, that led to Chinese relaxation of their vigilance over border controls, which made Voitinsky's visit possible. This was not a coincidence. According to Allen Whiting, the Karakhan Declaration was forwarded to the Chinese government through the Irkutsk office of the Comintern of which Voitinsky was the chief.[13] If the document was intended to pave Voitinsky's way, its success was obvious.

The question of the role of Chinese nationalism in the emergence of Communism must be approached with caution, for it lends itself readily to facile explanations that make nationalism the cause of Communism, and Communism a surrogate for nationalism. While Chinese nationalism played an important part in shaping attitudes toward Communism at this time (and later), the revolutionary nationalism of Chinese radicals must not be reduced to a one-dimensional nationalism that makes no room for extra-nationalistic revolutionary aspirations. All Chinese were in some sense nationalists, yet also something other than nationalists; their perceptions of the problems of Chinese society were as crucial in determining the nature of their nationalism as their nationalism was in qualifying their various revolutionary ideologies. If in 1920 some Chinese responded favorably to Voitinsky's message out of a nationalistic sense of gratitude to the Soviet Union for the Karakhan Declaration, they did not therefore all become Communists. Dai Jitao was a good example. Chinese historians have stated that his sympathies for the Soviet Union were entirely a product of his nationalist sentiments; yet he was one of the first to reject the relationship with the Soviet Union when it assumed the form of a Communist party linked to the Comintern. Others who were enthusiastic about Communism, such as Chen Duxiu, nevertheless felt uncomfortable with the implications of the alliance when it seemed to compromise their autonomy. As has been evident repeatedly since 1920, while nationalism has reinforced Chinese attraction to Communism, it has also militated against it. This contradiction rose to the surface as soon as Communism became a reality of Chinese politics. Thus nationalism does not serve sufficient explanation for radicals' response to Voitinsky.

Voitinsky's visit played a more significant part in the establishment of the Party than is suggested by the metaphor of "catalyst"; available evidence supports Xiang Qing's conclusions. Voitinsky did not simply convert Marxist intellectuals who were already prepared for such conversion; he organized the Party out of radical material that was quite unprepared for Communism. The founding of a Communist party was greeted with conflicting responses, and required considerable organizational effort on the part of Voitinsky and his Chinese followers. Similarly, Voitinsky's personal qualities as an organizer, and his efforts to interpret the October Revolution in Chinese terms, persuaded some, but not all.

Voitinsky's success, in other words, was conditional on the circumstances he found at hand. Historians such as Xiang Qing, in their insistence that the Party was a product of Comintern activity, ignore the significance of these circumstances. If Chinese radicals did not have a clear predisposition to Marxism or Communism before Voitinsky's arrival, neither were they an inert mass waiting to be molded into Communism. The contradictions in May Fourth radicalism already discussed had, by spring 1920, created fertile grounds for the acceptance of Voitinsky's message. The Comintern did not *create* this situation; rather, it *redirected* May Fourth radicals, who in spring 1920 found themselves at a crossroads. This is quite evident in the case of the two leaders of communism in 1920, Chen Duxiu and Li Dazhao.

Chen Duxiu and Li Dazhao

In January 1920 Chen Duxiu decided to leave Beijing for Shanghai to escape government harassment, which had made life difficult for him since his release from jail in September 1919. Li accompanied his friend and colleague to Tianjin to see him off to Shanghai. According to Deng Zhongxia, who was with them, on the way to Tianjin the two men discussed the possibilities of establishing a political party.[14] This is the first recorded instance we have of a discussion concerning the founding of a Communist party in China. Over the next few months, however, such discussion was to become commonplace in Beijing and Shanghai.

It is difficult to say what either Li or Chen might have had in mind. By early 1920, Li was a confirmed promoter of Marxism. His writings from this period show his historical outlook already dominated by the materialist conception of history. In Beida he taught courses on Marxism, and, under his intellectual leadership, the university had become a hot spot for discussions of Marxism. By late spring some of his students, such as Luo Zhanglong and Liu Renjing, had become quite adept themselves as students of Marxism. Li's rooms at the Beida library (the "Red Chamber") were open to his more intimate students, and they often gathered there for reading and discussion of Marxism and socialism.[15]

Li's Marxism, and especially his political identity, however, retained ambiguities. His first applications of the materialistic conception of history to the analysis of Chinese society retained his eclectic understanding of Marxist historical theory, freely blending Marxist concepts with ideas derived from geographical determinism.[16] Even more problematic was his attitude concerning contemporary political solutions. He had long held that political solutions that did not address basic questions of economic structure would be of no avail, but he was quite ambivalent on what the right solutions might be. While he occasionally proclaimed the inevitability of class struggle, he had not given up his hope in alternatives. In September 1919, he still expressed agreement with the Young China Association's advocacy of social transformation through the agency of "small groups."

The "youth movement" of the "Young China" that I hope for is a movement that seeks to transform both the mental and the material, both body
and soul, a movement that gets rid of the intellectual class, that enters
labor unions, that seeks to establish small groups on the basis of villages,
and aims to establish a broad union that takes the world as one big
family.[17]

He reiterated this position as late as December 1919, when he wrote: "I
hope very much that each profession and each group in the country makes
itself into a small organization [*xiao zuzhi*] and unites with others in a large
federation [*da lianhe*] to establish the basis for real democracy."[18]

Nothing in these sentiments distinguished Li from the guild socialists or
anarchists. Indeed, in late 1919 and early 1920, he supported with enthusiasm
the labor-learning movement in Beijing. He retained a theoretical interest in
the functioning of such groups. In January 1920, he published in *Weekend
Review* an essay based on Morris Hillquit's discussion of nineteenth-century
American utopian communities in his *History of Socialism in the United
States.* The essay discussed the mode of operation of these communities and
the reasons for their ultimate failure, but it was the editor of *Weekend Review,* Shen Xuanlu, not Li, who drew the conclusion that all these societies
had been destroyed by forces beyond their control.[19] Recall that when the first
labor-learning group in Beijing collapsed in March 1910, Li shared Hu Shi's
observation, against Dai Jitao's Marxist analysis, that its members were responsible for the failure.

Li, moreover, retained an academic, antipolitical stance on Marxism.
Though he seems to have discussed party organization with his students after
his initial discussion with Chen, even when party organization was under
way in the summer of 1920, according to Zhang Guotao, he continued to
express doubts about converting Marxist study groups into a political party,
on the grounds that they did not know enough Marxism.[20] This may well be
a reflection of Zhang's efforts to exaggerate his importance in the founding of
the Party nucleus in Beijing. It is nevertheless suspicious that in Beijing, the
location of the first Marxist study society led by China's "first Marxist" and
his radical students, the founding of a Communist nucleus lagged behind not
only Shanghai but Hubei and did not take place until sometime in October/
November 1920. Li's reluctance was also consistent with his appreciation,
deeper than most of his colleagues', of Marxism's difficulties. Zhang Shenfu,
a Beida instructor who was close to Li personally, provides at least indirect
confirmation of Zhang Guotao's claims, pointing to the indecision of Li, and
Chen, concerning the new party's name.[21] Li's political attitudes as a Marxist
retain some mystery, not the least indication of which is his failure to attend
the founding congresses in 1921 and 1922.

Now that the political animus against Chen Duxiu that has long dominated Chinese historiography has subsided, at least relatively speaking, Chinese scholars admit that Chen Duxiu, not Li Dazhao, was responsible for the
founding of the Party in 1920–1921. Chen's initiative also proves beyond
doubt that the quest for an effective political organization was far more im-

portant in the founding than any abstract ideological attraction to Marxism. Chen was by early 1920 an angry man, frustrated by the failure of the May Fourth Movement—which he had done so much to provoke as the acknowledged intellectual leader of the New Culture Movement—which was compounded by his maltreatment at the hands of the authorities. By his own admission, he knew little about Marxism when he initiated the founding activities. He was too impatient to wait upon a prolonged theoretical preparation. The time had come, he believed in 1920, for political action; theory could be learned in the course of it.[22]

This is not to suggest Chen's attitude toward the question of the party was free of ambiguities. Like Li, Chen failed to appear at the first congress in 1921 because he was "too busy," even though he was the acknowledged leader of the Communist movement, and was elected the first general secretary of the party in absentia. During the first year of the Party's existence, moreover, he had rocky relations both with the Comintern advisor Maring and with his own subordinates, at least partially because he found himself unable to submit to Bolshevik discipline. His party-building activities did not stop him from engaging in activities hardly consistent with the Bolshevik beliefs he professed, such as his continued support for labor-learning experiments well into the summer of 1920.[23]

As the editor of *New Youth* magazine and a professor at Beijing University, Chen was the undisputed leader of the New Culture Movement and, by the time of the May Fourth Movement, China's most distinguished radical. While he promoted radical causes, however, he did not himself play any significant role in the discussion of Marxism and socialism in the aftermath of the May Fourth Movement—possibly because he was in jail as that discussion was gathering speed. In a brief essay he penned for *Weekly Critic* in April 1919, he described the "Russian Revolution of the twentieth century" as "the key to the transformation and evolution of human society," but there is no evidence to indicate that in the early May Fourth period he was anything but a radical democrat.[24]

Chen was arrested in June 1919 for distributing pamphlets on a Beijing street corner, and spent the following three months in jail, despite popular outcry. His incarceration, rather than intimidating him, seems to have strengthened his resolve. Whether or not it also radicalized him, or got him thinking on the establishment of a party, is more difficult to say. While there is evidence of a shift in his thinking following his release, it is almost certain that before his move to Shanghai in January 1920, he was still not thinking of political organization in terms of a Bolshevik party, and Marxism was not a significant component of his thinking. In late 1919 he still owed more to John Dewey and Bertrand Russell intellectually than to Marx and Lenin.

Yet a shift in Chen's thinking starting about this time perhaps gives a hint, if only embryonic, of his turnabout in the spring of 1920. His writings before the May Fourth Movement had stressed New Culture themes of intellectual and cultural change. After his release, two themes appeared in his writings with increasing regularity, and significance; a concern for economic change as the basis for all other change in society; and for the population beyond intellectuals, especially labor. As with the reformist socialists of the time, this change initially was an extension of New Culture goals to the population at large, coupled with a concern for social reorganization to strengthen the basis for democratic institutions. Chen still appeared primarily as a radical democrat, but his democratic radicalism was now pushing him toward socialism.

Chinese historians have pointed to the Manifesto of the New Youth Society published in December 1919 as evidence of Chen's radicalization. The Manifesto, which criticized the hypocrisy of old thought, of "Mammonism and warlordism," read, in its relevant sections,

> Our ideal new era and new society are to be honest, progressive, free, equal, creative, beautiful, full of universal love and mutual assistance [*sic!*], and pleasant labor; in short, happiness for the whole society. We hope that the hypocritical, the conservative, the negative, the bound, class-divided, conventional, ugly, vicious, warring, restless, idle, pessimistic elements, happiness for the few—all these phenomena will gradually diminish and disappear.
>
> The new youth of our new society certainly will respect labor; he should according to his ability and interest treat labor as free, pleasant and beautiful rather than consider such a sacred thing a mere means for maintaining a subsistence. . . . We advocate mass movements and social reconstruction, absolutely cutting off any relations with past and present political parties.[25]

The Manifesto, in its concern for mutual aid, labor, mass movements, and social reconstruction, was certainly more radical than the initial program of *New Youth* magazine, restricted to the intellectual improvement of radical youth. Nevertheless, it contained no hint of Bolshevik or Marxist leanings. It represented the ideas of the liberal-radical democratic coalition that still edited *New Youth,* and its most radical ideas were the dominant anarchist themes of the period.

Much the same could be said of Chen's opinions in a short piece he published in his "Random Notes" in *New Youth* in December 1919, "The Extremists and World Peace" ("Guojipai he shijie heping"). The piece offered a very brief account of the background of Bolshevism in Russia, and defended the Bolsheviks against the charge of undermining world peace. The real enemies of peace, Chen pointed out, were those who still retained the aggressive ideology of militarist states, those who could not let go of "the self-aggrandizing thinking of a class or a nation."[26] It was not Bolshevism as political ideology he defended, but rather the right of the Soviet Union to self-determination.

There was nothing in these pieces published in December 1919 that could not be found in the writings of reformist socialists of the day such as Dai Jitao and Zhang Dongsun. Chen's position in 1919 was closest, by his own admission, to that of Zhang Dongsun, as is evident in the most important piece he published in December, "How to Establish a Foundation for Democracy" ("Shixing minzhidi jichu"), written under the influence of John Dewey.[27]

The article was important for articulating Chen's new emphasis on the priority of economic change. The goal of change, he stated from the beginning, was to secure "the progress of social life." Considerations of democracy entailed both political and economic democracy. Politics, however, was only a means, because the more fundamental realm of change lay in economic organization: "If the problems of the social economy are not resolved, no major political problem can be resolved; the social economy is the foundation of politics."[28] The means toward resolution, Chen insisted, were moderate rather than social revolutionary, and took as their premise the existing social system. Indeed, since one of the fundamental problems he identified in existing society was class-based pursuit of self-interest, he opposed class struggle. Rather, like other socialists of the day, he argued that the best way to reorganize Chinese society was from the bottom up, proceeding from small groups (professional and neighborhood associations that cut across class lines) to nationwide organization through a hierarchical system of representation. Chen, uncharacteristically, even alluded to the virtues of backwardness at one point, stating that Chinese society already had a tradition of self-government (*zizhi*) which, purged of some of its undesirable aspects, could support a new political and economic system based on local self-government.[29] The problems of Chinese politics since the founding of the Republic in 1912, in his view, arose out of an undue emphasis on central-provincial relations that ignored local self-government. A note acknowledged Chen's debt to Zhang Dongsun for inspiration, and even recommended an article by him as a companion piece. Chen's ideal of small groups, like Li Dazhao's, was probably also responsible for his enthusiasm toward the labor-learning movement in late 1919.

If Chen remained opposed to class struggle, his radicalized notion of democracy, now extended from political to economic questions, did lead him to a greater emphasis on class. In an essay in *Morning News* in the same month, "To the Workers of Beijing" ("Gao Beijing laodongjie"), he presented democracy as an instrument of the oppressed in their pursuit of liberation. In the eighteenth century democracy had been the banner of the bourgeoisie in its search for liberation from the aristocracy. *"Demokelaxi* of the twentieth century," he continued, "is the banner of the oppressed working class against the oppressor class of financiers, merchants, and industrialists."[30]

Chen still did not advocate class struggle, but the extension of his idea of democracy to questions of economic democracy, and his discovery of labor, was to result in a visible radicalization of his thinking by the time he moved to Shanghai in early 1920. Possibly also his new inclinations found expression in Marxism through his association with socialists in Shanghai, especially Dai Jitao and the *Weekend Review*. His emphasis on economic questions and his attention to labor both intensified following his move there; more importantly, he increasingly expressed his ideas in a Marxist language. His important essay "On Suicide" ("Zizha lun") in *New Youth* in January 1920 pointed to social and economic oppression, both spiritual and physical, as a major cause of the increase of suicide in the contemporary world. While this was only one kind of suicide, it showed a definite increase with the advance of "civilization":

"The more advanced the material civilization, the more the power over wealth is concentrated in a few hands and the misery of the economically oppressed deepened; therefore, the rate of suicide is much higher among the civilized than among the backward peoples."[31] Chen offered social reorganization as the only remedy.

Chen's stress on economic organization as the root cause of all social problems was also evident in his critique of Malthus in April 1920, "The Demographic Theories of Malthus and the Problem of Population in China" ("Maersaise renkou lun yu Zhongguo renkou wenti").[32] The essay criticized Malthus' emphasis on population increase, and suggested that the root cause of poverty was the system of private ownership: capitalists, who concentrated in their hands the means of production, deprived laborers of their surplus production, hence held the power of life and death over them. As far as laborers were concerned, surplus production was not really surplus because they could not afford to purchase the fruits of their own labor. In capitalist society, surplus production led to periodic crises of overproduction, as a result of which capitalists had no alternative but to seek markets elsewhere, which resulted in imperialism and militarist states.

This essay is the first I know of in which Chen used a Marxist vocabulary explicitly, and hinted at a Leninist analysis of imperialism. Whether or not he already had access to materials Voitinsky had recently brought must remain an open question; but the essay leaves no doubt that by April 1920, Chen had begun to familiarize himself with basic Marxist concepts, and utilized them readily in his social analysis.

This turn to a theoretical Marxism was accompanied by an increasing interest in the working class and socialism. It is possible that Chen got under way in early 1920 the survey activities that culminated in the special commemorative labor issue of *New Youth* in May. In February, Chen was invited to Wuhan to give a series of lectures; in his lectures at the Culture University (*Wenhua daxue*) in Wuchan, which dealt mainly with education, Chen advocated a "common people's socialism" (*pingmin shehui zhuyi*).[33] He encouraged students at this university to engage in labor surveys. About the same time, he began himself to collect materials concerning a debate that erupted in Changsha in February over the issue of Hunanese women workers in the Housheng (Enrich the Masses) Textile Factory in Shanghai. Women workers in Changsha were being recruited for the Shanghai factory of the prominent national capitalist Mu Ouchu. In February 1920, editorials in Changsha began to criticize the recruitment practices of Mu's representative there, and the conditions offered in Mu's factory. The debate soon involved Mu himself (who pleaded that China's industrial development required sacrifices by all), and spilled over to Shanghai, drawing the attention of people such as Zhu Zhixin. This debate was the basis for Chen's first significant article on the labor question, published in the special issue of *New Youth*. The article consisted of a compilation of the various contributions to the debate, with a commentary by Chen which shows the important place Marxist analysis had come to occupy in his thinking. As in his essay on Malthus, he took up the question of surplus value (which seemed to fascinate him, among others), this time citing Marx openly. Chen argued against Mu's plea for understanding, on the grounds that laborers deserved to share in their surplus. While wages were held down in the name of developing national industries, he pointed out, stockholders' income continued to climb. In response to Mu's plea that working hours had to be kept long in order to increase production, Chen argued that labor time should be calculated as social, not individual; the factory could hire more people and decrease labor time for individuals. Chen's comments, as with other critics of Mu in the debate, were quite moderate, possibly because of Mu's reputation for enlightment. What is important here is that his reasoning was by May 1920 infused with Marxist concepts and vocabulary, however deficient he may have felt theoretically.[34]

Chen's efforts to promote the translation of Marxist works into Chinese are also direct evidence of his attraction to Marxism in spring 1920. After his arrival in Shanghai, he was responsible, with Dai Jitao, for encouraging Chen Wangdao to translate the *Communist Manifesto;* to help Chen along, he even provided him with an English version from the Beida library to compare with the Japanese.[35] Also in February, during his visit to Wuchan, he persuaded Yun Daiying to undertake the translation of Kautsky's *Class Struggle.*[36] Chen Wangdao's translation appeared in August 1920, Yun's in 1921. Aside from Kautsky's discussion of *Capital,* which had appeared in Chinese in 1919, these were the first important Marxist works to become available in Chinese for the education of Communists.

Chen may not have been as knowledgeable as Li Dazhao concerning Marxist theory, but by spring 1920 he had embraced Marxist ideas enthusiastically. His own frustrations had already pointed to the necessity of a political party; as Zhang Guotao tells us, he was itching for action.[37] While his admiration for the working class in May 1920, when he declared manual labor superior to mental labor, was by no means unqualified in practice, he was also deeply concerned by this time with their problems. When Voitinsky arrived in Shanghai in April, Chen was ready—even readier than Li had been in Beijing.

The Establishment of Communism

The Communist Party of China came into being in skeletal form during fall 1920, starting with the Shanghai nucleus, which was probably established in August. Chen Duxiu and the young radicals gathered around him in Shanghai played key roles, not just there but around the country. Party organization spread out of Shanghai, reaching as far as France, built upon the personal relationships of the Shanghai nucleus, especially Chen.

There is still considerable uncertainty concerning the origins of Communism in 1920. For lack of other materials, we must rely on the participants' recollections. They do not always coincide; hence it is not always clear exactly when the various nuclei were established or by whom. In addition to the ravages of time on memory, there is also a tendency in some sources to exaggerate their own role or denigrate their opponents'. In some cases not even the participants were always aware of what was going on; some in the Marxist study societies, for example, were not privy to the establishment of the Communist nuclei for which the societies served as a front. There is not even agreement as to what these groups were called initially: "party" (*dang*), "nucleus" (*xiaozu*), or "party branch" (*dangzhibu*). In spite of these uncertainties, the sources agree on the outlines of the process, and the key actors.

The Beijing "Society for the Study of Marxist Theory"

The first organization devoted to the study of Marxism was established in March 1920 at Beida, coincident with Voitinsky's visit. Named the Society for the Study of Marxist Theory (*Makesi xueshuo yanjiuhui*), it was led by Li Dazhao and its initial membership was recruited from the students Li had invited to participate in the discussions with Voitinsky, mostly members of the Common Peoples' Education Lecturing Corps: Deng Zhongxia, Luo Zhanglong, Huang Rikuei, Liu Renjing, and Gao Shangde. Luo Zhanglong in his memoirs includes Zhang Guotao in the list, but Zhang was in Shanghai when the society was established and joined it sometime after his return to Beijing in April.[38] These students were already close to Li Dazhao, and constituted a group not only through their activities in the Lecturing Corps, but through their common residence in the Morning Garden Society, which they had established the previous August; they now simply remade themselves into a Marxist study group. Others would join the society shortly afterwards, including the anarchists at Beida with whom Li's students had long cooperated. By late summer anarchist members included Huang Lingshuang, Yuan Mingxiong, Chen Derong, Zhang Bogen, Hua Lin, and Wang Jinglin. According to one account, Qu Qiubai, himself still inclined toward anarchism, was a member. If Zhang Guotao's account is accurate, on the eve of the founding of the Communist nucleus in Beijing, anarchists outnumbered others in the society.[39]

The Society for the Study of Marxist Theory was a secret society when first founded. Not until November 1921, after the formal establishment of the Party, did it make its existence known publicly, with blessings from the chancellor of Beida, Cai Yuanpei. While it would come to have more than two hundred members after it became open, it was initially small, restricted to radical students closely associated with Li Dazhao.[40]

After it became public, the society assumed three tasks: organization of members for the study of Marxism, translation of Marxist works, and organization of public forums for the discussion of Marxism and socialism. It is likely that while the society remained secret, the first two tasks were its most important functions. Members in Beijing concentrated on translations from European languages (unlike their counterparts in Shanghai, whose translations were restricted to Japanese).[41] A 1922 list indicates a collection of about forty volumes of works on Marxism in Chinese and English, among other titles, including a copy of "The Infantile Sickness of 'Leftism' in Communism" (*sic*), one of the works Voitinsky had rumoredly brought.[42] Marx, Engels, and Kautsky were represented by several works. Works on the Soviet Union, judging by the list, were still relatively sparse.

"Kangmuni" (from "communist") library, as the members called their reading room, served as their gathering place; but it is difficult to tell from existing accounts whether the founding of the society made any real difference for the Beida radicals, who had already become tightly knit in the course of their radical activities. The group seems to have operated at first as a genuine study society. Its establishment probably represented nothing more than a commitment to the organized study of Marxism, as is suggested by anarchists' willingness to join it. Possibly its immediate tangible effect was to test its members' commitment to such study, and to provide a forum for it. Important as this was, it did not represent as radical a shift as the group in Shanghai; that group came to serve almost immediately as a forum for the establishment of a political nucleus.

The "Marxist Research Society" in Shanghai and the Establishment of the First Communist Nucleus in China

The Marxist Research Society (*Makesi zhuyi yanjiuhui*) was established in Shanghai in May 1920, shortly after Voitinsky's arrival there. Its immediate effect was to bring together disparate radicals and socialists there who were already in informal contact with one another. Initial membership included representatives from every major group of radicals in Shanghai, including, in addition to Chen Duxiu, Dai Jitao, Shen Xuanlu, and Li Hanjun from *Weekend Review,* Zhang Dongsun, the guild socialist, from *Reconstruction,* Shao Lizi from *Awakening,* the Zhejiang radicals, and other young radicals (such as Li Da) associated with Chen.[43]

The Shanghai group was never a study society in the sense that the Beijing Society was. Almost immediately following its formation, Voitinsky seems to have engaged it in considering the possibilities for founding a Communist party. The first effort in June was apparently a failure, as it met with objections from senior radicals such as Dai Jitao and Zhang Dongsun, who had been willing to participate in a discussion society but not to see it converted into a political organization.

The Communist nucleus in Shanghai was established in August 1920 in a meeting with Voitinsky that seems to have deliberately left out opponents. Shi Contong remembers the founding members to have been Chen Duxiu, himself, Li Hanjun, Yu Xiusong, and Chen Gongpei.[44] By early fall the nucleus included about ten members. In addition to the above, Li Da, Shao Lizi (who was also a Guomindang member), Chen Wangdao, Shen Yanbing (Mao Dun), Li Qihan, and Yang Mingzhai were inducted. Shi himself had by that time already left for Japan, having given up his earlier professed intention to become a worker!

The formation of the nucleus rendered irrevocable the division that had set in among Shanghai radicals since the first discussion of party organization in June. Zhang Dongsun had already disassociated himself from the group and would shortly turn against Marxism and socialism. The same was true of Dai; Yang Zhihua recalls that when she returned to Dai's house one evening in the fall (probably August), she heard Dai crying over what his associates had done.[45] Whether or not he withdrew voluntarily is not clear; at least one account suggests that Sun Yatsen gave him a dressing-down when he heard of his involvement with Communist-related activities, and compelled him to withdraw.[46] Whatever the case, the impact on Dai seems to have been traumatic; according to Bao Huiseng, he attempted to take his own life when he left Shanghai for Sichuan shortly after the founding of the Communist nucleus.[47] Within the next couple of years, Dai turned against the Marxism he had done so much to spread and emerged as a leader of the Guomindang right. Others who withdrew from Marxism in response to the founding of the Communist nucleus included some of the more anarchist-oriented radicals from Zhejiang. Dai's coeditor on *Weekend Review,* Shen Xuanlu, another Guomindang member involved with the founding of the nucleus, however, retained his association with the Communist party until the mid-1920s.

How things proceeded after the first meeting in June is not very clear. It appears that with the withdrawal of his senior associates, Chen Duxiu came to rely almost exclusively on his younger colleagues, chief among them Li Da, also a knowledgeable Marxist only recently back from Japan, and Shi Contong and other Zhejiang group members. Zhang Guotao, once again in Shanghai during summer 1920, claims to have discussed a party program extensively with Chen. Voitinsky was a very frequent visitor at Chen's residence, and it would seem, judging by the results of the efforts during that summer, that he had a crucial role in founding a program for the budding party.[48] This should not be taken to mean that Voitinsky wrote the program himself; Shi Contong remembers that for lack of concrete models, the nucleus had to rely on books in drawing up a party platform.[49] Voitinsky's guiding hand was visible in giving direction to party activities, not in the specifics of the party program.

According to Zhang Guotao, his discussions with Chen that summer emphasized not a long-range political program but immediate tasks necessary to launch the party. These included questions of membership and propaganda. They agreed that membership should be open to all persons of integrity, including anarchists, so long as they sympathized with or believed in Marxism and were willing to work actively for the Communist cause. They also agreed that they should stress the recruitment of workers, since the party was to be one of workers, but at the same time strive to recruit young radicals and awakened women intellectuals. The urgent tasks then would be to establish various organs for propaganda and organization, and to launch Communist nuclei in other cities. Organizationally, Chen "advocated adoption of the more democratic committee system by the CCP [Communist Party of China] with a secretary elected from among the committee members to serve as coordinator. In addition to the secretary, there should be members holding responsibility for such tasks as propaganda, organization, etc. He contended that he recommended this organizational structure not only because the Russian Communist party used it, but also because it was suited to conditions in China."[50]

When the Communist nucleus was established in August, with Chen as its secretary, it had a brief outline of a program. The only items of programmatic significance were, according to Li Da, "the dictatorship of laborers" (*laogong zhuanzheng*) and "cooperative production" (*shengchan hezuo*).[51] Shi Contong was to remark later that these items were of "anarchist" and social democratic orientation.[52] This vague program was to serve as a guide until the more comprehensive "Manifesto of the Communist Party of China" ("Zhongguo gongchandang xuanyan") was put together in November.

Zhang Guotao has recalled in his memoirs that these activities took two directions: the launching of Communist nuclei elsewhere, and the organization of Communist activity and propaganda in Shanghai. Efforts to launch Communist organizations in other cities were already under way by the end of the summer. The activities in Shanghai determined the direction of central policy and served as models for the other nuclei as they were formed over the next few months.

The activity the Shanghai nucleus devoted itself to most was propaganda; this consisted of the systematic discussion of communism, the Soviet Union, and labor movements around the world. With its September 1920 issue *New Youth,* already moved to Shanghai from Beijing, became a propaganda front for this nucleus, publishing extensively on these topics. A new section was introduced with the anarchist Yuan Zhenying (a former student of Chen's from Beida) in charge, which published systematic reports on the Soviet Union, possibly based on the materials Voitinsky had brought. Between fall 1920 and spring 1921, *New Youth* would publish over one hundred "Marxist-related" pieces. Chinese readers were for the first time exposed to systematic reporting on the Soviet Union.

New Youth was an open publication. On November 7, 1920, coinciding with the third anniversary of the Bolshevik revolution, the Shanghai nucleus began to publish *The Communist* (*Gongchandang*), the first journal in China devoted exclusively to the propagation of Communism. It was an internal party organ; Li Da became the editor. It published Lenin's theoretical works, including *State and Revolution,* for the first time in China, and in it Communists were to articulate their ideology. Through this journal they also launched their attacks against other socialists in an effort to define their distinctive position on socialist politics (more on this later).

Other Shanghai publications devoted to promoting Communism were *Awakening* and *The World of Labor* (*Laodong jie*). The former, still formally a Guomindang paper, became under Shao Lizi's editorship a major organ for the surreptitious spread of Communist ideas. The latter, starting publication on August 15, 1920, was the first Communist organ devoted to reaching laborers. Unlike its anarchist predecessor, *Labor*, it was written in a simple language laborers could understand. It combined simplified discussion of theory with surveys on labor conditions, short stories, and labor songs, both to awaken laborers to their condition and to praise the value of labor. The opening piece by Li Hanjun gave as the reason for publication the need "to teach laborers what they ought to know" so that they could improve their condition, for "laborers were the most miserable people in the world."[53] The journal promoted the idea of "the sanctity of labor," as Chen had meant the term in May. Chen Duxiu was a major contributor; so were Shen Xuanlu, Chen Wangdao, and the anarchist Yuan Zhenying. As late as October 1920, it published a piece by Dai Jitao. While the message that came through was not always Marxist, the journal devoted itself to revealing to laborers the misery of their lives(!), their role in the production of value, and the need for organization, cautioning them against the falseness of existing "yellow" unions.

The Communist nucleus also undertook publication through its own printing press. This press published the first important Marxist and socialist works in China in 1920–1921, including Chen Wangdao's translation of the *Communist Manifesto,* Li Hanjun's *Introduction to Marx's Capital* (*Makesi zibenlun rumen*), Li Ji's translation of Kirkup's *History of Socialism* (*Shehui zhuyi shi*) and, in 1921, Yun Daiying's translation of Kautsky's *Class Struggle.*

How effective the propaganda was in recruiting members is difficult to say, but Communist organizational efforts had already met with some success by late in the year. Li Qihan (a member of the Green Gang in Shanghai) undertook the labor organization and, possibly because of his gang connections, showed considerable success. In early fall a school was established for textile workers. In November, mechanics from several Shanghai factories got together to establish the first Communist union in China, Shanghai Mechanics' Union (*Shanghai jiqi gonghui*), led by the Communist worker Li Zhong. Taking advantage of workers' strikes, which had been on the rise since early 1920, Communists in the ensuing months recruited more workers, including those in printing, textiles, and transportation. The mechanics' union almost immediately began to publish its own journal, *The Mechanist* (*Jiqi gongren*). The printers' union, with upwards of one thousand members, also published a journal, *Friends Pictorial* (*Youshi huabao*). A workers' exhibition held in December 1920 drew nearly four hundred workers. On May Day 1921, in striking contrast to the previous year, about ten labor unions were represented in the activities.[54]

Activities among youth and women also proceeded apace. Already in the summer of 1920, Communists had organized the Foreign Language Institute (*Waiguoyu xueshe*) headed by Mme. Voitinsky and Yang Mingzhai. This school was to serve as a recruiting ground for students to go to the Soviet Union; in the fall the first group departed, among them Liu Shaoqi, Ren Bishi, Peng Shuzhi, and the anarchist Hua Lin.[55]

At the same time, in August, Yu Xiusong was placed in charge of the newly founded Socialist Youth Corps (*Shehui zhuyi qingniantuan*), with a program of its own (later distributed to other Communist groups as a guide). The corps recruited its members mainly from youth who had abandoned their homes and come to Shanghai in search of prominent radicals such as Chen Duxiu, Dai Jitao, and Shao Lizi. By early fall it had about ten members.[56]

Women were recruited through the Common People's Women's School (*Pingmin nuxue*) headed by Li Da. Its students were also recruited from among women who had left their homes; they were enrolled on a work-study basis. Chen Duxiu, Chen Wangdao, and Shao Lizi all served as lecturers. Among its first matriculants was the later prominent novelist Ding Ling.[57]

Another institution used for inducting members lends insights into the recruitment activities in Shanghai and elsewhere: the bookstore. According to Chen Wangdao, Communists operated a bookstore in Hangzhou (initially headed by Shi Contong) which served as a means not only of spreading Communist ideas, but also of recruiting—from among customers.[58] How important this was in Shanghai is difficult to say, but similar bookstores in Changsha and Jinan would play a crucial role in recruitment there.

In November 1920 Chen Duxiu left Shanghai for Guangzhou upon the invitation of Chen Jiongming to serve as the commissioner of education in Guangdong. In his absence, Li Hanjun assumed secretarial duties for the nucleus. Li Da continued as editor of *The Communist;* Chen Wangdao assumed editorship of *New Youth.* Chen Duxiu would be away from the party center over the next year.

Chen's departure may have been typical of early participants in the Communist movement who were as yet unwilling to sacrifice education and career to the tasks of party-building (Chen himself at one point expressed his disapproval of professional revolutionaries). Nevertheless, the organization and propaganda apparatus Chen left behind him was well established, capable of continuing with the tasks he had initiated. Before he left, he had also overseen the formulation of the Party's first major programmatic document, the Manifesto of the Communist Party of China.

Whether or not this document existed in Chinese originally is problematic. It was translated into Chinese in late 1921 by a certain "Chang" (probably Zhang Tailei), from an English original the Chinese acquired in Moscow during the Conference of the Toilers of the East. It was originally dated November 1920. These circumstances suggest that it might have been put together by Voitinsky, who left China shortly after November.[59]

The Manifesto analyzed the ideals of Communism into three components: economic, political, and social. The economic ideal was the socialization of the means of production (*shengchan gongyou*). This would eliminate the basis of exploitation in society, the appropriation of "surplus value" (*shengyu jiazhi*) (given Chen's fondness for this idea, he may have had a hand in the formulation). The political ideal was to abolish political power (*zhengquan*) and get rid of the military and legal systems which protected the minority in society. The social ideal was to abolish classes, or to leave in existence only the working class, which amounted to the same thing.

The Manifesto then discussed the means to achieve Communism. Having established that the capitalist state could only be overthrown through violence, it pointed to class struggle as "the means of overthrowing capitalism." Class struggle was a universal law of history, but it was particularly sharp under the capitalist system. It was necessary "to organize and concentrate the power of this class struggle"; in other words, the Communist party would carry out propaganda among workers, peasants, and sailors (*shuishou*), and unify them for class struggle. The task was identical to that of the Russian Revolution of 1917: to transfer power to the party of the working class. This transfer would be brought about, in the last instance, by a "general strike" (*zongtongmeng bagong*).

The Manifesto then reaffirmed the "dictatorship of the proletariat" (*wuchanjiejidi zhuanzheng*) as the only way to establish Communism. While this had been established in Russia as a principle, it was universal in its implications, since the overthrow of capitalism would necessarily require a period during which its remnants would have to be suppressed. Hence in every capitalist society the same problems prevailed, and the same solutions were in order:

> The dictatorship of the proletariat in Russia is a manifestation of the worldwide class struggle between the proletariat and the bourgeoisie of the world. A partial victory in this struggle has already been achieved. . . . This is not a peculiarity of Russian history, but a general characteristic of world history. Every country in the world must go through these circumstances of class struggle.[60]

The Russian (Voitinsky, or the books he brought) input into the document is obvious, not least in the inclusion of "sailors" who, in China, with hardly a navy to speak of, did not constitute a significant target for propaganda. Whether Voitinsky or his documents might have been responsible for the ideals of abolishing laws and the military is more difficult to say. Like the "general strike" as the ultimate tactic, these were important elements in the anarchist program. Stated as ultimate ideals they are not necessarily inconsistent with Marxism or Bolshevism. Possibly, however, their inclusion in this program was a concession to the anarchists whom the Communists still hoped to convert.

By the time Chen Duxiu left Shanghai in November, the Communist nucleus had committed itself to a political program in which Russian inspiration, and possibly direct Russian writing, had played an evident role. This program in essence presaged the one the party adopted when it was officially established the following July. While the budding Communists were still in the process of deciphering the meaning of Marx and Marxism, in other words, they were already committed to a political program defined by the Bolshevik interpretation of a proper Marxist revolution. Voitinsky's visit had been a roaring success.

The Network of Communism: The Formation
of Communist Nuclei in Other Cities

Before Chen Duxiu left Shanghai, he had also initiated party-building in other cities. The process, as Bao Huiseng confirms in his memoirs, was directed from Shanghai.[61] The ideological and organizational pattern in Shanghai was emulated by the new nuclei in other cities.

The first Communist nucleus outside of Shanghai was established in Hubei sometime in September 1920 in a meeting held at Dong Biwu's Wuhan Middle School. The Shanghai nucleus participated directly. Liu Baihua arrived in Wuhan with instructions to establish a Communist group. Li Hanjun, Dong's "Marxism teacher," himself wrote to Dong directly to inform him of developments in Shanghai. Dong responded immediately; in a meeting held at his school, the Communist nucleus was established. Its members included all those who had cooperated with Dong in radical organizational activities during the previous year: Chen Tanqiu, Bao Huiseng, Liu Bochui (a lawyer), and Zhang Kaiqing—the only worker among them, who had been initiated in the course of his janitorial duties in the Culture Bookstore.[62]

The following month Shanghai sent Voitinsky's assistant, Mamanev, to help with organizational activities. Shortly thereafter, Li Hanjun arrived to consult with and lecture to the group. Both he and Mamanev joined them in efforts to recruit Yun Daiying. He remained adamantly opposed to political activity, however, and refused to join in.

In October, Beijing followed suit. Li Dazhao had kept abreast of the developments in Shanghai through his regular correspondence with Chen Duxiu; according to Zhang Shenfu, Chen had even consulted with him and Li concerning the name of the new party.[63] If Li had earlier been reluctant to establish a party, his reluctance was now overcome by the example of Shanghai, as well as pressure from his students.

The Beijing nucleus' initial membership was recruited mostly from among the Beida students who were already members of the Society of Marxist Theory. The nucleus had a membership upwards of twenty, including two workers—Deng Pei, a Tangshan laborer, and Shi Wenbiao, a railroad worker from Zhangxindian. Some, like Miao Boying, He Mengxiong's wife, were persuaded to join in spite of their initial opposition (she was an anarchist). When the nucleus was founded, the anarchists in the study society stayed on.[64] Indeed, they initially carried responsibility for the publication of the nucleus' labor journal, *The Voice of Labor (Laodong yin)*. Also at their insistence, the group initially eschewed strict organization, especially the appearance of hierarchy.[65]

The establishment of the other nuclei, outside the mainstream of radical activity that had led to the founding of the Shanghai group, was a more arduous process. In Hunan a Communist group came into existence sometime between October and December 1920, with only three members known for certain; Mao Zedong, He Shuheng, and Peng Huang. Before long, however, others, mostly from the New Citizens' Study Society, would join this original core.

The Hunan nucleus, too, was established at the urging of Shanghai, where both Mao and Peng Huang had connections. Nevertheless, the delay here requires some explanation. It illustrates the different sources that fed the making of this nucleus, reflecting its earlier legacy.

Mao Zedong was the key person. His petition trip to Beijing and Shanghai earlier in the year had coincided with the founding of the Marxist study societies in those cities. Whether or not he was aware of them is not known; there is no indication that he either participated in their meetings, or knew about them (though, according to Luo Zhanglong, he did visit the Morning Garden commune in Beijing). Nevertheless, it is possible, as he later claimed, that during this visit he not only met with Chen Duxiu in Shanghai, but also had a chance to look at the literature on Communism that had become available recently. After he returned to Changsha, he praised Chen as "our teacher," and "the pioneer of the thought revolution."[66]

Upon his return to Changsha, Mao founded in August 1920 the Russian Research Society (*Ilosi yanjiuhui*), which was devoted to the study of the Russian Revolution, and began to publish articles in Changsha papers praising the Revolution and Lenin. At about the same time, he was busy with efforts to launch the Culture Bookstore (*Wenhua shushe*), which was formally inaugurated in early September with financial aid from a broad range of supporters in Changsha. The bookstore immediately became a major source of radical literature, including in its collection such titles as *The World of Labor, Studies of New Russia,* and the *Government of Workers and Peasants in Russia,* all of which are strong evidence of ties to the Shanghai nucleus.[67]

Yet there is also clear evidence that not Shanghai but Cai Hesen in France finally converted Mao to Marxism and Communism, and laid the groundwork for his initiating the nucleus in Changsha. A meticulous survey of Mao's writings and speeches from this period by Gao Jinsou has concluded that he did not finally abandon anarchism in favor of Marxism until the end of 1920.[68] Indeed, Mao's praise of the Soviet Union in early fall 1920 gives little clue to his ideological orientation, since he used the most general terms, expressing admiration mostly for the success of the revolutionaries in carrying out a "common people's revolution" (*pingmin geming*).

By mid-1920, Mao had already come to believe in the necessity of a "commonly shared ideology," which he compared to a "banner": "Once the banner has been erected, people will have a direction, know which path to take and which to avoid."[69] His correspondence with Cai shows that it was Cai who provided him with a "banner" and guided him to Marxism. Cai had spent the first six months of his stay in France feverishly reading socialist literature. By the summer of 1920, he had convinced himself of the superiority of Marxism to all other socialist alternatives. In the July meeting in Montargis of the Work-study Promotion Association, he pasted an inscription from the *Communist Manifesto* behind the speakers' platform.[70] Members of the New Citizens' Study Society had been busy for some time trying to decide on a way "to change China and the world" (*gaizao Zhongguo yu shijie*). Cai had finally decided, and was able to convince many other members of the society, that "socialism was the way to change the world . . . and China could not be an exception."[71] Comparing the socialist revolutions in Germany and Russia, moreover, he had come to the conclusion that the Russian model was the only viable one. He wrote to Mao in August:

> Socialism is the product of capitalism; its main mission is to destroy the capitalist economic system. Its method is the dictatorship of the proletariat, to use political power to establish a social economic system. . . . The consequence of class struggle must be a class dictatorship; without dictatorship there is no way to change society or protect the revolution. Class struggle is in essence a political struggle; because present politics is nothing but politics of the capitalists, who use political power, law, and the military to oppress workers, if the workers desire to achieve their liberation, they have no choice but to grasp political power themselves. In other words, they must first destroy the state apparatus of the middle class (whether it is constitutional monarchy or parliament), and then establish the political organ of the proletariat—the Soviet. The working class cannot resolve its economic fate without achieving political power.[72]

It took Mao some time to respond favorably; Cai's radicalism had already divided members of the New Citizens' Study Society in France, and Mao was getting contradictory messages from his comrades. Nevertheless, his own letters show that he was gradually giving up hope in anarchism because of its impracticality, "the impossibility of a society without authority and organization." Sometime after October, he wrote to Cai that he "agreed completely" with his views.[73] Shortly thereafter, he initiated the Communist nucleus in Changsha.

The Shanghai and Beijing nuclei cooperated in the launching of Communist organization in Jinan. The Shanghai nucleus apparently worked through Wang Leping, the Guomindang member in Jinan (and a relation to Wang Jinmei) whose bookstore had promoted radical activity there in the aftermath of the May Fourth Movement. But the Beijing nucleus may have played the major role. Already in April 1920, when Voitinsky had left Beijing for Shanghai, Li Dazhao had arranged for him to stop briefly in Jinan to talk with radicals there. In late winter 1920, the Beijing nucleus dispatched to Jinan Chen Weiren, who launched there, through Wang Jinmei and Deng Enming, a Society for the Study of Marxist Theory (the name was identical to that in Beijing, and different from Shanghai's—to avoid the authorities' inteference by making it appear theoretical, it was claimed). This society also served as the Communist nucleus in Jinan. With the exception of Deng, all five members were surnamed Wang, which suggests that kinship ties may have played an important part. Jinan was to serve as the headquarters of the Communist nucleus in Shandong; but about this same time the Beijing nucleus also launched in Tianjin a branch of the Socialist Youth Corps, which incorporated some Awakening Society members who were still in China.[74]

The nucleus in Guanzhou was not established until early 1921. Guangzhou perhaps provides the most interesting case of the complex politics involved. Guangzhou had always been an anarchist center, and the anarchists from Beida and Fujian were once again gathered there in 1920. The first Marxist society in Guangzhou was established in early fall 1920, and consisted of two Russian advisors and several anarchists, including the most prominent in China: Ou Shengbai, Liang Bingxian, Huang Zunsheng, Liu Shixin, and Yuan Zhenying. Ou Shengbai, whom the Russian advisors had contacted with an introduction from Huang Lingshuang in Beijing, apparently played the key role in founding this group. Tan Pingshan and Chen Gongbo refused to join this group, even though they cooperated with the anarchists in the publication of *The Masses*. It was Chen Duxiu himself who took over the establishment of the "real" Communist nucleus in Guangzhou after he arrived there in November 1920. By early 1921, there was a non-anarchist Communist nucleus in Guangzhou whose membership was recruited from the editorial board of *The Masses,* led by Tan Pingshan and Chen Gongbo.[75]

The two nuclei abroad that completed the organization of Communism at the time of the founding of the Party require only brief comment. The one in Tokyo, established early on, consisted of two members, Shi Contong and Zhou Fohai, who had already participated in party-building activities in Shanghai in the summer of 1920. The nucleus in France, which actually came into existence after the official establishment of the Party in July 1921, was also organized by those who were already members in Shanghai and Beijing. In the fall of 1920, Zhang Shenfu (Beida professor and friend of Chen and Li), about to depart to teach at the Sino-French University in Lyons, was delegated by his colleagues to establish a party branch in France. At about the same time two other party members left for France—Chen Gongpei and Zhao Shiyan. It was these three men who undertook to establish the nucleus there. The two other members initially inducted in France were Zhou Enlai and Liu Qingyang, who were both members of the Awakening Society in Tianjin, and had known Zhang Shenfu back in China (Liu was already Zhang's lover and would shortly become his wife). Other radicals, including some members of the New Citizens' Study Society, would join the party there later.[76]

Chinese Communism in 1920–1921

The Shanghai organization was the "key link" that held together the Communist nuclei that came into existence in 1920–1921. Shanghai initiated organization in other areas of China and abroad, and served as a model for others with varying degrees of success.

While ideological ambiguity was by no means eliminated from Communist writings, including those emanating from Shanghai, Shanghai made available for the first time an organized body of material with a coherent ideology of revolution. It presented its immediate aim as the establishment of a dictatorship of the proletariat, made class struggle the inevitable heart of revolutionary strategy, and affirmed the working class, represented by the Communist party, as the main force of revolution. This ideology was propagated not only in *The Communist* but in the open publications from Shanghai, *New Youth* and *The World of Labor,* as well as the materials on the Soviet Union Voitinsky had brought. This literature, distributed to Communist groups around the country, provided them with reading and discussion. They in turn initiated their own publications to propagate the same ideas in their own areas. The nucleus in Wuhan in the fall of 1920 began to publish *Wuhan Weekend Review (Wuhan xingqi pinglun)*, which served as a Communist front. As Communist groups formed, labor publications began to proliferate around the country. Shortly after its founding, the Beijing nucleus began to publish *The Voice of Labor.* Guangzhou had already started publishing a labor journal, *Laborers (Laodongzhe)*, in October; in February 1921, it was joined by another labor magazine more directly connected with the Communist nucleus, *Labor and Women (Laodong yu funu)*. In the summer of 1921, the Shandong group began to publish the *Shandong Labor Weekly (Shandong laodong zhoukan)*. As far as is possible to tell, the Hunan group was the only one in China not to publish a labor journal. But it did publish several pamphlets on labor, and Mao used such popular publications as *The Public (Dagongbao)* to spread ideas of "the sanctity of labor." These publications, it is worth noting, also stimulated the publication of smaller journals by laborers themselves.[77]

These publications echoed the line on labor established in Shanghai, but depending on their editors, they did display some variation in the themes and ideology they promoted. The one that deviated most conspicuously was *Laborers* in Guangzhou, which was actually published by the anarchists in the "Marxist" study society, and promoted an anarchist line on labor that opposed laborers' participation in political activity.[78] While *The Voice of Labor* in Beijing, also edited by the anarchists in the Communist nucleus, took a position on labor much closer to *The World of Labor,* it, too, inserted anarchist ideas into its discussions, namely Tolstoy's laborism.[79]

The most unusual of the publications on labor was possibly *Labor and Women,* the journal of the Communist nucleus in Guangzhou, to edit which Shen Xuanlu moved from Shanghai to Guangzhou. Shen and Dai Jitao had earlier promoted in *Weekend Review* the view that under capitalism, women and laborers constituted the most oppressed groups in society, and that the same mechanisms were at work in the oppression of both groups. Women, however, were oppressed by males, in addition to their social oppression. If laborers were to be liberated, a new economic system was necessary; if women were to be liberated from their double oppression as producers for capitalist society and for males, they needed to achieve economic independence. This, now, was the line Shen promoted in *Labor and Women,* which sought to awaken in laborers and women a consciousness both of their common problems and of the complex differences between their modes of oppression, so that they could organize themselves for liberation.[80]

All these differences nevertheless, appeared within a common united front. The various labor journals that came into existence in late 1920 shared a common format, covered similar themes (the centrality of labor to social existence, conditions of labor, and the need for labor organization), and advocated class struggle. They assumed greater uniformity, moreover, as Communist organization assumed greater coherence. Ideological issues would be clarified further when the party center in Shanghai launched a campaign in November to secure ideological unity within its various branches.

Organizationally, too, Shanghai set the pattern. The organizational regulations drawn up there to guide labor and youth work were distributed to other nuclei as models. How closely these were followed is difficult to say. There is direct evidence (in memories anyway) that initially only Beijing and Wuhan conscientiously followed the pattern.[81] All that may be asserted with any confidence is that observable variations were more a consequence of confusion or varying local circumstances than unwillingness to follow Shanghai—except among the anarchist members, of course. The ideological confusion was eliminated rather rapidly, I will argue, as the organization of the Party took shape. Variation according to local circumstances would continue long into the Party's history.

Party work proceeded at differing speeds. Most successful was Beijing, where the Socialist Youth Corps, established with the founding of the nucleus, recruited around fifty members by the end of the year. Labor work, too, proceeded rapidly there, building on the basis Beida radicals had established in the spring. By the end of the year, a Communist-directed school for laborers in Zhangxindian taught children during the day and adults in the evenings. Major Communist leaders such as Deng Zhongxia, Zhang Tailei, and Zhang Guotao all participated in the school. Communists were also able to make inroads among railroad and mining workers in such locations as Zhangxindian, Fengtai, and Tangshan. More than a thousand workers participated in the May Day celebration in Zhangxindian in 1921; many of them soon joined the Communist-led Zhangxindian Labor Union.[82]

Other nuclei initially showed less success with labor than youth activity. By the end of the year, most of the nuclei had established branches of the Socialist Youth Corps, usually consisting of ten to twenty members (membership in nucleus and corps often overlapped).

Labor work seemed more difficult. In Changsha and Guangzhou, anarchist domination of the existing labor movement made it difficult for the Communists to gain influence.[83] Mao in 1921 began to cooperate with the anarchist labor leaders Huang Ai and Peng Renquan and was able, through this connection, to increase Communist influence in the labor movement in Changsha. In Guangzhou, Communists in 1921 made inroads into the anarchist-controlled Barbers' Union, and were able to establish a Construction Workers' Union in Foshan with over one thousand members.[84] As Deng Zhongxia admitted in his memoirs, however, because of anarchist competition, Communists did not register significant success in labor organization in Guangzhou until 1925. In early 1921, Chen Duxiu himself responded to a suggestion that the party center follow him to Guangzhou with the words: "Anarchists are all over this place, spreading rumors about us. How can we move to Guangzhou?" Chen was especially upset by the anti-Communist activities of two of his former students from Beida, "the little devil" Ou Shengbai and "the madman" Zhu Qianzhi.[85]

The only other place Communists were able to make some headway in the labor movement was Wuhan. Hubei Communists at first restricted their activities to labor surveys, which they had initiated a year earlier. In March 1921 they were able to take advantage of a strike by coolies to organize them.[86] Outside of Shanghai and Beijing, however, major Communist labor activity would get under way only in late 1921, following the official establishment of the Party. In this activity, moreover, Communists returned from abroad, such as Li Lisan and Liu Shaoqi, would play major roles, having benefited from their experiences with labor organization abroad.

Communists were not tightly organized in early 1921 but they were organized (a tight organization would not be achieved until the second party congress in 1922), which already gave them an edge over their radical competitors in terms of effective activity. At the beginning of 1921, there were still more anarchists than Bolsheviks in China, judging by the number of anarchist publications, which peaked in 1922.[87] Anarchists also continued to command influence among youth and laborers. Communist organization, however, had already given the Communists a distinct identity that was lacking in the case of the anarchists who were still unable to organize themselves for unified action, and whose ideological advocacy, therefore, retained the same diffuseness that had characterized it during the May Fourth period. Some anarchists were so frustrated by their inability to unite that they were beginning to look to the budding Party as a more viable alternative for carrying out social revolution. A few of them already worked with the Communists, without necessarily abandoning their anarchist beliefs.[88]

The organization of the Party also gave Chinese Communists an identity which, against the backdrop of the diffuse Marxism of the immediate May Fourth period, represented a crucial change in Chinese radicalism. By early 1921, it was possible to speak of a Marxist ideological identity in China. This was not merely a matter of the greater availability of information on Marxism and Bolshevism to Chinese radicals, or even of a better understanding of Marxism. The ideological sophistication of the Communists still lagged behind their organizational achievements. Li Da recalled that at the time they still did not undesrtand the "dialectic," or even what "national revolution" might have meant in Marxist terms.[89] Zhang Guotao echoed him when he remembered that in his discussions with Chen Duxiu in the summer of 1920, they were not sure of the connection between national revolution and proletarian world revolution.[90] According to Dong Biwu, Li Hanjun—the "Marxism teacher" and author of *Introduction to Marx's Capital*—was not certain when he lectured on Marxism in Wuhan whether the *"Introduction to the Critique of Political Economy* [sic] was capitalist or imperialist capitalist."[91]

Beyond such confusion, it is also clear that there was no clear-cut agreement on the relationship of Marxism to Communism. In the same lecture, Li told his listeners that Bolshevism, social democracy, and guild socialism were all different manifestations of Marxism—which, if accurate, was nevertheless inconsistent with Bolshevik beliefs. There was even some ambiguity in the message propagated by the Communist journals; the labor journals especially, did not always speak with one voice on immediate policy issues. *The World of Labor* promoted class struggle and the centrality of laborers to it, but also published pieces with a clearly economistic bias, and even praised the ideas of Bertrand Russell, who was at the time giving anti-Bolshevik lectures in China.[92] Chen himself on occasion expressed the belief that Chinese labor did not yet have the educational preconditions for political participation, and advocated instead concentration on economic issues. There were, furthermore, differences over party policy, such as Chen's advocacy of a centralized party against Li Hanjun, who favored decentralization.

What made for Marxist identity was not agreement on policy or a shared understanding of theory, but an ideology of action, which rested in the Party's political program. The question of a shared ideology of action was urgent, and this question, rather than the education of members in Marxist theory, in late 1920 occupied the attention of the party leadership. After its initial organizational phase, the party center in Shanghai launched an ideological campaign to ensure that only committed Communists would stay on. While this campaign was mainly directed at socialist competitors, its most important goal was the streamlining of internal party ideology. With this campaign, the Party would establish ideological criteria for distinguishing proper Communist belief from analogous socialist ideas. The ultimate criterion was "belief in Communism," which meant, in effect, commitment to an organizationally defined interpretation of Marxism. As ambiguities were clarified, Communists were to part ways with other socialists with whom they had continued to cooperate even in the founding of the nuclei. In fall 1920, anarchists left the Party. Over the following year even some of the Marxists in the party would leave, unable to confine their Marxism within the interpretive boundaries imposed by the organizational imperatives of the party they had helped create.

10

The Parting of the Ways:
The Ideological Emergence of Communism

The emergence of a Communist organizational identity was accompanied by division in the ranks of May Fourth radicals who had cooperated in the propagation of socialism for over a year. The division was immediate in some places, more gradual in others. It was finalized in the controversies over socialism in late 1920 and early 1921, which drew a clear boundary between the political beliefs of the Communists and their ideological competitors on the left.

The division was immediate in Shanghai and France. As we have already noted, socialists such as Dai Jitao and Zhang Dongsun withdrew from the Marxist Research Society in Shanghai as soon as it was suggested that it convert to a party nucleus; they were accompanied by those among the Zhejiang radicals of anarchist persuasion. At about the same time, in July, members of the Labor-learning Promotion Association in France held a three-day meeting in Montargis which was the scene of heated debates between a radical faction led by Cai Hesen, who had now become a Bolshevik and advocated political activity, and a more moderate faction led by Xiao Zisheng (the formal head of the New Citizens' Study Society), who wanted the group to continue with its original work-study (*gongdu*) goals. The disagreement divided the membership of the resilient New Citizens' Study Society. In August, the radical faction (which also included Xiang Jingyu and Cai Chang) split from the main body to establish its own Labor-learning World Association.[1]

In other places in China, Marxists and anarchists continued to cooperate in the activities that led to the establishment of Communism well into the fall of 1920. As far as I am aware, this cooperation was extended to the admission of anarchists into the Communist nucleus only in Beijing; in other places, such as Jinan, Changsha, and Guangzhou, the cooperation ended as the Communist nuclei were formed. In Beijing the nucleus not only made a concession to anarchist sentiments by relinquishing formal organization and hierarchy, but even handed the editorship of its labor publication, *The Voice of Labor,* to its anarchist faction. In November the nucleus finally decided to establish a stricter organization and tighten itself ideologically. Anarchists objected, since they were opposed to "national and regional leadership, officials of any kind, or any form of discipline." Secondly, they rejected "the dictatorship of the proletariat" which the group now decided to adopt as its guiding principle. According to Zhang Guotao, at the meeting held in November to "thrash out differences" between the anarchists and the Marxists, Liu Renjing argued that the dictatorship of the proletariat was "the essence of Marxism," and anarchists in response withdrew from the nucleus. This was a "blow to Li Tachao's hope that all socialists could unite."[2]

Similar division occurred elsewhere. In Jinan, the decision to establish a nucleus led to heated debates within the Promote the New Society; the anarchists believed in "individual freedom" (*geren ziyu*) and the Marxist believed in "group freedom" (*tuanti ziyu*).[3] In Changsha, according to Angus McDonald, the anarchists and the Marxists engaged in "fierce competition" for new members.[4] In Guangzhou, cooperation in the publication of *The Masses* gave way to struggle when the Communist nucleus was established in early 1921.[5] Similar conflict between Marxists and anarchists erupted in France when the communist nucleus was established in late 1921. During the following year, the Communist party publication *Youth* (*Shaonian*) engaged in prolonged ideological struggle against the anarchist journal *After Work* (*Gongyu*), led by Zhou Enlai and Ren Zhouxuan (Ye Qing). The "victory" the Communists achieved over the anarchists by early 1923 was probably more tangible than elsewhere: they were able to attract away from anarchist ranks Chen Duxiu's two sons, Chen Yannian and Chen Qiaonian, who had hitherto held back in favor of anarchism over Marxism![6]

As the case of Beijing illustrates, these splits were less a consequence of a conscious policy to purge the anarchists than of Communist efforts to achieve organizational and ideological coherence. Li was not the only one who nurtured hopes in the unity of all socialists. Comintern advisors possibly felt the same way, if for different reasons. The conciliatory attitude toward the anarchists was possibly a consequence of a desire to convert them. Comintern advisors, as is evident from their overtures to the Guomindang and to Chen Jiongming and his anarchists, wanted to unite Chinese radicals, not divide them. Some anarchists were included in the first group of students to go to the Soviet Union for study in fall 1920. As late as 1922, Chinese anarchists (Huang Lingshuang among them) were invited to participate in the congress of the Toilers of the East.[7] Even after a split occurred, as we shall see, Communists extended to the anarchists a conciliatory attitude they denied to other socialists.

Nevertheless, the split was a foregone conclusion once party organization and a coherent ideology was placed on the agenda of radical poliitcs. November 1920 was a turning point in this regard. The formulation in that month of the Manifesto of the Communist Party of China, and the publication of *The Communist,* which immediately began to propogate the "doctrine of the dictatorship of the proletariat" as "the essence of Marxism," left no uncertainty about the Party's ideological direction. The split between the anarchists and the Marxists coincided with this redirection of the Communist groups. The two goals, unity among socialists and a tightly organized Communist party with a tightly defined organizational ideology, were mutually inconsistent, unless other socialists were willing to adapt their socialism to that of the Party. It was a situation of in—or out.

Chinese historians have described the debates that got under way in November 1920 between the Communists and their anarchist and guild socialist opponents as two of the three important debates that accompanied the emergence of Communism, the first one being the debate over "problems and isms" between Li Dazhao and Hu Shi in the summer of 1919. That debate had marked the "victory" of Marxism over liberalism; the last two marked the "victory" of Marxism over socialist "heterodoxy," and gave a clear direction to Communism.[8]

Whatever the merits of this evaluation, the debates in late 1920 and early 1921 were extremely significant in the ideological emergence of Communism. The debates were also the third major discussion of socialism in China, having been preceded by the debate between Liang Qichao and the Revolutionary Alliance in 1905–1907, and the debate between Shifu, Jiang Kanghu, and Sun Yatsen in the early Republic. They marked the unambiguous emergence of Communism on the Chinese socialist scene.

While the Communists' debate with the guild socialists (led by Zhang Dongsun) must be distinguished from the debate with the anarchists, the two were part and parcel of the same process: the organizational emergence that brought Communists into conflict with anti-Bolshevik socialist ideologies. Moreover, as I shall argue, while the debate publicly sought to discredit anarchists and the guild socialists and thereby to prove the superiority of Bolshevism, in actuality it was directed as much, if not more, toward the internal party membership. This was especially true of the debate against the anarchists, which took place on the pages of the internal party organ, *The Communist,* and did not become public until March 1921 when, in the rejuvenated anarchist organ *People's Voice (Min sheng),* Ou Shengbai launched a counterattack. An important goal of the debate was to ensure ideological purity among members of the nuclei, many of whom were still tainted by pre-Bolshevik ideological inclinations, by clarifying for them the meaning of Communism.

The polemics against other socialists were led by the Shanghai center. Li Dazhao made one or two minor contributions, but the major spokespersons for the Communist cause were Chen Duxiu and the young but theoretically sophisticated Li Hanjun, Li Da, Shi Contong, Zhou Fohai, and Chen Wangdao. Chen Duxiu and Li Da (as the editor of *The Communist*) played the key roles in the polemics against the anarchists. Aside from *The Communist,* most of the Communist contributions to the polemics were published in *New Youth* and, to a much lesser extent, in *Awakening.* (These contributions were later complied in *A Compendium of Discussions on Socialism* [*Shehui zhuyi taolunji*] published by New Youth Press in 1922.) Arrayed against them were writers of *Reconstruction,* the organ of the guild socialists, renamed *Reform* (*Gaizao*) in fall 1920; Zhang Dongsun was the chief spokesperson for this group. In March 1920, *People's Voice,* the former journal of Shifu, was rejuvenated, and in it Ou Shengbai led the anarchist counterattack on the Communists, resulting in a prolonged debate between Chen Duxiu and his former student. The repercussions of this debate would continue into early 1922, but it reached its climax in early 1921, by which time most of the issues had been set forth clearly.

Communist historians in general present these polemics as a defense of Marxism against its opponents. There is no doubt some truth to this interpretation, but only partial, because it overlooks the crucial significance of the debate for the ideological unification of the Party itself. According to this view, anarchists had been on the attack against Bolshevism since 1919, and Communists now took up the cudgel to defend their ideology. While as we have seen, anarchists were critical of developments in the Soviet Union and opposed to "the dictatorship of the proletariat," this view ignores the fact that Communists cooperated with them well into fall 1920 and that some anarchists, as in Beijing, were even members of the Communist nuclei initially. Besides, the attack was launched against the anarchists in the internal party organ, *The Communist,* which suggests that it was initially directed not at anarchists in general but anarchists in the party and, even more importantly, non-anarchist party members who had not yet shed the "taint" of anarchist ideas. As we shall see, the tone of the discussions confirms this interpretation.

The polemics against guild socialists do suggest a defense of Marxism, though there were ambiguities. This debate was provoked by two articles Zhang Dongsun published in *Current Affairs Daily (Shishi xinbao)* on November 6 and 7. While seeming innocuously brief, the articles contained a hidden attack against the Communists. Since he had withdrawn from the Marxist Research Society in June 1920, Zhang had moved away from socialism, turning against not only Bolshevism (which he had opposed all along) but even his own socialist ideas of the May Fourth period. His move to the right was possibly encouraged by the return from Europe of Liang Qichao, who disapproved of his disciple's flirtation with socialism, and now sought to bring members of the Research Clique into line. Finally, Bertrand Russell had just arrived on a lecture tour at the Clique's invitation, and his anti-Bolshevik sentiments exerted considerable influence on writers connected with *Reform.*

That Zhang provoked the controversy is also supported by the fact that the Communist response did not seem preplanned. By the end of the year there was a coordinated attack on Zhang's position. Initially, however, the attack came from individuals angered by his statements in his *Current Affairs Daily* articles: Li Da was so angered that he penned an immediate response to them on the very day they were published. (His response appeared in *Awakening* the following day.)[9]

Nevertheless, we must place this debate, as well as that with the anarchists, within the context of ideological developments that had accompanied the establishment of the Communist nucleus in Shanghai. Starting in September 1920, with the issue that marked its conversion into a Communist front, *New Youth* had initiated a firm, if gentle, criticism of other socialists. Chen

Duxiu's article "On Politics" (*"Tan zhengzhi"*), published in this issue, the first important piece to signal the ideological break within Chinese socialism, must be the point of departure for any evaluation of the controversy that broke out in November. (It was no coincidence that when the proceedings of the controversy were compiled in 1922 in the *Compendium of Discussions on Socialism,* this article led the volume.) A response to Chen's article might have been anticipated at any time from socialists who had parted ways with the Communists, and in whose move to the right not just ideology but personal resentment against former comrades played at least some part. It came in November from Zhang, who had been ambivalent about socialism all along anyway, and now returned from a tour of the interior with the conclusion that socialism was irrelevant to China.

The polemics with the guild socialists, too, had important implications for the ideological purification of the Party. Members of the Research Clique were not the only admirers of Russell in China. Zhang Shenfu, a philosopher by profession and member of the nucleus in Beijing, considered himself a disciple of Russell's. Chen Duxiu himself was quite excited by Russell's lectures. Articles in *The World of Labor* praised Russell and even bemoaned the fact that Chinese workers' ignorance prevented them from appreciating fully what he had to say.[10] Here, too, clearly, ideological uncertainties still deeply prevailed among Communists; for what Russell had to say was to warn Chinese against following the Bolshevik path!

"On Politics"

Chen's article is significant because it not only shows how far he had traveled politically since writing "How to Establish a Basis for Democracy" in December 1919, but also—because it articulates the political views of the acknowledged leader of Communism in September 1920—gives an indication of the issues that drew the attention of the budding party organization. "On Politics" was not merely, as Chow Tse-tsung says, an indication of Chen's longstanding interest in politics, which surfaced as he abandoned culture as the means to changing China, but a statement on socialist politics by the leader of the new Communist party.[11]

The article did not simply discuss politics, but presented a case for what Chen considered correct politics. While Chen did not refer explicitly to Communism, Bolshevism, or the Soviet Union, his conception of correct politics clearly reflected a Bolshevik, or revolutionary Marxist, approach. Indeed, while the argument was presented as a broad discussion of politics, a close reading shows that its primary purpose was to expose the deficiencies of anarchist and "revisionist Marxist" (*Magesi xiuzhengpai*) conceptions of politics.

The article started off defending the need to discuss politics against an unnamed person in *New Youth* who opposed political discussion. Politics is an inevitable component of human life, Chen stated; even if we ignore politics, politics will not ignore us. It was no use, therefore, to rail against political discussion.

Chen addressed himself, on the one hand, to those who were opposed to discussing politics and, on the other hand, to those who advocated it. In the first group he included scholars such as Hu Shi and Zhang Dongsun, merchants of the Shanghai chamber of commerce, and the anarchists. His main concern was with the anarchists. He believed that the first two groups' opposition was temporary and relative, based on fear of warlords; anarchist opposition to politics, on the other hand, was fundamental, absolute, and systematic, and called for careful consideration.

Anarchist opposition to politics, Chen conceded, had considerable validity. Their criticism of the state and "naked force" (*giangquan*) in politics was based on plausible evidence. The states of the past (he cited Franz Oppenheimer) had indeed usurped people's rights by the use of political authority. The anarchist position was also supported by Bertrand Russell, who had argued in his *Principles of Social Reconstruction* that while the state was in theory the concentrated expression of popular sovereignty, in reality it constituted itself as a power outside of and above society.

Chen agreed with anarchist views on past and present states, but disagreed with their extrapolation from past to future. Anarchists argued that no matter how the state and its laws were reformed, they would still be based on coercion; no fundamental change was possible, therefore, that did not reject absolutely the state and its laws. Against this Chen offered two arguments, one "theoretical," the other "factual." Theoretically, he argued that "anyone who understands evolution theory" ought not to speak of fundamental or nonfundamental, since denying reasons to the reality of the world made it impenetrable by action.[12] Moreover, indiscriminating opposition to "force" (*giangquan*) was unscientific. Humans used force daily in their efforts to conquer nature; there was nothing wrong with force that served human ends. "Whether or not force is evil depends on how it is utilized"; "evil does not inhere in force itself."[13]

"Factually," Chen presented three arguments in favor of using force. First, human misery was a product of the oppression of the many by the minority bourgeoisie; since the latter would not relinquish its power voluntarily, violent class struggle was necessary. Secondly, the bourgeoisie was experienced in the manipulation of power; even after its overthrow, therefore, force would be necessary to control it. Finally, force would be necessary even to direct the people at large. Human nature had a bad as well as a good side. Whatever original human nature had been, laziness and selfishness had by now become second nature to human beings. This would not change overnight with revolution, but would require the use of coercion for some time to come.

Chen's concluding message to the anarchists was that those who were opposed to the state and the laws of the working class might as well "be viewed as friends of the bourgeoisie."

Those who favored politics, according to Chen, could also be divided into two groups, the "old group" (*jiupai*) which held a superstitious awe of politics, and the "new group" (*xinpai*) which viewed the state as no more than an instrument, yet upheld it as the means to changing human society. He was concerned mainly with the latter group, in which "Marxist revisionists," such as the German social democrats, were the most prominent. There were not many of these people in China yet, he observed, but their numbers would surely increase with industrial development. In their reliance on the state and laws, the revisionists had become allies to the capitalists in England, Germany, and France. They called themselves state socialists but were in reality nothing other than state capitalists. They advocated a system where the state would be the only capitalist, which was sure to make the lives of the working people more, not less, miserable.

The worst deviation of this group, according to Chen, was its abandonment of class struggle in the name of democracy and humanitarianism. Without class struggle, democracy could never be anything but a tool of the bourgeoisie. Chen backed up this argument with the authority of the *Communist Manifesto;* some of his ideas also suggest that he was familiar with the *German Ideology*.

In conclusion, Chen summarized his own views on politics as follows:

> I recognize that humanity cannot abandon politics; I do not recognize the kind of politics that consists of struggle over position or the private usurpation of power.
>
> I recognize that the state can only be a tool, not a principle [*zhuyi*]. . . .
>
> Although I hold that we need not abolish root and branch the state, politics, and laws, I do not recognize that the bourgeoisie of the present (the state, laws, and politics of the usurping class) has the capability for sweeping away existing social ills.
>
> I hold that the greatest need for the present is to utilize the method of class struggle to establish a state of the working class, the producing class, and create laws and a politics that do not permit usurpation either at home or abroad. What it will be like afterwards is not for us to anticipate at this point.[14]

Anarchists were quick to perceive the implications. In the following issue of *New Youth* letters from two anarchists, Zheng Xianzong and Ke Qingshe, criticized Chen's views on laws and politics, especially his implicit defense of the dictatorship of the proletariat. Zheng criticized Chen's seeming defense of a perpetual existence for the state. The state, he argued, represented only one stage in human progress and should not be viewed as eternal. He rejected Chen's distinction between the past and the future, arguing that the state by its very nature prevented human fraternity by dividing people. Perhaps necessary in the past, it was now no more than a relic.

Zheng further criticized Chen for his assertion that anarchists rejected violence. Only some anarchists inspired by Tolstoy rejected violence, he pointed out, otherwise most agreed that violence was necessary to achieve liberation. But the need for violence would disappear with the success of the revolution. Capitalism would have no hope of resurrection once private property had been eliminated. If further suppression became necessary, it should be only on a temporary, transitional basis. Zheng also challenged Chen's view that force would be necessary to overcome ingrained habits of laziness and selfishness. In his opinion, Chen confounded the evils of one historical period with the eternity of human nature. Besides, he observed, even if some people did not work, it would be very difficult to establish standards for the correct application of violence that did not violate the rights of others. Zheng, in other words, preferred to err on the side of freedom from coercion.

The other respondent, Ke, agreed with Chen for the most part, adding only that one need not worry too much about the state since, with the abolition of property, the state would disappear automatically.

Not surprisingly, what seemed to bother the two anarchists the most was Chen's suggestion that the state, the dictatorship of the proletariat, might be as permanent a fixture in the future as in the past. In his response to Zheng, Chen denied that he had assigned permanence to the state. The major difference between himself and his two critics lay in the time period they assigned to the transition to a stateless society. He believed the state would have to exist for a fairly long time, since it would take effort, laws, and coercion to purge people of the hold of the past. As for standards, he argued, equal sharing of responsibilities and the periodic shifting of unpleasant tasks provided sufficient means for resolving the distribution of labor.

To Chen, revolution was not a single act but a continuing process, since he was unsure how long it would take for "reason to conquer instinct." What ultimately distinguished his reply from his anarchist respondents was its greater, pervasive pessimism. The state and coercion would be necessary for the foreseeable future (the only future he was willing to speak of) because there was no reason to be overly optimistic about human nature. Nor was it very meaningful to speak of "fundamental" transformations, since the task at hand required piecemeal resolution of problems inherited from the past. Revolution was not a single enormous effort followed by an eternity of ease, it was a task that required continuing, and arduous, work. The recognition of this—of the material constraints imposed by society and history on human action—was to Chen the distinguishing characteristic of the scientific against the utopian socialist.

Chen's answer to Ke was brief, as Ke's letter had been brief. Many opposed proletarian dictatorship, he pointed out, because it was not democratic; how democratic was it for workers not to be free in the present society?[15]

This initial clash was carried out in a courteous tone that would characterize such debates in 1920–1921. The debate itself appeared to be within the camp of radicals who agreed on the purpose of revolution if not the means. The clash between the Communists and the guild socialists which soon followed was different.

The Communists against the Guild Socialists

Chen's essay had included "revisionist" Marxists among its targets. Whether this had anything to do with provoking *Reform* socialists to attack Communism is hard to say since, when the debate erupted between the two groups in November, there were no direct references to this essay. There is no question, however, that the ideas Chen had advocated in his essay were prominent among the ideas *Reform* socialists sought to refute.

This debate was over the relevance of socialism to China, or the relative virtues of capitalism and Communism as means to resolving China's problems. We need to use the term "socialist" with caution in describing the political stance of *Reform* authors, who did not share a common vision of the future. Among the various authors who contributed to the debate, Zhang Dongsun, Xi Liuji, and Yang Ruiliu were the most insistent that they were criticizing Communism from a socialist perspective; the socialism that most appealed to them was English-style guild socialism. Zhang Junmai advocated German-style social democracy, while Peng Yihu and Lan Gongyan defended capitalist development modified by Bismarckian social legislation. Liang Qichao did not participate—except through an open letter criticizing Zhang Dongsun's zeal for socialism—but his ideas were ever-present in the writings of *Reform* authors.[16] He had been an anti-socialist ever since his debate with Revolutionary Alliance socialists in 1905–1907; his own ideas most resembled those of the advocates of capitalist development with social legislation. Nevertheless, the description of the *Reform* position as "socialist" is justified by the role Zhang Dongsun played: as the debate's initiator and in the cogency of his arguments. It was also his ideas that drew the greatest attention from the Communists since, in claiming a socialist position, he most seriously challenged the advocacy of Communist revolution. Zhang's evaluation of contemporary Chinese society, and his critique of Communism, were shared by all *Reform* writers.

Zhang provoked the controversy with two short essays in *Current Affairs Daily* on consecutive days in early November: "A Lesson Derived from Travels in the Interior" ("Yu neidi luxing er dezhi yi jiaoxun") and "Another Lesson Derived from Travels in the Interior" ("Yu neidi luxing dezhi youyi jiaoxun"). Zhang had spent the previous two months traveling in central China, and had concluded that China's greatest problem at present was poverty, exacerbated by warlord and bandit disorder. A statement he made in his second essay, quoting from a friend's letters, became the immediate cause of the controversy.

Shi Xincheng has told me: "Chinese at the present are not qualified to discuss or institute and ism [*zhuyi*], since no place in China has enough (of anything)." I also feel that this statement is valid, and painful. Except for a few in cities and treaty ports, at present most Chinese have not even achieved a "human existence" [*rendi shenghuo*]. Mu Zhushan has written to me from the United States saying that American farmers are better off than the Chinese middle class. . . . If we are to speak of an ism that can help Chinese achieve a "human existence," that ism is not a Western-derived socialism, statism, anarchism or Bolshevism [*duoshu-paizhuyi*]. We would do well to look elsewhere for it.[17]

Zhang had decided that the needed increase of wealth meant the development of industry. He described as empty talk any ism that could not "help Chinese achieve a 'human existence'." He had, in fact, returned to a position he himself had criticized earlier in the year: that only industrialization could change China (*shiye jiuguo*).

In response to the immediate furor these articles created, Zhang was asked by Liu Nangai to elaborate his views, which he did in "The Present and the Future" ("Xianzai yu jianglai"), published in the December issue of *Reform*. This essay was the most comprehensive exposition of the *Reform* position.

The structure of Zhang's argument is plainly visible in his summary of his position at the end of the essay: First, China has two tendencies at the present: the emergence of a gentry-merchant class (*shenshang jieji*) and tendencies toward the violence of a "false worker-peasant" (*wei laonong*) revolution. The first is slow, the second is rapid; the first is necessary (*biran*); the second is possible (*keneng*). Second, it will be possible to distinguish worker and capitalist only with the emergence of the gentry-merchant class. The adverse effects of this emergence will be felt only after a period of development—an idea have been inspired by Marx's notion of social relations turning from motive force to "fetters" of development. Third, the emergence of the gentry-merchant class will bring definite advantages: wealth and education will increase, those without a livelihood will become a proletariat, and warlord domination will be terminated. Fourth, on the other hand, if "false worker-peasantism" (*wei laonong zhuyi*) wins out, it can only be destructive and add to disorder. Fifth, "we" (i.e., socialists) must understand the limits of our power. We can neither increase wealth nor stop the advance of the gentry-merchant class, or put an end to warlordism. If we call for "worker-peasantism," we will only succeed in creating "false worker-peasantism." Sixth: therefore, socialists' task at present is to engage in cultural and educational work, study socialism, and promote "cooperativism." Seventh, our ultimate mission is to replace the gentry-merchant class, but that will be in the future. Zhang added, finally, that his argument rested upon "the theory of natural stages in history" (*lishidi ziran jieduanshuo*) and "the theory of human creativity" (*renwei chuangzaoshuo*). It was also inspired by Russell's lectures in China, as he pointed out at the beginning. What was most remarkable about the essay, however, was his use of what were clearly Marxist ideas of historical development (from the preface to *An Introduction to the Critique of Political Economy*, especially) to refute the possibility of revolution.[18]

The argument Zhang presented might have warmed the heart of any capitalist or landlord in China; yet he insisted that he was presenting the argument in the best interests of socialism (guild socialism, which he took to be the most advanced that had grown out of Marx's ideas). Indeed, his argument rested on a conclusion he drew from "the theory of natural stages" Marx had taught "us all": that the establishment of socialism must await the full development of capitalism. China at the present did not have the economic or social preconditions for socialism; if it were to be established now, it could only be "false worker-peasantism"—by which he meant, as did other *Reform* writers, Bolshevism.

Zhang had already sounded this theme in his earlier pieces—that the outstanding characteristic of Chinese society was its poverty. Oppression in China was not of class but of poverty. Chinese society, he averred, suffered from four "diseases": ignorance (*wuzhi bing*), poverty (*pinfa bing*), military and bandit chaos (*bingfei bing*), and foreign oppression (*waili bing*). If China had classes, they consisted of the peasantry and the military class. There was hardly a bourgeoisie or an urban class (*shimin*). There was no proletariat to speak of; what passed for the proletariat was no more than unemployed "vagabonds" (*yumin*), who were the creation of poverty, and who fed militarism and banditry. Since there were no classes, there was no class oppression. What workers there were suffered not from the oppression of the bourgoisie but from the oppression of "labor bosses" (*gongtou*). In agriculture, landlords and tenants shared income; if there was oppression, it was due to bandit and warlord oppression. Finally, foreigners' control of the economy oppressed all Chinese equally.[19]

Under the circumstances, Zhang argued, China's most essential need was for development. On the basis of present trends, there were two possible alternatives for development: capitalism and socialism. To Zhang, development under capitalism was the only viable alternative, since what went under the name of socialism not only did not have the power to develop the country, but could only lead to "false worker-peasantism," betraying its own socialist goals.

Since his basic intention was to refute Communist claims, he devoted most of his discussion to showing why socialism would not only not help, but even harm the country. Aside from his argument that there was no economic basis for socialism, he rested his conclusion on the observation that there was no social basis for it either. His premise was that any ideology, to be instituted, required the backing of a class. The democratic aspirations of the 1911 revolution had been frustrated, he observed, because there had not been a middle class to support democracy. The same problem existed with socialism. Its advocates were a few intellectuals; there was no genuine working class to provide the basis for socialism. There were only a few genuine workers in China and, with a few exceptions, they were unorganized and backward educationally. (Ironically, he pointed to the Communist-organized mechanics' union in Shanghai as the example of organized workers!) The rest were vagabonds. A socialism established on this basis could only be "false worker-peasantism" and add to disorder. Such disorder would not help China's develment; indeed, it could only play into the hands of warlords, and the foreigners who desired to intensify their economic domination.[20]

Zhang brought other arguments to bear. Dictatorship, he argued, was unviable in China because no one was qualified to assume the role of dictator. Besides, even dictators needed the support of a class, and in China there was no "working class" to support such a dictatorship. If one were established, the vagabonds would simply turn to struggle against one another. Thirdly, dictatorship did not suit the Chinese national character; while there was a strain that favored it, a contrary strain opposed centralized rule. Finally, social and political trends indicated that the present tendency was toward local self-determination, not centralization.

The national character argument, which Zhang had rejected a year earlier, played another important part in his anti-Bolshevik reasoning: Chinese were by nature opposed to rapid changes, and would not tolerate the kind of changes advocated by "false worker-peasantists." If they did, on the other hand, they would desire rapid results and, if such results were not forthcoming, turn against the changes overnight. Chinese were by nature, as Zhang presented them, at once patient and impatient!

Finally, Zhang played the foreign threat card: socialism was impossible because foreigners would not permit it. Whatever Chinese might desire, foreigners, who had a keen interest in China's economic fate, were not going to sit idly by and watch China go socialist.

Zhang, therefore, concluded that China's only hope lay with the other trend of contemporary society: the gradual emergence of a gentry-merchant class. There were signs that such a class was emerging in Chinese cities; there were even signs that some of the "military lords" (*bingfa*) were turning into "finance lords" (*caifa*). This new class offered the best hope of overcoming warlords and developing China economically. It could also anticipate foreign help, since foreigners were desirous of seeing China develop economically. The development under this class would be slow, but certain. Socialists should welcome the emergence of this class, since it would create a working class and prepare the basis for socialism.

In other words, capitalism, in both theoretical and practical terms, was the best hope. Socialists, in the meantime, should engage in cultural work, improve their understanding of socialism (which was currently quite primitive), and wait for the day when they could lead the working class to replace the gentry-merchant class. Perhaps with this kind of development the working class itself would acquire capitalist tendencies, Zhang conceded, but at least it would be educated; after all, there was no point in offering *Capital* to a working class that could not even read! The only social activity socialists could engage in presently was to promote consumer cooperatives, both to ease life for the working class, and to lay the groundwork for producers' cooperatives of a higher stage.[21]

Whatever his insistence that he was speaking in the best interests of socialism, Zhang's precocious argument (Plekhanovite in its determinism) denied in effect that socialism had any immediate relevance to China, and relegated it to a meaninglessly distant future in favor of a contemporary capitalism. Other writers for *Reform* went even further, rejecting socialism, especially Marx's socialism, as a viable path at all. Some rejected Marx's class analysis, arguing that social organization and political attitudes were too complex to be confined within the concept of class.[22] They pointed to the Soviet Union to argue that the overthrow of the capitalist class did not mean an end to exploitation and oppression, since these still persisted there.[23] Whatever their subtle differences, these authors were at one in concluding that for the foreseeable future, capitalist development was the only path open, and the best that could be done for the working class was to ameliorate its condition through social legislation, cooperative organization when and where possible, and, above all, education. Recalling arguments of the immediate May Fourth period, some suggested that the capitalist class be called upon to educate the working class, since it had a stake in that process.[24]

How all this was to be achieved under conditions of extreme poverty and disorder, *Reform* writers were not willing to say. This omission, and their denial of a basis for socialism in Chinese society, became the targets of the Communists.

Zhang's initial articles in *Current Affairs Daily* were immediately attacked by Li Da, Chen Wangdao, and Shao Lizi in *Awakening*. In the December issue of *New Youth,* Chen Duxiu compiled these articles, as well as responses by Zhang and others in the *Reform* camp, and published them as "The Discussion of Socialism" ("Guanyu shehui zhuyidi toalun"), adding a couple of contributions by himself. In ensuing months, *New Youth* published numerous articles by Chen Duxiu, Li Da, Li Ji, Zhuo Fohai, and others criticizing Zhang. In February 1921 *Reform* responded with a series of articles of its own, published in a new section of the journal entitled "The Examination of socialism" ("Shehui zhuyi yanjiu"). The controversy lasted through spring 1922, but the basic positions were clear enough by early 1921. As is evident in the February issue, the polemics drove *Reform* writers even farther to the right, eventually an almost unquestioning defense of capitalism, even though Zhang continued to insist on his basic socialist commitments.

The immediate Communist response focused on Zhang's failings as an individual. Li Da accused him of "ideological instability."[25] Chen Wangdao, recalling Zhang's December 1919 essay "Why We Must Discuss Socialism," wondered aloud why Zhang now made socialism into a cause of social misery when he had only recently praised it for its humanitarianism.[26]

Over the next two or three months, however, a more substantial critique of Zhang emerged that most of the Communist participants shared. Not surprisingly, they devoted the greatest effort to refuting the suggestion that capitalism was superior to socialism in considerations of China's development. The most systematic arguments against capitalism were formulated by Chen Duxiu in a speech he gave at the Law and Political Science University in Guangzhou, which was published in the July 1921 issue of *New Youth* under the title "A Critique of Socialism" ("Shehui zhuyi piping"). Almost predictably, Chen's critique was based upon Marx's idea of surplus value and his analysis of crises in capitalist society, themes Chen had first utilized in his criticism of Malthus in early 1920. Capitalism, Chen argued, had already created the crisis in European society; for China to adopt capitalism would simply be a blind adherence to European development. Capitalism was defective in both production and distribution. Capitalist production had two defects, private property and overproduction. The concentration of the means of production in private hands had resulted in the bifurcation of society into two classes, a "vagrant" (*yusui*) class that controlled production and a "miserable laboring" (*laoku*) class that sold its labor. Secondly, *laissez-faire* economy resulted in the constant, unplanned pumping of capital into production, which led to periodic overproduction and crisis. In distribution, surplus value (*shengyu jiazhi*) was usurped from laborers by the capitalist class.[27]

This problem was to Chen proof of the ultimate hopelessness of the capitalist system. In a system of private ownership, surplus value could not be distributed to the working class or utilized for social purposes. The value capitalists absorbed (capital, in other words) was pumped back into production, resulting in a surplus product that could not be absorbed by social consumption, because the same usurpation of surplus value deprived laborers of the ability to consume the products of their own labor. The economic crisis created by this process, Chen (citing Marx) argued, doomed the capitalist system to extinction. The crisis of capitalism (hence of revolution) had been averted by capitalist expansion and the creation of colonies. Marx's predictions concerning revolution in capitalist society had not been wrong, because capitalism had merely prolonged its life temporarily through colonialism. In the process, however, capital had allied with the military to create the militarist state, which had been responsible for the recent world war. Wilson's principle of self-determination had failed, according to Chen, because the American president had failed to understand this alliance between capital and the military.[28]

Chen's argument was not original, but was remarkable in that it showed familiarity not only with Marx but possibly with Lenin. *Imperialism* (as far as I am aware) was not yet available in Chinese, though Chen might have had access to it in another language. Related ideas were available in other writings of Lenin published at this time, such as the text of his speech at the second congress of the Communist International, which was published in *The Communist*. Possibly Chen got his analysis not from Lenin but Hobson, whose *Imperialism* was available in Chinese and was even cited by one of the *Reform* contributors to the debate. Whatever the source, the issue of imperialism was a new feature of the debate on socialism in China, as was another related idea—that capitalism was international and it was therefore meaningless in the contemporary world to speak of whether or not it existed in any one country.[29]

This theoretical appreciation of capitalism gave Communist writers the basis they needed to refute Zhang. Zhang had claimed that because only a few people in China led a comfortable existence while the rest were oppressed by poverty, there were no classes. In an open letter to Zhang in the December issue of *New Youth,* Chen suggested that those few who lived comfortably got their comfort off the backs of the working class.[30] Poverty in China, he (and others) argued, far from being the source of oppression, was the consequence of capitalist exploitation. The "vagabonds" Zhang spoke of, Li Da pointed out, were nothing but unemployed workers, deprived of their livelihood by capitalism.[31] Capital, Chen argued, created poverty by depriving workers of their jobs both in the city and the countryside. Technological development had made possible the unprecedented expansion of production, but also made laborers superfluous. Capitalist factory production, undermining handicrafts industries, eliminated an important source of livelihood for the agricultural population. Capital had an even more direct hand in agricultural unemployment: capitalist investment in land expropriated peasants' land, condemning them to vagabondage.[32] Capitalism, in other words, had come to play an important part in the Chinese economy, not only in the cities but also in the countryside—this argument, like so many in this debate, anticipated the later Trotskyist analysis of Chinese society. In his contribution, Li Ji drew upon evidence from Chinese society to argue that China had many capitalists, big and small. There were many workers, but because of the poverty capital condemned them to they appeared at times as "vagabonds."[33]

An article in the April issue of *The Communist* directly addressed the issue of oppression in the agrarian economy. The author denied that distribution was equitable in Chinese agriculture, and went on to divide the agrarian population into four classes: landlords who owned land but did not till it themselves, instead renting it out to the tillers (*tucaizhu,* he called them, or "landed finance lords"); a "middle peasantry" (*zhongdeng nongmin*) which tilled the land it owned and even rented land from others; "low peasants" (*xiaji nongmin*) who had some land but mostly rented from others; and the poorest, who owned no land and had to sell their labor. Not only was distribution unequal, the author argued, but there was a tendency in agriculture toward the concentration of land, similar to the concentration of capital in industry.[34]

While this article was addressed to the peasantry, calling on them to rise and join the revolution, in the process it also sought to refute the argument that there was no class consciousness or class conflict among the peasants. The author was particularly incensed at the ascription of agrarian conflict to outside agitators, pointing to the Pingxiang uprising of fifteen years earlier. Outside agitators, he argued, had no power to create class consciousness (which was a product of economic conditions) but could only speed up its articulation. Communism would be a real possibility in China, he concluded, if Communists could mobilize the peasantry, who already showed signs of class consciousness, since the suffering of the Chinese peasant was no less serious than that of the Russian peasantry on the eve of the October Revolution.[35]

Another article in the same issue, "The Self-government Movement and Social Revolution" ("Zizhi yundong yu shehui geming"), challenged the idea that the gentry could serve as a means for modernizing China. (This article, curiously, was a translation, with no indication of who its author was.) The author did show a grasp of the situation in China: that the gentry themselves were producers for warlords, that their effort to establish self-government was intended to enhance their own power and promised little benefit to the common people, and that they were no more powerful than anyone else against the warlords. On the other hand, the article argued its case mainly on general theoretical grounds, drawing on the example of revolutions in Europe. The "third class" (*disan jieji*), the author argued, had always relied for its power on the "fourth class" (*disi jieji*), but had also ended up betraying the latter. Even if the Chinese gentry managed to make itself into a middle class, it would do the same with laborers. It made much more sense, therefore, for laborers to carry out their own revolution and establish their own power through a social revolution than to participate in the self-government movement which would inevitably benefit the gentry alone.[36] This issue was important for the Communists since until only recently, some of them (including Mao) had participated enthusiastically in the self-government movement. Others (such as Chen Duxiu) who had rejected provincial self-government had advocated, in the May Fourth period, local organizations that cut across class lines.

Finally, Communists argued that industrialization in and of itself was unlikely to resolve the question of poverty, and might even exacerbate it. The history of Europe, as well as Chinese treaty ports, showed that industrialization made life worse for the majority of the people. Besides, they pointed out, socialists, too, advocated industrialization. In an open letter to Bertrand Russell, Chen Duxiu argued that both industrialization and the education of the worker could be achieved more efficiently under socialism. In the same context, he criticized *Reform* writers' assumption that capitalists should be trusted more than the state to achieve these goals. In an interesting, and perhaps self-contradictory, twist of his argument, he asserted that socialists only rejected capitalists, not capitalism, since socialism was itself capitalism without capitalists (he cited Dai Jitao in his support)![37]

The most interesting aspect of the Communist response to Zhang was the upholding of socialism's relevance in contemporary China. Most fundamental was the argument that it was meaningless to speak of whether or not capitalism existed in China, since in the age of international capital, no distinction could be made between Chinese and foreign capitalism or capitalists. This argument (again an important Trotskyist argument later on in the decade) was shared by all Communist participants in the debate, including Li Dazhao who, in his only contribution, insisted that there were no economic boundaries in the contemporary world.[38] There was an accompanying argument, again one that Li Dazhao and Chen Duxiu shared. While insisting on the unity of world capitalism, Chen argued that all Chinese held the position of laborers vis-a-vis foreign capital! China could not develop because Chinese capitalists were under the sway of foreign capital; real economic independence could only be achieved, therefore, through a workers' revolution. This argument also underlay his belief that while the movement for liberation was to be international, existing nations must first provide the point of departure. While these arguments served to refute Zhang's views on capitalist development, and his assertion that socialism would be impossible under conditions of foreign domination, they also pointed to a tension between Communist thinking on contemporary global capitalism and on China's particular needs. The advocacy of a Communist revolution required for its justification that China had already moved into capitalism. But this "capitalist" China, capitalist because part of global capitalism, was also a "proletarian" nation. The two ideas, not easily reconcilable, would provoke much debate and division in Communist party ideology in later years.

Equally interesting were the arguments countering Zhang's deterministic interpretation of Marx: that socialism must await the prior development of capitalism. In his open letter to Russell, Chen Duxiu argued that backwardness was itself a virtue, since it would enable the Chinese to avoid the mistakes of Western and Japanese development. Chen also argued that Zhang's determinism led him to overlook the role of human will in the development of society. Revolution was not merely a consequence of social evolution, but an act of will.[39] Revolution and evolution, Zhou Fohai added, recalling anarchist arguments, were not mutually exclusive; revolution merely hastened evolution and provided it with direction.[40] Chen believed that revolution was especially important in backward societies, which could not afford to wait for "natural" evolution to take its course. But perhaps the most "unorthodox" view (for a Communist, at least) was offered by the later Trotskyist Li Ji, who argued that Marx had after all been only a man, and that not all of his ideas were valid for all time. Times had changed since Marx had formulated his historical theory, and new times required new explanations and solutions.[41]

Chen Duxiu's conclusions in his "Critique of Socialism" summarized the Communist position. First, capitalism had already created a crisis in European society, pointing to its lack of viability as a model for China. Second, all Chinese were laborers vis-a-vis the West: only a workers' revolution could secure independent development for China. Third, the tendency toward internationalism was very pronounced in the contemporary world, but development, to be placed on a firm basis, must still start with individual nations. Fourthly, capitalism had already been shaken by the world war; hence it was necessary to unite with comrades around the world to bring about its downfall. Finally, unless foreign capital was overthrown, there could be no independent development for China, since foreigners would inevitably interfere with economic development.[42]

Implicit in these ideas was the social revolutionary premise that characterized Chinese Communist ideology in later years: that class struggle was part and parcel of China's liberation from imperialism. Having evaluated all the available socialisms in the second part of his long talk, Chen concluded that only Bolshevism offered a viable alternative for China because, of all the socialisms Marx's ideas spawned, only Bolshevism upheld Marx's commitment to class struggle. Bolshevism also reaffirmed the centrality to revolution of the dictatorship of the proletariat which, as was implicit in the Communist reasoning, was the only way to guarantee the success of revolution under the circumstances of Chinese society.

The debate with the guild socialists was crucial not only because it offers us a glimpse of Communist ideology as it unfolded following the establishment of the Party in mid-1921, but also because it played an important part at this time in articulating the Communists' position on capitalism and revolution. Whether or not they succeeded in convincing others outside their camp is beside the point; it clarified for those in the Party the implications of two ideas already central to Communist ideology: class struggle and the dictatorship of the proletariat. It also offered guidelines for the Communists' interpretation of Marx, which was already Leninist in character, although a full Leninist articulation emerged only after the Party's founding. Chinese historians sometimes express dissatisfaction with the "unorthodox" suggestion (by Li Da, for example) that Marxism was not restricted to Bolshevism. They recognize, nevertheless, that "the debate exposed the counterrevolutionary nature of guild socialism, and drew a clear line of demarcation between guild socialism and Marxism, and put an end to this counterrevolutionary way of thinking."[43] Primarily in the Party, we might add, where many had earlier found a great deal of value in guild socialism, and continued to express admiration for its greatest proponent in China, Bertrand Russell, even after they had committed themselves to Bolshevism. Most importantly, with this debate revolutionary intellectuals first committed themselves to the idea of class struggle, which until then they had viewed with considerable suspicion.

The Communists against the Anarchists

The attack on anarchism was even more clearly an internal party affair and, considering anarchism's widespread influence among party members, more crucial to their education in Bolshevism.

If there was an immediate cause for the discussion of anarchism that got under way almost with the first issue of *The Communist,* it was the tightening of party organization in November 1920 which was to result in the exodus of anarchists from the party. Initially, moreover, the discussion was a one-sided affair. To repeat what we have already stated, some anarchists had been attacking Bolshevism since early 1919, but it would be erroneous to view these attacks as the provocation for the discussion that started in *The Communist* in November 1920. Other anarchists had been members of the Communist groups since that summer, and in the initial period of party formation, Communists and anarchists cooperated all over China. The Communist criticism starting in November is best viewed, therefore, as an effort to clarify issues of Bolshevik versus anarchist revolution, over which there was still considerable confusion; most members of the Communist groups had been under the sway of anarchist ideas until only recently. The discussion in *The Communist,* moreover, was not addressed to any group or individual but asserted the superiority of Bolshevism to anarchism in general. Unlike the debate with the guild socialists, whom Communist writers freely described as the running dogs of capitalism, the journal's tone adopted toward anarchists was one of extreme friendliness, intended more to persuade them to abandon their "wrongful" ways than to discredit them. This tone persisted even when the ideological differences broke out in public debate between Chen Duxiu and his former student Ou Shengbai in the spring of 1921. Communist-anarchist polemics would not assume a tone of acrimony until 1922, by which time the inevitability of the break between the two groups had become obvious to all. (We might add that the issues raised by Ou Shengbai at this time would provide the basis for anarchist attacks on the Communists for the rest of the decade, by the end of which anarchism had disappeared from the Chinese scene as a significant ideological alternative.)

The Communist was the first Bolshevik propaganda organ in China, and the first publication to propagate systematically a revolutionary Marxist ideology. In its six issues, published between November 1920 and July 1921, its readers (mostly party members) were exposed for the first time to Lenin's ideology of revolution, mainly through translations of foreign works on Lenin and the October Revolution. It was here that sections of *State and Revolution* were first translated into Chinese, and Chinese Marxists first became cognizant of Comintern discussions on world revolution. Most of the journal was devoted to reports on Bolshevik-inspired movements around the world, labor movements in various countries (including long reports on the IWW), and conditions of labor in China. In addition, the journal published the first serious discussions in China on the relevance of Bolshevism to the Chinese revolution. These articles, most of them written by Li Da, Zhou Fohai, and Shi Contong, were to lay the basis for discussions of Bolshevism in later years. At the time, however, anarchism seemed the most important issue to them.

The editorial introduction to the journal's first issue enunciated the political line it would propagate as an organ of the Party. Affirming the priority of economic change over all other change, the editorial presented capitalism and socialism as the only economic alternatives in the contemporary world. Capitalism had developed in Europe, and was already in decline. Socialism, on the other hand, was still on the emergence; Russia had become a "laboratory" for socialism. Communist parties around the world followed the Russian example, and so should China, where the evil effects of capitalism were already being felt. Chinese laborers filled the world; those abroad were slaves to foreign capital, those in China slaved for foreign and Chinese capitalists alike. If they were to be saved, the example of the Russian Revolution provided the only course. The editorial rejected parliamentary means unequivocally as a "lie" intended to deceive laborers. Laborers could only liberate themselves by wresting power from capitalists through class struggle and establishing their own power. The ultimate goal was the creation of a stateless society, which would follow once it was guaranteed that the capitalist class had no hope of revival. The conclusion was a call upon the anarchists to join the Communist party. Anarchists, too, opposed private property and capitalism; hence they must participate in the struggle to transfer power to the working class. To do otherwise was to serve the capitalists whom they desired to overthrow.[44]

The agenda laid out in this editorial set the course for the ensuing issues. The basic issue was that of social revolution: in particular, differences between an anarchist and a Bolshevik strategy of social revolution (now identified with "Communism"). In *The Communist* a new idea emerged in Chinese socialism of social revolution that integrated politics and the social movement in its process. The state corporatist solutions some socialists had favored (including Guomindang socialists, state socialists, and "Jiang Kanghu socialism") had eschewed class struggle in the name of an immediate political revolution, leaving the task of social transformation to the period after the latter. Anarchists and the "social corporatist" guild socialists, on the other hand, had rejected politics in the name of a social movement that would gradually transform society, and thereby abolish politics altogether or create a new kind of politics as the case might be. The Communist idea gave equal importance to politics and the social movement, conceiving of them in a dialectical relationship. Writers in *The Communist* dismissed offhand all the alternatives except the anarchist idea of social revolution, with which they expressed a sense of kinship. They presented what differences there were as being within the same revolutionary camp, pertaining to the means rather than the ends of revolution.

The author who went farthest in reaffirming the essential unity of Marxism and anarchism was Shi Contong, who asserted in his "How We Must Carry Out the Social Revolution" ("Women zemmayang gan shehui geming") that he believed in all the goals of anarchism ("free organization," "free association," and the principle of "from each according to his ability, to each according to his need") even though he was not an anarchist.[45] Shi portrayed "Communism" and anarchism as merely different stages of history, with the one serving as the means to the other: "As I see it, if one wants to realize anarchism, one must first institute Communism; only when Communism has been fully developed can there be anarchist Communism."[46] Shi, however, was not the only one to identify the two. Li Da, who may have stood at the other end of the spectrum from Shi in his suspicion of the anarchists, nevertheless stated in his important essay, "The Anatomy of Anarchism" ("Wuzhengfu zhuyizhi jiepei"), that even if the anarchists were not the Communists' comrades, they were still friends, since they shared the goal of overthrowing capitalism. The problem with anarchists was that they had no method for doing so and acted out of emotion rather than reason. It was revealing that Li noted not only the popularity of anarchism, but that the number of anarchists was still on the rise. He invited them to join Communist ranks so to as to speed up the overthrow of capitalism and the establishment of socialism. Li agreed with Shi that Communists and anarchists desired to achieve the same kind of society; like Shi, he added that the achievement of that society (where the principle of "from each . . . to each" would prevail) must await the realization of "limitless" economic abundance, its material precondition.[47]

Against the anarchists, then, Communists argued the greater realism and rationality of their method of social revolution. Their reasoning took three related directions: that Communism had superior plans for economic development, which was essential to revolution and particularly important to backward China; that in accepting organization, it offered a better means of class struggle, which would otherwise have no direction; and finally, that Communism was more realistic in accepting the necessity of politics.

In his "Considerations on the Social Revolution" ("Shehui gemingdi shangjue"), Li Da offered the most comprehensive argument for the economic superiority of Communism over anarchism. Revealing a clearly Marxist appreciation of the problem, Li stated that while anarchists were concerned mainly with the problem of distribution, Communists focused on production, which was essential to the creation of an economic basis for socialism. In advocating a "centralist" (*jizhong*) approach to production, Communism promised a means to achieving this end. Anarchists, on the other hand, with the economic "dispersal" (*fensan*) they favored, offered no means to balance production against consumption, or to increase the wealth of society. For a socialist society, economic development required central intervention. This should be especially obvious to anarchists who proposed a society that presupposed "limitless" abundance.[48]

Li argued further that Communism was superior in the realm of distribution as well. Distribution had two aspects, income and consumption. Anarchists desired to equalize the latter, Communists the former. Anarchists desired to abolish money, and distribute goods according to need. While this might be possible in the future, it could not be instituted at the present, when there were not enough goods to go around. Li did not say how income equalization would prove superior in this respect, except to note that with the continued use of money, it would be possible to regulate production and consumption. What he had in mind, presumably, was the continued existence of a commodity economy where people would have a choice on how to spend their money.

Whatever the problems suggested by Li's own alternative, the difference was clearly between the immediate creation of a Communist society, which stressed freedom of production and consumption, and a society which postponed its Communist goals until productive abundance had become a reality. Until then, state direction and control of the economy would be necessary to increase production. Shi Contong, who believed that the appropriate material conditions were essential to the creation of any society, reaffirmed this position in arguing that machine production in both agriculture and industry was the precondition for a socialist economy. In Western capitalist societies, with their advanced production, the grounds were already ready for the establishment of socialism. In China, this must await the development of production. People who thought that socialism would be easier to achieve in China because of the underdevelopment of capitalism, Shi argued, were misguided because they overlooked the material conditions necessary to socialism.[49]

This argument also provided a major reason for the Communists' favoring the continued existence of the state. Especially because China was economically backward, argued Shi, the task of development must devolve upon the state. But politics was also important for the success of the revolution, as Zhou Fohai argued in two articles published in May and June 1921 respectively, "Why We Advocate Communism?" ("Women weishemma zhuzhang gongchanzhuyi") and "Seizing Political Power" ("Douqu zhengquan"),[50] which used Leninist arguments against the anarchist opposition to power (*qiangquan*) and the state. Recalling Chen Duxiu's statement in "On Politics" that politics did not leave alone even those who wanted to leave *it* alone, Zhou argued that without the use of power, there would be no way to achieve revolutionary success or to defend revolution against a bourgeois resurgence. A dictatorship of laborers was necessary not just to keep the bourgeoisie down after the revolution, but also to transform society and purge it of its past legacy. This would take a long time. Anarchists were too optimistic about the "good-heartedness" (*liangxin*) of people who, they believed, would abandon all their selfish habits after the revolution. Shi Contong added that the free, self-governing bodies the anarchists advocated as the basis for Communist society would be crushed right away unless there was a power to defend them.[51] Ironically, these authors conceded that organized state power was all the more important in the creation of socialist society in backward China where it was not even clear that the majority of the population favored revolution![52]

Finally, Communists argued that while social conditions existed in China for revolution, organization was necessary for the conversion of class consciousness into a weapon of revolution. In his "Considerations on Social Revolution," Li Da argued that there were already classes in Chinese society: there had long been class division in agriculture; with industrial development a class division had emerged between the bourgeoisie and the proletariat. While the Chinese bourgeoisie was small in numbers, it was indistinguishable from the foreign bourgeoisie, and the proletariat suffered at the hands of both. There were many possibilities for the organization of the proletariat, ranging from economistic trade unions to politically motivated organization. The possibility of these alternatives indicated that class consciousness as a social phenomenon did not necessarily lead to spontaneous unity of this class in class struggle. The only way to achieve such unity was through political organization. It was necessary to unify workers, peasants, soldiers, and intellectuals whenever possible, and engage in "direct action" against the ruling classes and their state. While "direct action" was a Sorellian idea (and *The Communist* did publish a piece by Sorel on Lenin) that anarchists also shared, what Li had in mind was the style of "direct action" that had led to Bolshevik success in 1917. Anarchist belief in spontaneous, free association, Communists believed, offered no means to unifying class consciousness into the political force necessary for revolutionary success.[53]

In the absence of debate, Communist writers felt no compunction to explain how the goals they professed to share with anarchists could be achieved through means that clearly stood at odds with these goals. A basic anarchist proposition throughout had been that means and ends were inseparable in the process of social revolution, that undesirable means would inevitably lead to undesirable ends, that freedom could not be achieved through dictatorship. The question of ends and means would be important in anarchist attacks on the Communists later on in the decade. For the time being, they were irrelevant to *The Communist's* advocacy of revolution, which was concerned not with ultimate goals but with immediate revolutionary strategy, and whose primary goal was to purge from the Party any continuing qualms about a Bolshevik strategy. What Communist authors argued, with considerable justification and self-consciousness if not wisdom, was that noble though the goals of anarchism were, it offered no means to achieving them. Whether or not this required the rejection of anarchist considerations on method is a moot question, at least historically. The immediate concern in early 1921 was to draw with unambiguity a distinction between Bolshevism and anarchism. *The Communist's* criticism of anarchism may have achieved this purpose; its inevitable concominant, however, was to drive the Communists themselves into an ideological corner which obviated the need for a critical appraisal of the revolutionary methods they advocated. Anarchism may have been impractical, as they claimed, but whether or not it was therefore irrelevant in the consideration of revolutionary strategy is another question. The refusal to entertain this question, which had been of central importance to May Fourth radicals, was the most cogent indication of how rapidly Bolshevism had taken hold of the Communists' revolutionary imagination.

When an anarchist response came in March 1921, it was not to arguments within *The Communist* (of which the anarchists were presumably unaware, since *The Communist* was semi-secret as an internal organ of the Communist groups), but to Chen Duxiu's public criticism of anarchism. The first debate between Marxists and anarchists that followed the establishment of the Communist nuclei erupted in March 1921, when Ou Shengbai responded in *People's Voice* to statements Chen had made in his lecture at Guangzhou in the Law and Political Science University ("The Critique of Socialism"). The exchange of letters that followed (restricted to Guangzhou, as far as is possible to tell) marked the first public debate between Communists and anarchists.

It is not necessary here to recount in detail this debate which, unlike *The Communist* polemics against anarchism, was carried out at a very abstract, hypothetical level. Neither Chen nor Ou enunciated its concrete implications until the very end, when Chen finally stated outright what had been in their two minds all along. Until then, they both danced around the issues with hypothetical examples to prove or disprove the viability of anarchism, with charges and countercharges of misrepresentation, and mutual charges of inconsistency.

The issue that provoked and dominated the debate was whether or not anarchism was compatible with group life. Chen had stated in his lecture that while anarchism had much of value to say with regard to individual conduct, it was irrelevant where social organization was concerned because the anarchist advocacy of "absolute freedom" (*juedui ziyu*) was incompatible with group existence.[54] In his open letter to Chen, Ou took exception to this statement. He criticized Chen for blurring important distinctions among anarchists. While some anarchists such as Stirner had advocated "absolute freedom" for the individual, they were the exception. Anarcho-communists (with whom he identified himself) did not object to group life, or even to the interference of the group in individual lives; what they rejected was the despotism of the group over the individual, of the kind that was implicit in the use of abstract laws to coerce individuals. What they advocated on their part was voluntary association (*lianhe*) that recognized the individual's right not to participate in the group's activities, and the substitution for abstract laws of flexible "public will" (*gongyi*) that would determine the group's functioning but, unlike laws, would be subject to change. Anarchists objected to indiscriminating interference in individual life without regard to whether the individual was good or bad. They themselves believed in the necessity of interference with individuals whose activities impinged on the rights of others, or threatened group existence. Instead of coercion, however, anarchists believed in education to change people for the better. In order to prove his case, Ou cited examples of voluntary association in the contemporary world. His examples, curiously, did no service to his argument; they included not only temporary associations such as cooperation in firefighting, but even associations of capital established to build railroads in Europe! They were, at any rate, rather easy for Chen to dispose of.[55]

The rest of the debate was devoted to thrashing out these issues. Chen conceded that there were indeed differences among anarchists on the issue of freedom, but he insisted that all anarchists suffered from a basic contradiction over this issue; indeed, he observed, anarchists such as Stirner were preferable because they at least recognized the contradiction, whereas Anarcho-communists such as Kropotkin tried to cover it up under a guise of Communism. Chen was not sympathetic to the other arguments Ou had presented. The insistence on the freedom not to participate in group activity, he argued, would only make group life impossible and unpredictable; what would happen to production, for instance, if individuals decided all of a sudden not to participate in production? While voluntary association might be possible on a contingent basis, as Ou's examples indicated, Chen believed no basis was provided for sustained social existence, which inevitably demanded coercion, and the sacrifice of individual rights to the welfare of the group. (What is the need for anarchism, he inquired sarcastically, if capitalism already provided the grounds for free association?) As for public will, Chen felt that it was unreliable because subject to the vagaries of "mass psychology," which could lead to terror as easily as association. Chen had considerable praise for laws as elements in human progress; international laws, he pointed out, had made possible for the first time in history the creation of a global society.

Public will, on the other hand, smacked to him of primitive society, which had been based on the despotism of the tribe over the individual. He rejected the distinction Ou had drawn between laws and "contract" between individuals on the grounds that the one was undesirable because above society, while the other was desirable because it was based on individual consent; to Chen, contracts were just another form of law, and would be meaningless without the backing of "abstract laws."[56]

These arguments became ever more elaborate. Two differences, however, were evident throughout the debate. Chen believed that individual rights must be sacrificed to the interests of the group; Ou did not. It followed also that Chen believed in the inevitability, and functionality, of coercion in social existence; while Ou believed that laws prevented people from doing what they would do naturally—associate with one another freely—since he believed as firmly as Chen that "social existence was the premise of individual freedom." Ou was hopeful that education would gradually correct anti-social behavior by purging people of their acquired habits. Chen thought the anarchist position excessively optimistic about the goodness of human nature, and was especially suspicious of the possibility of effective education for social ends within the context of a "bad" society. Perhaps nothing illustrates better how far Chen had traveled ideologically since the May Fourth period than his skepticism over the potential of education for social change, a belief he had done so much to instill in his students and followers (including Ou) as a leader of the New Culture Movement.

Ultimately, however, this debate over the relationship of the individual to the group was over revolutionary strategy. In his last response to Ou, Chen finally drew out the practical implications, when he drew a distinction between different kinds of coercion. He himself was equally opposed to coercion, he stated, where it deprived people of their humanity. Such was the case with class oppression, where one class deprived another class of its humanity, or with gender oppression, where the humanity of women was sacrificed in the interests of men. But these standards did not apply where the interests of the individual coincided with the interests of the group. Where interest was not private but public, there was no need to speak of coercion since any sacrifice of the individual represented a sacrifice for the welfare of the group of which the individual was an integral part, which, therefore, merely added up to sacrifice for one's own self. To Chen, the rights of labor unions under capitalism and Communism illustrated this distinction. In capitalist society, labor unions had the right to strike in defense of their rights because they represented the self-interest of laborers against the self-interest of the capitalists. In Communist society, however, there would be no need for the right to strike for workers because all production would be for society, and its benefits would accrue to members of the society equally. For laborers to strike then would be equivalent to striking against themselves.[57]

A double standard, perhaps, but one that pointed to the dilemmas of both Communists and anarchists, who shared an organic conception of society

where, once the evils of class division had been overthrown, any conflict between private and public interest would gradually disappear. As in the case
of *The Communist* criticisms of anarchism, the difference between Chen and
Ou concerned not the ends but the means of revolution. Ou believed that
revolution could be achieved without coercion, through education; indeed, to
introduce coercion was to nip in the bud the promise of a good society. Chen
Duxiu, having lost his faith in the power of education, thought other means
were necessary to bring about the seamless society whose individuals had
long lost the ability to associate freely, if indeed they had ever had it. Ou
demanded a consistency that transcended history; Chen saw in consistency an
obliviousness to history that would only perpetuate human oppression at the
hands of the past.

The differences between Chen and Ou, as with Marxists and anarchists in
general, were not simply political but philosophical. In his critique of anarchism in *The Communist,* Zhou Fohai had argued that anarchists were overly
optimistic about human nature, which flawed deeply their conceptions of
change. Not only did they have unduly optimistic expectations of human beings in the future, they could not explain the emergence of social evils in history; if people were naturally good and sociable, there was no way to explain
the historical emergence of social division and oppression.[58] Chen brought
similar arguments to bear against Ou when he criticized Ou's claim that people would be good in anarchist society because it was in their nature to be
good, that their very sense of shame would prevent them from doing evil.

Their skeptical view of human capability for good, the Communists believed, made their approach to change more realistic. This was to some extent
true, but the differences were relative rather than absolute. While some anarchists in China held an unqualified optimism concerning the goodness of human nature, such optimism was not shared by anarchists such as Ou Shengbai.
Ou was not against interference with individual human beings, he was against
coercion. What distinguished him from Chen in this debate was his insistence
that education could achieve all the improvement in human behavior that was
necessary for the establishment of a good society; even where education proved
helpless, denial of social participation to recalcitrant individuals would do the
job. What he criticized about present-day society was its immediate resort to
coercion and punishment in the name of abstract laws which left no room
for individual improvement. Ou was even willing, as Chen was to recognize
in the end, to consider the possible necessity of a transitional period of Bolshevism to prepare society for anarchism.

Communists, on the other hand, rejected the goodness of human nature
only in an immediate sense, as a sufficient precondition of social revolution.
They shared the belief that ultimately socialism, in its anarchist expression,
was a possibility: to deny that possibility would in fact have been to deny
the vision that legitimized their own revolutionary effort. They assigned priority, however, to the achievement of appropriate material conditions they
believed necessary to the functioning of Communist society. Once that had
been achieved, Communism would become a possibility. The human per-

sonality they deemed necessary to a Communist existence did not otherwise differ significantly from its anarchist counterpart.

The differences nevertheless pointed to a fundamental philosophical and epistemological problem that has long plagued anarchists and Marxists, in China and elsewhere; the problem of how to describe post-revolutionary society in the political language of bourgeois society. Richard Saltman has argued perceptively that this was a problem for Bakunin in his confrontation with Marx, and accounts for most of the inconsistencies in his anarchism.[59] Marx himself was deeply aware of the problem when he wrote in his *Eighteenth Brumaire of Louis Bonaparte* that "the beginner who has learnt a new language always translates it back into his mother tongue, but he has assimilated the spirit of the new language and can produce freely in it only when he moves in it without remembering the old and forgets in it his ancestral tongue."[60] The problem for both Marxists and anarchists in this debate was how to speak in a new language without losing touch with reality. This was ultimately what divided Chen and Ou, the Marxists and the anarchists, in China. Chen observed somewhere along the line that anarchists accused him of being unable to appreciate anarchism because he looked to the future through the spectacles of the present. How are we to create the future, he retorted, if we do not start with present reality?[61] In his observation was captured the pathos of both Marxism and anarchism in this initial confrontation.

Perhaps because of their mutual appreciation of this problem, the debate between Chen and Ou, as with the prior criticism of anarchism in *The Communist,* retained a certain level of courteousness and mutual respect in spite of an occasional note of acrimony. In his concluding lines to the debate, Chen had nothing but praise for his former student. Even if Ou was an anarchist, he noted, he recognized the necessity of class struggle and revolutionary activity, and even of a transitional stage in the revolution. He was, moreover, a follower of Kropotkin and a sincere revolutionary youth, unlike some of the "low-quality" Chinese-style anarchists (Zhu Qianzhi?). "I only regret," he concluded, "that there are few like him among Chinese anarchists."[62] His words might have been an epitaph to the May Fourth Movement.

And they were. We should not let the general implications of the debate blind us to its specific, historical significance. It was, in the first place, a debate over social and cultural approaches to social revolution. Anarchists in China had all along given priority to cultural change as a means to social revolution. This had accounted for the influence of anarchism during the New Culture movement. It would also identify the anarchist position over revolution in the 1920s. Now, however, the anarchists effort to uphold cultural revolution against the Communists would increasingly make them sound like voices from a no-longer relevant past as grounds for revolution shifted, and the once-revolutionary advocacy of cultural revolution appeared increasingly as opposition to the genuine social revolution that was under way.

And Chen Duxiu, the erstwhile champion of cultural revolution, had now given up on that hope and turned to what he now considered to be a more fundamental realm of change: society. Unless the social structure, embedded in economic organization, was first transformed, he now believed, cultural change would be of no avail. Indeed, he no longer seemed to believe even in the possibility of cultural change within the context of a "bad" society.

But there was another shift in Chen's thinking, as with all the other Communist writers we have discussed. If they no longer had faith in the ability of culture to change society, they did not display much faith either in the revolutionariness of the classes whose cause they promoted: skepticism over the possibilities of "human nature" pointed also to a skepticism concerning the vision that justified revolution, and the ability of the oppressed to remake themselves in revolution. There was something disturbingly authoritarian in the conception of revolution that Chen and the other Communists promoted: that revolution itself was in some ways coercion, coercion of the oppressed to remake themselves in spite of themselves. Many of the Communists intended "the dictatorship of the proletariat" not just to suppress the bourgeoisie but also to coerce the working class into a revolutionary mold. The idea is clearly Bolshevik, but not necessarily Marxist. Chinese became Communists before they were ever Marxists, as I suggested at the beginning of this study. It is quite clear from this perspective that in the debates that marked the emergence of Communism in China, the issue was not to defend Marxism against its critics, or even to produce a revolutionary Marxist analysis of Chinese society, but to rewrite the scenario of the Chinese revolution in the self-image of an organizational ideology that was quite prepared, in the name of revolution, to call into question its own theoretical and philosophical premises.

With these debates in late 1920 and early 1921, it becomes possible, I think, to speak of the emergence of a Communist identity in China. The polemics with the guild socialists clarified questions of organization and politics that had so far blurred the distinctions between Bolshevik and democratic socialist approaches. The polemics with the anarchists were even more fundamental, because they served to clarify revolutionary strategy within the camp of social revolutionaries, not least for the members of the emerging Communist organization. These polemics enunciated for the Communists an idea of social revolution that represented a newcomer on the scene of Chinese socialism, irrevocably different from those that had prevailed in the early May Fourth period. For radicals who opted for Communism, this new idea signaled a break with the May Fourth Movement, in which their radicalism had first taken shape.

The appearance of an exclusive Communist identity that brooked no ideological "confusion" does not imply that the identity of every participant in the early Communist movement was therefore transformed, and purged of the legacy of the past. What is at issue here is not the identity of every individual Communist, but the emergence of an organizational and ideological identity that clearly demarcated the boundary between Communist and non-Communist, and brooked no eclecticism or pluralism. It is clear from the language of the debates discussed above that even the term Communist, identified vaguely with anarchist ideals in the May Fourth period, was now captured for a Bolshevik identity. This redefinition would continue to create problems for individual Communists. What was no longer problematic was the question of what it meant to be a Communist. Individuals were free to accept or reject this definition. But for those who were not willing to accept it, the implications were clear: they, too, must part ways with "Communism," following in the footsteps of their former socialist associates of the May fourth period who had already, with the founding of the Communist nuclei, seen the writing on the wall.

Epilogue

The Communist party of China was formally (and secretly) established in July 1921 in Shanghai. The first congress formalized the organization that had been created over the previous year, and adopted an official party ideology. Shanghai was confirmed as the party center, with Chen Duxiu as general secretary, Zhang Guotao as head of the organization section, and Li Da as head of propaganda. The Communist nuclei around the country were converted into party branches, each with a local secretary: Hunan (Mao Zedong), Guangzhou (Tan Pingshan), Wuhan (Bao Huiseng), Beijing (Luo Zhanglong), and Jinan (Wang Jinmei). Shanghai had its own executive branch headed by Chen Wangdao; in Beijing Li Dazhao would play an unofficial leadership role. Zhang Shenfu and Zhao Shiyan were named correspondents of the party affiliates (before they became official branches) in Berlin and Paris respectively. While the local branches were granted some autonomy, they were to be under central supervision in "finance, activity, and policy." Party membership was to be open without regard to "gender or national origin" to all "sincere people" who "recognized the party program and policies."[1] New members were to be introduced by one party member and, before joining the Party, cut off all affiliation with other parties and groups.

The congress adopted as official party ideology the political line the Communists had been propagating for the previous year. The "revolutionary army" was to unite with the proletariat to overthrow the political power of the bourgeoisie, and establish a dictatorship of the proletariat that would last until all classes had been abolished. All private property in industry, land, and productive resources was to be abolished. The party would establish a "Soviet" system of management and become a branch of the Third International. Labor organization and propaganda work were singled out as the two most important tasks. There would be some flexibility in labor organization depending on local circumstances, but overall organization was to be supervised by a labor secretariat. Similarly, while local branches could publish their own ideological organs, all propaganda work was to be supervised from the party center.[2]

Both in organization and in ideology, the first congress formalized the Bolshevik assumptions that had guided the founding from the beginning. Yet this congress did not end the problems of the fledgling party. In Communist historiography, the first congress has held a dubious place in the history of the Communist Party of China. A truly stable party organization was not established until the second congress in July 1922. Indeed, a closer look at the events surrounding the first congress reveals that while it was a very significant event in the history of Communism in China, it was also fraught with problems, as Chen Tanqiu would later observe.[3] Some of these events raise questions as to whether or not the founders were fully aware of the implications of the organization they had brought into being. At least eight of the thirteen participants in the first congress wrote down their recollections of it in later years. These recollections coincide in all the important details, and give us a glimpse of the problems brought forth.

The major issues in the first congress concerned the relationship of the Party to the Communist International, party policies, and the nature of party organization. The congress was divided from the beginning between a "right" wing represented by Li Hanjun (supported on some issues by Chen Gongbo and Zhou Fohai) and a "left" wing represented by the Beijing representatives, Zhang Guotao and Liu Renjing. Li Hanjun, "the Marxist theorist," argued for some measure of independence from the Comintern, at least where it concerned the activities of the Party in China. He also objected to the immediate adoption of a Bolshevik constitution. He felt that Chinese Communists were not knowledgeable enough about Marxism to engage in political activity, and recommended study of Marxism and ideological propaganda as the immediate task. He went so far as to recommend that before adopting a constitution, the Party should send delegates abroad to study the constitutions of the Bolshevik party in the Soviet Union and the social democrats in Germany to decide which suited China's conditions best. Li, moreover, had close relations with the Guomindang in Shanghai, and did not approve of cutting off relations with other parties. He was supported in this by Chen Gongbo and Zhou Fohai; especially Chen, who himself was deeply involved in Guangzhou, not only with the Guomindang but also with Chen Jiongming. This group also objected to the condemnation of Sun Yatsen as just another politician whose activities were even more harmful than those of warlords because they deceived the masses. Finally, Li objected to the overly centralized organization of the Party. Li had come into conflict with Chen Duxiu over this same issue as early as February 1921, when Chen had sent to Shanghai a party program that had advocated centralization. Now at the congress, he continued to stick to his guns over this issue.[4]

Against Li, on the extreme left, was Liu Renjing, the later Trotskyist, who argued for the immediate adoption of the policies of class struggle and the dictatorship of the proletariat. Liu recalled that at the time he had just finished reading Marx's critique of the Gotha program of the German social democratic party, and was hot under the collar in his radicalism.[5] He not only opposed Li on every count, but even argued that the Party should stay clear of intellectuals, and make itself into a pure party of the proletariat. He was supported most fervently by Zhang Guotao.

The congress, which was dominated throughout by the Comintern representative Maring, decided in the end to support the radical position of the Beijing delegates, which was reflected in the final draft program. But the debate points nevertheless to uncertainties over the mission and organization that had not been eradicated in the period of preparation. The disagreements produced divisions, in fact, that resulted within the next few years in the exodus from the Party of most of those who had played a crucial part in the founding, including about half the representatives to the first congress.

The nature and consequences of the first congress point to several problems. First were problems of membership; in other words, the seriousness with which the first Communists took their obligations to the Party. As is clear from the cases of Chen Gongbo and Zhou Fohai, at least some refused to give priority to party affairs over their personal commitments and careers. Zhou and Chen left shortly after the congress for Japan and the United States, respectively, to continue their education, largely unconcerned with party affairs. That they later went over to the Guomindang has provided *prima facie* evidence for some Communist historians of their lack of seriousness, or worse, from the beginning. But such lack of seriousness was not restricted to them. Most problematic indeed were the cases of Chen Duxiu and Li Dazhao, the two most important leaders in the Party, neither of whom attended the first congress. Much is unknown in their cases, and the best we can offer for the present are speculations, but it is far too simple, in the light of problematic evidence, to attribute their absence to their being too busy to attend, which only suggests that in their case, too, the party may not have taken top priority. Liu Renjing, while he notes that Li was busy with too many things at Beida, adds surprisingly that Li was not elected to the Beijing committee as a representative which, given Li's influence in Beijing, can only be attributed to an unwillingness to be elected on his part.[6] Chen's case is even more curiout in that he left Shanghai in November 1920, in the midst of party organization, to take up a position in Guangzhou. Even after he returned to Shanghai at the end of 1921, after being elected general secretary in absentia, he told Bao Huiseng that he objected to party members becoming "professional revolutionaries."[7] Whatever else one might say about the behavior of Chen and Li, it is quite obvious that it is not the kind of behavior one associates with a Lenin or a Trotsky!

Secondly, attitudes toward Marxism and the Party's relationship to the Comintern that were expressed in the first congress point to even deeper, more clearly ideological problems. Li Hanjun, who had been a central figure in the founding of the nuclei, was recognized by his colleagues as the "foremost theorist" among them, and served as Chen's substitute after the first congress as general secretary. Yet he was obviously not convinced at the time that the Bolshevik interpretation of Marxism was the only correct one. We have already referred to his talk in Wuhan in fall 1920, when he had observed that Marxism had many manifestations, including social democracy and guild socialism. His position at the first congress indicates that he had still not abandoned this view, which was shared by at least one other important delegate,

Li Da.[8] Indeed, the only one at the congress to hold an unequivocally Bolshevik position was Liu Renjing, "little Marx" from Beijing.

The question of the relationship to the Comintern points to another significant area of ideological uncertainty. While the Party had unquestionably come into being under Comintern guidance, it is is difficult to say if the Chinese founders shared the same conception of their relationship to the Comintern as did their Comintern advisors. Li Hanjun was not the only one concerned about Comintern domination; Chen Duxiu shared his concerns.

These concerns were shaped by personal relationships to Maring, a kind of advisor entirely different from Voitinsky. Voitinsky had been cognizant of the sensibilities of his Chinese constituency and able to establish an excellent working relationship with them. Maring was domineering, more of a Communist missionary. Even Zhang Guotao, who was relatively sympathetic to Maring, recalls he viewed himself as "an angel of liberation to Asian peoples."[9] Li Hanjun was convinced from his very first meeting with Maring that he looked down on Chinese revolutionaries.[10] Chen Duxiu felt the same way after his return from Shanghai. Li Da recalls that Chen did his best to avoid Maring, even refusing to appear at scheduled weekly meetings where Maring expected him to give progress reports on party work.[11] The relationship was personal, but its deterioration only pointed to the sharpening of the question of independence for the Party. The first congress was convened by Maring shortly after his arrival in China; Chen Duxiu, secretary of the Shanghai nucleus and nominal leader of the Party before he formally became general secretary, first found out about the planned congress from Shanghai.[12] The question of authority became even more serious after the first congress.

Thirdly, while the first congress created a centralized organization, the center does not seem to have functioned as much of a center. Most of the work was undertaken by Li Da and Zhang Guotao. The new labor secretariat under Zhang Guotao would rapidly emerge as the most important undertaking of the Party; otherwise, the center does not seem to have provided much leadership. Li Da recalls that after Chen Duxiu returned to Shanghai, he behaved quite erratically. He often moved his residence without informing others of his address. He showed an inclination to throw temper tantrums when his wishes were not carried out. Li Da interprets this behavior as a personal quirk, which has received some confirmation from Yuan Zhenying, the anarchist Chen had recruited to the Party, who recalls that Chen's "despotism" reached unbearable proportions.[13] It is hard to say if this behavior was typical of Chen who all his life had commanded the respect of those close to him. It is possible that his behavior was at least partially a response to his problematic relationship to Maring.

The Party itself, however, may have been part of the problem. The rest of the membership in these early years seems to have behaved equally erratically, though for them the behavior took the form of gradual exodus. Key figures of the party in Shanghai, Li Da and Chen Wangdao, quit the party over the next two years (following the second congress). Li Hanjun was expelled from the Party at its fourth congress in 1925 (which did not prevent the Guomindang from executing him in 1927). Chen Congbo, Zhou Fohai, Shi Contong, Bao Huiseng, and Luo Zhanglong would all quit the party within the next few years. By the mid-1920s, only a few of the first congress participants were still in the party. Chen Duxiu and Liu Renjing went over to the Trotskyist camp after 1927. Zhang Guotao quit later, though his reasons lay more with Mao Zedong's leadership than doubts concerning the Party's relationship to the Comintern.

Only three of the representatives to the first congress were among the delegates to the second. Chen himself was present. The twelve delegates represented 195 members around China. The most significant membership increases were registered in Shanghai, Guangzhou, Changsha, and Wuhan, the latter two with the return from France of the New Citizens' Study Society members and the recruitment finally of Yun Daiying's Benefit the Masses Society.

It was this congress that firmly established the Party and brought it under direct Comintern control. And following this congress the decision was made, on Comintern instructions, to establish a united front with the Guomindang, which was formalized over the following year. Li Da recalls that representation in this congress was determined not by elections by the local branches, but by appointment from the center. Prominent among the delegates were Communists who had recently returned from abroad. The most important part in the congress was played by those who had recently returned from study in the Soviet Union, or participation in the Congress of the Toilers of the East in Moscow.[14] If Li's recollections are accurate, nearly ten years before the episode of the "Twenty-eight Bolsheviks," it had become clear to the Comintern leadership that the problem of control in the Communist party of China could best be resolved by instituting in party leadership those who had been touched directly by Moscow. Zhang Guotao's description of his attitudes following his return from Moscow lends credibility to this view.

From the perspective of later developments, the continued uncertainty concerning the ideology and organization of the Party that plagued the first congress may seem to render it an insignificant event. In some ways, the first congress belongs in the "prehistory" of the Party rather than the "history" which started with the second congress. The May Fourth legacy of Chinese Communism was still very much in evidence at the time of the first congress. Zhang Guotao recalls that many of his colleagues in the Party at this time retained a scholarly attitude toward party activities. They were still unable, we might add, to completely abandon the personal and intellectual associations they had formed in the heyday of May Fourth socialism. They seemed plagued with doubts concerning the organization they had created; ironically, such doubts were expressed most explicitly by those who seemed to be the most knowledgeable Marxists. And there is some suggestion in the evidence that it was precisely these people, who appeared to be "too intellectual," who were the least trustworthy in the eyes of Comintern advisors. Only with the second congress did the Party embark in earnest on the path of practical revolution. And for that the Comintern would rely most on young intellectuals who had purged themselves in activities abroad, however brief.

Nevertheless, the second congress represented not so much a new beginning as a completion of the tasks and trends that had gotten under way before even the first congress during the summer of 1920 when party organization had been initiated in Shanghai. Comintern domination was implicit from the very beginning in the organization of the Party under direct Comintern intervention. The ideological presuppositions of the Party were articulated in the very process of its organizational formation. Even the idea of a united front with the Guomindang, which seemed to contradict the opposition to Sun Yatsen in the first congress, had been implicit in the Party's initial ideology and organization. As Li Dazhao had hoped all the way into fall 1920, the founders had hoped to bring together in the Party all the radical socialists of the May Fourth period, including the anarchists. Organizational exclusiveness did not mean keeping out those who did not have a prior commitment to Marxism, by which standard even the founders would have had to be excluded, but rather drawing a boundary between those who professed a commitment to party goals and those who refused to do so. This was quite in keeping with the policies of the Comintern, which from the beginning had gone to China shopping for radicals. Understanding of Marxism was not a precondition for party membership; it was possibly even a liability. What was essential to begin with was "belief" in Bolshevik goals and methods.

From the perspective of May Fourth socialism, this profession of commitment was what constituted the break with the past. The Party was to provide the home which radicals had earlier sought elsewhere. May Fourth radicals had created "homes" for themselves in the many organizations that had come into being with the May Fourth Movement. But these organizations had lacked a clear ideological direction. What they had in common was attraction to a vague socialism dominated by anarchist values. They were attracted to Marxist explanations of China's problem and intrigued by the success of the Soviet Union, but knew little about either. While they found in Marxism abstract explanations to social problems, the values that guided their radical activity, including their efforts at social mobilization, were derived from anarchism, which they not only knew better than they did Marxism, but which was also more in keeping with their everyday problems and utopian longings. They were also oppressed, and in search of a means to fight their oppressors. And they were already weary of the more democratic, open activities of the May Fourth Movement, which seemed to have led them to a dead end with the population and left them at the mercy of unscrupulous authorities. They were also tired of their own intellectualism, which seemed to keep them apart from the oppressed masses with whom they wished fervently to identify.

The Party offered May Fourth radicals a new "home," and a new basis for activity; Bolshevism promised a concrete point of departure for action, which other socialisms did not match. If membership required a reconstruction of their prior ideological commitments, they were commitments of whose ineffectiveness they had already tired. They entered the Party as friends, teachers, and students; only those who were willing to remake themselves into comrades stayed on. Some took longer than others in making the decision; not a few proved unable to achieve the ideological reconstitution they suggested for the masses they hoped to lead. Those who succeeded inevitably parted ways with not only their former friends and associates, but their former selves as well.

11

Paths to the Future: Communist
Organization and Marxist Ideology

I can best recapitulate the argument of this study by providing a summary account that contrasts with the account which (I suggested in the introduction) has heretofore dominated our views.

The Communist movement in China got under way in the spring of 1920, at a moment of crisis in Chinese radicalism, when the ideological and organizational premises that had informed radical activity during the preceding years seemed to have run into a dead end. Comintern intervention in the Chinese revolution in March 1920 brought to Chinese radicals the organizational principles of Bolshevism, which promised to resolve urgent problems of the social revolution radicals sought to bring about. The response to the promise was immediate. Within eight months, the core of a Communist movement had taken shape in China.

The emergence of a Communist movement at this time resulted from a conjuncture of internal and external developments. In 1918–1919, socialism appeared as a world political tide, nourished by the successful October Revolution in Russia, labor and social revolutionary movements in Europe and North America, and national liberation movements in colonial societies that found inspiration in socialist ideas. In China, the maturation of urban capitalism during World War I brought forth a labor movement, which first expressed itself politically during the May Fourth Movement spearheaded by students. The political emergence of labor had a traumatic effect on Chinese intellectuals and turned them rapidly to consideration of questions of socialism and social change. In a situation where China had become a part of a world market of commodities and ideas, socialism appeared immediately relevant to the resolution of social problems that had attended the emergence of capitalism there. In 1919 socialist ideas spread rapidly in China. Marxism appeared on the Chinese intellectual scene at this time as part of a still eclectic interest in socialism.

Nevertheless, the formation of a Communist movement was the work of radical activists mobilized by the New Culture and May Fourth movements of the late 1910's. These years witnessed the emergence of a radical intelligentsia which articulated its new-found self-consciousness in demands for a cultural revolution. In the course of the intellectual and patriotic ferment of these years, the intelligentsia organized itself in "study societies" of various kinds around the country, centered around new educational institutions and journalistic endeavors. These societies served in 1919 as the cores for ideological and social mobilization. They were the institutional embodiments of a new culture of radicalism that was ideologically eclectic, and blended immediate patriotic with utopian aspirations, and cultural revolutionary ideals with hopes for social transformation. Anarchist ideas appeared in 1919 as the foremost inspiration for the activities of these societies.

These societies served as the vehicles for the organization of Communism in China in 1920. The establishment of Communism, however, required a break with the May Fourth legacy that had produced them. By the winter of 1919–1920, the radical fervor of the May Fourth Movement had given way to disillusionment. The mass movement had receded. Authorities around China were engaged in suppression of radical activism. The communal movement of 1919 had run into grave difficulties. And even the culturally radical intellectuals who had done so much to instigate student radicalism had grown suspicious of a movement that threatened to open up a social radicalism that went beyond what they had initially intended. Radical intellectuals showed signs of having lost their faith in intellectuals' ability to effect serious social change, and were drawn increasingly to search for ways to ally with the working class, which seemed to continue to register successes in its economic struggles.

This search was answered by the promise of Bolshevik organization that Comintern advisors brought to China in the spring of 1920. Under the leadership of Chen Duxiu, former study societies were quickly converted into a new political organization during the summer and fall of 1920. These societies at first preserved their mixed composition and ideological eclecticism. The process of organization, however, was accompanied by the gradual elimination of socialist competitors who were unable or unwilling to make an exclusive commitment to a Bolshevik organization and program, and ideological controversies which for the first time brought clear distinctions into the eclectic socialism of the May Fourth period. By late 1920, socialists had parted ways, and a group had emerged that identified with Bolshevism. From then on the official founding of the Communist party of China was a matter of time. It was accomplished in July 1921 under the direct guidance of the Communist International; the Communist movement in China was under way.

Perspectives and Perceptions: Teleology and Contingency in the Origins of Chinese Communism

In the introduction to this study, I suggested that giving voice to the silences in our past understanding of the origins of Communism in China means a radical rewriting of existing accounts. How radically the account I have offered here departs from earlier ones is best left to others to judge. It is important to note, however, that this account does not negate earlier ones, but rather incorporates them into a more comprehensive analytical and narrative framework; the surface reading of the origins of Communism, which still retains its validity *as* a surface reading, appears here against another reading, which has sought to come to terms with the ideological and social structures that provided the contemporary context. Whether or not this changes the surface reading, it offers, at the very least, explanations for inconsistencies and anomalies that reading has suppressed.

Indeed, one of these anomalies, in my opinion the most fundamental one, provided the point of departure for this study: that the Communist Party of China was founded by radicals who only imperfectly appreciated Marxism as revolutionary and social theory, and were only tenuously committed to it as a political ideology. This is something students of Chinese Communism have always known but chosen to explain away. Communist historians whose recognition of the problematic status of Marxism in May Fourth thinking has not shaken their real or apparent conviction in the self-evident truths of Marxism have continued to hold that once Chinese radicals had acquired familiarity with the new ideology, it was merely a matter of time before they converted to Communism; if they were insufficiently appreciative of Marxism when they founded the Party, it was because of the persistence of petit-bourgeois scruples. And if for some such scruples seemed to persist past the founding, it was because they were incorrigibly petit-bourgeois. Students of Chinese Communism in the West, the majority of whom do not share a similar conviction in Marxism's truths, have nevertheless found in China's circumstances variegated reasons for radicals' attraction to Marxism, and consequently turning to Communist politics, as the only means to resolve the problems of Chinese society. If the attraction to Communism had sources outside of Marxism, there is even less reason to inquire too deeply into the relationship between their Marxism and their eventual conversion to Communism—except in one significant area: the impact on Chinese Marxism and Communism of the parochial concerns of the Chinese revolution, which were responsible in the first place for the Chinese attraction to Communism.

In light of this, it is interesting that the same historians have exerted considerable effort to demonstrate that there was a definite relationship between Marxism and Communism in the origins of Chinese Communism; that the October Revolution provoked interest in Marxism which laid the foundation for the conversion to Communism, however shaky a foundation it may have been. Given how rapidly both ideology and the radical movement unfolded in 1917–1921, it has not seemed necessary to make too fine a point concerning the inconsistencies in the relationship between ideology and radical activity in these years. The trends seem to have been fairly clear, at least from what (as I have described it earlier) the foreshortened perspective of a later vantage point.

A deeper ideological poblem is, however, revealed in historians' reluctance to pursue these inconsistencies, and tendency even to dismiss them: the assumption of a teleology between Marxism and Communist organization. The teleology is most clearly evident with Communist historians, who refuse to recognize the seriousness of any Marxism that does not culminate in Communist politics, and deduce a prior Marxist commitment, however shaky, from participation in Communist politics (subject, of course to the possibility of revisionism, which permits a selective application of the teleology in accordance with shifting criteria of orthodoxy). But non-Communist historians, though the motivations here are more complex, also assume a teleology between Marxism as theory and Communist politics. The assumption runs the whole gamut of the political spectrum; indeed, it is fundamentally ideological as an essential component of contemporary political culture. The right may insist on it; the left is embarrassed by the possible necessity of rejecting it. Hence, I think, the tendency of Western scholars to insist on an ideological foundation in Marxism for the founders of the Party, despite their recognition that this Marxism was of a tenuous nature.

Ideology-based explanations of the origins of Communism in China are problematic not because ideology was unimportant in the process, but because of the one-dimensional, abstract approach to ideology that has rendered these explanations teleological. To insist on the anomalousness of a Party founded by radicals who had little or no appreciation of Marxism may indeed seem strange, since this phenomenon seems typical of much Communist politics. The underlying purpose in presenting this commonplace phenomenon as an anomaly is, really, to draw attention to the need to make a distinction between Marxism and Communism.

I mean not to suggest here that Marxism was irrelevant to the founding, but rather to dramatize the need to challenge the ideological teleology that has not only disguised significant questions about the origins of Communism in China, but has also distorted our understanding of the relationship between Marxism and Communism. This study's close scrutiny of the implications of this "anomaly," by calling into question the ideological explanations for Chinese radicals' conversion to Communism, has forced us to reexamine the ideological and social conditions, but above all the conditions of radical experience, that provided the context for the origins of Communism in China. The reexamination has revealed, I hope, that the passage to Communism was neither easy nor one-dimensional but required, for the individuals involved, difficult ideological choices and personal confrontations. It has also called our attention to intellectual and social developments during this period that have previously appeared at best marginal.

This is not to say that the emergence of the Communist movements at this time was accidental. Given China's circumstances in 1919–1920, the emergence of a Communist movement was probably inevitable. In a world intellectual context where socialism seemed to be on the political agenda of societies worldwide, Chinese radicals would have been blind not to perceive its significance. In a society where emerging capitalism had already produced the first signs of class confrontation between labor and capital, this political ideology had an immediate relevance. The October Revolution in Russia, moreover, dramatized for Chinese radicals, as for radicals worldwide, the path to a social revolution that promised success where other socialisms had failed.

This kind of broad historical teleology, however, points to inevitability merely as a potential; it does not tell us much about alternative resolutions of the problem which were available to the subjects of history, or the considerations that went into the choices they made. While we may argue that the emergence of a Communist movement in the post–May Fourth period was inevitable, we also need to remind ourselves that very few people made the choice to become Communists. Grand teleologies tell us little about how that small group made their choices, the processes whereby the choices were forced upon them, and the uncertainties that accompanied the choices they made; in other words, what the choices meant to those who made them. To bring the question to the level of the individual—authentically individual, not individuals as paradigms—is not to trivialize questions of politics. On the contrary, the historicization of the question offers the possibility of getting at certain issues of universal import that are disguised by grand social and ideological teleologies. The forest need not be lost from sight for the trees; it is merely a matter of whether we deduce the trees from the forest, or the forest from the trees.

The Ideology, Organization, and Social Context of Communism

The rejection of ideological teleology presents an obvious problem for the explanation of the origins of Communism in China: if Marxism was not a central, or even significant, factor in attracting radicals to Communism, how then do we explain the turn to Communism in 1920? Comintern intervention in China, which has served as the basis for explanation in some approaches to this question, only points to an opportunity, not a cause. Above all, it does not explain the rapidity of the Party's formation in China. To deal with this problem, we must account for two processes. One is what I have described as the dialectic between ideology and organization. Ideology is important not as an abstraction but in its translation into practice, because it is finally human activity, not ideas, that makes revolution, and that activity requires an organizational context. In the case of Chinese Communism, this is rendered even more necessary because it is difficult to identify ideological commitments that, before 1920, pointed inexorably to Communist organization. Organization, on the other hand, does not on its own point to the direction revolutionary activity would take. Only when May Fourth radical associations reorganized in accordance with Bolshevism did they move toward a clearly identifiable mode of radical activity.

Equally important is the dialectic between social context and radical association, which I have encompassed in the term radical experience. While social context on its own does not explain who becomes a revolutionary, and how or why, without the social context it is difficult to explain the variation in the social and political dimension of revolutionary activity. It is ultimately from social context that revolutionary organization derives its meaning and its possibilities. And it is this social context that endows competing revolutionary ideologies with practical significance as they claim revolutionaries' attention and give direction to their activities.

The process of the establishment of the Communist Party of China is a revealing historical case of the process whereby radical social activity transmuted a vague embryonic radical consciousness into a revolutionary consciousness. I must emphasize that the question here is neither the sociology of revolution—the dynamics of the societal processes which provide the broad context for revolution—nor the psychological idiosyncrasies that predispose certain individuals to rebellion. Both societal processes and individual psychologies no doubt contribute to the making of the revolutionary. The question is why, of all those who may be inclined by social contradiction or psychological predisposition to become rebels, only a handful become revolutionaries who organize themselves to engage in revolutionary activity. This requires that we look at the organization of the Party above all as a social process; a process of articulation of social relationships that come into existence in the course of radical activity.

Radical experience and the social relationships that were formed in the process of radical activity were crucial in the making of the Communists who were to found the Party in 1921. There was nothing "spontaneous" either about the organization of the Party, or even about the ideological conversion of Chinese intellectuals to Marxism; indeed, the two were part and parcel of the same process. In an abstract sense, the conditions of Chinese society were such that it predisposed radical intellectuals to look favorably upon the Marxist theory of society and revolution, especially following the successful example of the October Revolution in Russia. But there were other elements of Marxist theory that rendered the same intellectuals suspicious. Marxism acquired meaning for radical intellectuals in the course of radical activity and organization that was itself informed by their own "petit-bourgeois consciousness."

In spite of an increasingly radical rhetoric of revolution, the May Fourth Movement was motivated by a yearning for unity. There were patriotic reasons for this yearning: China's national plight rendered young radicals acutely aware of the dangers to national existence of continued division; the May Fourth Movement was originally motivated by disillusionment with a political legacy that seemed to prefer the satisfaction of private interest to the public good. The yearning for unity, however, represented an even deeper utopian longing. Unity against division, public interest over private interest, and a communitarian egalitarianism had been basic to the vision of the New Culture Movement, on which the Chinese intelligentsia of the May Fourth period had been nourished. It was on these grounds that the intelligentsia criticized the particularistic values of the past; and it was on these same grounds that it sought to create a new future. May Fourth individualism was conditioned by this vision of organic community.

Especially important for the May Fourth intelligentsia was the legacy of

anarchism which, resonant with the social ideals of the New Culture movement, reached the apogee of its popularity in China in 1919–1922. Anarchism
has received considerable attention from Chinese historians in recent years,
possibly because of increasing evidence that for the younger intellectuals of
the May Fourth period, it served as the midwife to Communism. To appreciate the significance of anarchism at this time, it is necessary to think of it
not simply as a formal ideology but also as a mood, a style, and even a
social-cultural moment of everyday life. The culture of radicalism that assumed shape with the New Culture and May Fourth movements drew inspiration from anarchism not simply as a set of ideas but as the fountainhead for
quotidian values; these promised a social reconstruction that would be total
but bloodless, rejected reliance on the state in favor of individual effort (not
a minor consideration at a time when the state itself seemed a major source of
social problems), pointed to individual liberation as a means to the creation
of authentic community, promised to abolish social divisions without threat-
ening democracy, and made cultural change the means of achieving social
change.

All socialism has one eye on the past and another on the future. A product
of capitalist society, socialism is at once modernist and futurist. It is also
informed, however, by a vision that promises the possibility of recapturing
the spirit of community that had once existed. Among socialisms, anarchism
may be the most consistent in offering the promise of recapturing this lost
past without sacrificing present gains, which is implicit in the basic premise of
anarchist philosophy—that individual liberation and egalitarian community,
rather than being antithetical, are mutually interdependent.

This promise had a strong appeal among an intelligentsia who, at the
moment they discovered their autonomy, had also realized their separateness
from society, especially labor, of which fact they were made painfully aware
with the mass mobilization of the May Fourth Movement. The communal
movement of 1919–1920 was motivated by a desire to overcome this separa-
tion, to create a new society which would not only make possible a new life
but create a communitarian unity in which all private interest would disappear. Anarchist values served not only as the inspiration for the communal
movement, but also as the organizational principles of the communes Chinese
youth established to realize this goal. The appeal of these values was not
restricted to youth. In the aftermath of the May Fourth Movement the ideal
of achieving social unity through "small group" organization was widely
shared by radicals of all ages and persuasions. Indeed, if there was a common
ground to socialism at this time, it is to be found in anarchism, the ideas and
values of which found their way into the socialism of as diverse radicals as
Li Dazhao, Dai Jitao, and Zhang Dongsun.

Radical encounters with society were to play a crucial part in nurturing
the awareness that would turn Chinese intellectuals from their self-absorption
to social radicalism. The greatest challenge to radical intellectuals in 1919
was the political emergence of labor in the course of the May Fourth Movement, which brought the issue of class ineluctably to the forefront of their

thinking. The dramatic turn to socialism in the summer of 1919 was a product not of external "influence," but of the appearance on the Chinese political scene of this unmistakable evidence that capitalism, with all its social implications, had arrived in China. Socialism had appeared in the aftermath of World War I as a world tide and, therefore, as a possible alternative in China's social reorganization. The appearance of labor, however, was what forced on Chinese radicals the realization that socialism was of immediate relevance to their society. The issue was no longer one of an abstract socialism for the future, but the immediate need to avoid the prospect of class division and conflict.

The issue of class was to transform the nature of socialism in China. It is important to note, however, that the immediate response to the prospect of class struggle among Chinese radicals was not enthusiasm, but fear. Chinese radical intellectuals were traumatized by the appearance of labor as a political force. What accounts for the sudden proliferation of interest in socialism in the summer of 1919 is above all fear of the threat to unity this radical new development in Chinese society posed, not an outpouring of welcome at the prospect of class struggle; socialism suddenly gained urgency because it seemed the only means to achieve class reconciliation before class division violently tore society apart. It was not yet valued as a strategy of class struggle

This was true not just of the anti-revolutionary socialists, whose previous understanding of socialism predisposed them against class struggle, but of later Communists as well. Li Dazhao's sympathy for the plight of labor preceded the May Fourth Movement and, much more than his writings on Marxism, distinguished him among contemporary radicals. But there is little evidence that he viewed class struggle as anything other than a necessary evil. This may be the reason he, like every other prominent radical intellectual of the time, invested so much in the communal movement of 1919–1920. In his case, as in the others', there may be a suggestion of intellectuals as a group concerned with their leadership role in the revolutionary movement. The communal movement was motivated by a broad social vision, but it was essentially an elitist movement of intellectuals. While it aspired to make intellectuals into better people by making them into laborers, it nevertheless assumed that intellectuals would retain their role as the vanguard in the creation of a new society. The anarchist notions of labor which inspired this movement glorified labor, but not necessarily the laborer. It was one thing to make labor in the abstract into a goal of humanity; it was altogether another thing to make laborers the vanguard of revolution.

This broad context of socialism, based in a very real way in the social contradictions that appeared in the aftermath of the May Fourth Movement, helps us grasp radicals' "reading" of the October Revolution and of Marxism in a contemporary context. The basic considerations that turned Chinese radicals to socialism in 1919 rested in a concern to achieve a social transformation, bloodless if at all possible, that would resolve the problems of a society in the process of capitalist transformation. As Chinese historians readily concede, these considerations were of such a nature as to create suspicion of the October Revolution, as well as of the most basic premises of Marxism. The same intellectual circumstances that facilitated Marxism's entry into radical thinking, in other words, also obstructed its unqualified acceptance.

This context helps explain the equivocalness of May Fourth attitudes toward the October Revolution and Marxism. We have seen that the initial enthusiasm for the Revolution was based on a misreading of its nature, or rather a reading informed by anarchist social revolutionary ideas that distorted Bolshevism. By early 1919, this reading was replaced by one that came close to the realities of the Revolution. Throughout, there was sympathy for the Russian revolutionaries, accompanied by resentment toward imperialist efforts to squash the Revolution. The question of the Revolution's relevance to China was, however, a good deal more complicated. While admiration was widespread for the Bolsheviks' achievements, it was coupled with a tendency to portray the violence of the Revolution as a negative example for China of what might happen if much-needed social reforms were not instituted immediately. This was as true of Li Dazhao as of Dai Jitao and Zhang Dongsun. Finally, Chinese radicals were woefully ignorant of the details of the Revolution and of its ideological basis in Leninism. They would acquire such knowledge only in 1920, after the initiation of Bolshevik activities in China.

Much the same was the case wth Marxism. The Bolshevik Revolution no doubt helped trigger interest in Marxism among Chinese radicals, but Marxism entered China as part of a general interest in socialism, and was subject to evaluation in that context. What most impressed Chinese intellectuals in 1919 were the materialism and the economism of Marxism. The Marxism they encountered, thanks largely to their sources, was not that of Lenin but of Kautsky, a Marxism most striking for its economic evolutionism rather than its virtues as a revolutionary ideology; Li Dazhao, China's "first Marxist," would even suggest that Marxism, in its economic determinism, subverted revolutionary consciousness. Within the context of May Fourth thinking, with its preoccupation with consciousness and ethical questions, Marxism was found wanting for its apparent failure to address such questions.

On the other hand, to the extent that Chinese radicals associated Marxism with revolutionary class struggle, they were hesitant to embrace it. The appearance of the possibility of class struggle in China was an important element in intensifying their interest in Marxism, but only with mixed feelings. As with their response to the October Revolution, they were wary of the implications of class division and conflict; at best, with Li Dazhao, they viewed class struggle as a necessary evil in a society that promised few other alternatives. But a good society required other values than class loyalty, and these values they continued to locate in other socialisms, especially anarchism. Possibly the greatest importance of Marxism in 1919 was to introduce into radical thinking concepts which enabled them to see and to analyze social problems in a new way. Until 1920, however, they continued to look for the solutions to those problems in stategies of social revolution that promised not to divide but to unite.

Given these uncertainties, the prevailing attitude toward Marxism before 1920 was one of confusion. This was a matter not merely of ignorance, but of an eclecticism that sought to minimize differences between Marxism and other socialisms and, thereby, to "humanize" Marxism, bringing it closer to the values of May Fourth radical culture. At worst, Chinese radicals were suspicious of Marxism for its basic premises; in particular the idea of class struggle. At best, they sought to modify its premises with the aid of other socialisms. It is difficult, at any rate, to find a Marxist in 1919 who discovered "utopia" in the Marxist promise, and an acceptable strategy of social revolution in its theoretical premises.

Interest in Marxism, moreover, must not be confounded with a Marxist identity or attraction to Communist politics. Communism would be established in 1920 by radicals who, with the solitary exception of Li Dazhao, had shown little interest in Marxism earlier; the question of Marxist identity is highly problematic even in the case of Li. On the other hand, Guomindang theorists such as Dai Jitao and Hu Hanmin, who did much to propagate Marxism in 1919–1920, had other political affiliations and were opposed to Communism and Communist politics. It is even possible to suggest, on the basis of available evidence concerning later Communists such as Li Hanjun, Chen Wangdao, and Yun Daiying, that there seemed to be an inverse relationship between appreciation of Marxism and willingness to participate in the founding of the Party. It certainly is very difficult to argue for a teleology between Marxism and Communism: that interest in Marxism pointed to necessary conversion to Communism.

In his *Chinese Communism and the Rise of Mao* Benjamin Schwartz noted the appeal of Bolshevik organization to at least one radical intellectual interested in Marxism, Dai Jitao. Available evidence suggests that this was the case for all the radicals who participated in the founding of the Party; perhaps all the more so in their case since, when it came to actually organizing a Bolshevik party, Dai Jitao was one of the first to shy away from the idea.

This appeal of Bolshevik organization, however, must itself be perceived within the context of May Fourth radical activity, and the ideological contradictions to which it gave rise. Comintern intervention in China coincided with a moment of gloom in Chinese radicalism, when radical activists were beginning to realize that the May Fourth Movement, if it had not failed to achieve its radical cultural goals, had at least fallen far short of the vision of social change it had inspired. By early 1920, radical activity lacked direction. Radicals not only found themselves without a mass following, but suffered at the hands of the counterrevolution that was beginning to assert itself. The final disappointment came when the illusoriness of the communal movement of 1919 became apparent as the labor-learning groups, in which radical activists had invested much intellectual and emotional energy as a means of changing society, failed. Radical activists were cut off not only from the public at large, but felt alienated from their earlier bases in educational institutions—where even formerly radical intellectual leaders had begun to express impatience with continued radical activity.

Chinese radicalism in 1920, in other words, was all dressed up with nowhere to go. The May Fourth Movement had created a radicalism without a future. The failure of radical experiments, and the sense of alienation it created, were also responsible for increasing impatience, if not disillusionment, with the anti-revolutionary socialism, including anarchism, which had dominated socialist thinking in 1919. The failure of radicalism only underlined the remoteness of these socialisms from the concrete, everyday realities of Chinese society. Into this situation stepped the Comintern with an unequivocally class-based revolutionary ideology, and an organizational form that showed the way to its realization in practices. The response was immediate.

Communist historians in China, while recognizing these developments, have stopped short of incorporating them fully into their explanations of the origins of Communism. There are obvious reasons for this reluctance, for these developments suggest that the early Communists were attracted to Communism not out of their recognition of the self-evident truths of "Marx-Leninism," but out of hopelessness, even desperation.

While radical disillusionment was a very important factor in the turn to Communism, however, it was not the only one. The radicals who established the Party may not have been very adept at understanding Marxism, but there was an important ideological factor, not theoretical but a direct product of their radical experiences, that predisposed them to the Bolshevik message. This was the growing attraction to the labor movement in the spring of 1920. Consciousness of the "people," and the need to incorporate them in the revolutionary movement, was a product of May Fourth radicalism. Of immediate relevance in the spring of 1920, however, was the apparent growth of the labor movement which, in a number of significant successful strikes at this time, demonstrated unequivocally that laborers were a power to be reckoned with.[1] The growth of the labor movement, in other words, presented a striking contrast to the receding movements of students and the bourgeoisie. Labor, which had appeared to May Fourth intellectuals as a source of individual moral regeneration, had by early 1920 become in their eyes the most promising source of social regeneration as well. If radical intellectuals did not quite place all their faith in laborers, they were nevertheless presented with striking evidence that laborers might be the only source of hope (and power) for a social revolution.

This increased importance assumed by the labor movement in radical thinking in early 1920 may have done more than anything else in underlining the importance of Marxism which, of all the socialisms available to Chinese radicals, was the most unequivocally class-based in its politics, at least in its Bolshevik interpretation. The shifting attitude toward the questions of class and class politics in early 1920, while still not free of ambiguities and uncertainties, was possibly the most important immediate factor, in other words, for the ideological receptivity to the message Voitinsky brought to China in March 1920. Combined with the organizational promise, which showed the way to an alliance with laborers, the appeal of the message to radical intellectuals was immediate.

The organization of Communism would have been much more arduous, and not nearly as effective, had it not been for the prior existence of May Fourth radical associations which had earlier served as testing grounds for radicalism, and now came to serve as the cores for Communist organization. The Communist movement in 1920 took shape around a national network of radical organizations that had come into being in the course of the May Fourth Movement and were held together less by ideology than by personal relationships. In the process, however, these associations had to be reorganized, and given a new identity as part of a new political network. This organizational transformation also provided the social-institutional basis for the ideological transformation of May Fourth socialism. It was in the course of this process, during the summer and fall of 1920, that lines of demarcation were drawn between Marxism and other socialisms, and a Marxist identity began to emerge in China.

It is important to reiterate here who the early Communist were. What identified them before 1920 was neither a common ideology, nor even a common purpose, but rather radical activity and experience. Communists were few in number, but the few who decided to opt for Communism in 1920 included activists who had distinguished themselves during the May Fourth Movement in various parts of China as foremost radical leaders. It was they who were most sharply aware of the failure of May Fourth activism. And it was they who were the most deeply committed to the perpetuation of radical activity. Their frustrations were an important element in turning them to Communism because it was they who suffered most at the hands of the counterrevolutionary suppression of radical activity in 1919–1920.

These radical experiences were crucial in 1920–1921 in bringing together the radical intelligentsia who founded the Party and would serve in ensuing years as its core. The question of radical experience also offers insights into a problem posed at the beginning of this study: the problem of ideology and organization in the emergence of organized activity, viewed within the broader social context of such activity.

Not a common ideology, or even a shared purpose, initially brought May Fourth radicals together in radical associations, but rather, vague dissatisfactions and yearnings which freely blended public with private concerns, national salvation with individual liberation, social with cultural ideas. They came together in haphazard associations based on personal networks in and around contemporary educational institutions. It was in the course of talking and acting together that common purposes emerged, and the associations acquired some internal coherence. And it was in the course of radical encounters with society that an ideology of social revolution gradually took shape as the binding ideological force of radical associations, preparing the ground for their eventual conversion to Bolshevism, and Marxism.

This is not to suggest that these associations could have served as vehicles to Bolshevism regardless of their social and ideological context. A comparison here with an earlier radical organization in China, the Restoration Society founded in Shanghai in 1904, for which we have documentation, might be instructive. In the revolutionary atmosphere that prevailed during the last decade of the Qing dynasty, radical intellectuals in Shanghai had gone through experiences similar to those of the May Fourth period, organizing themselves around educational institutions with similar feelings of discontent and yearning. Associated activity in their case, too, had a radicalizing effect on them, and culminated in the conversion of "educational" associations into a political organization in 1904, the Restoration Society. This society represented radical intellectuals' final commitment to revolutionary political activity, as they moved from a diffuse radicalism to determined political action, underground if necessary to cope with political oppression.[2]

The Restoration Society, however, remained limited in its political ideology and social vision. In the end, its activities remained divorced from the people at large, and took the form of conspiratorial efforts at assassination and political terrorism. Even after the establishment of an organizational framework, its members were unable to draw clear distinctions between effective revolutionary action and acts of revolutionary heroism.

For the radicals of the May Fourth period, the situation was significantly different. The social mobilization of society at large provided them with a revolutionary context in which the political significance of social activity impinged deeply upon their consciousness, driving them upon a social revolutionary course. The Bolshevik ideology that was available to them provided them with an ideology of social revolution. Bolshevism, too, may be viewed as a form of revolutionary conspiracy designed to cope with problems of revolution in an oppressive political environment, but it is a conspiracy designed not as an end in itself but above all as a vehicle of social mobilization and organization. The Communists in 1920 were engaged in labor organization before they had even completed the task of party formation. It is a moot question here whether Bolshevik ideology or the social context of the labor movement in China was responsible for turning radical associations to Bolshevism. The latter was part of the direct radical experience with society, the former served to explain the realities they encountered in the course of their radical activity, in its Marxist social analysis, and to give direction to those activities, in its organizational principles. Within this context, however, it was in the final analysis the radical experience—the collective confrontation of the social and cultural problems of revolution—that informed the process whereby radical intellectuals turned within a very brief period from a pursuit of "the meaning of life" to the establishment of a political organization in which all question of meaning was subsumed within the single-minded goal of making revolution.

Into the Future

This study has criticized approaches to the origins of Communism in China that have read its past from the perspective of its future. I will say a few words in conclusion about what the origins of the Party may have to tell us about its future. This strategy, too, has its pitfalls, as indicated by some Chinese historians' efforts today to discover in the Party's origins everything from its continuing authoritarianism to the persistence in it of anti-organizational anarchist tendencies. It is inappropriate to read from the Party's origins its future course, therefore ignoring the very significant historical forces that at every moment in its history have mediated the relationship between its past and its future. Once a party organization had come into being, it served as a locus of historical change, providing some continuity in the Party's history, but the Party would not remain the same either in organization or in ideology. The Communist party that came into power in 1949 was vastly different from what it had been in 1921. We may discover in the origins suggestions of things to come, but never a blueprint for the future.

Accordingly, some insights into problems in the Party's subsequent history are suggested by the context of its formation and process of establishment. These insights are direct for the immediate aftermath of the founding, and much less tentative for later years.

First is the question of Comintern domination in the Party's early years. The ready acquiescence of early Communists in Comintern direction may seem puzzling if we ascribe the origins of Communism in China to a nationalistic attraction to Communism, or an independent appreciation of Marxism. It seems much less so when we recognize that the Party's formation was a direct product of Comintern intervention. This is not to suggest that the passage was an easy one for individual Communists. Comintern domination did not appear to be a problem so long as they dealt with Voitinsky, who impressed them with his good will; it was much more difficult when it came to dealing with Maring, the domineering "angel of liberation" to Eastern peoples. As early as the founding conference of the Party, Comintern direction emerged as a problem for some of the founders. The problem, with all the dilemmas it presented to Chinese radicals, was expressed more in the form of personal than ideological resistance, for the founders were in no position to challange their Comintern advisors on ideological grounds. For some, the initial dissatisfaction eventually culminated in parting ways with the Party they had helped establish. Such was the case with Li Hanjun, Chen Wangdao, Bao Huiseng, Zhou Fohai, and Shi Cuntong. For others, resistance took the form of erratic behavior, as was the case with Chen Duxiu, who quite evidently was unable to reconcile his nominal position as party secretary with the actuality of Comintern power. Chen's case, more than any other, illustrates the conflict between the vision that had led Chinese radicals to Bolshevism, and the realities they discovered after they had subjected themselves to Bolshevik organization. The Comintern's apparent decision in 1922 to try and enforce its will through younger radicals who had been initiated into Communism abroad, especially those who had rubbed elbows with Comintern leaders in Moscow, shows that the mistrust was mutual. The Communist party of China was founded by radical intellectuals whose loyalties to Bolshevism were conditioned by revolutionary ideals inspired by sources other than Communism. They could serve the cause of Bolshevism in China, as long as they remained faithful to the new organization, but they could not be trusted indefinitely. The tension between ideology and organization persisted throughout the 1920s, and came to a head when the revolutionary movement ran into severe obstacles in 1927.

A byproduct of Comintern domination was the alliance between the Guomindang and the fledgling Communist party that was proposed in late 1922 and realized in 1923. It is by now beyond any serious doubt that the idea of an alliance orginated with the Comintern, and was pushed through the Party against the will of some of its older leaders (namely Chen Duxiu) but with the aid of younger members who had been persuaded in Moscow of the importance of such an alliance.

The process whereby the Communist party of China was founded suggests that there was another dimension of this alliance. There was, in fact, an alliance between radicals associated with the two political groupings before there was a Communist party or a formal alliance between the two parties. These alliances were formed in the course of the radical activities of the May Fourth period, when party affiliation seemed much less important than personal ties and common purpose. In Shanghai, most prominently, and in other places such as Jinan, Wuhan, Guangzhou, and Changsha, radical members of the Guomindang associated freely with May Fourth radicals; out of this association emerged groups that served as the basis for Communist organization in 1920. Ideological lines were blurred in the immediate May Fourth period by the simple fact that there was no clear ideology that separated one radical from another with any definiteness. Guomindang radicals were more "Marxist" in 1919–1920 than most later Communists. Even later, after organizational lines had been drawn with the founding of the Party, important local leaders of the Guomindang such as Shen Xuanlu and Shao Lizi continued to cooperate with the Communists. We sometimes overlook the fact that many members of the Guomindang were radicalized by developments in the aftermath of the May Fourth Movement, and throughout the twenties Marxism would remain as a force in the Guomindang, creating much confusion about political identity, just as many Communists remained uncertain of their identity because of their basic commitment to national goals. When the united front (or "reorganization") was established in 1924, it already had a social basis in the association locally between Communists and members of the Guomindang.

The organizational basis upon which Communism was established is a third area where the origins of the Party shed some light on its early development. Following 1921 the Communist party emerged quickly as a real force on the Chinese political scene and commanded a power out of all proportion to its small numbers. Much of this power the Party owed to the strength of its local organizations, the former May Fourth radical associations upon which it had been established, which had deep roots in their environment. At the same time, however, these local organizations had their own local concerns which did not always coincide with those of the Party as a national organization; their very power helped curtail the power of the center. Part of the reason for the continuing weakness of the party center in Shanghai was that real power throughout the twenties rested with Comintern advisors in Guangzhou; what little power it had it derived from its function as a communications center for the party network. But the nature of party organization was another reason; localism was implicit in the Party's establishment upon the basis of existing local radical associations, which was both a help and a hindrance to the consolidation of Communist power.

Finally, possibly the most important insight yielded by the origins of the Party pertains to the relationship between Marxist theory and Communist organization, which provides us with a context within which to evaluate these other problems.

The questions raised by this relationship point to the fundamental problem of the relationship between theory and practice in Marxism. The problematic nature of this relationship was captured with characteristic acuity by Lukacs:

> While for pure theory the most diverse views and directions can live side by side peaceably, while their oppositions assume the form merely of discussions which can take place placidly within the framework of one and the same organization without threatening to disrupt it, the same questions, when they are given as organizational orientation, present themselves in the sharpest manner as directions which are mutually exclusive. Every "theoretical" direction or divergence of views must immediately be transformed into an organizational issue if it is not to remain mere theory,or abstract opinion, if it really has the intention of showing the path to its realization.[3]

This cogent presentation of the relationship between revolutionary theory and revolutionary organization, while brilliant in its economical description of a basic dilemma of Marxism, is nevertheless striking for glossing over two questions of the most fundamental significance. While it tells us that theoretical inquiry and debate must be restricted in order to enable revolutionary organization, it does not tell us if the nature of revolutionary organization is itself subject to debate and inquiry—a serious oversight, especially in light of the fact that the choice of one revolutionary organization over another implies automatically the choice of one version of theory over another. The question, moreover, is not merely a question of revolutionary strategy, but impinges directly and obsessively upon the question of the goal of revolution: what does the restriction of open-ended theoretical debate in the name of organizational coherence imply for the ideological aspirations to democracy which are built into Marxism as a critical theory of society?

These questions, to which the origins of the Communist party of China (as the origins of Bolshevism earlier) compel our attention, were to persist in the history of Chinese Communism, as they have persisted in Marxism in general.

One Chinese historian has remarked recently that the Communist party of China in its origins had no original Marxist thinker comparable to Lenin or Plekhanov who could address problems of the Chinese revolution; the Party's practice, therefore, suffered from its crude grasp of theory, and an inability to apply theoretical insights to the revolutionary analysis of China's peculiar circumstances.[4] This, in many ways, is an understatement; not only was there no one comparable in theoretical stature to a Lenin or Plekhanov, but the founders of the Party had little awareness of the intricacies of Marxism. The most that can be said of their Marxism is that it reflects some of the parochial concerns of the Chinese revolution. These concerns did not lead them into any original theoretical insights into Marxism, or any breakthroughs in the interpretation of Marxist theory Chinese Marxism, such as it was in the twenties, was wholly derivative of Bolshevism.

The organization of Communism before there was any significant appreciation of Marxist theory, or its application in revolutionary analysis, was to be an obstacle to the Chinese understanding of Marxism, as the more knowledgeable among the founders of the Party, such as Li Hanjun, perceived readily. Bolshevik organization obviated the need for theoretical inquiry and analysis. The radicals who founded the Party became Communists before they were Marxists, and once they had done so, an organizationally defined ideology became for them a substitute for theoretical analysis: being in no position to analyze Bolshevism from a broader Marxist perspective, they readily accepted the Bolshevik claim to be all that was worthwhile in Marxism, which was no doubt aided in the 1920s by the rapid political success Bolshevik organization seemed to guarantee. This was reflected in the literature on Marxism. With the founding of the Party, Chinese Communists seemed to lose all interest in European Marxist literature; the works on Marxism that found their way in China between 1921 and 1927 were almost exclusively of Bolshevik origin. What there was in the way of independent Marxist literature came not from the Communists, but the Marxists in the Guomindang. Not until after 1927, when the revolutionary movement encountered a serious crisis with the split between the Guomindang and the Communists, did Communists once again discover Marx, as part of an urgent effort to reevaluate and analyze what had gone wrong. Only after 1927, in other words, did they acquire a genuine familiarity with Marxism, and begin to apply it to the analysis of Chinese society in order to discover a revolutionary strategy appropriate to the circumtances of that society.[5]

Their lack of familiarity with Marxism left Chinese Communists at the mercy of Bolshevism. This is not to denigrate the Bolshevik contribution; Lenin's insights into imperialism represented a major contribution to Marxism, especially within a non-European context, and his views on revolutionary organization (Bolshevism) around the turn of the century restored revolution to Marxism. These were crucial to the organization of revolution in China.

Unlike Japanese Marxists, with their preoccupation with the metaphysical questions of Marxism, Chinese Marxists discovered in Bolshevism an ideology of action that quickly moved them into revolutionary practice.

It is also clear, however, that the revolutionary model provided by Bolshevism obviated concrete social analysis of the kind Lenin himself had undertaken. In China, the cliches of Bolshevism substituted for independent analysis. The practice inspired by those cliches seemed to work as long as there was a general mobilization of Chinese society to sustain it; its weaknesses became readily apparent in 1927, when the revolution ran into trouble. The most crucial issue, where revolutionary strategy was concerned, was that of agrarian revolution. While there is some evidence that Communists paid greater attention to this issue in the 1920s than we have suspected, the Comintern-defined strategy in China nevertheless presented the issue of agrarian revolution as at best secondary. The few people in the 1920s who genuinely appreciated the centrality of rural revolution to the Chinese revolution, such as Peng Pai and Yun Daiying, began to engage in revolutionary activity in the countryside while still going through their flirtation with anarcho-communist ideas.[6] For the rest of the Party, rural revolution did not appear as a real, and necessary, alternative until after the revolution had encountered deep problems in urban China. Even then, there was considerable ideological opposition to it among those loyal to the Bolshevik model of revolution.

Equally significant is the question of democracy, both within the Party and in the Party's relationship to society in the process of revolution. The same writer has observed that the problem of democracy, which plagues the Party to this day, was created at the Party's origins with the despotism exercised by Chen Duxiu.[7] Chen is here once again made a scapegoat for problems that were implicit in the Bolshevik organization of the Party. It is important to remember, moreover, that a "despotic" organization was forced upon May Fourth radicals by circumstances of oppression; it is a difficult question how a democratic party could have coped with the problems of revolution in China. Very few political organizations in twentieth-century China could be described as democratic. Under the circumstances, Bolshevism, which itself was a product of despotism in Russia, was well equipped to deal with the problems of the Chinese revolution.

The question of democracy is worth raising, however, because if the exigencies of revolution may call forth such an organization, it is also possible for revolution to serve as an excuse for Party dictatorship over society after those exigencies have disappeared. This is evident in the reluctance of Communist parties in power, including in China today, to seriously consider democratic Marxist alternatives to Bolshevism simply by denying the authenticity of any Marxism that is not Bolshevik.

While the relationship of Bolshevism to Marxism, or the authenticity of non-Bolshevik Marxisms, may be subject to debate, what is not debatable is that the Marxist conception of socialism is not restricted to Bolshevism. Indeed, the extension of democracy beyond its political definition to include social and economic democracy is crucial to Marxism. If this creates problems for Marxism and socialism, the problems ought nevertheless to be confronted directly. This is systematically ignored when Marxism is confounded with Bolshevism which, by its own explicit premises, has curtailed democracy in the name of revolution. The Chinese Communist party, when it was established in 1920–1921 on Bolshevik premises, represented a political organization whose dictatorial nature conflicted with the democratic aspirations that had motivated May Fourth radicals, and could be justified only in terms of coping with an oppressive political environment. Yet what had been a choice made out of necessity eventually turned into a definition of orthodoxy and an object of political celebration. The confounding of Bolshevism and Marxism at the origins of the Party not only disguised contradictions between Marxist goals and Bolshevik organization, but was also the point of departure for the ideological consolidation of Bolshevik orthodoxy in later years. Early Communists in China were not equipped ideologically to deal with these contradictions. To point to the distinction is important, nevertheless, because the distinction points to continuing problems in Chinese Communism. To refuse to do so is to deny to Marxism the democratic impulse tht lies at its very origins.

In recent years, the question of party origins has been raised in Chinese historiography from another perspective, this time involving the role anarchism played in the ideology of early Communists. In spite of all "Marxist" efforts to stamp it out, one author has observed, anarchist thinking survived in the Party to undermine Marxism. Some have blamed the "anti-Party" activities of the Cultural Revolution upon anarchism. Others have placed anarchist influences in post-Mao years, blaming anarchist "libertarianism" for demands for democracy that enjoyed a brief hearing in 1978–1979.[8]

If we must speak of lingering anarchist influence in the Communist party of China, other evidence of anarchist "influence" could be invoked. Anarchists were not simply "anti-Party," they were also anti-bureaucracy and anti-dictatorship, which have continued to be live issues in Chinese Communism. On the positive side, they were proponents of "mutual aid," which idea has bequeathed its name, if not its reality, to social organization in post-1949 China. Most important may have been the anarchist ideal of labor-learning, which sought to abolish social inequality by making intellectuals into laborers and laborers into intellectuals, an idea that found strong echoes in the "red-expert" ideals that were enunciated in the late 1950s and into the 1970s as a means of creating a socialist culture. Indeed even the "populism" that some students of Chinese Communism such as Meisner have identified as a distinguishing feature of Chinese Communism from Li Dazhao to Mao Zedong drew from the beginning upon contemporary anarchist ideas and values. This populism, needless to say, counteracted the Bolshevik principles of the Party, and made the Communist party of China a relatively more open organization than its counterparts elsewhere.

These ideas and values, moreover, were not restricted to Mao Zedong, but were diffused widely among the early Communists, especially those who received their baptism in the work-study programs sponsored by anarchists in the May Fourth period, among them Zhou Enlai, Deng Xiaoping, and a host of less well-known Communist leaders who were active after 1949 both in the Party and in cultural work.

Whether or not the appearance of such ideas and values in later years can be ascribed to a persisting anarchist influence is highly problematic. While they were most fervently advocated by anarchists in the May Fourth period, they are not necessarily restricted to anarchism but are common to socialism in general. Their re-emergence at a later time, moreover, was due to particular problems encountered in the course of the revolution, such as bureaucratic elitism. As presented in later years, they were divorced from any kind of anarchist conceptualization of society, for there is little evidence, in the case of Mao at any rate, that the promotion of anarchist-sounding ideas and values were intended to undermine the Party; indeed, that they were utilized to serve an authoritarian political structure may account for the unanarchist consequences they led to during the Cultural Revolution: a power structure rendered even more arbitrary than usual by its own ideological incoherence.

Nevertheless, the question is an intriguing one. The fact that anarchism prevailed in the origins of the Party, not simply as an ideology but in the culture of radicalism upon which the early Communists were reared, suggests that it may have had some staying power even in the thinking of those who rejected it ideologically. And, even if such anarchist ideas and values are not restricted to anarchism, the fact that within the context of socialist discourse in China it was the anarchists who promoted them with the greatest insistence and consistency suggests, at the very least, that those who advocated them at a later time were at least aware of the association, even if they had no anarchist intention.

What meaning may be assigned to the question of anarchism within the context of the post-1949 state is another matter. Anarchist influence may be condemned for provoking "anti-Party" attitudes, but this is justifiable only from a perspective that identifies party rule with socialism; it is only a continued commitment to Bolshevik principles that makes any effort to ameliorate party domination of society, or at democratization, appear subversive of socialism. The same perspective, in its political conservatism, is responsible for the vulgarized portrayal of anarchism merely as an ideology of disorder.

George Lukacs once observed that "Marxism is the self-criticism of the bourgeoisie." In the same vein, we might suggest that the legacy of anarchism is the conscience of socialism. While the anarchist effort to remain true to socialist ideals in political practice goes a long way toward explaining why anarchists, in their refusal to face up to the realities of power, have been condemned to political ineffectiveness, it has also distinguished anarchism as the only socialism to uphold consistently the vision that lies at the point of departure of all socialism: the vision of community, equality, and democracy. The vision offers us a yardstick from within socialism against which to evaluate the claims to socialist authenticity of socialists, of no matter what political orientation.

There is little question that however effectively Bolshevik organization served as an instrument of revolution in China, the choice of Bolshevism over its competitors in 1920–1921 also represented an attenuation of the democratic and egalitarian ideals that had been the motivating forces of May Fourth radicalism, which anarchism had done so much to nourish. Indeed, anarchists believed deeply that a revolution could be only as good as the radical organization that brought it about; in revolutionary organization, in other words, rested the paradigm of revolutionary society. An organization that was dictatorial internally, and in its relationship with the social forces it led, could never bring about a democratic or egalitarian society. Anarchists may have been naive as revolutionaries; they were not wrong in their perception of this crucial relationship between revolutionary organization and the revolutionary society of the future.

To recall these origins, rather than subvert socialism, may from this perspective help put socialism in China on the right track once again. To condemn the role anarchists played in the origins of the Communist party of China is to deny the vision that inspired May Fourth radicals to embark upon their long revolutionary quest in the first place. The very act of remembering may restore to Chinese socialism its long-forgotten origins in a democratic vision that was not just political, but social and cultural as well.

For the student of Chinese Communism, this same act of remembering is a reminder of the distance Chinese radicals were to travel on the road to Bolshevism. Bolshevism in China took shape rapidly in simple chronological terms: four years, if we start with the October Revolution, slightly over a year if we start with the May Fourth Movement. The rapidity of the conversion to Bolshevism makes the process appear effortless, if not predestined. We need to remember the immense intellectual and emotional territory that lay between where they started and where they finally ended up, to be reminded that the road in between was long and arduous. For some, it was to be endless.

NOTES

Abbreviations to Notes

DFZZ   *Dongfang zazhi* [Eastern Miscellany]

YDQH   *Yida qianhou* [The Period of the First Congress], 2 vols. Beijing: Renmin chubanshe, 1980.

LDZXJ   *Li Dazhao xuanji* [Selected Works of Li Dazhao]. Beijing: Renmin chubanshe, 1978.

WSSQQKJS   *Wusi shiqi qikan jieshao* [Introduction to Periodicals of the May Fourth Period]. 6 vols. Beijing: Sanlian shudian, 1979.

XQPL   *Xinqqi pinglun* [Weekend Review].

JFGZ   *Jiefang yu gaizao*, later *Gaizao* [Reconstruction].

WSSQST   *Wusi shiqidi shetuan* [Societies of the May Fourth Period], 4 vols. Beijing: Sanlian shudian, 1979.

XQN   *Xin qingnan* [New Youth].

Chapter 1

1. Maurice Meisner, *Li Ta-chao and the Origins of Chinese Marxism* (Cambridge: Harvard University Press, 1967), p. 13.

2. Ibid., pp. 13–14.

3. Martin Bernal, "Chinese Socialism Before 1913," in Jack Gray, ed., *Modern China's Search for Political Form* (New York: Oxford University Press, 1969), p. 67, and Li Yu-ning, *The Introduction of Socialism to China* (New York: Columbia University Press, 1971).

4. Robert Scalapino, "The Evolution of a Young Revolutionary: Mao Zedong in 1919–1920," *Journal of Asian Studies* 42 (November 1982):29–61.

5. Arif Dirlik, "The New Culture Movement Revisited: Anarchism and the Idea of Social Revolution in New Culture Thinking," *Modern China* 11 (July 1983):251–300.

6. Benjamin I. Schwartz, *Chinese Communism and the Rise of Mao* (Cambridge: Harvard University Press, 1951), p. 8.

7. Meisner, *Li Ta-chao*, p. 114.

8. "Wusi shiqi lao tongzhi zuotanhui jilu" [Record of round-table discussion by old Comrades of the May Fourth period], in *Jinian wusi yundong liushi zhounian xueshu taolunhui lunwen xuan* [Collection of discussions in celebration of the sixtieth anniversary of the May Fourth Movement] (Beijing: Chinese Academy of Social Sciences, 1980), 1:29–30.

9. See, for example, Chen Duxiu, *Duxiu wencun* [Collection of works by Chen Duxiu], 2 vols. (Shanghai, 1922), 2:117–119.

10. Schwartz, *Chinese Communism*, p. 33.

11. See Chapter 10. Also see Cai Wei, *Wusi shiqi Makesizhuyi fandui fan-*

Makesizhuyi sichaodi douzheng [The struggle between Marxism and anti-Marxism during the May Fourth period] (Shanghai: Renmin chubanshe, 1979).

12. Lucien Bianco, *Origins of the Chinese Revolution,* trans. Muriel Bell (Stanford: Stanford University Press, 1971), p. 54.

13. Sheweilaofu(?), "Zhongguo gongchan dang chengli shi" [History of the founding of the Communist party of China], in *Dangshi yanjiu ziliao* (Materials on Party History), nos. 6, 7 (joint issue) (June 20, 1981), pp. 26–36. Original published in *Problems of the Far East,* no. 4 (1980) (Moscow).

14. Schwartz has suggested that for the Guomindang theoretician Dai Jitao, the main appeal of Marxism lay in its organizational promise. The thesis in this study is that this was the attraction of Bolshevism for all Chinese Communists at this time.

Part I

Prologue

1. Morris Hillquit, "Socialist Russia vs. Capitalist World," in Philip Foner, ed., *The Bolshevik Revolution: Its Impact on American Radicals, Liberals, and Labor* (New York: International Publishers, 1967), pp. 217–218.

2. "Jinrizhi Mading Lude" [The Martin Luther of our day]. Trans. from *New York Times.* In DFZZ 15 (April 15, 1918):66–69.

3. Chen Gongbo, "Chen Gongbo huiyi Zhongguo gongchan dangdi chengli" [Chen Gongbo recalls the founding of the Communist party of China], in YDQH, 2:419.

Chapter 2

1. Fang Hanqi, "Shiyue geming zai Zhongguo baokan (1917–1921) shangdi fanying" [The reflection of the October Revolution in Chinese periodicals and newspapers (1917–1921)], in *Xinwen yewu* (Journalism), no. 11 (1957), p. 98.

2. "EFa geming yitong lun" [Similarities and differences between the Russian and French revolutions], DFZZ 15 (August 15, 1918):22–32.

3. Ying Po, "Eguo nu gemingdangkuei chuihua lu" [The record of a Russian woman revolutionary leader], DFZZ 14 (December 1917):23.

4. Jun Shi tr., "Eguozhi tudi fenqi wenti" [The problem of land distribution in Russia] (trans. from Japanese), DFZZ 15 (September 1918):43.

5. Liu Dajun, "Shehui zhuyi" [Socialism], DFZZ 15 (November 1918):190–198, and Jun Shi, "Eguo xianzaizhi zhengdang" [Political parties in contemporary Russia], DFZZ 15 (February 1918):61–65.

6. Liu, "Shehui zhuyi."

7. For examples, see "FaE gemingzhi bijiao guan" [Comparison of the French and Russian revolutions] and "Shumindi shengli" [The victory of the common people], LDZXJ, pp. 101–104 and pp. 109–111 respectively.

8. Maurice Meisner, *Li Ta-chao and the Origins of Chinese Marxism* (Cambridge: Harvard University Press, 1967), pp. 60–70.

9. Ibid., p. 56.

10. Gail Bernstein, *Japanese Marxist: A Portrait of Kawakami Hajime, 1879–1946* (Cambridge: Harvard University Press, 1976), part 2.

11. According to Zhang Guotao, in 1912 Li Dazhao even translated a book

entitled *Outline of Tolstoyism*. See Chang Kuo-t'ao, *The Rise of the Chinese Communist Party, 1921–1927* (Lawrence: The University Press of Kansas, 1971), p. 692, n.75.

12. "Daiai pian" (The Great Grief), LDZXJ, pp. 1–3. For Liu Shipei's anarchism, see Arif Dirlik, "Vision and Revolution: Anarchism in Chinese Revolutionary Thought on the Eve of the 1911 Revolution," *Modern China* 12 (April 1986):121–161.

13. For the relationship between anarchism and populism, see Franco Venturi, *Roots of Revolution* (New York: Grosset & Dunlap, 1966), and A. Walicki, *The Controversy Over Capitalism* (London: Oxford University Press, 1969).

14. Yi Cun, "Eguo guojipai shixingdi zhenglue" [The political strategy of the extremists in Russia], *Laodong* [Labor] 1 (April 12, 1918):9.

15. *Laodong*, 2, p. 25.

16. Quoted in WSSQQKJS, 2a:170.

17. Lao ren, "Ouzhan yu laodongzhe" [The European war and laborers], *Laodong* 1 (March 12, 1918):17.

18. WSSQQKJS, 2a:177–178.

19. " 'Wuyi' May Day [*sic*] yundong shi" [History of the May Day movement], LDZXJ, pp. 311–326. For the reference to *Laodong*, see pp. 323–324.

20. Zhu Chengjia, ed., *Zhonggong dangshi yanjiu lunwen xuan* [Selected essays on the history of the Communist party of China], 3 vols. (Changsha: Hunan remnin chubanshe, 1983). See vol. 1, p. 161.

21. Shao Lizi, "Dang chengli qianhoudi yixie qingkuang" [Certain circumstances surrounding the establishment of the Party] in YDQH, 2:70.

22. Meisner, *Li Ta-chao*, p. 142.

23. Arif Dirlik and Edward Krebs, "Socialism and Anarchism in Early Republican China," *Modern China* 7 (April 1981):117–151.

24. *Jinhua* [Evolution] 1 (February 1919):7–9.

25. Huang Lingshuang, "Ping *Xinchao zazhi* suowei jinri shijiezhi xinchao" [Criticism of the so-called contemporary world tide of *Renaissance Magazine*], *Jinhua* 1 (February 1919): 13–17.

26. Dirlik and Krebs, "Socialism and Anarchism."

27. Ge Maochun, Jiang Jun, and Li Xingzhi, eds., *Wuzhengfu zhuyi sixiang ziliao xuan* [Selection of materials on anarchist thought], 2 vols. (Beijing: Beijing daxue chuban she, 1984). See vol. 1, pp. 439–441, 472–473.

28. "Laodong jiedi zhuci" [In celebration of Labor Day], *Beijing daxue xuesheng zhoukan* [Beijing University student weekly], no. 14 (May 1, 1920):3.

29. "Shijie zuixinzhi liang da zuzhi" [Two great organizations in the contemporary world], in Ge, et al., eds., *Wuzhengfu zhuyi*, 1:410–421.

30. *Wusi yundong zai Shanghai* [The May Fourth Movement in Shanghai] (Shanghai: renmin chubanshe, 1980), pp. 533–535.

31. WSSQQKJS 2:475–485 (indices).

32. Ibid., pp. 444–448.

33. *Wusi aiguo yundong dangan ziliao* [Archival materials on the May Fourth patriotic movement] (Beijing: Zhongguo shehui kexue chubanshe, 1980), pp. 614–615.

34. Ibid., pp. 634–636.

35. Ibid., pp. 632–633.

36. *Jinhua* 1 (February 1919):28.

37. Arif Dirlik, "The New Culture Movement Revisited: Anarchism and the

Idea of Social Revolution in New Culture Thinking," *Modern China* 11 (July 1983:251–300.

38. "Zailun wenti yu zhuyi" [Another discussion of problems and isms], LDZXJ, pp. 231–232.

39. "Guojipaizhi yinxian" [Clues to extremism], LDZXJ, pp. 151–152.

40. "Zailun wenti yu zhuyi," LDZXJ, p. 232. Also see reference in WSSQQKJS, Ia:130. For an explanation of the incident, see Jerome Davis, "Nationalization of Women: A Hoax," in Foner, ed., *The Bolshevik Revolution*, pp. 163–164.

41. WSSQQKJS, Ia:131.

42. LDZXJ, pp. 155–157 and 216–218.

43. WSSQQKJS, Ia:132–133.

44. "Duifu 'Buerseweike' di fangfa" [How to deal with "Bolshevism"] XQPL, no. 3 (June 22, 1919), p. 4.

45. "Eguodi jinkuang yu lianheguodi duiE zhengce" [Present conditions in Russia and the Allied policy toward Russia], XQPL, no. 26 (November 30, 1919), p. 1.

46. Jitao, "Laonong zhengfuzhi xiadi Eguo" [Russia under the worker-peasant government], XQPL, no. 39 (February 29, 1920), p. 1.

47. *Wusi yundong zai Shanghai*, pp. 533–535.

48. WSSQQKJS, Ia:189.

49. *Wusi yundong zai Shanghai*, pp. 80–93.

50. WSSQQKJS, Ia:131, 133. I thank Tetsuo Najita for his help in identifying this journalist.

51. For Fuse's opposition to Marxism, see Huang Lingshuang, "Ping *Xinchao zazhi*," p. 15.

52. Quoted in WSSQQKJS, Ia:131.

53. "The Bullitt Report," in Foner, The Bolshevik Revolution, p. 202.

54. Ibid., p. 114.

55. Ibid., p. 201.

56. Luo Jialun, "Jinrizhi shijie xinchao" [The contemporary world tide], *Xinchao* [The Renaissance] 1 (1919):19–24.

57. WSSQQKJS, IIIa:281–282, 283.

58. Xiang Qing, "Zhongguo gongchandang chuangjian shiqidi Gongchan guoji he Zhongguo geming" [The Comintern at the time of the founding of the Communist party of China and the Chinese revolution], Zhu, ed., in *Zhonggong dangshi*, 1:297.

59. "Yuan Zhengyingdi huiyi" [Memoirs of Yuan Zhenying], in YDQH, 2:474.

60. Ding Shouhe, *Shiyue geming dui Zhongguo gemingdi yingxiang* [The influence of the October Revolution on the Chinese revolution] (Beijing: renmin chubanshe, 1957), p. 44.

Chapter 3

1. Originally entitled "Xin minzhu zhuyidi zhengzhi yu xin minzhu zhuyidi wenhua" [The politics and culture of New Democracy], *Zhongguo wenhua* (Chinese culture) 1 (February 1940):19.

2. Wang Laibing, "Guanyu Zhongguo gongchan dang zaoqi zuzhi jige wenti" [Some questions on the early organization of the Communist party of China], in Zhu Chengjia, ed., *Zhonggong dangshi yanjiu lunwen xuan*, 3 vols. (Changsha: Hunan renmin chubanshe, 1983), 1:213, 223.

3. Liu Renjing, "Huiyi wo zai Beida Makesi xueshuo yanjiu huidi qingkuang" [Remembering circumstances of the Society for the Study of Marxist Theory at Beida], in *Dangshi yanjiu ziliao* [Materials on party history], 3 vols. (Chengdu: Sichuan renmin chubanshe, 1982), 1:64. This collection should be distinguished from the serial to which I also refer in this study. The two carry the same title, presumably because the former represents selections from the latter.

4. See Part III, Epilogue. The reference to Li Hanjun is in Chang Kuo-t'ao, *The Rise of the Chinese Communist Party, 1921–1927* (Lawrence: The University Press of Kansas, 1967), p. 115. In his memoirs, Guo Moruo refers to having met in 1922 a Li Shanting who was then known as "China's Marx." This was probably Li Hanjun. See *Geming chunqiu* [Annals of Revolution] (Shanghai: New Art and Literature Society, 1951), pp. 104–5.

5. Maurice Meisner, *Li Ta-chao and the Origins of Chinese Marxism* (Cambridge: Harvard University Press, 1967), p. 115.

6. *Makesi Engesi zhuzuo zai Zhongguodi chuanpo* [The propagation of Marx and Engels' works in China] (Beijing: Marx-Engels Research Institute, 1983), p. 247.

7. Chang, *Chinese Communist Party*, p. 692, n.77.

8. Liu Renjing, "Huiyi 'wusi' yundong, Beijing Makesi zhuyi yanjiu hui he dangdi 'yida,'" [Remembering the May Fourth Movement, the Beijing Marxist Research Society, and the first Party congress], YDQH, 2:114.

9. Li Rui, *Mao Zedong tongzhidi chuqi geming yundong* [The early revolutionary activities of comrade Mao Zedong] (Beijing: Zhongguo qingnian chubanshe, 1957), p. 94. Meisner accepts the existence of this society.

10. Edgar Snow, *Red Star over China* (New York: Grove Press, 1961), p. 150. It is interesting that in the recent revised edition of Li Rui's book, the reference to this society no longer appears. Indeed, it is interesting what Li Rui says of Beida during Mao's first visit: "At this time Marxism had still not been introduced systematically, and petit-bourgeois thinking, particularly anarchism and Tolstoy's pan-laborism, had a very big market. People could not distinguish Marxism from them. There were a few people such as Li Dazhao who already recognized that China must follow the Russian path, and understood the necessity of grasping the Marxist theory of class struggle (following the May Fourth Movement, Li would teach a course on "the Materialist Conception of History"), but even they could not use the concept of class struggle to analyze problems, or even rid their thinking of the influence of non-Marxist or petit-bourgeois thought. . . . During the May Fourth Movement, many people encountered Marxism in the course of a transition through anarchism. At the time, some anarchists were engaged in anti-imperialist and anti-feudal propaganda and activity. While Mao Zedong was in Beijing, he also read several books on anarchism, had contact with anarchists at Beida, and discussed with them the possibility of realizing anarchism in China." *Mao Zedongdi zaoqi geming huodong* [The early revolutionary activities of Mao Zedong] (Changsha: Hunan renmin chubanshe, 1980), pp. 179–180.

11. "Wodi Makesi zhuyi guan," LDZXJ, pp. 173–211.

12. "Jieji jingzheng yu huzhu," LDZXJ, pp. 222–225. Quotation on p. 224.

13. *Makesi Engesi zhuzuo zai Zhongguodi chuanpo*, p. 249. Also see Li Xin, *Weidadi kairui* [The great beginning] (Beijing: Zhongguo shehui kexue chubanshe, 1983), p. 205, n.1.

14. Li, "Wodi Makesi zhuyi guan," p. 194.

15. Li Longmu, "Li Dazhao tongzhi he wusi shiqi Makesi zhuyi sixiangdi xuan-

chuan" [Comrade Li Dazhao and the propagation of Marxist thought during the May Fourth period], *Lishi yanjiu* [Historical Studies], no. 5 (1957), p. 11.

16. WSSQQKJS, Ia:14, n.

17. Li, "Wodi Makesi zhuyi guan," p. 195.

18. Meisner, *Li Ta-chao,* p. 93.

19. Ibid., p. 94.

20. Li, "Wodi Makesi zhuyi guan," p. 176.

21. Gail Bernstein, *Japanese Marxists: A Portrait of Kawakami Hajime, 1879–1946* (Cambridge: Harvard University Press, 1976), pp. 38–39, 103–123.

22. "Jingzheng yu huzhu" [Competition and mutual aid], XQPL, no. 6 (July 13, 1919), p. 3.

23. Fang Hanqi, "Shiyue geming zai Zhongguo baokan (1917–1921) shangdi fanying," *Xinwen yewu,* no. 11 (1957):102.

Part II

Prologue

1. James Joll, *The Second International, 1889–1914* (New York: Harper Colophon Books, 1966), p. 4.

2. Jean Chesneaux, *The Chinese Labor Movement, 1919–1927,* trans. H. M. Wright (Stanford: Stanford University Press, 1968), part 1.

3. Ibid., p. 377.

4. Bureau of Social Affairs, The City Government of Greater Shanghai, *Strikes and Lockouts in Shanghai Since 1918* (Shanghai, 1932). Chart on p. 96.

5. Priscilla Robertson, *The Revolutions of 1848: A Social History* (Princeton: Princeton University Press, 1967). See part 1 for a discussion of the French working class at this time.

6. It is noteworthy that Chinese literature describes the May Fourth Movement as an "enlightenment" (*qimeng*) movement. A few words may be in order here concerning this term which is crucial to the interpretation of the Movement. While the intellectuals' search for "enlightenment" was a basic motivation of the New Culture Movement, and would have a formative effect on May Fourth thinking, it should be evident from the analysis here that I view it as only one aspect of these movements. Undue emphasis on "enlightenment" (and the patriotic motivations of the May Fourth Movement in its immediate origins) disguises the *social* aspects of the Movement, and the social turn May Fourth radicalism took in May/June 1919 in the process of intellectuals' confrontation of the "people." This emphasis is largely a consequence, I think, of viewing these movements from the top, in terms of the thinking of the major intellectuals who led the New Culture Movement, which on the whole yields a view of that movement as a liberal "enlightenment" movement, compounded with nationalist concerns. This view shaped Chow Tse-tsung's seminal *The May Fourth Movement* (Stanford: Stanford University Press, 1967). The Communists have long challenged this rather elitist view, claiming the May Fourth Movement for their own without, however, giving a satisfactory account for the claim (see reference to Mao's 1940 statement cited in Chapter 3). Now that Chinese Communism has abandoned its social radicalism, commentators on the May Fourth Movement in China also seem to recall the Movement as a patriotic "enlightenment" movement. For a recent rewrite of the Movement, based rather uncritically on this contemporary evidence, see Vera Schwarcz, *The*

Chinese Enlightenment Movement (Berkeley: University of California Press, 1985). The interpretation offered here stresses the *social* aspects of the Movement, which is the aspect that appears when the Movement is viewed through ground-level radical activism and experience. This also underlines the importance of socialism (especially anarchism), which drew its appeal from its promise to resolve the contradictions thrown up by the extension of "enlightenment" to the people at large, but especially the challenges presented by the political emergence of laborers in June 1919.

Chapter 4

1. "Women weishemma yaojiang shehui zhuyi" [Why must we discuss socialism], JFGZ (December 1919):2.

2. Feng Ziyou, *Zhongguo shehui zhuyizhi guoqu ji jianglai* [The past and future of Chinese socialism] (Hong Kong: Shehui zhuyi yanjiusuo, 1919), p. 2. The reference was to the Anfu clique.

3. For an example, see *Shehui zhuyi pingyi* [Critique of socialism] (n. p., 1919), Preface says it was sponsored by the Chinese Merchants' Association in Guangzhou.

4. WSSQQKJS, 3, p. 756.

5. It is worth noting that anarchists used these terms in juxtaposition on a regular basis. *Qiangquan* was used as the translation for "naked force," as well as "authority," which, needless to say, added up to the same thing in anarchist eyes.

6. Zhou Fohai, "Zhongguozhi jieji douzheng" [China's class struggle], JFGZ 1 (December 1919):14.

7. *Zhongguo zhigong yundong jianshi* [A brief history of the Chinese labor movement]. Selection in *Wusi yundong huiyi lu* [Reminiscences of the May Fourth Movement], 3 vols. (Beijing: Zhongguo shehui kexue chubanshe, 1979). See vol. 2, p. 632.

8. Wu Zhihui, "Lun gongdang buxing youyu gongxue busheng" [Absence of a workers' party rests in the stagnation of work-study], *Laodong* 1 (March 20, 1918):2.

9. "Qingnian yu nongcun" [Youth and villages], LDZXJ, pp. 146–150.

10. WSSQQKJS, Ia:104–105.

11. Ibid., pp. 105–106.

12. Chen Wangdao, "Huiyi dang chengli shiqidi yixie qingkuang" [Recollections of certain circumstances surrounding the founding of the Party], in YDQH, 2:19.

13. Dai Jitao and Shen Xuanlu would seem to have been the foremost advocates of this line of thinking. See Dai, "Laodongzhe jiefang yundong yu nuzi jiefang yundongdi jiaodian" [Comparable points about the liberation of labor and the liberation of women), *Jianshe* [Construction] (March 1920):269–287.

14. "Tangshan meikuangdi gongren shenghuo" [The lives of Tangshan coal miners], LDZXJ, pp. 153–154.

15. "Xiaxiangdi xuesheng" [A student in the countryside] and "Pingmin jiaoyu jiangyantuan he laodong buxi xuexiao" [The Common People's Education Lecturing Corps and part-time schools for laborers], in WSSQST. See vol 2, p. 262.

16. See, for instance, Jerome Grieder, *Chinese Intellectuals and The State* (New York: The Free Press, 1983).

17. "Shixing minzhudi jichu" [The foundation for instituting democracy], *Duxiu wencun,* 2 vol. (Shanghai, 1922), 1:375.

18. Jitao, "Laodong yundongdi fasheng ji qi guiqu" [Origins and goals of the labor movement], XQPL, no. 41 (March 14, 1920), pp. 1–4. Also see Zhang Dongsun "Women weishemma," and Zhou Fohai, "Zhongguozhi jieji douzheng."

Chapter 5

1. WSSQQKJS, Ia:321.

2. Ibid., pp. 188–189.

3. Eric Hobsbawm, *Revolutionaries* (New York: New American Library, 1973), p. 87.

4. Richard Saltman, *The Social and Political Thought of Michael Bakunin* (Westport: Greenwood Press, 1983), p. 25.

5. Chu Minyi, "Xu Wuzhengfu shuo" [On anarchy], *Xin shiji* [New era], no. 34 (February 15, 1908), p. 4.

6. Li Shizeng, "Da pangguanzhe" [Response to the onlooker], *Xin shiji,* no. 8 (August 3, 1907), p. 1.

7. Huang Lingshuang, "Benzhi xuanyan" [The declaration of this journal]. *Jinhua* 1 (January 20, 1919). In WSSQST, 4:186.

8. Jue sheng, "PaiKong zhengyan" [Proof of need to overthrow Confucius], *Xin shiji,* no. 52 (June 20, 1908), p. 4.

9. Ibid.

10. "Hunan qu wuzhengfu zhuyizhe tongmeng xuanyan" [Declaration of Hunan Anarchist Federation] (1925). In Hudson Collection (n.d.), Box 4 Package 6, part 2, Item 1.

11. Li Shizeng, "Sangang geming" [Revolution against the three cardinal principles], *Xin shiji,* no. 11 (August 31, 1907), p. 2.

12. Arif Dirlik and Edward Krebs, "Socialism and Anarchism in Early Republican China," *Modern China* 7 (April 1981):133–134.

13. Wu Zhihui, "Lun gongdang buxing youyu gongxue busheng," *Laodong* 1 (March 20, 1918):2.

14. "The New Era," Enclosure to Dispatch no. 306 from the Amoy Consulate of the U.S., in *Records of the Department of State Relating to Internal Affairs of China* (Washington, D.C.: National Archives, 1960), roll 7. As far as is possible to tell from the translation, this was Shifu's "Wuzhengfu qianshuo" [Anarchy explained simply].

15. In Hudson Collection, "Hunan qu wuzhengfu zhuyizhe."

16. See Edward Krebs, "Liu Ssu-fu and Chinese Anarchism, 1905–1915" (Ph.D. diss., University of Washington, 1977), chapter 5.

17. Li Shizeng and Chu Minyi, "Geming" [Revolution] (Paris: Xin shiji congshu, 1906). For Huang, see n. 7.

18. Chu Minyi, "Xu wuzhengfu shuo," *Xin shiji* 40 (March 28, 1908), p. 2.

19. Qian Xing, "Lun zhishi yiwai wu daode," *Xin shiji* 79 (December 26, 1908).

20. In WSSQST, 4:162.

21. WSSQQKJS, 3:494–495.

22. Shifu, "Wuzhengfu gongchandangzhi mudi yu shouduan" [The goals and methods of anarcho-communists], *Shifu wencun* [Collected works of Shifu] (n.p.: Gexin shuju, 1927), pp. 45–52.

23. Ibid., pp. 49–50.

24. In WSSQST, 4:164.

25. Ibid., p. 167.

26. Peter Kropotkin, "Anarchist Morality," in *Kropotkin's Revolutionary Pamphlets*, Roger Baldwin, ed. (London: Benjamin Blom, 1968), p. 91.

27. WSSQQKJS, 3a:216–217.

28. Ibid., p. 216.

29. *Cai Jiemin* [Cai Yuanpei] *xiansheng yanxinglu* [Record of Mr. Cai Jiemin's speeches] (Beijing: Beijing daxue chubanshe, 1920), pp. 539–541.

30. *Shifu wencun*, pp. 49–50.

31. Quoted in Paul Clifford, "The Intellectual Development of Wu Zhihui: A Reflection of Society and Politics in Late Qing and Republican China" (Ph.D. diss., London University, 1978), p. 325.

32. "Jiu sixiang yu guoti wenti" [Old thinking and the question of national formation], XQN, no. 3 (May 1, 1917), pp. 1–3.

33. Quoted in Ma King-sheuk, "A Study of Hsin Ch'ing-nien (New Youth) Magazine, 1915–1926" (Ph.D. diss., London University, 1974), p. 67.

34. Quoted in Chow Tse-tsung, *The May Fourth Movement: Intellectual Revolution in Modern China* (Stanford: Stanford University Press, 1967), p. 304.

35. "Hunan qu wuzhengfu zhuyizhe."

36. Shifu, *Shifu wencun*, p. 36. Also see Ming Chan, "Labor and Empire: The Chinese Labor Movement in the Canton Delta, 1895–1928" (Ph.D. diss., Stanford University, 1975).

37. *Shifu wencun*, pp. 56, 81–83.

38. WSSQQKJS, 3a:193–203.

39. Hu Shi, "Gongdu huzhutuan wenti" [The problem of work-study mutual aid groups], XQN, no. 7 (April 1, 1920), p. 2.

40. Huang Liqun, *Liufa qingong jianxue jianshi* [Brief history of diligent work frugal study in France] (Beijing: Jiaoyu kexue chubanshe, 1982), p. 41.

41. "Gongxue zhuyi ji fangfa" [The ideology and method of labor-learning], *LuOu zhoukan* [Weekly of Chinese Students in Europe], no. 45 (September 12, 1920), p. 1.

42. Quoted in WSSQQKJS, 2a:178.

43. "Gongxue huzhutuandi da xiwang" [The great hope for labor-learning mutual aid groups], *Cai Jiemin xiansheng yanxinglu*, p. 58.

44. "Laogong shensheng" [Labor is Sacred]. Original published in *Beijing daxue rikan* [Beida student daily], November 27, 1918. Reprinted in *Zhongguo xiandai shi ziliao xuanpian* [Compendium of source materials on modern Chinese history], 3 vols. (Shenyang: Heilongjiang renmin chubanshe, 1981), 1.

45. *Cai Jiemin xiansheng yanxinglu*, pp. 58–59.

46. Cang Fu, "Laodong zhuyi" [Laborism], DFZZ 15 (August 15, 1918), pp. 1–4.

47. WSSQST, 4:360–528, *passim*.

48. An "extensive" discussion of the "new Village" movement is available in Ding Shouhe, *Cong wusi qimeng yundong dao Makesi zhuyidi chuanpo* (Beijing: Renmin chubanshe, 1978), pp. 215–219. For a comparison of "new Village" principles with the principles of *gongxue* organizations, see WSSQQKJS, 3a:299–300.

49. Mo Chipeng," "Memoirs of Shifu" (n.d.). I am indebted to Edward Krebs for making this ms. available to me.

50. Ding, *Cong Wusi*, pp. 215–219.

51. Wang Guangqi, "Gongdu huzhutuan" [Labor-learning mutual aid groups], *Shaonian Zhongguo* [Young China], no. 1 (January 15, 1920). Reprinted in WSSQST, 2:379.

52. Quoted in WSSQQKJS, 27a:297.

53. Zhushan zuiweng[!], "Ping 'Gongdu zhuyi,'" JFGZ (February 1, 1920):3.

54. Shen Xuanlu, "Wo duiyu zuzhi 'Gongdu huzhutuan' di yijian" [My views on organizing 'labor-learning mutual aid groups'], XQPL, no. 30 (December 28, 1919), pp. 1–3.

55. WSSQQKJS, 3a:279.

56. "Tongmenghui yu wuzhengfu dang" [The Revolutionary Alliance and the anarchist party], *Duxiu wencun*, 2:44.

Chapter 6

1. Xu Xingzhi, "Dang chengli shiqi Zhejiangdi gongnong yundong" [The worker-peasant movement in Zhejiang at the time of the founding of the Party], in YDQH, 2:38.

2. Gail Bernstein, "The Russian Revolution, the Early Japanese Socialists, and the Problem of Dogmatism," *Studies in Comparative Communism* 9 (Winter 1976):327–348.

3. Yuan Quan, "Jinshi shehui zhuyi bizu Makesi zhi fendou shenghuo" [The life of struggle of Marx, the founding father of modern socialism], in Lin Daizhao and Pan Guohua, eds., *Makesi zhuyi zai Zhongguo* [Marxism in China], 2 vols. (Beijing: Qinghua University Press, 1983), 2:1–6.

4. T.T.S. (Shi Cuntong?), "Makesi yihua yijie" [A paragraph from "Idle words on Marx"], XQPL, special New Year's issue (January 1920), part 2, p. 4.

5. "Makesi zhuan" (Biography of Marx), in ibid., p. 3.

6. Jitao, "Deguo shehui minzhu dangdi zhenggang" [The political program of the German Social Democratic Party], XQPL, no. 10 (August 10, 1919), pp. 2–3.

7. "Bolshevism di shengli" [The victory of Bolshevism], LDZXJ, p. 114.

8. Liu Binglin (Nangai), "Makesi zhuanlue" [Brief biography of Marx], in Lin, et al., *Makesi zhuyi zai Zhongguo,* 2:22.

9. "Duifu 'Buerseweike' di fangfa," XQPL, no. 3 (June 22, 1919), p. 2.

10. She, "Gongchandang xuanyan" [Manifesto of the Communist party], in Lin, et al., *Makesi zhuyi zai Zhongguo,* 2:7.

11. David McLellan, *Karl Marx: His Life and Thought* (New York: Harper Colophon Books, 1973), p. 220.

12. Leszek Kolakowski, *Main Currents of Marxism,* 3 vols. (New York: Oxford University Press, 1981); see vol 2, p. 33.

13. See end of this chapter.

14. "Wodi Makesi zhuyi guan," LDZXJ, pp. 173–211.

15. Ibid., pp. 177–180.

16. Ibid., p. 208.

17. Gail Bernstein, *Japanese Marxist: A Portrait of Kawakami Hajime, 1879–1946* (Cambridge: Harvard University Press, 1976), p. 39.

18. "Makesi di weiwu shiguan," trans. Yuan Quan, in Lin, et al., *Makesi zhuyi zai Zhongguo,* 2:16.

19. Kolakowski, *Main Currents of Marxism,* 2:31–32.

20. Bernstein, *Japanese Marxist,* pp. 109–113.

21. Quoted in ibid., p. 40.

22. "Wodi Makesi zhuyi guan," LDZXJ, p. 189.

23. "Makesi weiwu shiguandi piping." WSSQQKJS, 1a:116–117.

24. Bernstein, *Japanese Marxist,* pp. 93–98.

25. "Weiwu shiguan di jieshi" [Explanation of the materialist conception of history], XQPL, special October 10 issue (1919), part 1, p. 3.

26. "Wodi Makesi zhuyi guan," LDZXJ, pp. 175–176.

27. Iibd., p. 194.

28. "Women weishemma yaojiang shehui zhuyi," JFGZ 1 (December 1919): 10.

29. For a discussion of this piece and other works applying the Materialist conception of history to Chinese society, see Arif Dirlik, *Revolution and History: Origins of Marxist Historiography in China, 1919–1937* (Berkeley: University of California Press, 1978), chapter 2.

30. "Jin," LDZXJ, p. 95.

31. Gerald Cohen, *Karl Marx's Theory of History: A Defense* (Princeton: Princeton University Press, 1978).

Chapter 7

1. See Philip Schmitter and G. Lembruch, eds., *Trends Toward Corporatist Intermediation* (Beverly Hills: Sage Publications, 1979).

2. See the entry under "Jieji tiaohe lun" in *Jianming shehui kexue cidian* (Shanghai cishu chubanshe, 1982), p. 421. Another dictionary gives us " 'ge jieji hezuo' zhuyi" (ideology of cooperation between all classes). See *Xin YingHan cidian* [New English-Chinese dictionary] (Shanghai: Shanghai yiwen chubanshe, 1982), p. 258.

3. Xuanlu, "Shanghai bagongdi jianglai" [The future of the Shanghai strikes], XQPL, no. 2 (June 15, 1919), p. 2.

4. Jitao, "Laodong yundongdi fasheng ji qi guiqu," XQPL, no. 41 (March 14, 1920), p. 1.

5. Ibid., p. 2.

6. Taoji, "Gongren jiaoyu wenti" [The question of workers' education], XQPL, no. 3 (June 22, 1919), pp. 2–3.

7. Ibid., p. 2.

8. Ibid.

9. "Fang Sun xianshengdi tanhua" [Conversation with Mr. Sun during a visit], XQPL, no. 3, p. 3.

10. This was the text entitled "Bingren xuzhi" [What soldiers ought to know]. For the text and government responses to it, see *Zhongguo wuzhengfu zhuyi he Zhongguo shehui dang* [Chinese anarchism and the Chinese Socialist Party] (Nanjing: Jiangsu renmin chubanshe, 1981), pp. 19–28.

11. "Jieji douzhengdi yanjiu" [An examination of class struggle], *Jianshe* 2 (August 1920):15.

12. Ibid., pp. 11–13.

13. "Geming jixudi gongfu" [The task of continuing the revolution], XQPL, special October 10 issue (1919), part 2, pp. 1–4.

14. Cited in "AA zhi AD" (From AA to AD), in Ge Maochun, Jiang Jun, and Li Xingzhi, eds., *Wuzhengfu zhuyi sixiang ziliao xuan,* 2 vols. (Beijing: Beijing daxue chuban she, 1984), 1:472–473.

15. Zhu Zhixin, "Meiyou gongzuodi rendi 'shengcunquan' he 'laodongquan' "

[The right to existence and the right to labor of the unemployed], XQPL, no. 37 (February 15, 1920), p. 1.

16. See Phillip Schmitter, "Still the Century of Corporatism?" in Schmitter and Lembruch, eds., *Corporatist Intermediation,* pp. 7–52.

17. This journal, originally entitled *Jiefang yu gaizao* [Liberation and reform], was renamed simply *Gaizao* (Reform) when Liang Qichao took over its editorship from his errant disciple Zhang Dongsun in late 1920.

18. Zhou Fohai, "Zhongguodi jieji douzheng," JFGZ 1 (December 1919): 19–20.

19. WSSQQKJS, 3a:282.

20. Ibid., p. 283.

21. Ibid., p. 277.

22. Ibid., p. 293.

23. Ibid., p. 296.

24. "Gongtuan zhuyi (Syndicalism) zhi yanjiu" [An examination of syndicalism], JFGZ 1 (September 1919): 1–11.

25. Ibid., p. 11. This was a goal shared by advocates of guild socialism, syndicalism, and other proponents of "small group organization."

26. Yu Shang, "Jierte shehui zhuyi" [Guild socialism], JFGZ 1 (October 1919):2.

27. Ibid., pp. 2–3.

28. Ibid., p. 4.

29. "Women weishemma yaojiang shehui zhuyi," JFGZ 1 (December 1919):7.

30. Ibid., p. 11.

31. Ibid.

32. Zhang Dongsun and Zhang Junmai, "Zhongguozhi qiantu Deguo hu? Eguo hu?" [Which is China's future? Germany or Russia?], *Gaizao* 2 (July 15, 1920):13.

33. "Women weishemma," pp. 13–14.

34. "Zhongguozhi qiantu Deguo hu?," p. 17.

35. Ibid., p. 16.

36. Ibid., pp. 13–14.

37. "Shehui zhuyizhi gaizao" [The transformation of socialism], JFGZ 2 (July 15, 1920):49.

38. *Jiang Kanghu yanjiang lu* [Lectures of Jiang Kanghu], 2 vols. (Shanghai: Nanfang daxue, 1920).

39. Jiang Kanghu, *Jinshi sanda zhuyi yu Zhongguo* [The three great ideologies of the modern world and China] (Nanfang University, 1924) (Pamphlet), p. 44.

40. "Zhongguo shehui dang" [The Chinese Socialist Party], in *Zhonghua minguoshi ziliao conggao* [Draft of historical materials on the history of the Chinese Republic], compiled by the Modern History Institute of the Chinese Academy of Social Sciences (Beijing(?): Zhonghua Shuju, 1976), pp. 1–23.

41. Ibid., p. 22.

42. Deng Yingchao, "Huiyi Tianjin 'Juewushe' deng qingkuang" [Remembering the "Awakening Society" in Tianjin and other matters], in YDQH, 27:236.

43. *Jiang Kanghu yanjiang lu,* part 3, p. 11.

44. "Xin minzhu zhuyi," ibid., pp. 4–9.

45. Ibid., pp. 11–20.

46. See ibid. Also see Arif Dirlik and Edward Krebs, "Socialism and Anarchism in Early Republican China," *Modern China* 7 (April 1981):117–151.

47. LDZXJ, p. 233.

48. Ibid., p. 148.

49. "Women weishemma," p. 12.

50. See "Duifu 'Buerseweike' di fangfa" [How to deal with Bolshevism], XQPL, no. 3 (June 22, 1919), p. 4.

51. Zhang, "Xianzai yu jianglai" [The present and the future], in *Zhongguo xiandai shi ziliao xuanpian*, 4 vols. (Shenyang: Heilongjiang renmin chubanshe, 1981), p. 62.

Epilogue

1. The intellectual issues involved in ideological eclecticism should not blind us to the fact that for the readership of these ideological discourses, at least, ideological confusion may have been imbedded in simple confusion over terminology. Anarchism, for example, was variously called *wuzhengfu zhuyi* (no government), *wuzhi zhuyi* (no rule), *ziyou shehui zhuyi* (libertarian socialism); guild socialism was called *jierte shehui zhuyi* (guild transliterated), *zizhidi shehui zhuyi* (self-rule socialism) or *gonghui shehui zhuyi* (labor union or syndicate socialism).

2. WSSQQKJS, 1a:125.

3. Ibid., pp. 189–191.

4. For the distinctions drawn by a later Marxist, see the essays by Li Da, "Shemma Jiao shehui zhuyi" [What is Socialism?] (June 1919), and "Shehui zhuyidi mudi," [The goal of socialism] (June 1919), in *Li Da Wenji* [Collection of Li Da's writings], 2 vols. (Beijing: Renmin chubanshe, 1980) 1, pp. 1–5.

5. WSSQQKJS, 1a:105.

Part III

Prologue

1. For Voitinsky's visit, see Xiang Qing, "Guanyu gongchan guoji he Zhongguo geming jianli lianxidi tantao" [An investigation into the establishment of relations between the Communist International and the Chinese revolution], in *Dangshi yanjiu ziliao*, 3 vols. (Chengdu: Sichuan renmin chubanshe, 1982), 3:129–130. For his trip to Fujian, see Liang Bingxian, *Jiefang bielu*, n.p., n.d., pp. 21–22.

2. There is some terminological confusion concerning the appellations of these groups. They are described in the literature variously as *xiaozu* (small group), *xuehui* (study society), and *dang* (party). *Xiaozu* would seem most appropriate, since they were no longer study societies, strictly speaking, and not yet a party. I describe them as study societies or cells, depending on their place in the process of organization toward a party.

3. "Li Dazhao yu Buerteman" [Li Dazhao and Borstelman], *Dangshi yanjiu ziliao*, nos. 6, 7 (June 20, 1981), p. 25. According to an anarchist, Huang Lingshuang, Chen Duxiu and Li Dazhao formed in 1919, with the intermediation of a Russian named "B," a "socialist alliance" (*shehui zhuyizhe tongmeng*) which was replicated elsewhere, and served in 1920 as the basis for communist organization. See Zheng Peigang, "Wuzhengfu zhuyi zai Zhongguodi ruogan shishi" [Some historical facts concerning anarchism in China], *Guangzhou wenshi ziliao* [Historical and literary materials on Guangzhou] 7 (April 1963): 171–208. See p. 191.

4. Zhang Jingru, "Lun wusi shiqi juyou chubu gongchan zhuyi sixiangdi zhishi fenzi" [A discussion of May Fourth intellectuals subscribing to a rudimentary communism], *Beijing Shifan daxue xuebao* [Journal of the Beijing Normal University], no. 4 (1978), p. 6.

5. Ibid., p. 5.

6. Ibid., p. 6.

7. *Dangshi yanjiu ziliao*, 2:205–206.

8. Luo Zhanglong, "Huiyi dangdi chuanli shiqidi jige wenti" [Recalling some questions concerning the period of the Party's founding], in YDQH, 2:197.

9. Chang Kuo-t'ao, *The Rise of the Chinese Communist Party, 1921–1927* (Lawrence: The University Press of Kansas, 1971), pp. 89–94.

10. Shen Qinglin, "Guanyu gongchan zhuyi xiaozu" [On the Communist cells], *Dangshi yanjiu ziliao*, no. 17 (December 20, 1979), p. 11.

11. Shi Fuliang (Cuntong), "Zhongguo gongchandang chengli shiqidi jige wenti" [Some questions concerning the period of the founding of the Party], in YDQH, 2:33.

12. See Louis Althusser, "Contradiction and Overdetermination," in Louis Althusser, *For Marx*, Ben Brewster, tr. (New York: Vintage Books, 1970), pp. 89–128.

Chapter 8

1. Luo Zhanglong, "Huiyi Beijing daxue Makesi xueshuo yanjiu hui" [Recollections of the Society for the Study of Marxist Theory in Beijing University], in YDQH, 27:187–188.

2. For documentation concerning the Young China Society, see WSSQST, 1:211–572.

3. For this society, see ibid., 2:4–40.

4. Luo, "Huiyi Beijing daxue," p. 186. Also see Edgar Snow, *Red Star over China* (New York: Grove Press, 1961).

5. For this society, see WSSQST, 2:134–266. A further discussion of the society may be found in Vera Schwarcz, *The Chinese Enlightenment Movement* (Berkeley: University of California Press, 1985), pp. 87–93.

6. "Beida pingman jiaoyu hui jiangyantuan zai 'wusi' qianhou suoqidi zuoyong" [The role played by the Beida Common People's Education Lecturing Corps at the time of the May Fourth Movement], WSSQST, 2:254.

7. Shao Lizi, "Dang chengli qianhoudi yixie qingkuang," YDQH 2:68.

8. "Yang Zhihuadi huiyi" [Recollections of Yang Zhihua], in YDQH, 2:25.

9. Ibid., p. 27. Also see the following reference.

10. Xu Xingzhi, "Dang chengli shiqi Zhejiangdi gongnong yundong," in YDQH, 2:38–43.

11. Chen Wangdao, "Huiyi dang chengli shiqidi yixie qingjuang" [Recollection of certain circumstances surrounding the founding of the Party], in YDQH, 2:19–24. Also see *Makesi Engesi zhuzuo zai Zhongguodi chuanpo*, (Beijing: Marx-Engels Research Institute, 1983), pp. 11–18.

12. WSSQQKJS, 2:434–435.

13. "Yang Zhihuadi huiyi," in YDQH, 2:25.

14. Chen, "Huiyi dang chengli," p. 19.

15. WSSQQKJS, 2a:435. See also Ni Weixiong, *"Zhejiang xinchao* di huiyi"

[Recollections of the *New Tide of Zhejiang*], in *Wusi yundong huiyi lu,* 3 vols. (Beijing: Zhongguo shehui kexue chubanshe, 1979) 2:737–741.

16. Jiang Danshu, " 'Feixiao' yu Zhejiang Diyi Shifandi fanfengjian douzheng" ["Against filial piety" and the anti-feudal struggle at Zhejiang First Normal], in ibid., pp. 57–58.

17. WSSQQKJS, 1a:332.

18. Liu Qingyang, "Juexingledi Tianjin renmin" [The awakened people of Tianjin], in *Wusi yundong huiyi lu,* 2:531–564. See also Chen Xiaocen, "Juewu she ji qi chengyuan" [Awakening Society and its members], in *Tianjin wenshi ziliao xuanji* [Selections from Tianjin historical and literary materials], no. 15 (Jinan: Shandong renmin chubanshe, 1981), pp. 156–194.

19. Liu, "Juexingledi Tianjin renmin." See also Chen Xiaocen, "Wusi yundong chanshengdi Tianjin Juewu she" [The Awakening Society, product of the May Fourth Movement], in *Wusi yundong huiyi lu,* 2:579–597, p. 591. For the quotation, see Chen Xiaocen, "Huiyi Tianjin 'wusi' yundong ji 'Juewu she' " [Recollections of the May Fourth Movement in Tianjin and the Awakening Society], *Tianjin wenshi ziliao xuanji,* no. 3 (1979), p. 23.

20. Liu Qingyang, "Duiyu 'Juewu she' deng wentidi jieda" [Answers to some questions on the Awakening Society and other matters], in YDQH, 2:230.

21. Deng Yingchao, "Huiyi Tianjin 'Juewu she' deng qingkuang" [Recollections of the Tianjin Awakening Society and other matters]," in YDQH, 2:236.

22. Lin Daizhao, "Makesi zhuyi zai Zhongguodi chuanpo he Zhou Enlai tongzhi" [The propagation of Marxism in China and comrade Zhou Enlai], *Beijing daxue xuebao* (Beijing University Journal), no. 2 (1978), pp. 2–3.

23. Ibid., pp. 3–4.

24. Gu Shiting, "Dang chengli shiqi Shandong jiqudi yixie qingkuang" [The situation in Shandong at the time of the founding of the Party], in YDQH, 2:396–399. See also *Wusi yundong zai Shandong xiliao xuanji* [Materials on the May Fourth Movement in Shandong] (Jinan: Shandong renmin chubanshe, 1980), pp. 444–562.

25. Ibid., pp. 444–447.

26. Ibid., pp. 444–447.

27. Ibid., p. 450.

28. Dong Biwu, "Chuangli Zhongguo gongchandang" [Founding the Communist party of China]. In YDQH, 2:292. See also *Wusi yundong zai Wuhan* (The May Fourth Movement in Wuhan (Wuhan: Hubei renmin chubanshe, 1981), pp. 330–338.

29. "Chen Tanqiu," in *Zhonggong dangshi renwu zhuan* [Biographies of Party members], 10 vols. (Xian: Shaanxi renmin chubanshe, 1983), 9:1–7.

30. Bao Huiseng, "Gongchan dang diyice quanguo daibiao huiyi qianhoudi huiyi" [Recollections of the period around the time of the first congress of the Communist party of China], in YDQH, 2:314.

31. Liao Huanxing, "Huiyi Liqun she shimo" [Recollections of the Benefit the Masses Society), *Wusi yundong huiyi lu,* supp. vol., pp. 368–373. See also Liao Huanxing, "Wuchang Liqun shushe shimo" [History of the Benefit the Masses bookstore in Wuchang], in YDQH, 2:296–302. For Chow, see *The May Fourth Movement* (Stanford: Stanford University Press, 1967), p. 189.

32. Ibid., pp. 296–298.

33. Ibid., p. 299. For Chen's visit, see *Wusi yundong zai Wuhan,* pp. 275–283.

Liao suggests that Yun undertook the translation for financial reasons, in order to support the Society.

34. Liao, "Wuchang Liqun shushe shimo," p. 300.

35. Luo Zhanglong, "Huiyi Xinmin xuehui" [Recollections of the New Citizens' Study Society], in YDQH, 2:256–284.

36. Zhou Shizhao, "Xiangjiangdi nukong" [The angry roar of the Xiang river], *Wusi yundong huiyi lu,* 1:417–465.

37. Luo, "Huiyi Xinmin xuehui," p. 266.

38. Wei Wei, et al., *Deng Zhongxia zhuan* [Biography of Deng Zhongxia] (Beijing: Renmin chubanshe, 1982), p. 28.

39. Angus McDonald, *The Urban Origins of Rural Revolution* (Berkeley: University of California Press, 1978), p. 131.

40. Tan Tiandu, "Huiyi Guangdongdi 'wusi' yundong yu gongchan xiaozudi jianli" [The May Fourth Movement and the founding of the Communist cell in Guangdong], in *Guangdong wenshi ziliao* (Guangzhou: Guangdong renmin chubanshe, 1979) 24:67–75. See also Deng Zengxiang, "Guangzhou xuesheng wusi yundong ji" [Recollections of the May Fourth Movement of Guangzhou students], *Wusi yundong huiyi lu,* 2:826–843.

41. Liang Furan, "Guangdong dangdi zuzhi chengli qianhoudi yixie qingkuang" [Some circumstances surrounding the founding of the Party organization in Guangdong], in YDQH, 2:443–457.

42. Marilyn Levine, "The Found Generation: Chinese Communism in Europe, 1919–1925." (Ph.D. diss., University of Chicago, 1985). See chapter 4. See also Wang Yongxiang, *LiuFa qingong jianxue yundong jianshi* [Brief history of the diligent work frugal study movement in France] (Harbin: Heilongjiang renmin chubanshe, 1982), pp. 68–73.

43. Ibid., p. 71.

44. Levine, "The Found Generation," p. 140.

45. Luo Zhanglong, "Huiyi Beijing daxue Makesi xueshuo yanjiu hui," in YDQH, 2:192–194.

46. Chang Kuo-t'ao, *The Rise of the Chinese Communist Party, 1921–1927* (Lawrence: The University Press of Kansas, 1971), p. 87.

47. Ibid., pp. 50–51.

48. Liu Qingyang, "Juexingledi Tianjin renmin," in *Wusi yundong huiyi lu,* II:554.

49. Chang Kuo-t'ao, *The Rise,* p. 43.

50. Liao Huanxing described the "method" as *huxiang chuandi,* "passing around to one another." See "Wuchang Liqun shushe shimo," in YDQH, 2:298. See also Xu Xingzhi, "Dang changli shigi," YDQH, II:38.

51. This observation, and the analysis presented in this chapter, owes some debt to the work of social psychologists on small group dynamics and their behavioral consequences. For a prominent example of this kind of work, see Muzaffer Sherif and Carolyn W. Sherif, *Reference Groups: Exploration into Conformity and Deviation of Adolescents* (New York: Harper and Row, 1964). The Sherifs use this approach to analyze conformity and deviation among adolescents. My interest here is in small groups as social spaces within which radical ideology and activity take coherent shape, and as social support groups which legitimize radical activity. I also place greater emphasis on the social environment than do most social psychologists, whose work too often overlooks this element, as well as the inclinations individuals bring to groups. The following statement by the Sherifs, however, is quite pertinent to my analysis: "The prevailing values [of the social

environment] do not mechanically determine the choice processes of individuals when there are alternatives; nor do individuals make decisions in quiet solitude through sheerly intellectual deliberation. An individual perceives the value alternatives in his setting through the web of interaction with other individuals, the filtering process acquiring its highest value among individuals who face common problems and interact with the desire to do something about them." (p. 259.) I am indebted to Bernard Silberman for calling my attention to this work.

52. For this society, see Liao Huanxing, "Wuchang Liqun," p. 299. For similar practices by the Morning Garden Society, see *Deng Zhongxia zhuan*, p. 25. The most famous, of course, was the New Citizens' Study Society, which kept up these practices even after the dispersal of its membership through the *Xinmin xuehui tongxin* (Correspondence of the New Citizens' Study Society).

53. Chang, *The Rise*, pp. 104–105.

54. For a discussion of this idea, see Fredric Jameson, *The Political Unconscious* (Ithaca: Cornell University Press, 1981), introduction.

55. "Dui 'Juewu she' deng wentidi jieda," in YDQH, 2:229.

56. Snow, *Red Star over China*, pp. 148–149.

57. Deng Yingchao, "Wusi yundongdi huiyi," *Wusi yundong huiyi lu*, 1:75.

58. *Wusi yundong zai Shandong*, p. 452.

59. Deng Yingchao, "Huiyi Tianjin 'juewu she' deng qingkuang," in YDQH, p. 232.

60. Liu Qingyang, "Juexingledi Tianjin renmin," *Wusi yundong huiyi lu*, 2:555. See also Chen Xiaocen, "Wusi yundong," p. 589–590. The Declaration of Awakening Society is available in WSSQQKJS, 1:415–416.

61. Mao Zedong, "The Great Union of the Popular Masses," trans. Stuart Schram, *China Quarterly*, no. 49 (1972), p. 79.

62. Wang, *LiuFa qingong jianxue yundong jianshi*, p. 69.

63. Li Da, "Zhongguo gongchandi faqi," p. 10.

64. Xia Yan, "Dang wusi langchao zhongdao Zhejiang shihou" [Encounter with Zhejiang in the midst of the May Fourth tide], *Wusi yundong huiyi lu*, 2:732. "Appeal to Youth" was possibly the most important text at the time in converting youth to anarchism.

65. Shi Fuliang, "Zhongguo gongchan dangdi chengli," p. 34.

66. For Qu, see Paul Pickowicz, *Marxist Literary Thought in China: The Influence of Ch'u Ch'iu-pai* (Berkeley: University of California Press, 1981). For Li Lisan, see "Li Lisan zhuanlue" [Brief biography of Li Lisan], *Beifang Luncong*, no. 1 (January 1984), p. 108.

67. Mao, "The Great Union," p. 79.

68. *Deng Zhongxia zhuan*, pp. 22–44.

69. Chang, *The Rise*, pp. 69–70.

70. *Deng Zhongxia zhuan*, pp. 27–28.

71. For the "numbers" for the group, see Chen Xiaocen, "Huiyi Tianjin 'wusi' yundong ji 'Juewu she,' " p. 20.

72. "Yang Zhihuazhi huiyi," in YDQH, 2:26.

73. Liu, "Juexingledi Tianjin renmin," *Wusi yundong huiyi lu*, 2:562.

74. The work was Hillquit's *History of Socialism in the United States* (1910; reprint ed., New York: Dover Publications, 1971), which Li put to more than one use. See Chapter 9.

75. Tan Tiandu, "Huiyi Guangdongdi," p. 71.

76. See *Xin qingnian* 7 (May 1, 1920).

77. "Shanghai Houshen shachan Hunan nugong wenti" [The problem of Hunanese women workers in the Housheng textile factory in Shanghai], *Duxiu wencun,* 1:453–550. Original in *Xin qingnian* 7, 6 (May 1, 1920).

78. See Angus McDonald, *Urban Origins,* chapter 4, and Lynda Schaffer, *Mao and the Workers: The Hunan Labor Movement, 1920–1923* (Armonk: M. E. Sharpe, 1982).

79. Liu, "Dui 'Juewu she' deng wentidi jieda," in YDQH, p. 229.

80. Chang, *The Rise,* p. 84.

81. *Deng Zhongxia zhuan,* p. 33.

82. Zhu Wushan, "Beida pingmin jiaoyu jiangyantuan zai 'wusi' qianhou suoqidi zuoyong," WSSQST, 2:253.

83. *Duxiu wencun,* 1:449.

84. WSSQST, 2:422.

85. See the discussion "Gongdu huzhutuan wenti" [The question of labor-learning mutual aid corps], *Xin qingnian* 7 (April 1, 1920).

86. "Gongdu huzhu tuandi shiyan he jiaoxun" [The experience and lessons of the labor-learning mutual aid corps], XQPL, no. 46 (special labor issue) (May 1, 1920), pp. 1–4.

87. Ibid., reprint in WSSQST, 2:424.

88. Ibid., p. 439.

89. Chang, pp. 91–92.

Chapter 9

1. Luo Zhanglong, "Huiyi dang chuangli shiqidi jige wenti," YDQH, 2:198–199.

2. *Dangshi yanyiu ziliao,* 1:203–206. See also Xiang Qing, "Zhongguo gongchan dang chuangli shiqidi gongchan guoji he Zhongguo geming," *Zhonggong yanjiu lunwen xuan* (Changsha: Hunan renmin chubanshe, 1983).

3. Shi Fuliang, "Dang chuangli shiqidi yixie qingkuang" [Some circumstances surrounding the founding of the Party], in YDQH, 2:36.

4. Wu Tingkang, "Zhongguo laodongzhe yu laonong yihuidi Eguo" [Chinese laborers and the labor-peasant government in Russia], *Dangshi yanjiu ziliao* nos. 6, 7 (June 20, 1981), pp. 3–4.

5. "Zhongguo gongchan dangdi faqi he diyice, dierce daibiao dahui jingguodi huiyi" [Recollections of the founding of the Communist party of China and its first and second congresses], in YDQH, 2:7.

6. Wang Laibing, "Guanyu Zhongguo gongchan dang zaoqi zuzhidi jige wenti" [Some questions on the early organization of the Communist party of China], *Zhonggong dangshi yanjiu lunwen xuan,* 1:204–208. Mme. Voitinsky was a teacher at the language institute.

7. Xiang Qing, "Zhongguo gongchan dang chuangli," *Zhonggong dangshi yanjiu lunwen xuan,* 1:296.

8. Ibid., p. 289.

9. Ibid., p. 297.

10. Luo, "Huiyi dang chuangli," in YDQH, 2:196–200.

11. *Dangshi yanjiu ziliao,* 1:205.

12. Li Da, "Zhongguo gongchan dangdi faqi," in YDQH, 2:6.

13. Allen Whiting, *Soviet Policies in China, 1917–1924* (Stanford: Stanford University Press, 1953), p. 142.

14. Zhou Yuxin, "Li Dazhao yu Zhongguo gongchan dangdi chuangli" (Li Dazhao and the Founding of the Communist Party of China). *Zhonggong dangshi yanjiu lunwen xuan*, 1:51.

15. Chang, *The Rise of the Chinese Communist Party, 1921–1927* (Lawrence: The University Press of Kansas, 1971), pp. 86–95.

16. Dirlik, *Revolution and History* (Berkeley: University of California Press, 1978), p. 26.

17. "Shaonian Zhongguodi shaonian yundong" [The youth movement of young China], LDZXJ, p. 230.

18. LDZXJ, p. 286.

19. Li, "Meilijian zhi zongjiao xincun yundong" [The religious utopian communities in the United States], XQPL, no. 31 (January 1920), p. 4.

20. Chang, p. 90.

21. Zhang Shenfu, "Jiandang chuqidi yixie qingkuang" [The situation in the early period of Party formation], in YDQH, 2:220.

22. Chang, *The Rise*, pp. 101–102.

23. "Shanghaizhi gongdu huzhutuan" [The labor-learning mutual aid corps in Shanghai], WSSQST, 2:451.

24. "Ershi shiji Elosidi geming" [The Russian Revolution of the twentieth century], *Meizhou pinglun* [Weekly critic], no. 18. Quoted in *Chen Duxiu pinglun xuanpian* [Critical discussions of Chen Duxiu] 2 vols. (Henan renmin chubanshe, 1982), 1:454.

25. Quoted in Chow Tse-tsung, *The May Fourth Movement* (Stanford: Stanford University Press, 1967), pp. 174–175.

26. *Duxiu wencun*, 2:67.

27. Ibid., I:373–391.

28. Ibid., 1:375.

29. Ibid., p. 377.

30. Quoted in *Chen Duxiu pinglun xuanpian*, 1:367.

31. *Duxiu wencun*, 1:402.

32. Ibid., pp. 431–448.

33. See *Wusi yundong zai Wuhan* [The May Fourth Movement in Wuhan] (Wuhan: Hubei renmin chubanshe, 1981), pp. 275–283, for the lectures. For "common people's socialism," see Liao Xinchu, "Hubei dang zuzhidi jianli jiqi chuqidi huodong" [The founding of the Hubei Party branch and its initial activities], in *Zhonggong dangshi yanjiu ziliao xuan*, 1:219.

34. For Chen and the Hubei labor surveys, see ibid., p. 130. For Chen's essay, see *Duxiu wencun*, 1:453–550.

35. *Makesi Engesi zhuzuo zai Zhongguodi chuanpo* (Beijing: Marx-Engels Research Institute), p. 14.

36. Liao, "Hubei dang zuzhidi jianli jiqi chuqidi huodong," p. 130.

37. Chang, *The Rise*, p. 102.

38. Since membership was in flux, membership lists vary slightly from source to source; there is general agreement among the sources, however, over the core membership.

39. Chang, p. 111.

40. Luo Zhanglong, "Huiyi Beijing daxuedi," YDQH, 2:190.

41. Ibid., pp. 192–193.

42. For a list of the holdings, see WSSQST, 2:278–281.

43. Shen Yanbing (Mao Dun), "Huiyi Shanghai gongchan zhuyi xiaozu"

[Recollections of the party nucleus in Shanghai], in YDQH, 2:44. See also Zhou Yangru, "Shanghai gongchan zhuyi xiaozu" [The Communist nucleus in Shanghai], in *Zhonggong dangshi yanjiu lunwen xuan,* 1:99–100.

44. "Zhongguo gongchan dang chengli shiqidi jige wenti" [Some questions on the timing of the establishment of the Communist party of China], in YDQH, 2:26.

45. "Yang Zhihuzahi huiyi," in YDQH, 2:26.

46. Li "Zhongguo gongchan dangdi faqi," p. 7.

47. "Gongchan dang diyice quanguo daibiao huiyi qianhoudi huiyi" [Recollections of the period around the first national congress of the Communist party], in YDQH, 2:312.

48. Chang, *The Rise,* p. 107.

49. Shi Fuliang, "Zhongguo gongchan dang chengli shiqidi jige wenti," in YDQH, 2:36. This is confirmed by Chang, *The Rise,* p. 101.

50. Ibid., p. 102.

51. Li, "Zhongguo gongchan dangdi faqi," YDQH, 2:7.

52. "Zhongguo gongchan dang chengli shiqidi jige wenti," in YDQH, 2:36.

53. For *The Communist,* see Li, "Zhongguo gongchan dangdi faqi," p. 8. The quotation from Li Hanjun is in WSSQQKJS, 2:533.

54. Zhou, "Shanghai gongchan zhuyi xiaozu," p. 106.

55. Li Da, "Guanyu Zhongguo gongchandang jianlidi jige wenti," in YDQH, 2:4. See also Shen Qinglin, "Guanyu gongchan zhuyi xiaozu" [On the Communist nuclei], *Dangshi yanjiu ziliao,* no. 17 (December 1979), p. 25.

56. Li, "Guanyu Zhongguo gongchan dang," p. 4.

57. Chen Wangdao, "Huiyi dang chengli shiqidi," in YDQH, 2:24.

58. Ibid., p. 22.

59. "Zhongguo gongchan dang xuanyan," in YDQH, 2:1.

60. Ibid., p. 4.

61. Bao, "Gongchan dang diyice," YDQH, 2:303–321.

62. Ibid., pp. 312–314. See also Liao Xinchu, "Hubei dang," *Dangshi yanjiu lunwen xuan,* 1:131–134.

63. See n.8 in this chapter.

64. Zhang Zhong, "Zhonggong 'yida' yiqiandi dangyuan mingdan chutan" [Investigation of party membership lists before the first congress], *Dangshi yanjiu ziliao,* no. 52 (November 20, 1981), pp. 8–17. Also Shen Qinglin, "Guanyu gongchan zhuyi xiaozu," *Dangshi yanjiu ziliao,* no. 17 (December 20, 1979), pp. 1–36.

65. Chang, *The Rise,* p. 211.

66. Huang Xianmeng, "Guanyu 'yida' qiandi Hunan gongchan dang xiaozu wenti" [The Question of the Communist nucleus in Hunan before the first congress], in *Zhonggong dangshi yanjiu lunwen xuan,* 1:123.

67. Ibid., p. 124. See also McDonald, *The Urban Origins,* p. 129, and *Wusi shiqi Hunan renmin geming douzheng shiliao xuanpian* [Revolutionary struggles of the Hunanese people during the May Fourth period] (Changsha: Hunan renmin chubanshe, 1979), pp. 310–335.

68. "Guanyu Mao Zedong tongzhi zhuanbian wei Makesi zhuyizhedi shijian" [On the timing of comrade Mao Zedong's conversion to Marxism], *Nankai xuebao* [Nankai University journal], no. 3 (1980), pp. 6–10.

69. For the quotation from Mao, see ibid., p. 9. See also *Wusi siqi Hunan renmin geming douzheng shiliao xuanpian* [Revolutionary struggles of the Hunanese people during the May Fourth Movement] (Changsha: Hunan renmin chubanshe, 1979), p. 451.

70. *LiuFa qingong jianxue yundong jianshi,* p. 69.

71. *Wusi shiqi Hunan renmin geming,* pp. 452–453.

72. Ibid., p. 453. Pp. 449–461 offer an illuminating analysis of the correspondence.

73. Ibid., p. 460.

74. Zhou Yuxin, "Shandong gongchan zhuyi xiaozu" [The Communist nucleus in Shandong], *Zhonggong dangshi yanjiu lunwen xuan,* pp. 147–152. See also Shen Qinglin, "Guanyu gongchan zhuyi xiaozu," pp. 15–16.

75. Ibid., pp. 10–13. See also "Chen Gongbo huiyi Zhongguo gongchan dangdi chengli" [Chen Gongbo recalls the founding of the Communist party of China], in YDQH, 2:412–419.

76. Shen, "Guanyu gongchan zhuyi xiaozu," pp. 16–17. See also Levine, "The Found Generation," chapter 5.

77. Shen, "Guanyu gongchan zhuyi xioazu," pp. 21–32.

78. WSSQQKJS, 2a:75–79. See also the recent reprint of this periodical: *Laodongzhe* (Guangzhou: Guangdong renmin chubanshe, 1984).

79. WSSQQKJS, 2a:61–70.

80. Ibid., pp. 80–85.

81. Shen, "Guanyiu gongchan zhuyi xiaozu" pp. 21–32.

82. Ibid., p. 31.

83. See McDonald, *Urban Origins,* and Schaffer, *Mao and the Workers.* For Guangzhou, see Ming Chan, "Labor and Empire: The Chinese Labor Movement in the Canton Delta, 1895–1928" (Ph.D. diss., Stanford University, 1975).

84. He Jinzhou, "Guangdong zuichu gongchan dang zuzhizhi yanjiu" [Investigation of the earliest Communist organization in Guangdong], *Dangshi yanjiu lunwen xuan,* 1:163–169.

85. "Bao Huisengdi yifeng xin" [A letter of Bao Huiseng], in YDQH, 2:434.

86. "Huiyi gongchan dang chuqi Wuhan laodong yundong yu Xiang Ying lieshi" [Recollections of the labor movement in Wuhan in the early period of the Communist party and the martyr Xiang Ying], in YDQH, 2:322–351. See also Shen, *Guanyu gongchan zhuyi xiaozu,* p. 31.

87. See WSSQST, 4:324–351, for a list of anarchist publications.

88. Yuan Zhenying, "Yuan Zhenyingdi huiyi" [Memoirs of Yuan Zhenying], in YDQH, 2.

89. "Zhongguo gongchan dangdi diyice," YDQH, 2:17.

90. Chang, *The Rise,* p. 101.

91. Dong Biwu, "Dong Biwu tan Zhongguo gongchan dang diyice quanguo daibiao dahui he Hubei gongchan zhuyi xiaozu" [Dong Biwu discusses the first congress of the Communist party of China and the Communist nucleus in Hubei], in YDQH, 2:370.

92. WSSQQKJS, 2a:69.

Chapter 10

1. *LiuFa qingong jianxue yundong jianshi,* p. 70.

2. Chang Kuo-t'ao, *The Rise of the Chinese Communist Party* (Lawrence: the University Press of Kansas, 1971), p. 113.

3. *Wusi yundong zai Shandong ziliao xuanji* [Materials on the May Fourth Movement in Shandong] (Jinan: Shandong renmin chubanshe, 1980), p. 509.

4. McDonald, *The Urban Origins of Rural Revolution* (Berkeley: University of California Press, 1973), pp. 134–135.

5. Liang Furan, "Guangdong dangdi zuzhi chengli qianhoudi yixie qingkuang" [The situation in Guangdong around the time of the founding of Party organization], in YDQH, 2:447–448.

6. Zhang Hongxiang and Wang Yongxiang, *LiuFa qingong jianxue yundong jianshi*, pp. 98–123.

7. Liang Bingxian, *Geming bielu*, p. 33.

8. Cai Shu, *Wusi shiqi Makesi zhuyi fan fandui Makesi zhuyi sichaodi douzheng* [The struggle of Marxism against anti-Marxism in the May Fourth period] (Shanghai: Shanghai renmin chubanshe, 1979).

9. Cai Shu, *Wusi shiqi Makesi zhuyi*, p. 52.

10. WSSQQKJS, 2a:69–70.

11. Chow Tse-Tsung, *The May Fourth Movement* (Stanford: Stanford University Press, 1967), p. 223.

12. "Tan zhengzhi," *Duxiu wencun*, 1:546.

13. Ibid., p. 546.

14. Ibid., p. 556.

15. For this exchange, see *Shehui zhuyi taolun ji* [Collection of discussions on socialism] (Shanghai: Xin qingnianshe, 1922), pp. 30–31.

16. For a discussion of Liang's views at this time, see Zhang Pengyuan, "Liang Qichao dui shehui zhuyidi renshi ji Zhongguo xiandaihuadi jianjie" [Liang Qichao on socialism and China's modernization], *Shihuo yuekan* [Shihuo monthly] 3 (January 1973):6–28. Liang's essay was "Fu Zhang Dongsun shu lun shehui zhuyi yundong" [Letter to Zhang Dongsun discussing the socialist movement], *Gaizao* 3 (February 15, 1921), in *Zhongguo xiandai sixiang shi ziliao jianpian*, 1, pp. 240–252.

17. Cai Gaosi, ed., *Zhongguo xiandai sixiang shi ziliao jianpian* [Collection of materials on modern Chinese thought], 3 vols. (Hangzhou: Zhejiang renmin chubanshe, 1982), 1:616.

18. "Xianzai yu jianglai," *Gaizao* 3 (December 15, 1920):35–36.

19. Ibid., pp. 35–36.

20. Ibid., pp. 25–29.

21. Ibid., pp. 33–34.

22. Lan Gongwu, "Shehui zhuyi yu ziben zhidu" [Socialism and the capitalist system], *Gaizao* 3, (December 15, 1920):51–54. Also "Shehui zhuyi yu Zhongguo" [Socialism and China], in ibid., pp. 26–34.

23. Lan, "Shehui zhuyi yu ziben zhidu."

24. Ibid.

25. *Li Da wenji* (Beijing: Renmin chubanshe, 1981) 1:24.

26. For this essay, and the prolonged exchange over this issue (which involved criticism of Bertrand Russell), see *Shehui zhuyi taolun ji*, pp. 32–74.

27. Ibid., pp. 74–96.

28. Ibid., p. 83.

29. "Yige shenshuo" [A further statement], *Gaizao* 3 (December 15, 1920): 54–58. For Li Dazhao, see "Zhongguodi shehui zhuyi yu shijiedi ziben zhuyi" [Chinese socialism and world capitalism] (1929), LDZXJ, pp. 356–357.

30. *Shehui zhuyi taolun ji*, pp. 62–63.

31. "Taolun shehui zhuyi bing zhi Liang Rengong" [Discussion of socialism in response to Liang Qichao], *Shehui zhuyi taolun ji*, p. 200.

32. Ibid., pp. 64–65.

33. "Shehui zhuyi yu Zhongguo" [Socialism and China], in *Shehui zhuyi taolun ji*, p. 320.

34. "Gao Zhongguodi nongmin" [To the Chinese peasantry], *Gongchandang*, no. 3 (April 7, 1921), pp. 5–6. The first page of this article was confiscated by the authorities.

35. Ibid., p. 7.

36. "Zizhi yundong yu shehui geming," trans. Sheng, *Gongchandong*, no. 3 (April 7, 1921), pp. 8–9.

37. *Shehui zhuyi taolun ji*, pp. 44–45.

38. "Zhongguodi shehui zhuyi yu shidiedi ziben zhuyi."

39. *Shehui zhuyi taolun ji*, p. 72.

40. "Jinhua yu geming" [Evolution and revolution], in ibid., p. 274.

41. Ibid., p. 325.

42. Ibid., p. 86.

43. WSSQQKJS, 1a:26.

44. *Gongchandang*, no. 1 (November 7, 1920), p. 1.

45. Ibid., no. 5 (June 7, 1921), p. 11.

46. Ibid., p. 17.

47. Ibid., no. 4 (May 7, 1921), pp. 14–15. See also "Shehui gemingdi shangjue" [Considerations on social revolution], ibid., no. 2 (December 7, 1920), p. 5.

48. Ibid.

49. Ibid., no. 5, p. 16.

50. Ibid., no. 4, pp. 23–30, and no. 5, pp. 3–9.

51. "Douqu zhengquan," ibid., pp. 5–7.

52. *Gongchandang*, no. 5, pp. 18–20.

53. "Shehui gemingdi shangjue," ibid., no. 2, pp. 8–9.

54. *Shehui zhuyi taolun ji*, p. 90.

55. This debate was originally conducted in *Xin qingnian* and the anarchist periodical *Min sheng*. It was reprinted in *Shehui zhuyi taolun ji*, pp. 97–154. Ou's response, pp. 97–101.

56. Ibid., pp. 102–108. See p. 147 for the statement on Stirner and Kropotkin.

57. Ibid., pp. 149–151.

58. Chen, "Women weishemma zhuzhang gongchan zhuyi," p. 26.

59. Saltman, *The Social and Political Thought of Michael Bakunin*, p. 5.

60. Karl Marx, *The Eighteenth Brumaire of Louis Bonaparte*, in Karl Marx and F. Engels, *Selected Works* (Moscow: Progress Publishers, 1973), p. 398.

61. *Shehui zhuyi taolun ji*, p. 139.

62. Ibid., p. 155.

Epilogue

1. "Zhongguo gongchandang diyice gangling" [The first program of the Communist party of China], in YDQH, 1:7.

2. Ibid., p. 6.

3. "Diyice daibiao dahuidi huiyi," in YDQH, 2:285–291.

4. See Chang, *The Rise of the Chinese Communist Party* (Lawrence: The University Press of Kansas, 1971), pp. 144–149; Li Da, "Zhongguo gongchan dangdi faqi," in YDQH, 2:10–15; Chen Tanqiu, "Diyice daibiao dahuidi huiyi," in YDQH, 2:374–383; Dong Biwu, "Dong Biwu tan," in YDQH, 2:365–369; Bao

Huiseng, "Gongchan dang diyice," in YDQH, 2:303–321; Liu Renjing, "Huiyi dangdi 'yida,' " in YDQH, 2:207–216; Chen Gongbo, "Chen Gongbo huiyi," YDQH, 2:412–431.

5. Liu, "Huiyi dangdi 'yida,' " p. 213.

6. Ibid., p. 211.

7. Bao, "Gongchan dang diyice," pp. 307–308.

8. Ibid., p. 313.

9. Chang, *The Rise,* p. 139.

10. Ibid., pp. 137–139. See also Bao, "Gongchan dang diyice," p. 307.

11. Li, "Zhongguo gongchan dangdi faqi," pp. 15–16.

12. Bao, "Gongchan dang diyice," p. 305.

13. Yuan Zhenying, YDQH, 2:475.

14. Li, "Zhongguo gongchan dangdi faqi," p. 17.

Chapter 11

1. For the successful economic struggles of Chinese labor during this period, see Chesneaux, *The Chinese Labor Movement, 1919–1927,* H. M. Wright, tr. (Stanford: Stanford University Press, 1968), pp. 156–159.

2. For a discussion of the processes of radicalism that produced the Restoration Society in 1904, see Mary B. Rankin, *Early Chinese Revolutionaries* (Cambridge: Harvard University Press, 1971), pp. 48–125.

3. George Lukacs, *History and Class Consciousness* (Cambridge: MIT Press, 1972), p. 299.

4. See *Zhonggong dangshi yanjiu lunwen xuan,* 3 vols. Changsha: Hunan renmin chubanshe, 1983) 1:223–234.

5. Dirlik, *Revolution and History* (Berkeley: University of California Press, 1978).

6. For a discussion of the ideological inclinations of Peng Pai, see Robert B. Marks, *Rural Revolution in South China* (Madison: University of Wisconsin Press, 1984), pp. 165–168. See also Fernando Galbiati, *P'eng P'ai and the Hai-Lu-feng Soviet* (Stanford: Stanford University Press, 1985), chapter 2 and 4.

7. *Zhonggong dangshi yanjiu lunwen xuan,* pp. 219–220.

8. For examples of the rather extensive discussion of anarchism in contemporary historiography, see Yang Ziming, "Wusi shiqi Makesi zhuyi he wuzhengfu zhuyidi douzheng" [The struggle between Marxism and anarchism in the May Fourth period], *Xibei shiyuan xuebao* [Journal of Northwestern Normal Academy], no. 2 (April 1984), and Li Zhenya, "Zhonguo wuzhengfu zhuyidi jinxi" [The past and the present of anarchism in China], *Nankai xuebao* (Nankai Journal), no. 1 (1980), For an extensive list of works published through 1980, see the bibliography in *Makesi zhuyi zai Zhongguo* (Beijing: Qinghua daxue chubanshe, 1983) 1:574–575.

BIBLIOGRAPHY

Althusser, Louis. "Contradiction and Overdetermination," in Louis Althusser, *For Marx*. Translated by Ben Brewster. New York: Vintage Books, 1970, pp. 89–128.

Beijing daxue xuesheng zhoukan [Beijing University student weekly] (1920).

Bernstein, Gail. *Japanese Marxist: A Portrait of Kawakami Hajime, 1879–1946*. Cambridge: Harvard University Press, 1976.

————. "The Russian Revolution, the Early Japanese Socialists, and the Problem of Dogmatism." *Studies in Comparative Communism* 9 (Winter 1976), pp. 327–348.

Bianco, Lucien. *Origins of the Chinese Revolution*. Translated by Muriel Bell. Stanford: Stanford University Press, 1971.

Bureau of Social Affairs, The City Government of Greater Shanghai. *Strikes and Lockouts in Shanghai Since 1918*. Shanghai, 1932.

Cai Gaosi, ed. *Zhongguo xiandai sixiang shi ziliao jianpian* [Collection of materials on modern Chinese thought]. 3 vols. Hangzhou: Zhejiang renmin chubanshe, 1982.

Cai Yuanpei. *Cai Jiemin xiansheng yanxinglu* [Record of Mr. Cai Jiemin's speeches]. Beijing: Beijing daxue chubanshe, 1920.

Cai Wei. *Wusi shiqi Makesizhuyi fandui fanMakesizhuyi sichaodi douzheng* [The struggle between Marxism and anti-Marxism during the May Fourth period]. Shanghai: Renmin chubanshe, 1979.

Chang Kuo-t'ao. *The Rise of the Chinese Communist Party, 1921–1927*. Lawrence: The University Press of Kansas, 1971.

Chen Duxiu. *Duxiu wencun* [Collection of works by Chen Duxiu]. 2 vols. Shanghai, 1922.

Chen Duxiu pinglun xuanpian [Critical discussion of Chen Duxiu]. 2 vols. Henan renmin chubanshe, 1982.

Chen, Joseph. The May Fourth Movement in Shanghai. The Hague: Mouton & Co., 1971.

Chevrier, Yves. "Utopian Marxism: 'Populist Strains' and Conceptual Growth Pains in early Chinese Communism, 1920–1922." Unpublished paper.

Chesneaux, Jean. *The Chinese Labor Movement, 1919–1927*. Translated by H. M. Wright. Stanford: Stanford University Press, 1968.

Chou Tse-tsung. *The May Fourth Movement: Intellectual Revolution in Modern China*. Stanford: Stanford University Press, 1967.

Clifford, Paul. "The Intellectual Development of Wu Zhihui: A Reflection of Society and Politics in Late Qing and Republican China." Ph.D. dissertation, London University, 1978.

Cohen, Gerald. *Karl Marx's Theory of History: A Defense*. Princeton: Princeton University Press, 1978.

Dangshi tongxun [Party history circular]. 1983.

Dangshi yanjiu ziliao [Materials on party history]. 1978–1982.

Dangshi yanjiu ziliao [Materials on party history]. 3 vols. Chengdu: Sichuan renmin chubanshe, 1982.

Deng Zhongxia. *Zhongguo zhigong yundong jianshi (1919–1926)* [Brief history of the Chinese labor movement]. Hong Kong: Wenhua ziliao gongyingshe, 1978; first published, 1930.

Deng Zhongxia zhuan [Biography of Deng Zhongxia]. Beijing: Renmin chubanshe, 1982.

Ding Shouhe. *Cong wusi qimeng yundong dao Makesi zhuyidi chuanpo* [From the May Fourth enlightenment movement to the propagation of Marxism]. Beijing: Renmin chubanshe, 1978.

———. *Shiyue geming dui Zhongguo gemingdi yingxiang* [The influence of the October Revolution on the Chinese revolution]. Beijing: Renmin chubanshe, 1957.

Dirlik, Arif. "Ideology and Organization in the May Fourth Movement: Some Problems in the Intellectual Historiography of the May Fourth Period." *Republican China* (Fall 1986), pp. 1–21.

———. "Vision and Revolution: Anarchism in Chinese Revolutionary Thought on the Eve of the 1911 Revolution." *Modern China* 12 (April 1986), pp. 121–61.

———. "The New Culture Movement Revisited: Anarchism and the Idea of Social Revolution in New Culture Thinking." *Modern China* 11 (July 1985), pp. 251–300.

———. *Revolution and History: Origins of Marxist Historiography in China, 1919–1937*. Berkeley: University of California Press, 1978.

Dirlik, Arif, and Krebs, Edward. "Socialism and Anarchism in Early Republican China." *Modern China* 7 (April 1981), pp. 117–151.

Dongfang zazhi [Eastern miscellany] (1917–1919).

Fang Hanqi. "Shiyue geming zai Zhongguo baokan (1917–1921) shangdi fanying" [The reflection of the October Revolution in Chinese periodicals and newspapers (1917–1921)]. *Xinwen yewu* [Journalism], no. 11 (1957).

Feng Ziyou. *Zhongguo shehui zhuyizhi guoqu ji jianglai* [The past and future of Chinese socialism]. Hong Kong: Shehui zhuyi yanjiusuo, 1919.

Fleming, Marie. *The Anarchist Way to Socialism: Elisée Reclus and Nineteenth Century European Anarchism*. London: Croom and Helm, 1979.

Foner, Philip, ed. *The Bolshevik Revolution: Its Impact on American Radicals, Liberals, and Labor*. New York: International Publishers, 1967.

Galbiati, Fernando. *P'eng p'ai and the Hai-Lu-feng Soviet*. Stanford: Stanford University Press, 1985.

Gao Jinsun. "Guanyu Mao Zedong tongzhi zhuanbian wei Makesi zhuyizhedi shijian" [On the timing of comrade Mao Zedong's conversion to Marxism]. *Nankai xuebao* (Nankai University Journal), no. 3 (1980).

Ge Maochun, et al., eds. *Wuzhengfu zhuyi sixiang ziliao xuan* [Selection of materials on anarchist thought]. 2 vols. Beijing: Beijing daxue chubanshe, 1984.

Gongchandang [The Communist] (1920–1921).

Gray, Jack, ed. *Modern China's Search for Political Form*. New York: Oxford University Press, 1969.

Grieder, Jerome. *Chinese Intellectuals and the State*. New York: The Free Press, 1983.

Guangdong wenshi ziliao. [Historical and literary materials on Guangdong]. Guangzhou: Guangdong renmin chubanshe, 1979.

Hillquit, Morris. *History of Socialism in the United States.* 1910. Reprint. New York: Dover Books, 1977.

Hobsbawm, Eric. *Revolutionaries.* New York: New American Library, 1973.

Huang Liqun. *Liufa qingong jianxue jianshi* [Brief history of diligent work frugal study in France]. Beijing: Jiaoyu kexue chubanshe, 1982.

Hudson Collection (n.d.). Box 4, Package 6, Part 2. The Hoover Institute.

Jameson, Fredric. *The Political Unconscious.* Ithaca: Cornell University Press, 1981.

Jianshe [Construction]. (1919–1920).

Jiang Kanghu. *Jinshi sanda zhuyi yu Zhongguo* [The three great ideologies of the modern world and China]. Nanfang University, 1924.

———. *Jiang Kanghu yanjiang lu* [Lectures of Jiang Kanghu]. Shanghai: Nanfang daxue, 1920.

Jianming shehui kexue cidian [Elementary social science dictionary]. Shanghai: Shanghai cishu chubanshe, 1982.

Jiefang ju gaizao, later *Gaizao* [Reconstruction]. (1919–1921).

Jinhua (1919).

Jinian wusi yundong liushi zhounian xueshu taolunhui lunwen xuan [Collection of discussions in celebration of the sixtieth anniversary of the May Fourth Movement]. 3 vols. Beijing: Chinese Academy of Social Sciences, 1980.

Joll, James. *The Second International, 1889–1914.* New York: Harper Colophon Books, 1966.

Kolakowski, Leszek. *Main Currents of Marxism.* 3 vols. New York: Oxford University Press, 1981.

Krebs, Edward. "Liu Ssu-fu and Chinese Anarchism, 1905–1915." Ph.D. dissertation, University of Washington, 1977.

Kropotkin, Peter. *Kropotkin's Revolutionary Pamphlets.* Edited by Roger Baldwin. London: Benjamin Blom, 1968.

Laodong [Labor]. (1918).

Laodongzhe [The laborer]. 1920. Guangzhou: Guangdong renmin chubanshe, 1984. Reprint #1–8.

Levine, Marilyn. "The Found Generation: Chinese Communism in Europe, 1919–1925." Ph.D. dissertation, University of Chicago, 1985.

Li Da, *Li Da wenji* [Collection of Li Da's writings]. 2 vols. Beijing: Renmin chubanshe, 1981.

"Li Da tongzhi shengping shilue" [Brief biography of Comrade Li Da]. *Wuhan daxue xuebao* [Journal of Wuhan University], no. 1 (1981), Special issue on Li Da, pp. 1–9.

Li Dazhao. *Li Dazhao xuanji* [Selected works of Li Dazhao]. Beijing: Renmin chubanshe, 1978.

"Li Dazhao yu Buerteman" [Li Dazhao and Borstelman]. *Dangshi yanjiu ziliao,* Nos. 6, 7 (June 20, 1981).

Li Longmu. "Li Dazhao tongzhi he wusi shiqi Makesi zhuyi sixiangdi xuanchuan" [Comrade Li Dazhao and the propagation of Marxist thought during the May Fourth period]. *Lishi yanjiu* (Historical Studies), No. 5 (1957).

Li Rui. *Mao Zedong tongzhidi chuqi geming yundong* [The early revolutionary activities of comrade Mao Zedong]. Beijing: Zhongguo qingnian chubanshe, 1957.

Li Rui. *Mao Zedong zaoqi geming huodong* [The early revolutionary activities of Mao Zedong]. Revised edition of *Mao Zedong tongzhidi chuqi geming yundong.* Changsha: Hunan renmin chubanshe, 1980.

Li Shizeng and Chu Minyi. "Geming" [Revolution]. Paris: Xin shiji congshu, 1906.

Li Xin. *Weidadi kairui* [The great beginning]. Beijing: Zongguo shehui kexue chubanshe, 1983.

Li Yu-ning. *The Introduction of Socialism to China.* New York: Columbia University Press, 1971.

Li Zhenya. "Zhonguo wuzhengfu zhuyidi jinxi" [The past and the present of anarchism in China]. *Nankai xuebao* (Nankai journal), no. 1 (1980),

Liang Bingxian. *Jiefang bielu* [An alternative record of liberation]. n.p., n.d.

Lin Daizhao. "Makesi zhuyi zai Zhongguodi chuanpo he Zhou Enlai tongzhi" [The propagation of Marxism in China and comrade Zhou Enlai]. *Beijing daxue xuebao* [Beijing University journal], no. 2 (1978).

Lin Daizhao and Pan Guohua. *Makesi zhuyi zai Zhongguo* [Marxism in China]. 2 vols. Beijing: Qinghua University Press, 1983).

Liu Jianqing and Zhang Hongxiang. "Cai Hesen zai Zhongguo gongchandang chuangli jianzhongdi diwei" [Cai Hesen's place in the founding of the Communist Party of China]. Nankai xuebao [Nankai journal], no. 3 (1980), pp. 1–5.

LuOu zazhi. [Journal of Chinese students in Europe]. (1916–1918).

LuOu zhoukan [Weekly of chinese students in Europe]. 1919–1920).

Makesi Engesi zhuzuo zai Zhongguodi chuanpo [The propagation of Marx and Engels' works in China]. Beijing: Marx-Engels Research Institute, 1983.

Ma King-sheuk. "A Study of Hsin Ch'ing-nien (New Youth) Magazine 1915–1926." Ph.D. dissertation, London University, 1974.

Mao Zedong. "The Great Union of the Popular Masses." Translated by Stuart Schram. *China Quarterly,* no. 49 (1972), p. 79.

———. "Xin minzhu zhuyidi zhengzhi yu xin minzhu zhuyidi wenhua" [The politics and culture of New Democracy]. *Zhongguo wenhua* [Chinese culture] 1 (February 1940), pp. 1–29.

Marks, Robert B. *Rural Revolution in South China.* Madison: University of Wisconsin Press, 1984.

Marx, Karl, and Engels, F. *Selected Works.* 3 vols. Moscow: Progress Publishers, 1973.

Mast, Herman. "Tai Chi-t'ao, Sunism and Marxism During the May Fourth Movement in Shanghai." *Modern Asian Studies* 5 (1971).

McDonald, Angus. *The Urban Origins of Rural Revolution.* Berkeley: University of California Press, 1978.

McLellan. *Karl Marx: His Life and Thought.* New York: Harper Colophon Books, 1973.

Meisner, Maurice. *Li Ta-chao and the Origins of Chinese Marxism.* Cambridge: Harvard University Press, 1967.

Meizhou pinglun [Weekly critic] (1918–1919).

Ming Chan. "Labor and Empire: The Chinese Labor Movement in the Canton Delta, 1895–1928." Ph.D. dissertation, Stanford University, 1975.

Min sheng [People's voice] (1913–1914).

Mo Chipeng. "Memoirs of Shifu" (n.d.). Unpublished manuscript.

"Ouzhan yu laodongzhe" [The European war and laborers]. *Laodong* [Labor] 1 March 12, 1918).

Pickowicz, Paul. *Marxist Literary Thought in China: The Influence of Ch'u Ch'iu-pai.* Berkeley: University of California Press, 1981.

Rankin, Mary B. *Early Chinese Revolutionaries.* Cambridge: Harvard University Press, 1971.

Records of the Department of State Relating to Internal Affairs of China. Washington, D.C.: National Archives, 1960.

Robertson, Priscilla. *The Revolutions of 1848: A Social History.* Princeton: Princeton University Press, 1967.

Saltman, Richard. *The Social and Political Thought of Michael Bakunin.* Westport: Greenwood Press, 1983.

Scalapino, Robert. "The Evolution of a Young Revolutionary: Mao Zedong in 1919–1920." *Journal of Asian Studies* 42 (November 1982), pp. 29–61.

Schaffer, Lynda. *Mao and the Workers: The Hunan Labor Movement, 1920–1923.* Armonk: M. E. Sharpe, 1982.

Schmitter, Philip, and Lembruch, Gerhard, eds. *Trends Toward Corporatist Intermediation.* Beverly Hills: Sage Publications, 1979.

Schwartz, Benjamin I. *Chinese Communism and the Rise of Mao.* Cambridge: Harvard University Press, 1951, p. 8.

Schwarcz, Vera. *The Chinese Enlightenment Movement.* Berkeley: University of California Press, 1985.

Shehui zhuyi pingyi [Critique of socialism]. N.p., 1919.

Shehui zhuyi taolun ji [Collection of discussions on socialism]. 2 vols. Shanghai: Xin qingnianshe, 1922.

Shen Qinglin. "Guanyu gongchan zhuyi xiaozu" [On the communist cells]. *Dangshi yanjiu ziliao,* no. 17 (December 20, 1979).

Sherif, Muzaffer and Sherif, Carolyn W. *Reference Groups: Exploration into Conformity and Deviation of Adolescents.* New York: Harper and Row, 1964.

Shifu wencun [Collected works of Shifu]. N.p.: gexin Shuju, 1927.

Sima Lu. *Zhonggongdi chengli yu chuqi huodong* [The founding and initial activities of the Communist party of China]. Hong Kong, 1974.

Snow, Edgar. *Red Star over China.* New York: Grove Press, 1961.

Tang Conliang. "Li Lisan zhuanlue" [Brief biography of Li Lisan]. *Beifang luncong* [Northern Essays], no. 1 (January 15, 1984), pp. 105–111, and no. 2 (March 15, 1984), pp. 105–112.

Tianjin wenshi ziliao xuanji (Selections from Tianjin historical and literary materials), no. 3, 15. Jinan: Shandong renmin chubanshe, 1981.

van de Ven, Hans J. "The Founding of the Chinese Communist Party and the Search for a New Political Order, 1920–1927." Ph.D. dissertation, Harvard University, 1987.

Venturi, Franco. *Roots of Revolution.* New York: Grosset & Dunlap, 1966.

Walicki, A. *The Controversy Over Capitalism.* London: Oxford University Press, 1969.

Wang Yongxiang. *LiuFa qingong jianxue yundong jianshi* [Brief history of the diligent work frugal study movement in France]. Harbin: Heilongjiang renmin chubanshe, 1982.

Wang Zonghua, Zhang Guangyu, and Ou Yangzhi. "Wusi shiqi Yun Daiying tongzhidi sixiang fazhan he geming shiji" [The development of comrade Yun Daiying's thought during the May Fourth period and his revolutionary practice]. *Wuhan daxue xuebao* [Journal of Wuhan University], no. 3 (March 27, 1979), pp. 22–39.

Whiting, Allen. *Soviet Policies in China, 1917–1924.* Stanford: Stanford University Press, 1953.

Wildman, Allen K. *The Making of a Workers' Revolution.* Chicago: The University of Chicago Press, 1967.

Wusi aiguo yundong dangan ziliao [Archival materials on the May Fourth patriotic movement]. Beijing: Zhongguo shehui kexue chubanshe, 1980.

Wusi shiqi Hunan renmin geming douzheng shiliao xuanpian [Revolutionary struggles of the Hunanese people during the May Fourth period]. Changsha: Hunan renmin chubanshe, 1979.

Wusi shiqi qikan jieshao [Introduction to periodicals of the May Fourth period]. 6 vols. Beijing: Sanlian shudian, 1979.

Wusi shiqidi shetuan [Societies of the May Fourth period]. 4 vols. Beijing: Sanlian shudian, 1979.

Wusi yundong huiyi lu [Reminiscences of the May Fourth Movement]. 3 vols. Beijing: Zhongguo shehui kexue chubanshe, 1979.

Wusi yundong yu Beijing Gaoshi [The May Fourth Movement and the Higher Normal in Beijing]. Beijing: Shifan daxue chubanshe, 1984.

Wusi yundong zai Shandong ziliao xuanji [Materials on the May Fourth Movement in Shandong]. Jinan: Shandong renmin chubanshe, 1980.

Wusi yundong zai Shanghai [The May Fourth Movement in Shanghai]. Shanghai: Renmin chubanshe, 1980.

Wusi yundong zai Tianjin [The May Fourth Movement in Tianjin]. Tianjin: Renmin chubanshe, 1979.

Wusi yundong zai Wuhan [The May Fourth Movement in Wuhan]. Wuhan: Hubei renmin chubanshe, 1981.

Wusi yundong zai Zhejiang [The May Fourth Movement in Zhejiang]. Hangzhou: Zhejiang renmin chubanshe, 1979.

Wu Tingkang. "Zhongguo laodongzhe yu laonong yihuidi Eguo" [Chinese laborers and the labor-peasant government in Russia]. *Dangshi yanjiu ziliao,* nos. 6, 7 (June 20, 1981).

Wu Zhihui. "Lun gongdang buxing youyu gongxue busheng" [Absence of a workers' party rests in the stagnation of work-study]. *Laodong,* no. 1 (March 20, 1918).

Xiao zhaoran. "Beijing daxue yu 'wusi' gianhou Makesi Leining zhuyi zai Zhongguodi chuanpo" [Beijing University and the propagation of Marxism-Leninism in China during the May Fourth period]. *Beijing daxue xuebao* [Journal of Beijing University], no. 3 (1979), pp. 2–11.

Xinchao [The renaissance] (1919).

Xin qingnian [New youth] (1916–1922).

Xin shiji [New era] (1907–1910).

Xin YingHan cidian [New English-Chinese dictionary]. Shanghai: Shanghai yiwen chubanshe, 1982.

Xingqi pinglun [Weekend review] (1919–1920).

Yanjiu Makesi Engesi zhuzuo he shengping lunzhu mulu [An index of writings relevant to research on Marx's and Engels' writings and lives]. (Beijing: Shumu wenxian chubanshe, 1983.

Yang Ziming. "Wusi shiqi Makesi zhuyi he wuzhengfu zhuyidi douzheng" [The struggle between Marxism and anarchism in the May Fourth period]. *Xibei shiyuan xuebao* [Journal of Northwestern Normal Academy], no. 2 (April 1984).

Yi Cun. "Equo quojipai shixingdi zhenglue" [The political strategy of the extremists in Russia]. *Laodong* [Labor] (April 12, 1918).

Yida Qianhou [The period of the first congress]. 2 vols. Beijing: Renmin chubanshe, 1980.

Zhang Hongxiang and Wang Yongxiang. *Liufa qingong jianxue yundongshi* [The diligent work frugal study movement in France]. Harbin: Heilongjiang renmin chubanshe, 1982.

Zhang Jingru. "Lun wusi shiqi juyou chubu gongchan zhuyi sixiangdi zhishi fenzi" [A discussion of May Fourth intellectuals subscribing to a rudimentary communism]. *Beijing Shifan daxue xuebao* [Journal of the Beijing Normal University], no. 4 (1978).

Zhang Pengyuan. "Liang Qichao dui shehui zhuyidi renshi ji Zhongguo xiandaihuadi jianjie" [Liang Qichao on socialism and China's modernization]. *Shihuo yuekan* (Shihuo monthly) 3 (January 1974).

Zhang Zhong. "Zhonggong 'yida' yiqiandi dangyuan mingdan chutan" [Investigation of party membership lists before the first congress]. *Dangshi yanjiu ziliao*, no. 1 (November 20, 1981).

Zheng Peigang, "Wuzhengfu zhuyi zai Zhongguodi ruogan shishi" [Some historical facts concerning anarchism in China]. *Guangzhou wenshi ziliao* [Historical and Literary materials on Guangzhou] no. 7 (April 1963).

Zhonggong dangshi renwu zhuan [Biographies of party members]. 10 vols. Xian: Shaanxi renmin chubanshe, 1983.

Zhonggong dangshi yanjiu lunwen xuan [Essays on party history]. 3 vols. Changsha: Hunan renmin chubanshe, 1983.

Zhongguo wuzhengfu zhuyi he Zhongguo shehui dang [Chinese anarchism and the Chinese Socialist Party]. Nanjing: Jiangsu renmin chubanshe, 1981.

Zhongguo xiandai shi ziliao xuanpian [Compendium of source materials on modern Chinese history]. 4 vols. Shenyang: Heilongjiang renmin chubanshe, 1981.

Zhonghua minguoshi ziliao conggao [Draft of historical materials on the Chinese republic]. Compiled by the Modern History Institute of the Chinese Academy of Social Sciences. Zhonghua Shuju, 1976.

Zhu Chengjia, ed. *Zhonggong dangshi yanjiu lunwen xuan* [Selected essays on the history of the Communist party of China]. 3 vols. Changsha: Hunan renmin chubanshe, 1983.

INDEX